Publications of
**The S. S. Huebner Foundation
for Insurance Education**

LECTURE SERIES

Life Insurance Trends and Problems—McCahan (Editor) (out
  of print)
Life Insurance Trends at Mid-Century—McCahan (Editor)
Investment of Life Insurance Funds—McCahan (Editor) (out
  of print)
Accident and Sickness Insurance—McCahan (Editor)
Pensions: Problems and Trends—McGill (Editor)
The Beneficiary in Life Insurance—McGill (Editor)
Life Insurance Sales Management—McGill (Editor)
All Lines Insurance—McGill (Editor)
Risk Management—Snider (Editor)
*Insurance, Government, and Social Policy: Studies in Insurance
  Regulation*—Kimball and Denenberg (Editors)
Investment Activities of Life Insurance Companies—Cummins
  (Editor)

STUDIES SERIES

An Analysis of Government Life Insurance—McGill (out of print)
Group Life Insurance—Gregg (out of print)
Group Health Insurance—Pickrell
Group Annuities—Black (out of print)
The Economic Theory of Risk and Insurance—Willett (out of print)
Life Insurance Housing Projects—Schultz
Life Insurance Investment in Commercial Real Estate—Snider
Total Disability Provisions in Life Insurance Contracts—Herrick
Insurance and Economic Theory—Pfeffer
Transition to Multiple-Line Insurance Companies—Bickelhaupt
*Compulsory Temporary Disability Insurance in the United
  States*—Osborn
*Development of Comprehensive Insurance for the
  Household*—Pierce

MONOGRAPH SERIES

Investment Activities of Life Insurance Companies

Edited by

J. David Cummins

Research Director
The S. S. Huebner Foundation
for Insurance Education

Published for

The S. S. Huebner Foundation
for Insurance Education
University of Pennsylvania

by

RICHARD D. IRWIN, INC.   Homewood, Illinois   60430

4 5 6 7 8 9 0   5 4 3 2

ISBN 0-256-01974-6
Library of Congress Catalog Card No. 76–57328
Printed in the United States of America

To

MILDRED ANN BRILL

*Friend, confidante, and counselor of
twenty-two classes of Huebner Fellows and
their families*

Nature and Purpose of the Foundation

The S. S. Huebner Foundation for Insurance Education is a Pennsylvania nonprofit corporation created for the purpose of promoting and strengthening insurance education at the college level in the United States and Canada. Established under a deed of trust in 1940 and incorporated in 1955, the Foundation is named in honor of Dr. S. S. Huebner, pioneer insurance educator acclaimed throughout the world as the "Father of Insurance Education." The organization is administered at the University of Pennsylvania, with which Dr. Huebner was associated for 49 years.

The major functions of the Foundation are (1) to increase the supply of qualified teachers of risk and insurance through providing financial assistance to graduate students and established teachers aspiring to insurance teaching careers at the college or university level, and (2) to enrich the literature in the area of risk and insurance through publishing the results of significant research carried out under the auspices of the Foundation.

The Foundation operates under the general direction of a rotating Board of Trustees, composed of nine executives of life insurance companies. The educational activities of the Foundation are supervised by an Administrative Board composed of persons holding academic appointments at the University of Pennsylvania and other educational institutions noted for their insurance programs. Responsibility for the active management of the Foundation is vested in an Executive Director, appointed by the President of the University.

Financial support for the Foundation is provided through annual contributions from approximately 110 life insurance companies and the proceeds from the sale of its publications, the latter being devoted to the costs of the publication program.

Preface

The economic and social role of the life insurance industry has undergone major changes in recent years. In earlier decades life insurance companies competed with a relatively limited group of other financial intermediaries for the consumer's economic-security dollar. Social Security and private pension plans were less prominent, and the industry occupied a more important position as a repository for the individual retirement savings of the public. In the securities markets, the industry faced much less competition for the relatively safe, high yielding investments which were its specialty. By present-day standards, the products of the industry were relatively uncomplicated and life insurance was heralded as the "cornerstone of family financial planning."

While many of the preceding statements about the life insurance industry are still true to a degree, there can be little question that major changes have occurred. The growth in the Social Security program and the increasing importance of private pension plans have reduced the role of individual life insurance in the provision of retirement income. As the relative importance of group life insurance, individual term insurance, and lower cash value policies has increased, the investment strategies of life insurers have shifted accordingly. The industry has introduced a multiplicity of new products, many of them equity based, in an attempt to meet rising competition in the economic-security field. Simultaneously, the companies have participated more vigorously in the competition for the management of corporate and individual pension plans. In general, the investment objectives of the sponsors of these plans differ significantly from those of the individual policyholders of an earlier day, leading to an increased emphasis on higher risk, higher yielding investments and to additional sophistication in investing procedures.

In the securities markets, the companies have faced increased competition from relatively new financial intermediaries such as corporate bond funds and real estate investment trusts. The growth and increased investment flexibility of other institutions such as state and local government retirement funds have resulted in unprecedented levels of competition for the privately placed bonds and certain other securities that have long been regarded as the insurers' special area of expertise. Finally, the ravages of inflation and the disintermediation accompanying the recurring monetary crises of recent years have affected both the competitive abilities and the investment strategies of the insurance industry.

The chapters in this book deal with many of these developments in the course of describing the current investment practices of life insurance companies. In addition to traditional life insurance investment topics such as privately placed bond and income property mortgage investment activity, chapters are included on scientific portfolio selection procedures and life insurance company cash flow forecasting. The emphasis on relatively new developments is reflected in the chapters on separate accounts, real estate investment trusts, and equity real estate investments of life insurers. Corporate social responsibility and the evolution of life insurance investment regulations are also subject to chapter-length treatment. Several additional chapters deal with other important aspects of life insurance company investment activities.

The forerunner of this book was another Huebner Foundation publication, *Investment of Life Insurance Funds*, edited by David McCahan and published in 1953. That book, which was based on series of lectures presented at the Wharton School in 1951 and 1952, proved to be one of the most successful Huebner Foundation publications. It went out of print in 1974, providing the impetus for the preparation of this volume. Needless to say, the many differences between the two books reflect the changes which have taken place during the past 25 years in the investment activities of life insurance companies.

Like its predecessor, this book consists of a series of papers originally presented as lectures at the Wharton School. The series began during the 1974–75 academic year and concluded during the fall term of 1975. The presentors were leading academic and insurance industry authorities on life insurance investments, and the audiences consisted of graduate students and faculty of the Wharton School as well as invited guests from the insurance industry. All of the lectures were especially prepared for the Huebner Foundation series, and only one of the papers has been previously published. (By prior agreement with the Foundation, the chapter entitled "The Social Responsibilities of Life Insurance Companies As Investors," by Robert Mundheim, appeared in the October 1975 issue of the *Virginia Law Review*.)

The participants in the lecture series were chosen after consultation with a number of academic and insurance industry experts. Especially helpful in this regard were Dan M. McGill, chairman of the Administrative Board of the Huebner Foundation, and Kenneth Wright, president of the American Council of Life Insurance. A number of those invited to participate early in the planning stages of the lecture series made valuable suggestions for other possible participants. J. Robert Ferrari of the Prudential was quite helpful in this regard. Although the book consists of 14 chapters covering nearly all aspects of life insurance company investing, there are other areas which could have been examined. A few such areas were considered, but because of problems of timing and the exigencies of the employment obligations of those invited to develop these areas, certain topics are not treated in separate chapters of the book. Nevertheless, the subjects which have been covered represent a very comprehensive view of the industry's investment process.

Because most of the contributors to this volume either hold fulltime positions in the insurance industry or have consulted extensively in the investments field, the book is primarily practical in its orientation. Extremely technical material has not been emphasized, and, where it does appear, an effort has been made to present it in a readable style. The book should thus be useful for educational programs in investments, either at the college and university level or in industry training programs. However, the depth of the material is such that practitioners in life insurance company investment departments should find the book to be valuable as a reference work. In addition, insurance and finance scholars can employ the book to familiarize themselves with the fundamentals of life insurance investing, and it provides a wealth of institutional information to assist in formulating econometric hypotheses.

The editor is grateful to a number of individuals for their contributions to the success of this project. Paramount among them are the authors, not only for their willingness to participate in the lecture series and prepare chapters for the book but because of their patient and cooperative attitude during the lengthy editing process. An attempt has been made to achieve a degree of consistency of style among the chapters and to avoid duplicative material. In some cases, this resulted in extensive editorial changes, and the authors involved are to be commended for their forbearance. Special thanks are also due to Dan M. McGill, who encouraged me to undertake this project and offered helpful advice on many occasions as the work progressed. Jerry Rosenbloom, executive director of the Huebner Foundation, was also very helpful and supported the project in every respect. His ability to minimize administrative complications and his willingness to provide the necessary support staff on a moment's notice speeded considerably the completion of the book.

Stephen Taylor and Judith Ziobro of the Flow of Funds section of the Board of Governors of the Federal Reserve System are deserving of thanks for their willingness to respond promptly to the numerous requests for data which accompanied the preparation of the book. The American Council of Life Insurance was also quite helpful in supplying data for the book. Mary McCutcheon deserves credit for accurately preparing the final typescript of the book in spite of the editor's illegible notations. Finally, thanks are due to Diana Krigelman and Clrissa Givens, both of the Huebner Foundation staff, for coordinating the proofreading of the manuscript and attending to numerous important details of the project.

Philadelphia, Pa.   J. DAVID CUMMINS
April 1977

Contents

1

Investment Strategy for the Life Insurance Company

By Robert A. Rennie*

The investment strategy of a life insurance company is concerned with changes in economic and financial conditions, particularly in view of their impact on the supply of savings available to the company and on the demand for investment funds by various sectors of the capital market. It is concerned also with the investment implications that result from shifts in the mix of life insurance and annuity products purchased by the public and with the ensuing changes in the contractual obligations of the company. And, finally, it is concerned with the unique set of strategic decisions arising from the forward commitment process, whereby a company makes firm loan authorizations at interest rates set currently for funds that will be received and disbursed many months in the future.

Since the first series of Huebner Foundation lectures on life insurance investments more than 20 years ago,[1] there have been major changes in the role of life insurance companies as financial intermediaries, in the types of life insurance and annuity products purchased by the public, and in the relative importance of private placements in the portfolios of life insurance companies. It is the intent of this chapter to measure the impact of these changes on the life insurance

---

* Robert A. Rennie is senior vice president—investments of the Nationwide Life Insurance Company.

[1] These lectures appear in David McCahan, ed., *Investment of Life Insurance Funds* (Philadelphia: University of Pennsylvania Press, 1953).

1

investment process and to suggest means to develop productive investment strategies for the future. The analysis focuses on the period from 1952 to the present time, covering developments since the first Huebner Foundation lectures on this subject and since the U.S. Treasury—Federal Reserve "Accord" of March 1951, which unpegged bond prices and modified significantly the investment strategy of life insurers.

THE ROLE OF LIFE INSURANCE COMPANIES IN THE CAPITAL MARKETS

Life Insurance Companies as Financial Intermediaries

As financial intermediaries, life insurance companies endeavor to meet simultaneously the financial requirements of policyholders and pension plan contributors, on the one hand, and, on the other, the preferences of issuers of securities (primarily borrowers) who wish to expand their holdings of real assets, e.g., plant and equipment, real estate, and inventories, beyond the limits of their present net worth. In the past, the managements of most life insurance companies operated on the assumption that policyholders preferred to have their insurance assets invested in fixed dollar instruments with negligible risk of default. However, the intense competition for pension plan deposits and the relative decline of permanent life insurance have tended to shift insurance investments toward variable value assets and to intensify the search for attractive life insurance products that would reverse the decline in the share of household savings flowing to life insurers.

Life insurance companies are a vitally important part of the highly developed capital market structure in this country. Over the years, they have provided policyholders with attractive and convenient instruments to accumulate retirement savings and to protect their families financially against premature death. Life insurance is one of the most widespread and efficient systems for mobilizing the funds of small savers. Having collected those savings, the insurers then allocate them among alternative types of investments. The assets of life insurance companies are primarily the obligations or the equities of those seeking capital funds. Conversely, the liabilities of life insurers are the assets of the policyholders and pension plan depositors. In general, the insurance and pension liabilities assumed by life insurance companies have greater predictability of value, smaller default risk, and greater liquidity than the assets held by the companies.

There are several reasons why life insurers can transform and transmute in this manner the risks they assume in the savings-investment process. As noted above, insurance companies provide efficient, low-cost means of collecting the relatively modest sums that most policyholders save each year. Life insurers are equally efficient in pooling these savings into meaningful amounts for future investment. Similarly, their investment departments can provide the professional skills needed to evaluate, appraise, and negotiate appropriate terms for investments and can service them effectively after they have been made. In addition, by diversifying their investments broadly among various types of capital market instruments, life insurance companies provide further protection for policyholders by reducing the delinquency and default risks on each dollar invested. Finally, additional safety is afforded through state insurance laws and regulations relating to investments and through periodic examinations of insurance company operations.

Because of the existence of intermediaries such as life insurance companies, borrowers can be accommodated at lower rates of interest and on easier terms than if they were forced to borrow exclusively from individuals. This is due to the fact that most individual investors would undoubtedly insist on higher rates of interest and stricter loan terms to offset the increase in risk and loss of liquidity, certainty, and convenience that they would incur if they invested directly in the securities of primary borrowers. In addition, the aggregate amount of funds available in the capital markets would decline as many investors would hold larger money balances for liquidity purposes. Thus, the efficiency of life insurance companies in attracting and allocating the savings of policyholders, reducing risk, increasing liquidity, and providing greater stability and certainty in the value of policyholders' savings has served to increase economic and social welfare.

Changes in Life Insurance Investments since 1952

Asset Holdings of Life Companies. The investments of life insurance companies have undergone major changes in scope and structure since 1952. As Table 1.1 reveals, the total financial assets of all U.S. life insurance companies rose from $71.5 billion at the end of 1952 to $279.9 billion on December 31, 1975, more than a three-fold increase. The proportions of various types of investments have changed significantly during this period. Despite the Treasury—Federal Reserve "Accord," U.S. government bonds declined sharply in both relative

TABLE 1.1
Distribution of Total Financial Assets of U.S. Life Insurance Companies

Year	Total Financial Assets (billions)	Percent of Total Financial Assets							
		Corporate Shares	U.S. Government Securities	State & Local Obligations	Corporate Bonds	Home Mortgages	Other Mortgages	Open-Market Paper	Policy Loans
1952	$ 71.5	3.4%	14.4%	1.7%	42.8%	16.5%	13.3%	—%	3.8%
1953	76.5	3.4	12.8	1.7	43.5	17.3	13.2	—	3.8
1954	82.2	4.0	11.1	2.2	43.1	18.5	13.1	—	3.8
1955	87.9	4.1	9.8	2.3	42.2	20.1	13.4	—	3.8
1956	93.2	3.8	8.2	2.5	42.2	21.6	13.8	—	3.8
1957	98.2	3.5	7.1	2.4	42.7	21.8	14.1	—	4.0
1958	104.3	3.9	6.9	2.6	42.5	21.5	14.1	0.0	4.0
1959	110.0	4.2	6.3	2.9	42.2	21.5	14.2	0.1	4.2
1960	115.8	4.3	5.6	3.1	41.5	21.5	14.6	0.3	4.5
1961	122.8	5.1	5.0	3.2	41.2	21.0	15.0	0.2	4.6
1962	129.2	4.9	4.9	3.1	41.1	20.4	15.9	0.3	4.8
1963	136.8	5.2	4.4	2.9	40.9	20.0	17.0	0.3	4.9
1964	144.9	5.5	3.9	2.6	40.2	19.7	18.4	0.2	4.9
1965	154.2	5.9	3.4	2.3	39.6	19.2	19.7	0.2	5.0
1966	162.3	5.4	3.2	2.0	39.1	18.6	21.2	0.2	5.6
1967	172.6	6.3	2.8	1.8	38.9	17.3	21.8	0.3	5.9
1968	183.1	7.2	2.6	1.7	38.7	15.8	22.3	0.3	6.2
1969	191.3	7.2	2.4	1.7	38.0	14.4	23.2	0.7	7.2
1970	200.9	7.7	2.3	1.6	36.9	13.3	23.7	1.1	8.0
1971	215.2	9.6	2.1	1.6	37.0	11.4	23.7	1.3	7.9
1972	232.4	11.5	2.0	1.5	37.3	9.6	23.5	1.3	7.7
1973	244.8	10.6	1.8	1.4	37.8	8.3	24.9	1.2	8.3
1974	255.0	8.6	1.7	1.5	37.8	7.5	26.4	1.6	9.0
1975	279.9	10.0	2.2	1.6	37.7	6.3	25.7	1.7	8.8

Source: Flow of Funds data, available from Flow of Funds section, Board of Governors of the Federal Reserve System.

and absolute terms, falling from 14.4 percent of total financial assets in 1952 to 2.2 percent at the end of 1975.

State and local government obligations followed a different course, rising steadily from 1.7 percent in 1952 to 3.2 percent in 1961. Thereafter, there was a persistent relative decline to 1.6 percent in 1975. The reduction in the relative importance of tax-exempt bonds income after 1961 was due in part to a shift in tax treatment. The Life Insurance Company Income Tax Act of 1959 permitted tax-exempt interest to be deductible only in the ratio of net investment income minus additions to reserves to net investment income. The subsequent growth of commercial bank assets accelerated the aggregate demand for municipal bonds and resulted in a decline in relative yields, further dimming the attractiveness of these issues for life insurers.

Corporate bonds exhibited a slight relative decline until 1970, falling from 42.8 percent of total financial assets in 1952 to 36.9 percent in 1970. Thereafter, the percentage of corporate bonds increased slightly to a level of 37.7 percent at the end of 1975. Open-market paper, which was a negligible holding of life insurance companies until 1969, had risen to $4.8 billion by the end of 1975. Corporate equities, which had accounted for only 3.4 percent of financial assets in 1952, began to climb rapidly in the 1960s and reached 11.5 percent by year-end 1972. Aggressive competition for pension plan deposits and the lure of common stocks to fund such plans during this period accounted for much of this increase in the corporate share category. The percentage of total assets invested in corporate equities declined to 8.6 percent by the end of 1974, primarily due to falling stock prices, but had recovered to 10.0 percent of assets by year-end 1975.

Home mortgages traced a somewhat different pattern, rising from 16.5 percent of assets in 1952 to 21.8 percent in 1957 and then declining to 6.3 percent at the end of 1975. Lower relative interest rates on home mortgages were responsible for the decline. On the other hand, commercial, multifamily residential, and farm mortgages as a group rose from 13.3 percent of assets in 1952 to 25.7 percent of assets by year-end 1975. Finally, policy loans, whose volatility has played a major role in investment decisions since 1965, rose from 3.8 percent of assets in 1952 to a high of 9.0 percent at year-end 1974. They had declined slightly to 8.8 percent of assets by the end of 1975.

Asset Acquisitions of Life Companies. More significant in terms of investment strategy, perhaps, is the record of net annual purchases of financial assets during the period. Information on this facet of life insurance investment activity is presented in Table 1.2. The table indicates that net acquisitions increased from $4.8 billion in 1952 to $20.6 billion in 1975. However, several major shifts in national monetary policy produced fluctuations in policy loan demand; and, after deducting such loans, there were absolute declines in the net purchases of *external* financial assets in 1957, 1966, 1969, and again in 1974.

Net purchases of corporate equities were comparatively insignificant in the 1950s. However, they rose to moderate levels in the first half of the 1960s, exceeded $1.0 billion for the first time in 1967, and reached $3.6 billion in 1971. Thereafter, net equity acquisitions subsided to $1.9 billion in 1975. Most of the increase in common stock acquisitions can be attributed to the growth of separate accounts. The percentage of common stocks in the regular portfolios was less at the end of 1974 than it had been in 1960.

There was a net disinvestment in U.S. government securities in almost every year until 1970. In the home mortgage category, acquisitions increased substantially during the early and middle 1950s; but, by 1967, amortization and repayments exceeded new acquisitions, and net disinvestment continued through 1975. Unlike home mortgages, commercial mortgages became relatively more important in recent years, increasing from 7.6 percent of asset acquisitions in 1952 to 34.2 percent in 1974. The decline in commercial construction in 1975 again reduced the share of such mortgages to 21.2 percent of total acquisitions. Multifamily mortgage acquisitions have been even more volatile. They comprised a very small percentage of net life insurance investment during the 1950s and early 1960s. However, beginning in 1964 and extending through 1970, multifamily mortgage acquisitions exceeded $1.0 billion each year and averaged 20.0 percent of net external investments. Since that time, investments in multifamily mortgages have declined significantly.

Net purchases of corporate bonds have accounted for a consistently high percentage of total external life insurance company investments since 1952 except in 1969, 1970, and 1974 when they represented only 24.3, 19.5, and 28.8 percent, respectively. During the remainder of the period, bond purchases always exceeded 31.0 percent and frequently exceeded 40.0 percent of external acquisitions. Much of the explanation for the drop in bond purchases in 1969 and 1970 stems from the sudden increase in policy loans, which accounted for 12.8 percent of total net investments in 1968, advanced to 26.3 percent in 1969, and still represented 22.2 percent of such acquisitions in 1970. Because the purchase of corporate bonds is frequently the residual item in life insurance investing, such investments were

TABLE 1.2
Distribution of Net Annual Purchases of Selected Financial Assets of U.S. Life Insurance Companies

	Billions of Dollars			Percent of Externally Acquired Financial Assets						
Year	Total Net Acquisitions	Less Policy Loans	Net Acquisitions of External Financial Assets	Corporate Shares	U.S. Government Securities	Corporate Bonds	Home Mortgages	Commercial Mortgages	Multi-family Mortgages	Open-Market Paper
1952	$ 4.8	$0.1	$ 4.7	3.5%	−16.6%	66.0%	24.4%	7.6%	5.5%	—%
1953	5.0	0.2	4.8	1.9	−8.8	56.3	30.0	7.9	1.6	—
1954	5.3	0.2	5.1	5.3	−14.9	41.2	38.4	9.7	0.8	—
1955	5.4	0.2	5.2	1.3	−9.5	32.7	48.2	11.3	2.8	—
1956	5.5	0.2	5.3	0.0	−19.3	41.5	46.6	15.2	1.2	—
1957	5.2	0.4	4.8	0.9	−11.0	56.3	27.3	18.7	−1.3	—
1958	5.4	0.3	5.1	1.5	4.0	47.1	18.3	16.0	−0.1	0.3
1959	5.5	0.4	5.1	3.8	−5.7	41.2	23.7	12.7	2.3	2.0
1960	5.7	0.6	5.1	6.9	−8.1	33.3	25.4	18.1	3.9	3.5
1961	6.2	0.5	5.7	8.2	−5.0	43.9	15.7	16.9	6.8	−1.8
1962	6.8	0.5	6.3	6.9	0.5	39.7	9.5	21.8	7.9	2.4
1963	7.0	0.4	6.6	3.7	−4.9	42.4	14.5	25.7	9.0	0.5
1964	7.9	0.5	7.4	7.4	−3.1	31.1	16.1	13.6	25.6	−1.8
1965	8.8	0.5	8.3	8.5	−5.3	33.7	12.8	20.5	19.0	0.5
1966	8.6	1.4	7.2	3.7	−1.8	33.3	8.9	28.6	20.5	1.2
1967	8.7	0.9	7.8	13.0	−3.1	48.7	−6.0	20.8	18.3	1.3
1968	9.4	1.2	8.2	16.5	−2.0	45.1	−8.9	23.4	12.6	0.6
1969	9.5	2.5	7.0	24.4	−3.4	24.3	−19.7	28.3	21.2	12.0
1970	9.9	2.2	7.7	25.8	0.8	19.5	−11.5	20.7	22.9	10.1
1971	12.7	1.0	11.7	31.1	−1.0	47.0	−18.1	21.7	6.4	5.4
1972	14.4	0.9	13.5	25.9	0.8	51.9	−17.3	23.0	4.4	1.6
1973	16.9	2.2	14.7	24.2	−1.6	40.1	−12.6	33.3	7.5	0.2
1974	16.6	2.7	13.9	16.5	0.8	28.8	−10.1	34.2	8.4	7.7
1975	20.6	1.6	19.0	10.1	9.0	47.9	−7.5	21.2	0.4	3.9

Source: Flow of Funds data, available from Flow of Funds section, Board of Governors of the Federal Reserve System.

"squeezed out" in many companies when policy loans rose rapidly during those two years. The drop in corporate bond acquisitions may also be explained in part by the appearance of the closed-end corporate bond funds during this period, many of which were launched by life insurance company affiliates.

The Effects of Competition among Financial Intermediaries

Competition for Consumer Savings. Life insurance companies have long faced increasing competition from other intermediaries for the current flow of savings,[2] and the empirical evidence suggests that their share of the savings market has undergone a slow but steady attrition.[3] This development is evident from a comparison of the relationship between the financial asset holdings of life insurance companies and those of all major financial institutions. Such a comparison is presented in Table 1.3. As the table indicates, life insurance companies held 21.2 percent of total assets with financial institutions in 1952. By 1975, however, their share had fallen to 13.1 percent.

Among the major institutions, state and local pension funds grew at the fastest relative rate, followed by savings and loan associations and private pension funds. Commercial banks, whose asset share declined until 1965, began to compete aggressively for savings deposits; and their proportion of assets has recovered substantially in recent years. The relative growth rates of non-life insurance companies and mutual savings banks were below the average of the group, whereas finance companies have maintained a relatively constant share of total assets. Credit unions have enjoyed the fastest rate of growth of any type of financial intermediary, but their share of total assets is small. On the other hand, mutual funds experienced a phenomenal growth record until the late 1960s but faded rapidly in subsequent years because of lower common stock prices and mediocre fund sales.

The growth rates of these financial institutions have had a significant impact on the portfolio composition of life insurance companies. The direct competition of non-insured retirement plans for pension fund deposits has forced life insurers to reexamine their investment

---

[2] James J. O'Leary, "The Flow of Savings through Life Insurance," Life Insurance Association of America, *Proceedings of the Fifty-Sixth Annual Meeting* (1962), pp. 197–206, 238.

[3] American Life Insurance Association, "Annual Growth of Selected Forms of Institutional Saving, 1947–1973," *Investment Bulletin No. 725,* June 13, 1974. This series compares the savings through life insurance to the savings flows of seven other major financial institutions, excluding commercial banks.

TABLE 1.3
Total Financial Assets of Financial Institutions

Institution				Percent of Total			
	1952	1955	1960	1965	1970	1974	1975
Life insurance companies	21.2%	20.8%	19.5%	16.7%	15.1%	13.1%	13.1%
Other insurance companies	4.2	4.6	4.4	4.0	3.8	3.6	3.6
Private pension funds	2.9	4.3	6.4	8.0	8.3	6.0	7.0
State and local retirement funds	2.0	2.6	3.3	3.7	4.5	4.6	5.0
Commercial banking	50.3	44.5	38.8	37.3	39.0	43.0	40.9
Savings and loans	6.7	8.9	12.0	14.1	13.2	15.1	15.9
Mutual savings banks	7.5	7.5	6.9	6.4	6.0	5.6	5.7
Credit unions	0.4	0.7	1.1	1.2	1.4	1.6	1.7
Finance companies	3.6	4.3	4.7	4.8	4.9	4.9	4.6
Mutual funds	1.2	1.8	2.9	3.8	3.6	1.7	2.0
REITs	—	—	—	—	0.3	0.9	0.5
Total	100.0%	100.0%	100.0%	100.0%	100.0%	100.0%	100.0%
Total assets of institutions (billions)	$336.8	$423.4	$593.4	$921.7	$1,330.3	$1,952.6	$2,134.5

Note: Percentages and asset totals are based on amounts outstanding at the ends of the years listed. Not shown in this table are the assets of money market funds, security brokers and dealers, and sponsored credit agencies and pools, which the Federal Reserve includes in its listing of financial assets of financial institutions.

Source: Flow of Funds data, available from Flow of Funds section, Board of Governors of the Federal Reserve System.

strategies and portfolio choices. Insurance portfolio managers appear to be increasingly yield conscious in the face of rising "new money" interest rate guarantees for pension plan deposits. Moreover, the well-publicized fact that life insurance is attracting a declining share of total savings has triggered a closer examination of the investment policies of insurers as well as a more intensive search for new, potentially attractive life insurance products.

Competition in the Investment Markets. The investment policies of life insurers have undergone reexamination in other respects as well. In the past, several of the major financial institutions—e.g., savings and loan associations, mutual savings banks, and commercial banks—have been rather tightly restricted in the types of investments they could make. Competition for many types of assets was limited. However, the emergence of new intermediaries and the liberalization of the investment requirements of some of the old ones has increased the competition for many of the traditional types of life insurance investments. In recent years, for example, banks, life insurance companies, and other financial intermediaries have sponsored a number of real estate investment trusts and corporate bond funds. There is some evidence that the emergence of these new types of institutions has modified the portfolio choices of life insurers, at least for brief periods of time.

Such changes in the structure of the capital markets have had a significant impact on the investment strategy and the flow of investment funds from life insurance companies since 1952. As Table 1.4

TABLE 1.4
Percentage of Total Financial Assets Held by Life Insurance Companies

Year	Corporate Bonds	Commercial Mortgages	Multifamily Mortgages	Home Mortgages	Corporate Equities
1952	62.2%	31.3%	28.6%	20.1%	1.3%
1955	61.0	30.8	26.3	20.0	1.1
1960	53.5	30.1	18.6	17.5	1.1
1965	49.6	30.3	23.1	13.4	1.2
1970	36.8	30.4	26.6	9.0	1.7
1974	34.3	28.2	19.7	4.2	3.4
1975	33.3	28.5	19.6	3.6	3.3

Source: Flow of Funds accounts, available from Flow of Funds section, Board of Governors of the Federal Reserve System.

indicates, at the end of 1952, life insurance companies held 62.2 percent of the corporate bonds, 31.3 percent of the commercial mortgages, 28.6 percent of the multifamily residential mortgages, 20.1 percent of the home mortgages, and 1.3 percent of the corporate equities outstanding. By the end of 1975, however, the share of corporate bonds held by life insurers had declined to 33.3 percent of the total, and the proportion of home mortgages had declined to 3.6 percent. The shares of commercial and multifamily mortgages had slipped moderately to 28.5 percent and 19.6 percent, respectively. Corporate equities was the only category of investments that moved upward, rising to 3.3 percent of the total outstanding assets at the end of the period.

Several factors help to explain the relative changes in asset holdings of life insurers. Certain shifts in investments, when compared with offsetting changes made by other types of investors, cast considerable light on the forces at work. As Table 1.5 indicates, for example, the purchase of corporate bonds by life insurers declined dur-

TABLE 1.5

Life Insurance Companies' Share of Total Net Annual Purchases of Private Securities and Mortgages

	Percent of Total Purchases				
Year	Corporate Bonds	Commercial Mortgages	Multifamily Mortgages	Home Mortgages	Corporate Equities
1952	62.4%	39.3%	30.6%	16.9%	5.3%
1953	58.3	32.4	11.7	18.9	4.0
1954	62.7	28.3	7.5	20.4	10.0
1955	49.0	28.7	17.9	19.9	2.4
1956	43.0	33.2	11.0	23.0	−0.1
1957	35.6	36.8	−11.7	15.2	1.1
1958	35.3	27.6	−0.2	9.3	1.9
1959	45.1	21.1	5.6	9.2	4.4
1960	31.7	29.1	9.5	11.7	11.4
1961	47.1	24.2	13.6	7.0	9.2
1962	44.8	28.7	16.0	4.1	18.8
1963	45.5	33.4	18.1	5.6	15.7
1964	34.3	26.4	41.6	7.0	15.3
1965	35.0	38.6	43.3	6.2	19.8
1966	21.2	36.2	48.3	5.3	5.6
1967	23.0	34.6	40.3	−3.3	18.3
1968	25.7	28.7	30.2	−4.2	20.8
1969	12.6	34.0	30.1	−7.6	16.8
1970	6.3	22.3	25.5	−5.9	18.9
1971	23.2	25.6	7.8	−6.9	24.3
1972	38.1	18.5	4.7	−5.3	26.4
1973	42.9	25.6	10.6	−4.2	38.7
1974	16.7	31.3	16.8	−4.2	47.3
1975	25.1	36.2	＊	−3.3	17.0

＊ There was a $47 million decline in the net flow of total multifamily residential mortgages in 1975. Life insurance companies did have token net purchases of multifamily residential mortgages equal to $83 million in 1975 compared to $1.17 billion in 1974.

Source: Flow of Funds accounts, available from Flow of Funds section, Board of Governors of the Federal Reserve System.

ing 1955. This occurred even though the net volume of bonds issued that year increased. The record shows that households, which had been net sellers of such bonds in the previous three years, reversed their stance and were net buyers of over $650 million dollars of corporate issues in 1955, almost one fifth of the net amount issued.

On the other hand, life insurers increased their net purchases of home mortgages that year by $574 million despite the fact that interest yields on bonds increased much faster than yields on home mortgages. Apart from the increase in bond purchases by households, the shift in investment strategy by insurers appears to be related to the $3 billion increase in the volume of home mortgage loans in 1955. Life investment managers felt considerable pressure at that time to accommodate the originators of their mortgage loans in handling the unprecedented volume of new home loan applications.

Table 1.5 also indicates that there was a sharp decline in net bond purchases by life insurers in 1960. This decrease, which totalled $359 million, took place despite a $807 million increase in total supply and seems to reflect, at least in part, the aggressive buying of corporate bonds on the part of both private pension plans and state and local retirement funds. These intermediaries increased their net purchases by $649 million in 1960 and accounted for 51 percent of all net purchases that year.

The clearest example of the impact on life insurance investments of actions taken by other financial intermediaries took place during 1969 and 1970. While the net cash inflow to life insurers decreased sharply in those years because of changes in monetary policy and the ensuing increase in policy loans, these changes do not explain fully the sharp curtailment in the purchase of corporate bonds, particularly in 1970. It was during this period that banks and life insurance companies, among others, were establishing corporate bond funds; and it is likely that several life insurers met some of their commitments to purchase bonds from these sources.

Because of the rising level of interest rates, households were using the proceeds of their policy loans and other resources to buy the bond funds and other issues directly. Household purchases of corporate bonds rose from $4.2 billion in 1968 to $9.5 billion in 1970. Thereafter, household purchases of corporate bonds tapered off sharply until high interest rates in 1974 and 1975 produced a resurgence of household bond purchases. Life insurance company acquisitions of these bonds recovered from the depressed figure of $1.5 billion in 1970 to $7.0 billion in 1972.

Keen competition for commercial mortgage loans among financial institutions has adversely affected the share of life insurance company investments in this area on two different occasions since 1952. In 1958, the savings and loan associations initiated an active program of acquiring commercial mortgage loans at the same time that commercial banks, mutual savings banks, and households were expanding their investments in this area. During that time, the life insurers' share of this market declined from 36.8 percent in 1957 to 21.1 percent in 1959.

Life insurers again faced a declining proportion of the commercial mortgage market after 1969. However, on this occasion, life insurance investment managers probably chose not to attempt to maintain their past share of the market. By 1973, the total flow of funds into commercial mortgages was $19.1 billion, more than triple the level of 1969. Although life insurance company investment managers increased their commercial mortgage loans from $2.0 billion in 1969 to $3.1 billion in 1972 and $4.9 billion in 1973, this expansion did not match the total rise in such loans. The balance of the additional funds needed came primarily from commercial banks, savings and loan associations, mutual savings banks, and real estate investment trusts, many of which were organized by life insurers during this period. After 1973, the total volume of commercial loans declined sharply, and by the third quarter of 1976 was down to an annual rate of $11.7 billion, of which the life companies acquired $3.0 billion. Life insurance investments in multifamily residential mortgages also experienced an irregular decline in the three years after 1970, both in relative and absolute terms. Here, too, the real estate investment trusts appear to have filled part of the gap.

Increased competition among financial intermediaries for types of investments long favored by life insurers appears to have modified the proportions of bonds and mortgages acquired for their portfolios at different times since 1952. Relative interest rates do not seem to have been the primary reason for such portfolio choices. For example, the growth of savings deposits in commercial banks increased greatly the banks' appetite for commercial and multifamily residential mortgages. Corporate bonds became a favorite investment of state and local pension funds in the 1960s and of mutual savings banks in 1967 and in 1970–1972. Savings and loan associations, which dominated the one-to-four family mortgage market throughout the entire 24-year period, moved aggressively into the multifamily residential mortgage market in the early 1960s and again in the late 1960s and 1970s. Finally, as indicated above, new financial intermediaries

—corporate bond funds and real estate investment trusts—aggressively entered the corporate bond and mortgage markets.

Affiliated Investment Activities

Faced with a declining share of individual savings, life insurers have organized or acquired a wide range of financial, real estate, and service institutions. This activity has been conducted either directly or through associated holding companies. Major efforts have been devoted to the development of mutual investment funds. By the end of 1975, 103 insurance companies or affiliated organizations had formed some type of association with 311 investment companies. The first major link between mutual funds and life insurance was forged in 1952, when the Nationwide Insurance Group acquired the management/underwriting company serving Mutual Investing Foundation, a mutual fund organized in 1933. One of the main reasons for forming this life insurance–mutual fund combination was to use an established financial institution (mutual funds) to help train the Nationwide agency force in the sale of the insurance-related equity products that were envisioned in the future.

Rapid progress in the development of the life insurance–mutual fund combination came after 1967. At the close of 1975, mutual funds associated with insurance companies had assets amounting to $18.6 billion, or 38.2 percent of the total resources of the mutual fund industry. Among the 185 mutual funds that had been organized directly by insurance companies were 85 whose shares are offered by insurance agents, dually licensed to sell both funds and insurance; 51 open-end separate accounts that are utilized to fund variable annuities or other types of pension and thrift plans; and 24 open-end companies that serve the same purpose but are organized as unit investment trusts under the Investment Company Act of 1940.[4]

In the late 1960s and early 1970s, life insurance companies also expanded the scope of their investment activities by sponsoring a relatively large number of real estate investment trusts and closed-end corporate bond funds. A preliminary survey of 25 such institutions sponsored by major life insurers indicated that they had total assets of $4.5 billion at the end of the most recent fiscal year.[5]

---

[4] Wiesenberger Services, Inc. *Investment Companies,* 36th annual ed. (New York, 1976), chap. 36, p. E–1.

[5] Life insurance company affiliated REITs are discussed in more detail in Chapter 7 of this volume.

Many of these affiliated financial institutions appear not to have fulfilled the expectations of their sponsors. Declining common stock prices, rising interest rates, serious overbuilding of commercial properties, and other economic uncertainties have tended to frustrate the achievement of desired results. In general, few of these newer types of financial products provide the predictability or stability in value that the average family is seeking for its savings. It appears that if life insurers are to attract a larger share of individual savings, they must design other products that meet more fully the public's desire for convenience, liquidity, high yield, and more protection against inflation.[6] The development of a "full service" savings product that combines the best features of the life insurance contract with those of a discretionary deposit account is overdue and is uniquely within the jurisdiction of the life insurance business.

INVESTMENT STRATEGY AND ASSET-LIABILITY MANAGEMENT INTERACTION

An insurer's choice of investments is necessarily influenced by the types of insurance policies it issues. The nature of its liabilities will vary, depending on whether its insurance portfolio is heavily weighted with permanent life insurance, health insurance, annuity and pension plan contracts, or term policies. Its investment strategy will vary in relation to the ordering of such liabilities and to its perceived risks in meeting those obligations. Each company's investment requirements are different, and an analysis of overall industry data will not determine all the strategic considerations involved in its investment decisions.

To explain more fully the investment strategies of individual companies over the past two decades, the author of this chapter has conducted a study of the investment behavior during that period of the 100 largest U.S. life insurance companies.[7] The smallest company in the study had assets of $250 million on December 31, 1973, and the largest had assets of almost $35 billion. The combined assets of these

---

[6] Roger F. Murray, "An Overview of the Life Insurance-Mutual Fund Combination," *The Journal of Risk and Insurance*, vol. 36, no. 4 (September 1969), pp. 423–24.

[7] To maintain an identical group of companies throughout the period, the ranking in terms of asset size was determined as of December 31, 1972, the latest date for which full information was available at the outset of the study. The 1973 data for those companies have been incorporated in the study. Two companies with life insurance charters but no life insurance in force were deleted from the group and were replaced by the next two companies in rank.

100 companies represented 95.3 percent of the industry total at the end of 1952 and declined gradually to 89.5 percent on December 31, 1973.[8] Thus, the investment decisions of these companies have accounted for a major part of the flow of life insurance funds during this period.

Portfolio Mix and Net Investment Yield

One phase of the study sought to determine the relationship between the net investment yields of the companies and the percentage of assets invested in different categories of investments. The correlation between the net investment yields of the companies and their asset size was also determined. Table 1.6 presents the correlation co-

TABLE 1.6
Relationship between the Net Investment Yield and the Investment Portfolio
Mix of the 100 Largest Life Insurance Companies

Investment Type	*Correlation Coefficients*				
	1952	*1963*	*1968*	*1972*	*1973*
Mortgage loans	0.3991†	0.3364†	0.0885	0.1749*	0.1521
Bonds	−0.4608†	−0.1873*	0.0323	0.2528*	0.2365*
Bonds and mortgage loans combined	−0.0455	0.4711†	0.3592†	0.4578†	0.4423†
Common stock	0.2973†	−0.4825†	−0.5958†	−0.5046†	−0.4062†
Preferred stock	0.0701	−0.3388†	−0.3021†	−0.2186*	−0.1934*
Policy loans	0.1131	−0.0450	0.1694*	0.0430	−0.0569
Cash	−0.4234†	−0.4140†	−0.4434†	−0.3700†	−0.5451†
Real estate	0.0804	−0.3456†	−0.3304†	−0.3778†	−0.4015†
Total assets	−0.0895	0.0669	0.0913	0.0493	0.0363

* Significant at the 5 percent level.
† Significant at the 1 percent level.
Source: *Best's Insurance Reports: Life-Health*, various years.

efficients among those variables for the 100 top companies for the years 1952, 1963, 1968, 1972, and 1973.[9]

Bonds and Mortgages. While a significant relationship existed

___

[8] All data in this study were secured from *Best's Insurance Reports: Life-Health* (Morristown, N.J.: A. M. Best Co., annual) for the respective years.

[9] Of course, in order to obtain conclusive results with regard to many of the relationships tested in this section, more advanced econometric techniques would have to be employed. Time constraints did not permit a study of this type to be conducted for purposes of this book.

between investment yield and the proportion of mortgage loans in the portfolios in 1952 and 1963, the relationship lessened substantially in more recent years. This change may be explained to some degree by the increasing role of high-yielding private placement issues in the portfolios in later years. In the bond category, there was a negative relationship in the earlier years, undoubtedly reflecting the large holdings of U.S. government bonds. However, some positive correlation appeared in the 1970s after government bond holdings had been reduced to modest levels. There is a significant correlation between investment yields and the combined total of the bond and mortgage loan categories beginning in 1963 and continuing throughout the period. These two investment categories accounted for 71.4 percent of regular portfolio assets in 1973. Companies appeared to purchase these two types of investments alternatively because there was a negative correlation of -0.6028 between bond and mortgage loan holdings in 1973.

Common and Preferred Stocks. Net investment yield was positively correlated with the percentage of common stock holdings in 1952, but the relationship was reversed by 1963, and the negative correlation persisted throughout the balance of the period. It should be recalled, however, that Best's net investment income concept omits realized and unrealized capital gains. An analysis of the average total yield of the ten companies in the group having the highest percentage of common stock holdings indicated that their net investment income as reported by Best's averaged 4.66 percent for the period 1964–1973, while their total yield was 5.33 percent. In other words, their net yield was supplemented by a 0.67 percent annual return from realized and unrealized capital gains.

On the other hand, a group of ten companies selected randomly from the population of 100 companies yielded only 0.01 percent annually from realized and unrealized capital gains. The ten companies with the lowest percentage of common stocks in the group had realized and unrealized losses of 0.14 percent of mean invested assets. The results of this phase of the study are presented in Table 1.7.

Total yield appears to be positively related to the amount of common stock holdings. Because of the negligible yield from realized and unrealized capital gains secured by the randomly selected group of companies,[10] it seems possible to use Best's net investment yield

---

[10] This does not mean that the companies have done poorly in the stock market, but rather that stocks represent only a small part of the total portfolio of the typical company.

TABLE 1.7
Relation of Investment Yield to Common Stock Holdings: 1964–1973

Company Group	Average Net Investment Yield (Best's)	Average Yield from Realized and Unrealized Gains	Total Yield
Ten companies with highest ratio of common stocks	4.66%	0.67%	5.33%
Ten companies with lowest ratio of common stocks	5.07	−0.14	4.93
Ten companies randomly selected from top 100	5.22	0.01	5.23
Total life insurance industry average yield	5.14		

figure as a surrogate for total yield for an average group of companies over a substantial time period. Many companies use realized stock gains to offset realized bond losses which they consciously initiate in their portfolios. The proceeds are then reinvested in higher yielding securities.

Preferred stock holdings are negatively correlated with investment yield. In this case, it should be observed that the dividend credit allowed under the 1959 income tax law increased the after-tax yields of preferred stock. Consequently, the relative holdings of preferred stock have been rising gradually since 1960.

Policy Loans, Cash, and Real Estate. Surprisingly, there has been little correlation between investment yield and the ratio of policy loans to total assets. Indeed, the correlation was moderately positive in 1968. It turned slightly negative in 1973, but not to a significant degree. Further analysis indicates that several of the companies with a relatively large percentage of policy loans have sought to overcome this disadvantage by pursuing a more aggressive investment policy. On the other hand, some of the companies with a negligible volume of policy loans are primarily health insurers, which tend to be characterized by investment yields below the industry average.

Investment yield is negatively correlated with cash balances to a significant degree, and the largest cash balances are held by health insurance companies. It is likely that such companies find it appropriate to maintain substantial cash balances with banks in the normal course of conducting their credit life and health insurance business.

Real estate investments have been negatively correlated with investment yield, at least since 1963. In part, this relationship is due to some difficult experiences that certain life insurers have had with real estate and mortgage loan programs. The results have tended to depress the investment yields of these companies while leaving them with relatively large holdings of non-income producing real estate. Conversely, several life insurance affiliates of multiple-line groups hold little or no real estate in their life portfolios. Often these companies have above-average yields, and the effect is to reinforce the negative correlation between real estate holdings and investment yields.

Impact of Size and Growth. No significant bivariate correlation exists between the size of a life insurance company and its net investment yield. Certain advantages enjoyed by the larger companies through their ability to reach special markets appear to be offset by the greater flexibility of smaller companies and their ability to take advantage of market situations that offer temporary or special yield differentials. There are observed differences within both large and small companies relating to management's attitudes toward risk that may increase or decrease current yield. Yet, all life insurers are subject to relatively uniform legal and regulatory constraints on their investment choices that tend to limit the range of risk and return among companies.

Finally, as expected, there is a significant correlation between the rates of asset growth and the net investment yields of the 100 top companies. During the period between 1952 and 1963, the relationship between asset growth and investment yield was negative, the correlation coefficient being -0.2746. This is probably due to the fact that interest rates declined during the recession of 1954 and again during the years 1961 and 1962. On the other hand, investment yields and asset growth were positively correlated (0.3095) during the interval between 1963 and 1973, when interest rates increased to significantly higher levels.

In general, the investment yields of the top 100 companies were significantly correlated over time, but the coefficients were not as high as might be expected. For example, the correlation coefficient of company yields for 1963 and 1973 was only 0.4171. On the other hand, the correlation of asset growth over different time periods was high. The growth in company assets over the years 1952–1963 relative to the growth during 1963–1973 had a correlation coefficient of 0.7898. Thus, high growth companies tend to project their superior performance over long time periods. This produces above-average cash flows and enables investment managers to achieve progressively higher investment yields during periods of rising interest rates.

Insurance Product Mix and Portfolio Strategy

The second phase of the analysis of the investment practices of the top 100 life insurers attempted to determine if the companies' investment strategies are related to their business mix. The record indicates that there have been major changes both in the composition of reserve liabilities and in the product mix of life insurance companies since 1952 and that these changes have modified the investment policies of life insurers.

Changes in Product Mix since 1952. Pension fund reserves accounted for only 11.4 percent of total life insurance company liabilities in 1952. By 1973, this figure had increased to 24.8 percent. Total life insurance reserves, on the other hand, had decreased from 80.3 percent to 61.6 percent of total liabilities. Of the net increase in liabilities recorded in 1973, pension fund reserve increases accounted for 34.0 percent, compared to 24.4 percent in 1952. The health insurance reserves of life insurers increased ten-fold during this period.

Changes in the distribution of life and health insurance writings were even more apparent. Group insurance, as a percentage of total life insurance in force, increased from 28.3 percent to 40.2 percent during the 22-year period. Purchases of term insurance accounted for 43 percent of all ordinary life insurance purchases in 1973, up from less than 30 percent in 1952. The ratio of health insurance premium receipts to the total premium receipts of life insurers more than doubled from 1952 to 1973, rising from 15.8 to 31.9 percent of the total.

Examined on an individual company basis, the changes are equally clear. In 1952, 78 of the 100 companies had one half or more of their insurance in force in the form of whole life or endowment policies. By 1973, only 35 companies met this criterion. In 1952, only eight companies had one third or more of their in-force business in the form of group insurance. By 1973, the number had increased to 37. And finally, in 1952 only five companies had as much as one third of their in-force business in the form of ordinary term insurance. By 1973, 12 of the top companies had issued this amount of ordinary term insurance.

Product Mix and Investment Behavior. To measure the relationship between product mix and investment policy, the 100 top life companies were divided into five different groups according to the distinctive character of their insurance reserve liabilities, their premium receipts, or their mix of business in force. The criteria for classification were as follows:

1. *Permanent Life Insurance*—life insurance reserves equal to 70 percent or more of total assets.
2. *Health Insurance*—premium receipts from health insurance equal to 65 percent or more of company premium receipts or health reserves equal to 15 percent or more of total assets.
3. *Annuities*—annuity reserves equal to 15 percent or more of total assets.
4. *Term*—ordinary term insurance equal to one third or more of total insurance in force.
5. *Balanced Product Mix*—companies with a balanced insurance portfolio not fitting any of the foregoing categories.

Most of the top 100 life insurers fitted readily into one of these classes. Five companies writing mainly employee benefits coverages qualified in two or more classes, usually in the health, annuity, or term categories. In such cases, these companies were included in the group where they had the greatest relative proportion of their reserves or coverages. Table 1.8 sets forth the distribution of the investment portfolios of the 100 top companies classified by the predominant type of their insurance reserves or writings. It seems clear that there is a definite relationship between the types of assets held by life insurers and the nature of their liabilities.

As expected, the writers of permanent insurance had a higher-than-average percentage of policy loans, although the amount was small and actually lower than the level of outstanding policy loans for companies with a balanced insurance portfolio. Their mortgage loan portfolios were above average, but the percentages of assets in preferred and common stocks were below average, and their separate account holdings were negligible. Otherwise, the distribution of their assets closely approximated the averages for all 100 companies. The asset growth of the writers of permanent insurance paralleled the growth of all companies in the study for the entire 1952–1973 period, but growth has lagged somewhat since 1968. Their net investment yield and the increase in that yield over the whole period are slightly below average. The 27 major writers of permanent insurance each held assets of $887 million on average at the end of 1973, compared to average holdings of $2,259 million for the average company in the group.

The distribution of investments of the ten health insurers is radically different from the holdings of other company groups. Tax considerations explain much of the difference. For example, only seven of the top 100 companies had net policy reserves below 60 percent of

TABLE 1.8
Distribution of Investment Portfolios of 100 Largest Life Insurance Companies by Predominant Product Type (year-end 1973)

Investment Category	Company Grouping*					
	Permanent Life	Health	Annuities	Term	Balanced Product Mix	All 100 Companies
Mortgage loans	35.2%	21.6%	35.6%	28.6%	31.2%	31.7%
Corporate bonds	34.6	26.9	36.6	37.0	33.4	34.2
Government bonds	5.3	13.3	4.1	9.7	5.0	5.9
Common stock	4.5	11.1	3.4	4.3	5.5	5.6
Preferred stock	2.1	6.0	1.2	4.1	3.0	3.2
Policy loans	9.3	4.9	6.2	7.3	10.9	9.0
Real estate	3.6	3.5	2.7	1.7	3.5	3.5
Cash	0.6	1.8	0.4	0.7	0.8	0.8
Separate accounts	0.3	4.2	4.8	1.4	2.8	2.0
Other assets	4.5	6.7	5.0	5.2	3.8	4.1
Yield	5.96	5.77	6.19	6.26	5.97	6.00
Asset growth						
1968–1973	36.6%	82.6%	35.6%	62.7%	38.4%	44.2%
1952–1973	730.6	3,154.7	313.6	682.6	394.8	753.5
Increase in yield						
1968–1973	22.6%	26.1%	23.0%	26.2%	20.7%	22.5%
1952–1973	72.4	97.2	84.9	88.0	75.7	79.5
Average size of company (millions)	$886.9	$670.9	$9,835.0	$891.0	$1,447.7	$2,259.0
Number of companies	27	10	13	9	41	100

Note: The percentage figures are unweighted averages of the percentage portfolio distributions of the individual companies within the groups.

* The definitions of the company groups are presented on p. 21.

Source: *Best's Insurance Reports: Life-Health*, 1974.

assets, and six of them were primarily health insurers. In several cases, the health insurers' investment policies seem to be patterned on the investment strategy of casualty insurance companies.

Mortgage loan and corporate bond holdings of this group are substantially below the overall average (21.6 and 26.9 percent, respectively). While the government bond holdings are high (13.3 percent), much of the difference is held in tax-exempt state and local bonds. Common and preferred stock investments were relatively high, particularly for certain individual companies. Health insurers had little trouble with policy loans—on the average this asset represented less than 5 percent of their total assets. Assets held in separate accounts were at twice the average level of all 100 companies, perhaps reflecting the employee benefit orientation of the health writers. As noted previously in this chapter, the high cash holdings may be related to operating policies involving group creditors' coverages. The net investment yield for this group was considerably below average, reflecting the significant holdings of tax-exempt and equity securities. On the other hand, the rate of asset growth of health insurers exceeded that of all other company groups over the entire period, and their increase in yields has been well above average.

The 13 annuity and pension plan writers had a distribution of investments that appears to harmonize with their contractual liabilities and with the highly competitive pension market in which they operate. Mortgage loan holdings were the highest of any group, accounting for 35.6 percent of total assets. This high figure indicates the desire of these companies to hold a significant volume of high-yielding assets whose regular amortization will coincide broadly with their annuity payment requirements. The annuity companies also demonstrated their emphasis on high yields by holding above-average percentages of corporate bonds and below-average amounts of government bonds and cash. The low government bond and cash holdings also probably reflect the fact that the liquidity requirements of the annuity writers are relatively less than those of some of the other company groups.

Annuity companies revealed in other ways a strong tendency to match their asset holdings with their particular insurance products. They had the highest percentage of assets in separate accounts of any class of insurer (4.8 percent). However, these companies have the lowest relative percentage of assets of any group invested in common and preferred stocks in their regular accounts (3.4 percent and 1.2 percent, respectively).

The investment yield of this group is high, despite the below-average increase in assets since 1952 and even since 1968. The average size of companies in the annuity group—$9,835 million in assets—compares with $2,259 million for all companies among the top 100 firms. This group includes seven of the ten largest life insurance companies, and the distribution and growth of assets are typical of such companies.

Term insurers had the highest net investment yield of any group in the study (6.26 percent) during 1973. A rapid growth in assets since 1968 seems to have contributed to this result. Five of the nine term life companies are the life affiliates of major multiple-line insurance groups, and in general, their assets are managed by highly skilled investment officers. The below-average size of the mortgage loan portfolios reflects in several cases the lack of a well-developed structure for originating mortgage loans. On the other hand, the percentages of corporate and government bonds are high. This bond concentration utilizes the investment skills and contacts developed within the broader investment staffs of the multiple-line groups. The average term life company, with $891 million in assets, is smaller than the mean firm in the study. Growth in assets since 1968 has been well above the average, but not for the entire period from 1952.

The investments of companies with balanced portfolios of insurance products match closely the average holdings of all companies. Policy loans are relatively high, reducing slightly the proportion of assets held in mortgage loans and bonds. Net investment yield is slightly below average, probably reflecting the high level of policy loans and the slower growth in assets, which have been very sluggish over the entire time span since 1952.

The Policy Loan Problem

Life insurance investment officers have faced five periods of recession and three "credit crunches" since 1952. These fluctuations in economic activity and in monetary policy have placed intense pressures on the investment operations of life insurers because the inflow of funds available for investment has been seriously depressed during recent periods of interest rate escalation.[11] Policy loans and mort-

---

[11] See George A. Bishop, *The Response of Life Insurance Investments to Changes in Monetary Policy: 1965–1970* (New York: Life Insurance Association of America, 1971).

gage prepayments-in-full are the two variables responding most sensitively to interest rate increases.

Through the periods of tight money in 1966, 1969–1970, and again in 1973–1974, the total volume of policy loans rose from $7.7 billion at the end of 1965 to approximately $22.9 billion at the end of 1974. During those years, when the market rate of interest increased above the contractual policy loan rates (5 to 6 percent for most companies), policyholders were motivated to borrow the cash values of their life insurance policies. Under the provisions of state insurance laws and the terms of their policies, policyholders can borrow those funds at their option. In the future, so long as the general level of interest rates remains substantially above policy loan ceilings, these loans can be expected to rise during periods of monetary restraint.

The major impact of monetary restraint on policy loans has been concentrated on a limited group of companies. Among the 100 top companies in this study, the trend in the ratio of policy loans to total assets is shown in the accompanying table.

Companies with High Percentages of Policy Loans to Total Assets

End of Year	10–15%	15–20%	20–25%	Over 25%	Total over 10%
1952	5	1	—	—	6
1963	6	—	—	—	6
1968	15	1	1	—	17
1972	19	12	—	1	32
1973	21	11	2	1	35

In the interests of policyholders and insurers alike, it seems imperative that efforts to solve the policy loan problem and its disruptive impact on cash flow be accelerated. Several major companies have increased the policy loan rates in their newly issued policies to a higher level, such as 8 percent. Another approach is to adjust the dividends on policies with outstanding loans to recognize the differential between the policy loan interest rate and rates available in the capital markets. A third alternative would be to utilize a formula which links policy loan interest rates to some generally accepted market rate of interest. Although the use of variable loan rates has thus far been forestalled by difficulties in obtaining regulatory approval, this method would be the most effective mechanism for minimizing disintermediation caused by monetary restraint and rising interest rates.

INVESTMENT STRATEGY OF AN INDIVIDUAL LIFE INSURER: AN ILLUSTRATIVE CASE

The foregoing analysis has sought to demonstrate that life insurers are major investors in a broad range of capital market instruments. No other type of financial intermediary has so many options to consider in designing its investment strategy. Not only does this wide spectrum of asset choice enable life insurers to secure broad diversification in their portfolios, but it also permits them to shift their emphasis from one sector of the capital market to another in response to competitive demand, relative yields, and the supply of attractive investments.

The preceding discussion outlined the different investment strategies pursued by various categories of insurers. It was concluded that the composition of assets varies among insurers, depending to a considerable degree upon the character of their reserve liabilities and the predominant types of insurance that they issue.

These general considerations shape the broad investment environment within which major segments of the life insurance industry function. But they illustrate only in part the specific factors that must be taken into account by an individual life insurer in formulating its own investment strategy. Consequently, this section is concerned with choosing an investment strategy that best fits the goals of such an individual company from among several alternative investment strategies. Specifically, an attempt is made to outline the steps that have been taken over the past five years to develop an explicit investment strategy for a medium-sized life insurance company of which the author serves as chief investment officer.[12]

The investment strategy of an individual company and its ability to undertake risk in its portfolio of assets are conditioned by three interrelated factors: (a) the relative financial strength of the company and the adequacy of its capital and/or surplus to meet future requirements; (b) the investment policies of the company and management's attitudes toward portfolio diversification and risk bearing; and (c) the forward commitment process and the timing and distribution of loan authorizations prior to the actual disbursement of funds.

---

[12] Nationwide Life Insurance Company had assets of $857.2 million on December 31, 1975, ranking 47th in asset size among U.S. life insurers. At year-end 1975, bonds comprised 36.0 percent of total assets; mortgage loans, 36.1 percent; common stocks, 2.0 percent; preferred stock, 2.6 percent; separate accounts, 11.1 percent; policy loans, 5.5 percent; and all other assets, 6.7 percent.

The Relative Financial Strength of the Company

Measuring the overall financial strength of a life insurance company is a complex, sometimes arbitrary process. There do not appear to be any broad "rules of thumb" that are acceptable for this purpose, including the frequently used relationship of capital and surplus to interest-bearing liabilities. In an effort to fill this gap, the company has developed a formula which, in essence, establishes the amount of surplus considered to be necessary for each line of business, with one of the major requirements being an amount estimated to be sufficient to adjust ordinary reserves to the net-level basis. The surplus requirements for all major lines are then aggregated to arrive at the total for the company. Actual capital and statutory surplus is then divided by the total requirements, and the resulting percentage is used to indicate the company's relative financial strength. The company objective is to achieve a 100 percent relationship.

Obviously, as the foregoing financial relationship rises above 100 percent, the investment policy of the company can become more aggressive, and higher-yielding securities and mortgage loans with longer maturities can be chosen for the portfolio. Conversely, as the percentages decline below 100 percent, the investment strategy of the company must become more conservative. Maturities must be shortened and higher-rated, less risky investments purchased for the company.

Investment Policies and Managerial Attitudes

The Investment Policy: Maximization through Flexibility. The company's investment policy seeks to maximize total long-term, after-tax investment income, subject to the relative financial strength and risk-bearing ability of the company, as outlined above, and also subject to the statutory and regulatory constraints imposed by insurance laws and regulatory agencies.[13] By implication, this policy instructs

---

[13] In general, the statutory and regulatory constraints have not been excessively restrictive. When changing economic or financial conditions have called for increased investment flexibility, the industry has usually sought legislative relief. Frequently, when the desired changes were clearly in the public interest, statutory modifications were made without delay.

On the other hand, it should be noted that the degree of regulatory discretion —as opposed to the provisions of insurance statutes—has grown in recent decades. See, for example, Spencer L. Kimball and Herbert S. Denenberg, "The Regulation of Investments: A Wisconsin Viewpoint," in *Insurance, Government, and Social Policy,* ed. Spencer L. Kimball and Herbert S. Denenberg (Homewood, Ill.: Richard D. Irwin, 1969), chap. 8. State insurance departments have

management to purchase, at any point in time, whatever forms of investment will produce the largest expected return to the company—bonds, notes, mortgages, common or preferred stock—as long as the constraints are not violated.

In the opinion of the company's executives, this degree of flexibility is required if top management hopes to achieve a superior investment performance. Rapidly shifting financial, economic, and social conditions call for specific investment decisions that must be made promptly as events unfold. For example, a rigid investment policy that prescribes fixed percentages of bonds, mortgage loans, and equities in the portfolio can put a competent investment manager in a strait jacket. Such a policy appears to be counterproductive, from the viewpoint of both the company's welfare and the economic health of the country as a whole.

Investment management has several levels of responsibility. In the first place, it must manage the portfolio in such a way as to meet the company's contractual obligations to policyholders. In some instances, this is a predetermined interest return. But because the company has issued a large volume of participating policies, it must also earn a sufficient return to help pay generous policyholder dividends. In addition, in the case of separate accounts, investment contracts, and many deposit administration pension accounts, investment management has to meet increased competitive pressures stemming from the comparative rates of return being cited to prospective clients by sales representatives of investment counselors, banks, and other life insurers. Secondly, in the case of a stock company, investment management must strive to make its contribution toward increasing the company's earnings per share. Often, rising investment income is the most important contributor toward earnings reports.

---

sometimes been slow to recognize the merits of investment innovations that they could authorize or prohibit by regulatory discretion. For example, during the 1950s, certain insurance departments were reluctant to approve the dual licensing of insurance agents to sell equity products as well as insurance.

More recently, at least one insurance department has opposed the leveraging of life insurance investment portfolios. In April 1972, the New England Mutual Life Insurance Company sold to the public $50 million of 7⅜ percent debentures due in 1997. This was the first such financing by a major mutual insurance company. The proceeds were used to increase the total investment potential of the company. In view of the subsequent escalation of interest rates, this innovation was clearly one that has served the interests of the company's policyholders. However, when another quality insurer sought clearance shortly thereafter from the insurance regulators in its own state of domicile to make a similar debenture issue, permission was refused, despite the fact that the department had previously concurred with the New England Mutual issue.

Finally, life insurance companies, as important institutional investors, have been a significant source of funds over the years, helping to finance capital formation and to increase the productivity of the economy. Life insurers also have a major role to play in maintaining efficient, orderly capital markets, thereby equalizing interest rates across those markets. To fulfill this function, funds should be invested in those sectors of the market where the rate of return is the highest. In other words, they should always seek to attain the maximum rate of return on their current investments.

Implicit in the foregoing objective is the ability to move rapidly from one type of investment to another in order to capitalize on differentials in yield. It has been noted that the relative volume of new bond and stock financing has conformed closely to changes in the relative costs of those two forms of financing.[14] As a purchaser of such securities, the company should be equally sensitive to the relative values and yields to be secured in the different sectors of the capital market if it is to help maintain equilibrium in that market. Only if flexibility is maintained in the company's investment strategy can it respond promptly to such changes in relative values. A policy of virtually fixed percentages of bonds, mortgages, and stocks in the portfolio would tend to frustrate the company's ability to perform one of the basic responsibilities that life insurers should assume in this complex economy. And of more immediate concern, such an inflexible investment policy reduces investment income below the amount the company could be earning at the same level of risk bearing.

The company's flexible investment policies are carried out within the framework of broad investment guidelines set at the monthly meetings of the investment committee of the board of directors. The investment staff presents a detailed report outlining its investment activities during the past month and secures authorization or ratification of certain major investment items. In turn, the investment committee frequently indicates its reaction to current staff investment strategy in the light of emerging economic, financial, and governmental trends and overall company operations. Although few formal

---

[14] Throughout most of the post-World War II period, when the cost of capital raised via bond issues has been high relative to the cost via common stock issues, the net volume of bond issues has been low relative to the net volume of common stock issued, and vice versa. During the period 1949–1974, for example, the correlation coefficient of the ratios of the cost of capital via common stocks (earnings/price ratio, Standard & Poor's 500 stocks) versus bonds (Moody's Baa) and the ratios of the net volume of common stocks versus corporate bonds issued was a significantly high −0.93.

directives are issued at the meeting, the staff reevaluates its strategy following each session. After a full review of investment committee deliberations and an examination of the cash flow forecasts relative to outstanding and prospective commitments, the senior investment staff resets its course for the next time period. Often the modifications in strategy are minor; but, occasionally, they lead to recommended changes in the basic investment policies of the company, which are reviewed and formally approved by the investment committee on an annual basis.

Attitudes toward Diversification and Risk Bearing. Considerable progress has been made in recent years in developing valid theories of portfolio risk and asset pricing. These developments have stemmed primarily from the work of H. M. Markowitz, William F. Sharpe, and a number of other researchers.[15] The capital asset pricing model developed by these investigators postulates an *efficient* capital market. An efficient market is one in which new information about a capital asset is immediately and costlessly available to all investors and potential investors and in which brokerage costs are zero. The model has been shown to possess considerable power in risk measurement and portfolio selection, and it has proven valuable to Nationwide in the management of its common stock portfolio.[16]

Unfortunately, however, the market for common stocks is the only one that might be considered to approximate an "efficient" capital market. Serious "inefficiencies" are present in the market for publicly issued bonds, and the secondary markets for private placements and commercial mortgage loans are very imperfect. However, the principles underlying the capital asset pricing model are equally applicable to those classes of investments and appear to offer the most productive starting point for life insurance companies in their future efforts to refine the measurement of portfolio risk.

Meanwhile, the company depends primarily upon the fundamental analysis, experience, and judgment of its mortgage loan underwriters and securities analysts in selecting good quality commercial

---

[15] H. M. Markowitz, *Portfolio Selection: Efficient Diversification of Investments,* Cowles Foundation Monograph No. 16 (New York: John Wiley & Sons, 1959); William F. Sharpe, "Capital Asset Prices: A Theory of Market Equilibrium under Conditions of Risk," *Journal of Finance,* vol. 19 (September 1964), pp. 425–42; James Lorie and Richard Brealey, eds., *Modern Developments in Investment Management* (New York: Praeger Publishers, 1972); and Eugene F. Fama and Merton H. Miller, *The Theory of Finance* (Hinsdale, Ill.: Dryden Press, 1972).

[16] The use of this type of portfolio analysis by life insurance companies is discussed in more detail in Chapter 4.

mortgage loans, private placements, and other securities. Specific loan terms and maturities are generally set or approved by the analyst or underwriter negotiating the loan. In the case of publicly issued bonds, the analysts' work is supplemented by an evaluation of the quality ratings assigned by the rating services. Frequently, the company attempts to buy securities in anticipation of an upward revision of the rating and, occasionally, to sell specific issues in the portfolio prior to the announcement of a lowered rating.

It is the responsibility of the respective department heads to maintain an optimum balance within the portfolios for which they are responsible. They are expected to maintain a wide diversification of investments among industries, to secure total yields commensurate with the risks involved, to scale the size of individual investments to those risks, and to construct portfolios whose maturity schedules will generate a regular cash flow from such maturities.

The Forward Commitment Process

The forward commitment process calls for many complex decisions on the part of investment management. Life insurers acquire most of their corporate bonds and mortgages by first extending commitments to the borrowers seeking such financing.[17] No other financial intermediary must cope with as many variables and constraints as are encountered by the life insurer in the forward commitment process. Separating the investment decision by many months from the actual disbursement of funds requires investment managers, implicitly or explicitly, to project future cash flows and interest trends by type of investment if they intend to pursue a rational, yield-oriented investment strategy.

Among the forecasts and other inputs involved in the forward commitment process are the following:

1. A projection is developed of the cash flows that will be available at different points in the future when funds must be disbursed to meet commitments made in prior time periods.[18]

---

[17] Forward commitments are discussed further in Chapter 2 of this book. For further reading on the subject, see James E. Pesando, "The Interest Sensitivity of the Flow of Funds through Life Insurance Companies: An Econometric Analysis," *Journal of Finance*, vol. 29, no. 4 (September 1974), pp. 1105–21; and W. Leigh Ribble, Jr., "The Portfolio Behavior of U.S. Life Insurance Companies" (Ph.D. diss., Massachusetts Institute of Technology, 1973), pp. 25–44.

[18] Cash flow forecasting is discussed in Chapter 10 of this book.

2. The interest rate trends that will prevail in the future must be projected. Management must also assign probability distributions to these forecasts. If rates are expected to rise in future quarters, for example, it would be shortsighted to commit funds now for future disbursement at current yields when, by deferring such commitments, higher yields can be secured later. Conversely, if interest rates are expected to fall, it would be equally short-sighted not to speed up commitments for the future delivery of funds at the current high rates.

3. Estimates are made of changes in the interest rate differentials between commercial mortgage loans and private placements that are expected to develop. Such changes will shift the proportion of commitments that are made for mortgage loans as compared to private placements and vice versa.

4. A decision must be made on the *minimum* proportion of cash flow that will be committed to mortgage loans and, alternatively, to private placements. A smoothly functioning commercial mortgage loan department cannot cease making forward commitments completely and sever ties with the originators of its loans merely because private placement bonds are currently producing a higher yield.

5. A decision must also be made on the extent to which forward commitments will be permitted to vary from their normal commitment patterns over time. For technical reasons, the duration of the lag between the commitment and the disbursement of funds is much longer for commercial mortgage loans than for private placements. At the same time, because the demand for capital funds is much greater than the funds available, a company can vary the percentage of both mortgages and private placements committed each quarter for closing at a subsequent time period.

6. The company must decide whether to commit in prior periods all the funds that are expected to be available at the time of closing. An alternative strategy is to hold some funds in reserve for investment either in public issues or for future investment. Or, the company could choose to overcommit the funds available, because some commitments will probably be cancelled before closing and/or because future interest rates are expected to be lower and a conscious policy of short-term borrowing is contemplated.

Currently, Nationwide's cash flow available for investments exceeds $150 million annually. Because policy loans are not a major factor in the cash flow projections at Nationwide,[19] the amount of funds available has been highly predictable. However, the forward commitment process is of major concern to the company's investment strategy because forward commitments account for approximately 90 percent of total investments. During the four-year period, 1971–1974, the company attempted to distribute forward commitments over time so that investment income would be maximized. Investments in commercial mortgage loans accounted for 53.7 percent and private placements for 46.3 percent of the total. However, the allocations of funds between these categories varied significantly from quarter to quarter. In the first three months of 1972, for example, privately placed bonds accounted for 91.0 percent of total closings. Commercial mortgages represented 73.2 percent of the total in the second quarter of 1974.

The average yield on all commercial mortgage loans closed during the four-year period was 8.78 percent, and for private placements it was 8.77 percent—a result that appears to be somewhat fortuitous. The spread in yields was much greater within individual quarters, ranging from 1.5 percent in favor of private placements in the second quarter of 1971 to 0.5 percent in favor of mortgage loans in the first quarter of 1973 and in the second quarter of 1974. In these and most other time periods, the preponderant share of funds was allocated to the type of investment with the favorable yield differential. On several occasions during the four-year period, short-term loans were secured from banks to take advantage of favorable interest rate trends. This policy was continued in 1975 and 1976.

The average percentage amount committed in each prior quarter for commercial mortgage loans and for private placement bonds during 1971–1974 is set forth in Table 1.9. Nationwide's schedule of prior commitments for commercial mortgage loans closely approximates the Pesando estimates for the life insurance industry. However, it appears that the industry's bond disbursement lag is much shorter than Nationwide's. The industry's data may include a higher percentage of publicly issued securities.

Because of the complexities involved in the forward commitment process, the company has developed a dynamic linear programming model which helps investment management distribute its commitments over time between commercial mortgage loans and private

---

[19] Nationwide has not experienced policy loan difficulties because of its rapid growth and the types of policies written.

TABLE 1.9
Amount Committed in Quarters Prior to Closing

Quarter Prior to Closing	Commercial Mortgage Loans			Private Placements		
	Percent in Quarter	Cumulative Percentage	Life Industry Estimate[*]	Percent in Quarter	Cumulative Percentage	Life Industry Estimate[*]
−8 or earlier	13.2%	13.2%	23.9%	1.4%	1.4%	—%
−7	8.8	22.0	27.4	2.7	4.1	—
−6	8.7	30.7	32.6	3.6	7.7	—
−5	6.1	36.8	39.5	2.2	9.9	—
−4	11.6	48.4	48.1	7.8	17.7	6.4
−3	8.8	57.2	58.5	9.5	27.2	19.7
−2	4.2	61.4	70.6	33.0	60.2	39.7
−1	22.0	83.4	84.4	28.0	88.2	66.5
0	16.6	100.0	100.0	11.8	100.0	100.0
Mean	4.38 quarters			2.08 quarters		
Standard deviation	1.61 quarters			0.69 quarters		

[*] These figures were derived from data presented in James E. Pesando, "The Interest Sensitivity of the Flow of Funds through Life Insurance Companies," *Journal of Finance*, vol. 29, no. 4 (September 1974), p. 1113.

placements.[20] Based on interest rate forecasts developed by the company, the model permits the simulation of the effects of various strategies which incorporate the minimum practical constraints involved in keeping an orderly supply of investment opportunities flowing from the originators of private placements and mortgage loans. It manipulates the cash flow and interest rate data statistically to produce the optimum commitment pattern for a specific strategy. The strategies are then compared by management, and the one which best fits company goals and policies is selected for implementation.

SUMMARY AND CONCLUSIONS

The investment strategies of life insurance companies have been shaped by factors that are both external and internal to the industry. Externally, the rapid growth of total family savings over the past quarter century has produced major changes in the forms in which the public prefers to hold those assets. Internally, in their competition with other financial intermediaries for the savings dollar, life insurers have intensified their search for new, potentially attractive life insurance products. Moreover, the fact that they are attracting a declining share of family savings has induced them to adopt more flexible, higher-yielding investment strategies. Increasingly, in their choice of investments, life insurers are also matching the types of investments and their maturities more closely with the nature of their contractual liabilities.

Externally, life insurance company investment strategies are being conditioned by changes in the structure of the capital markets. Established financial intermediaries—banks, savings and loan associations, mutual savings banks, and pension funds—are becoming dominant purchasers of investments that have traditionally been preferred by life insurers. A large volume of these favored portfolio choices have also been purchased in recent years by the new investment institutions—the bond funds and the real estate investment trusts. Internally, the rapid increase in policy loans during periods of monetary restraint has caused severe fluctuations in cash flow for many life

---

[20] The initial model was developed by Michael Schoch and James Demas, graduate students in the college of engineering at the Ohio State University. A technical description of the model is presented in a paper by Jacob M. Eschler and Robert A. Rennie, "The Nationwide Forward Commitment Model," *Investment Modeling: A Management Tool, Systems and Procedures*, Report No. 32 (New York: Life Office Management Association, November, 1976), pp. 13–17.

companies that rely heavily on the advance commitment process in implementing their investment programs.

Finally, the strategic investment decisions immediately confronting an individual life insurance company have been examined. These decisions are conditioned by the relative financial strength of the company, by top management's attitudes toward risk bearing, and by the unique set of considerations involved in the forward commitment process. The investment goal of the company is to maximize yield subject to an overall risk constraint and to the restrictions of state investment regulations. Markowitz-Sharpe portfolio analysis is helpful in selecting a diversified common stock portfolio, but "inefficiencies" in the markets for bonds and mortgages necessitate heavy reliance on traditional investment analysis to maintain diversification with respect to these types of investments. Forward commitments, which call for investment decisions many months prior to the actual disbursement of funds, are an especially challenging problem. Overall, flexibility, informed judgment, and the aid of quantitative modeling interact to enable the company to achieve its goals.

2

Developments in the Private Placement Market: The Changing Role of the Life Insurance Industry

By Eli Shapiro*

In every year of the postwar period through 1965, life insurance companies were the largest single net purchaser of corporate bonds. Throughout those years nearly all of the corporate bonds they acquired were privately placed. Three things happened between 1965 and 1974 to alter this pattern. First, the life insurance industry has at times temporarily shifted its bond acquisitions from the private to the public market, in response to cyclical changes in corporate demands for funds. Second, other institutions as well as individuals acting on their own behalf have responded to divergences in relative yield relationships by reducing net acquisitions in their more traditional investment areas in favor of corporate bonds. In so doing, they have at times toppled the life insurance industry from its preeminent role in the long-term corporate bond market. And third, commercial banks have increased their participation in the "term" loan area of commercial and industrial loans as a counterpart activity to their lengthened liability structure. As a result, commercial banks have become important new lenders to corporations of medium to long-term funds via instruments that by any criteria other than name would be classified as private placements.

* Eli Shapiro is chairman of the finance committee of the Travelers Insurance Companies.

Mrs. Barbara N. Opper, who was financial economist of the Travelers Insurance Companies at the time this chapter was written, provided invaluable assistance in the preparation of this material.

This chapter examines these three developments as they reflect the responsiveness of all parties—corporate borrowers, institutional investors, and individuals acting for their own accounts—to the fluctuations that have occurred in the capital markets. Before examining these flows into and out of direct placements, this chapter provides a definition for direct placements, analyzes their advantages and disadvantages, and examines the borrowers and lenders for whom direct placements are an appropriate instrument.

THE DEFINITION OF DIRECT PLACEMENTS

The Securities Act of 1933 (the 1933 Act) provided an important raison d'etre for direct placements. For any security offered interstate to the public, that act requires the disclosure of numerous material facts about the issuer in a so-called registration statement available to all interested investors. The effect of the act was twofold: (1) Investors became classifiable into two categories—the "public," the vast body of investors for whom the securities law was designed to afford protection, and "sophisticated investors," including most institutional investors, who were deemed able to obtain on their own the relevant information contained in a registration statement. (2) An important set of requirements was developed pertaining to facts that had to be disclosed in a registration statement and standards of conduct to be adhered to by principals to a publicly sold corporate issue during the period of time surrounding its sale.

The disclosure requirements and other legal restrictions connected with a public issue required the purchase of expensive talent to guide the issuer through the legal and accounting intricacies of the registration period. They also meant that a significant period of time had to elapse between the time of the decision to issue the security and its actual marketing. During this period, of course, market conditions or other relevant factors could change substantially.

The requirements of the 1933 Act are therefore the relevant considerations in defining a direct placement. A direct placement is a long-term corporate debt issue in which there is one or a small number of lenders, each of whom can reasonably be considered sophisticated and able to ascertain and evaluate the material facts about the borrower. These considerations also determine its advantages and disadvantages, at least for those firms with the option of issuing debt in the public market. For those smaller or weaker firms unable to issue debt publicly, direct placements offer the only significant means for borrowing at long-term. Consequently, the following comparison of advantages and disadvantages of direct placements and publicly issued debt is not meaningful for certain groups of firms.

THE ADVANTAGES AND DISADVANTAGES OF DIRECT PLACEMENTS

The advantages of a direct placement to a corporate borrower large enough and creditworthy enough to have access to either the public bond market or the private market are varied. They include costs (at least under some conditions), flexibility, and forward planning capability.

The cost of borrowing per se is not necessarily lower for either form of financing. It is generally true that the coupon interest rate on a private placement is higher than that on an otherwise comparable public bond. This differential shows some cyclical variation but has approximated, on average, 75 basis points. Balancing that higher coupon, however, is the avoidance of registration and underwriting fees provided by a private placement. Even if a private placement is sold through an agent, instead of through direct negotiations between the issuer and the lender, these costs typically have been negligible in comparison to the costs of issuing public bonds.

Thus, when comparing public and private bonds with all other factors equal, a range of issue sizes exists in which it is often true that, spread over the life of the bond, total financing costs (interest plus costs of issuing the debt) are lower with a private placement. Very small issues are, of course, effectively excluded from being issued publicly for the very reason of the large fixed costs associated with registration. And, in extremely large issues, the fixed issue costs become negligible when amortized over a 20- or 30-year term to maturity.

The flexibility and individualized tailoring provided by a private placement are distinct advantages to a borrower. Public bonds tend to be structured so as to adhere to specific sets of terms and covenants, especially within industry groupings of the issuers. This standardization tends to speed sales from the underwriting syndicate at time of issue, as lenders are thereby able to base decisions on a relatively limited set of specifics associated with each issue. For the same reason, standardization tends to ease secondary marketing. None of these considerations is very important to the buyer of a private placement, who typically intends to hold the bond until its maturity.

Similarly, with a public bond, the only way a borrower can be assured of the coupon is actually to issue the debt, which means that the proceeds are received whether or not there is an immediate long-term use for them. By contrast, the forward commitment process through which private placement terms are established provides that borrower and lender agree upon the terms and conditions of a loan (which generally reflect the capital market at the time of the agreement) and fix a mutually satisfactory date for disbursement of the funds that may be many months into the future.

Because the loan negotiations are carried out between the borrower and the final lender, private placements often allow a tailoring of loan terms to suit the individual needs or plans of both parties to the transaction. This kind of tailoring generally is not feasible in designing a public issue since it is to be purchased by a large number of individuals and institutions with perhaps very little mutuality of interest. The price to the borrower for this flexibility is that the indenture agreement on a private placement typically carries stricter terms than the provisions of a publicly offered bond. The call provision is almost always stricter on a private issue than in the public market, especially in terms of the number of years before any call or refunding may occur. Other provisions that also tend to be stricter on a private placement have to do with the borrower's use of bank credit and long-term debt, his expenditures on long-term leases, and any expansion or merger activity.

Extending the comparison between the flexibility of a private placement and a public issue, it is apparent that subsequent alteration of the indenture terms is measurably easier with a private placement. For one thing, there are far fewer lenders to contact in order to reach an agreement on new terms. For another, the lender or lenders on a private placement typically remain in very close association with the borrower and tend to be attuned to any needs for changing the terms of the loan.

For a lender, a private placement affords the opportunity to gain a higher coupon interest rate in return for less marketability than offered by an otherwise comparable public bond issue. Many of the other advantages and disadvantages to a lender of a private placement versus a publicly offered bond from the same borrower can be inferred from the preceding discussion of advantages and disadvantages to the borrower.

For a lender with a relatively predictable supply of loanable funds, such as a life insurance company or a pension fund, a reasonably orderly conversion of investable funds into long-term permanent investments is provided by the forward commitment process. As the use of forward commitments allows borrowers to plan more effectively the magnitude and timing of their capital expenditures, so also do forward commitments allow lenders to line up their long-term investments with terms and disbursement dates that fit their needs.

The need to deal directly with the borrower in tailoring the terms and in making any subsequent changes in the loan provisions can also be beneficial to the lender. This usually requires the lender to develop an expertise somewhat beyond that of a lender which purchases only publicly issued bonds (even within the same general credit ranking). But, it also implies that the lender can remain in close contact with the borrower and can follow closely developments in the borrower's business, thereby enabling the lender to be alerted to any changes in the borrower's credit standing or in his need for additional funds.

BORROWERS IN THE DIRECT PLACEMENT MARKET

All of the preceding advantages and disadvantages of a private placement have been stated in terms of the comparison between private and public issues. As noted above, this comparison is relevant only for the stratum of firms for which the public market is a real borrowing alternative. In general, firms that have a credit rating (or would merit a credit rating) of about Ba or better and would borrow some relatively large minimum amount do have these alternatives. By now that minimum is probably about $5 or $10 million. In the 1951–1955 period, it was about $1 million.[1]

In addition to the firms which can choose between public and private bond issues, a second group of firms exists for which private placements are the only effective means to obtain long-term borrowed funds. For them, the tailoring of loan terms to suit individual needs and the ease of amending loan terms as conditions change are extremely important. The analytical expertise of the institutional lender can at times benefit the smaller firm's management in much the same way that good commercial banking advice can. And the opportunity to obtain a forward commitment in which all terms, costs, and conditions are set forth can help to eliminate some of the

---

[1] Eli Shapiro and Charles R. Wolf, *The Role of Private Placements in Corporate Finance* (Boston: Division of Research, Graduate School of Business Administration, Harvard University, 1972), pp. 91–104, using data in U.S. Securities and Exchange Commission, *Cost of Floatation of Directly Placed Corporate Securities 1951–55* (Washington, D.C., 1957). The determining factors are the relatively fixed-dollar costs associated with registration and the receptivity of underwriting teams to handling such a small amount.

risk faced by smaller or weaker firms in planning capital outlays and other activities that give rise to the need for long-term funds.

This second group of private placement borrowers represents a business opportunity for institutional lenders. With their expert personnel and their diversified portfolios, they can accept the risks that might be associated with long-term loans to firms which are relatively small or have weaker credit ratings. In fact, they actively seek these borrowers as, on the whole, the risk/return trade-off in this kind of lending has been satisfactory.

LENDERS IN THE CORPORATE BOND MARKET

During the years 1969–1975, the life insurance industry apparently maintained its dominance as the major source of funds for privately placed bonds. At times, however, it was superseded in the overall bond market by other lenders. The dominance of life insurance companies in the private placement market can be inferred from the data in Table 2.1. The table indicates that life company private placement acquisitions as a percent of total private placements never fell below 48 percent during the period 1963–1975. In some years, life insurers may have supplied as much as 96 percent of total privately placed bond funds. In view of the fact that the total private placement series utilized in this analysis may not represent the universe of privately placed loans, these figures must be viewed with a degree of caution. However, they provide at least a preliminary indication that insurers play a preeminent role in the market for privately placed bonds.

Table 2.2 presents data on the acquisitions of corporate bonds by major lenders during the period 1946 through 1975. The shifts in the relative positions of the lender groups during this period were largely determined by changing yield differentials among financial instruments. For example, the behavior of households acting for their own accounts was a reaction to the declining returns available from common stocks and to the cyclical shifts in the relative attractiveness of deposit-type claims.

Between 1969 and 1975, yields on corporate bonds rose dramatically relative to those of other types of investments. As Figure 2.1 illustrates, the yield spread between corporate bonds and home mortgages became much more favorable to bond investments. Corporate bond volume also increased significantly during this period, a development which was, of course, associated with the sharp relative increases in bond yields. As a result of these developments, lenders such as mutual savings banks and individuals shifted funds from

TABLE 2.1
Acquisitions from Outstanding Forward
Commitments by a Sample of
Life Insurance Companies

Year	Life Company Acquisitions* (millions)	Percent of Total Private Placements
1963	$3,450	56.0%
1964	3,514	48.5
1965	4,050	49.7
1966	3,694	48.9
1967	4,111	59.0
1968	n.a.	—
1969	3,942	70.2
1970	3,776	76.6
1971	5,628	76.5
1972	8,101	93.1
1973	7,464	95.7
1974	5,893	95.7
1975	8,832	87.0

Note: Acquisitions include only those outstanding during the month prior to takedown; they exclude acquisitions from commitments made during the same month as the disbursement occurred. The acquisitions data have not been blown up to represent an industry total. The sample of companies represented by the above series accounted for ⅔ of industry assets before 1968 and 80 percent of assets after 1967. The data were not blown up because there are indications that the companies in the sample invest more heavily in private placements than those not in the sample.

* Includes state and local bonds and other noncorporate securities.

Sources: American Council of Life Insurance, "Forward Investment Commitments of Reporting Life Insurance Companies" (Washington, D.C., quarterly); and Securities and Exchange Commission data published in Federal Reserve Bulletin.

other assets into bonds. Other lenders, such as state and local pension funds, experienced sharp increases in their investable funds which would have enabled them to participate more actively in the corporate bond market even without significantly altering the composition of their portfolios.

In order to illustrate these developments, the net asset acquisitions of state and local pension funds and of households during the period 1946–1975 are presented in Tables 2.3 and 2.4, respectively. Table 2.3 demonstrates that state and local retirement funds grew rapidly during this period and substantially increased the proportions of their investable funds placed in the corporate bond market. Table 2.4 indicates that investment in corporate bonds by households has been extremely volatile. It also reveals that corporates were not a favored

TABLE 2.2
Net Acquisitions of Corporate Bonds by Lender Category (dollar amounts in billions)

Year	Life Insurance Companies		Private Pension Funds		State and Local Retirement Funds		Other Institutional Investors*		Individuals and Others		Total Corporate Bond Sales
	Amount	Percent	Amount	Percent	Amount	Percent	Amount	Percent	Amount	Percent	
1946	$1.8	180%	$0.3	30%	$ †	—%	$0.2	20%	$-1.3	-130%	$ 1.0
1947	3.0	100	0.3	10	†	†	0.4	13	-0.7	-23	3.0
1948	4.2	88	0.3	6	0.1	2	0.3	6	-0.2	-4	4.8
1949	2.6	79	0.3	9	0.1	3	0.4	12	-0.1	-3	3.3
1950	1.8	78	1.0	43	0.2	9	0.2	9	-0.9	-39	2.3
1951	2.7	69	0.7	18	0.1	3	0.1	3	-0.1	-3	3.9
1952	3.1	62	1.1	21	0.3	6	0.4	8	0.1	—	5.0
1953	2.7	59	1.1	24	0.5	11	0.4	8	-0.1	-2	4.6
1954	2.1	62	1.3	38	0.6	18	0.2	6	-0.2	-6	3.4
1955	1.7	47	0.9	25	0.6	17	-0.6	-17	1.2	33	3.6
1956	2.2	44	1.6	32	0.5	10	-0.1	-2	0.8	16	5.0
1957	2.7	36	1.9	25	0.9	12	1.0	13	1.2	15	7.5
1958	2.4	35	1.5	22	1.1	16	0.8	12	0.8	12	6.8
1959	2.1	46	1.2	26	0.9	20	*	—	0.3	7	4.6
1960	1.7	31	1.6	30	1.1	20	0.2	4	0.9	17	5.4
1961	2.5	48	1.2	23	1.7	33	0.1	2	0.2	4	5.2
1962	2.5	45	1.2	22	1.8	33	0.3	5	0.1	2	5.5
1963	2.8	45	1.5	24	2.1	34	-0.5	-8	0.4	6	6.2
1964	2.3	34	1.6	24	2.2	32	1.0	15	0.4	6	6.8
1965	2.8	35	1.5	19	2.3	28	0.8	10	1.2	15	8.1
1966	2.4	21	2.5	22	2.9	26	1.3	12	2.7	24	11.2
1967	3.8	23	1.1	7	3.7	22	3.6	21	4.9	30	16.6
1968	3.7	26	0.6	4	2.6	18	3.2	22	4.7	33	14.4
1969	1.7	12	0.6	4	4.0	29	1.3	9	7.5	54	13.8
1970	1.5	6	2.1	9	4.5	19	5.0	21	11.4	49	23.3
1971	5.5	23	-0.7	-3	3.9	17	6.0	26	9.7	41	23.5
1972	7.0	38	-0.8	-4	4.5	24	3.2	17	5.4	29	18.4
1973	5.9	43	2.1	15	6.0	44	-1.7	-13	1.6	12	13.6
1974	4.0	17	4.7	20	6.4	27	3.6	15	-0.7	-3	23.9
1975	9.1	25	2.8	8	5.0	14	8.5	23	9.5	26	36.3

Note: Due to the construction of the Flow of Funds accounts, the data in the table include foreign, as well as corporate bonds.

* This category includes commercial banks, mutual savings banks, other insurance companies, and open-end investment companies.

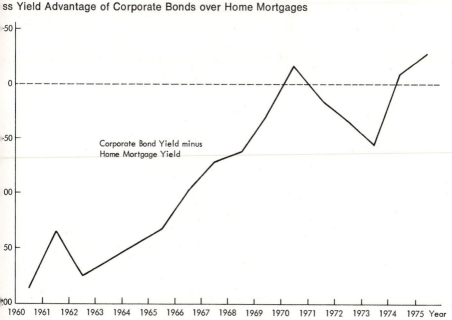

Sources: New (public) issue Aaa utility bonds with deferred call protection, *Federal Reserve Bulletin,* Table
New conventional home mortgages, FHA, *Federal Reserve Bulletin,* Table A45.

investment of households until the late 1960s and early 1970s. Corporates ranked no higher than third in terms of total household acquisitions until 1966. In the ensuing seven years, they ranked first
four times. This provides additional evidence of the increased competition faced by life insurers in the corporate bond market.

Yield differentials also had an impact on borrowing decisions. The
estimated average annual yield premium of private over public issues
is illustrated by the dashed line in Figure 2.2.[2] The solid line in this

---

[2] The "quality" premium was estimated as the difference between new, public deferred-call Aaa and Aa utility issues. That amount was subtracted from the
difference between Baa direct placement commitments and Aa utilities new deferred-call public issues. This is a rough measure since it assumes that the quality
differential between Aaa and Aa equals that between Aa and Baa issues, and between utilities and industrials. This is known to be an overstatement in the last
two years, as public concern over the plight of utility earnings has caused a widening in the differential between industrials and utilities. Moreover, since the
energy crunch, utilities with identical credit ratings sell at different yields depending, among other things, on the source of fuel for energy production. In
general, utilities with a lower dependence on oil as an energy input sell for lower
yields than comparably rated companies with a heavy oil dependency.

TABLE 2.3
Net Acquisitions of Credit Market Instruments by State and Local Government Retirement Funds (dollar amounts in billions)

Year	Corporate Bonds		Corporate Stock*		State and Local Obligations		U.S. Government Securities		Mortgages		Total Credit Market Instruments
	Amount	Percent	Amount	Percent	Amount	Percent	Amount	Percent	Amount	Percent	
1946	$ †	—%	$ †	—%	$0.1	33%	$0.2	67%	$ †	—%	$ 0.3
1947	†	—	†	—	0.1	33	0.2	67	†	—	0.3
1948	0.1	25	†	—	0.1	25	0.2	50	†	—	0.4
1949	0.1	20	†	—	0.2	40	0.2	40	†	—	0.5
1950	0.2	29	†	—	0.2	29	0.2	29	†	—	0.7
1951	0.1	14	†	—	0.2	29	0.4	57	†	—	0.7
1952	0.2	22	†	—	0.2	22	0.5	56	†	—	0.9
1953	0.5	42	†	—	0.2	17	0.5	42	†	—	1.2
1954	0.6	40	†	—	0.3	20	0.5	33	0.1	7	1.5
1955	0.5	38	†	—	0.3	23	0.3	23	0.1	8	1.3
1956	0.6	42	†	—	0.4	29	0.3	21	0.1	7	1.4
1957	0.8	50	0.1	6	0.4	25	0.1	6	0.1	6	1.6
1958	0.8	53	0.1	7	0.4	27	*	—	0.2	13	1.5
1959	0.9	45	0.1	5	0.3	15	0.5	25	0.3	15	2.0
1960	1.2	55	0.1	5	0.2	9	0.3	14	0.5	23	2.2
1961	1.7	71	0.2	8	—0.1	—4	0.2	8	0.4	17	2.4
1962	1.9	79	0.2	8	—0.5	—21	0.4	17	0.3	13	2.4
1963	1.9	79	0.2	8	—0.5	—21	0.4	17	0.4	17	2.4
1964	1.9	68	0.3	11	—0.4	—14	0.6	21	0.5	18	2.8
1965	2.1	64	0.4	12	—0.3	—9	0.4	12	0.7	21	3.3
1966	2.5	66	0.5	13	—0.1	—3	0.2	5	0.8	21	3.8
1967	3.4	97	0.7	20	—0.1	—3	—0.1	—29	0.5	14	3.5
1968	2.1	50	1.3	31	*	—	0.4	10	0.4	10	4.2
1969	3.6	66	1.8	33	—0.1	—2	—0.3	—6	0.6	10	5.6
1970	3.8	62	2.1	34	—0.3	—5	—0.3	—5	0.8	13	6.1
1971	4.2	68	3.2	52	0.1	2	—1.6	—26	0.3	5	6.2
1972	5.3	70	3.5	43	—0.1	—1	—0.6	—7	—0.3	—4	7.8
1973	5.9	64	3.9	42	—0.6	—7	0.1	1	—0.1	—1	9.2
1974	8.4	69	3.5	29	—0.6	—5	0.6	5	0.3	2	12.2
1975	5.7	48	2.6	22	2.1	18	1.0	8	0.5	4	12.0

Note: Components may not add to totals due to rounding.
* Including investment company shares as well as direct acquisitions.

Net Acquisitions of Credit Market Instruments by Households, Personal Trusts, and Nonprofit Organizations (dollar amounts in billions)

Year	Corporate Bonds		Corporate Stock*		State and Local Obligations		U.S. Government Securities		Commercial Paper		Mortgages		Total Credit Market Instruments
	Amount	Percent	Amount	Percent	Amount	Percent	Amount	Percent	Amount	Percent	Amount	Percent	
1946	$ −0.9	−300%	$1.1	366%	†	—%	$ −1.4	−466%	$ 0	—%	$1.5	500%	$ 0.3
1947	−0.8	−25	1.1	34	$0.4	12	1.1	34	0	—	1.3	40	3.2
1948	−0.1	−2	1.0	29	1.0	29	0.3	8	0	—	1.2	35	3.4
1949	−0.4	−13	0.8	27	0.7	24	1.1	37	†	—	0.7	24	2.9
1950	−0.8	−113	0.7	116	0.5	83	−0.6	−100	†	—	0.7	116	0.6
1951	†	—	1.6	80	0.3	15	−0.8	−40	†	—	0.9	45	2.0
1952	†	—	1.6	38	2.0	47	−0.2	−4	†	—	0.8	19	4.2
1953	−0.1	—	0.9	20	1.8	41	0.5	11	0.1	2	1.0	23	4.3
1954	−0.3	−13	0.7	30	2.5	108	−1.8	−78	−0.1	4	1.2	52	2.3
1955	1.0	10	1.1	11	3.5	38	2.5	27	†	—	1.2	13	9.2
1956	0.9	10	1.9	22	2.4	28	1.5	18	†	—	1.5	18	8.3
1957	1.1	16	1.5	22	1.7	25	0.6	8	†	—	1.9	28	6.7
1958	1.3	48	1.5	55	0.8	29	−3.2	−118	†	—	2.3	85	2.7
1959	0.3	2	0.6	5	3.3	28	5.7	48	†	—	1.8	15	11.7
1960	0.6	10	−0.4	7	3.5	61	†	—	†	—	2.0	35	5.7
1961	0.1	3	0.4	14	1.2	42	−0.5	−17	†	—	1.7	60	2.8
1962	−0.1	5	−2.1	105	−1.0	50	0.2	−10	†	—	1.0	50	2.0
1963	†	—	−2.9	−161	1.0	55	3.4	188	†	—	0.3	16	−1.8
1964	0.9	15	−0.2	3	2.6	44	3.1	52	†	—	0.3	5	5.9
1965	1.0	45	−2.2	−100	1.7	70	2.4	109	†	—	−0.8	−36	2.2
1966	2.1	12	−1.1	6	3.6	21	7.8	47	2.7	16	1.3	7	16.4
1967	4.6	−230	−4.5	225	−2.2	110	1.3	−65	−2.1	105	0.9	−45	−2.0
1968	5.2	89	−6.5	−112	−0.8	−13	5.6	96	0.7	12	1.5	25	5.8
1969	6.6	21	−3.8	12	9.6	30	12.8	41	4.8	15	1.1	3	31.2
1970	10.7	−366	−1.6	59	−0.8	30	−9.7	359	−1.5	56	0.1	4	−2.7
1971	9.3	−65	−5.2	37	−0.2	1	−14.4	101	−3.9	27	0.2	1	−14.2
1972	5.2	400	−5.2	−400	1.0	77	0.6	46	1.5	115	−1.8	−138	1.3
1973	1.1	5	−8.1	−37	4.3	20	20.4	94	3.5	16	0.5	2	21.7
1974	−1.7	8	−1.0	5	10.0	45	14.5	66	−0.5	2	0.8	4	22.1
1975	9.0	58	−1.2	8	7.0	45	1.4	9	−2.5	16	1.5	10	15.4

Note: Components may not add to totals due to rounding.

* Including investment company shares as well as direct acquisitions.

† Less than ± $0.05 billion.

Source: Flow of Funds accounts, available from Flow of Funds section, Board of Governors of the Federal Reserve System.

FIGURE 2.2

Responsiveness of Bond Issues to Yield Differentials in the Public and Private Markets

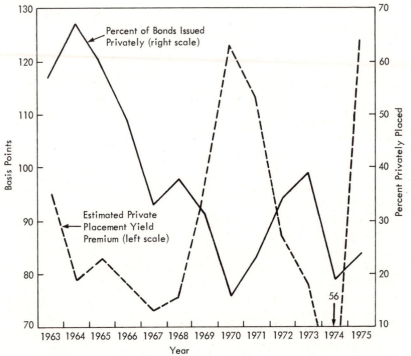

Sources: Percent of Bonds issued privately are Securities and Exchange Commission data, also published in *Federal Reserve Bulletin*, Table A38. The estimated private placement yield premium is derived from unpublished data produced by the American Council of Life Insurance and from the Salomon Brothers New Issue Aa Utilities yield series, published weekly by that firm.

figure represents the percentage of gross bond issues during the year that were privately placed. As would be expected, the relationship between this percentage and the yield differential is inverse. That is, when the yield premium of a private placement over a public bond increases, borrowers tend to shift to the relatively less expensive public market.

Such behavior can, of course, only be expected by those firms large enough and creditworthy enough to have access to the public bond market as a viable alternative. This kind of behavior was confirmed by Wolf in his analysis of the long-term debt issues of the *Fortune* 500 companies.[3] His statistical work supports the hypothesis that

---

[3] Charles R. Wolf, "The Demand for Funds in the Public and Private Corporate Bond Markets," *The Review of Economics and Statistics*, vol. 56, no. 1 (February 1974).

large, financially secure firms which can borrow in either market are more sensitive to the yield differentials than are other corporate borrowers when deciding between public and private issues.

BOND ACQUISITIONS BY LIFE INSURANCE COMPANIES

Although life insurance companies appear to have maintained their dominance over the private placement market, as was inferred from Table 2.1, at times between 1967 and 1975 they also became active in acquiring bonds from the public market. Although the data to examine this hypothesis are not direct measures of public bond acquisitions by life insurance companies, the estimating procedure yields results that, a priori, seem reasonable.

To estimate public bond acquisitions, sample data for life company monthly acquisitions of corporate securities from commitments outstanding during the prior month were inflated by the sample's representation of industry assets.[4] This produced an industry total of estimated gross takedowns of private placements. Not included in this private placement estimate were takedowns from commitments made within the month of takedown, because those takedowns appear to include some of the public bond acquisitions.[5] One further complication encountered when estimating gross private placement acquisitions is that the size of the sample of reporting life companies was increased in 1968; and in conjunction with that increase, data for one month were not released. That amount was estimated, and a continuous series representing industry private placement acquisitions was created.

The industry's public bond acquisitions were estimated by subtracting private acquisitions from data representing the gross long-term bond acquisitions of life insurance companies.[6] The series is shown in Table 2.5, which also presents the private and public bond split for all bond issuers. Comparison of the two series of gross public

---

[4] The data were obtained from American Council of Life Insurance, "Forward Investment Commitments of Reporting Life Insurance Companies" (Washington, D.C., quarterly).

[5] These were excluded because if they are included the resultant industry private placement gross acquisition series at times far exceeds the SEC series of gross private placement acquisitions that purports to represent all activity in this market, not just that of life companies.

[6] *The Tally* (New York: American Council of Life Insurance, monthly). Yet another source of "noise" in the public bond series is that the data from the *Tally* (total life insurance industry bond acquisitions in Table 2.5) reflect some valuation changes and accounting transactions, while the commitment acquisitions are in cash.

TABLE 2.5
Estimated Acquisitions of Bonds by Life Insurance Companies
(billions of dollars)

Year	Life Insurance Industry Bond Acquisitions			Gross Issues of Bonds		
	Total	Private	Public	Total	Private	Public
1963	$ 5.9	$ 5.1	$0.8	$10.9	$ 6.2	$ 4.7
1964	6.2	5.2	0.9	10.9	7.2	3.6
1965	7.0	6.0	1.0	13.7	8.2	5.6
1966	7.0	5.5	1.5	15.6	7.5	8.0
1967	8.8	6.1	2.7	21.9	7.0	14.9
1968	9.0	6.7	2.4	17.4	6.6	10.7
1969	6.5	4.9	1.6	18.4	5.6	12.7
1970	6.3	4.7	1.6	30.3	4.9	25.4
1971	11.2	7.0	4.2	31.9	7.1	24.8
1972	13.6	10.1	3.5	26.1	8.7	17.4
1973	12.1	9.3	2.8	21.0	7.8	13.2
1974	11.3	7.4	3.9	32.1	6.2	25.9
1975	16.6	11.0	5.6	42.8	10.2	32.6

Note: Public bond acquisitions of the life insurance industry are estimated as the difference between total and private acquisitions. The private placement data for the life insurance industry are based on a sample and have been blown up to approximate an industry total. The statistic for 1968 is especially tenuous, since the sample was increased in that year and some data are missing.

Source: Total life insurance industry bond acquisitions are from American Council of Life Insurance, *The Tally*. Private placement data are from American Council of Life Insurance, "Forward Investment Commitments of Reporting Life Insurance Companies." Gross issues of bonds are based on Securities and Exchange Commission data, also published in *Federal Reserve Bulletin*, Table A38.

bond activity suggests that some of the increases or decreases in the public bond acquisitions of the life insurance industry might be associated with like movements in the volume of gross public debt issued. The clear exception is the 1969–1970 period. The relationship seems, however, to be a coincidence of factors affecting the two series, rather than one of causality.

In Figure 2.3, another relationship is shown that seems to fit better into a cause and effect scenario. In the upper panel of Figure 2.3 are two series—the estimated gross public bond acquisitions of the life insurance industry and the industry's average uncommitted cash flow. The two series moved in similar patterns from 1966 through 1975. One force affecting public bond acquisitions by life companies would appear to be the volume of "free" investable funds on hand. As may be observed in the bottom panel of Figure 2.3, the absolute volume of loanable funds exerted little influence on the measure of public bonds acquired.

The motivations for life insurance company activity in the public

FIGURE 2.3
Life Insurance Industry Public Bond Acquisitions

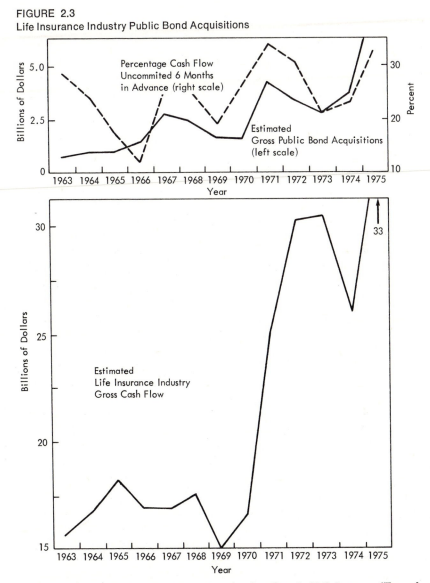

Sources: Uncommitted cash flow data are from American Council of Life Insurance, "Forward Investment Commitments of Reporting Life Insurance Companies." Data on gross cash flow are from Kenneth M. Wright, *Economic and Investment Report—1975* (Washington, D.C.: American Council of Life Insurance, 1975). Estimated public bond acquisitions are derived in Table 2.5, p. 50.

bond market for long-term (as opposed to trading-account) holdings may be explained by several forces. For one thing, public issues offer an investment opportunity for cash flows as they are received. This is especially advantageous when the outlook for loanable funds carries an unusually large degree of uncertainty. The penalties to a life insurance company for misforecasting its cash flow can be minimized if outstanding forward commitment takedowns are limited to a relatively small proportion of the predicted cash flow. Moreover, the opportunity costs of not having forward commitments in hand are minimized at those times when the private/public yield differential is narrow.

Another impetus to acquiring public bonds on a cyclical basis has been changing yield differentials among quality categories of bonds. These differentials have generally declined when the supply pressures of new bond issues were relatively large and when there was upward pressure on interest rates. At those times, the life insurance industry was able to acquire bonds in the public market that tended to be of higher credit quality than the average in their outstanding portfolios. In general, these issues were also more marketable, entailed no risk of misforecasting cash flows, and offered yields that were unusually close to those of bonds lacking these advantages. It was an opportunity to upgrade the quality and marketability of portfolios without relinquishing the usual yield penalty associated with those features.

An indication of the quality characteristics of private placements acquired by life insurance companies is presented in Table 2.6. The table apportions by quality classifications the new placement commitments made during the period 1960–1975. The risk/return preferences of the life companies are evident from the preponderance of commitments to borrowers in the Baa quality range. Some of these firms and many of the borrowers categorized as "other" in the table are those for whom the public bond market is not a viable financing alternative.

Another aspect of life insurance private placement behavior shown in Table 2.6 is the cyclical use of incentive features. These are private placement commitments that are convertible into common stock, have warrants attached, allow for participation in the borrower's earnings, or otherwise provide compensation to the lender in addition to the coupon interest rate.[7] They appear to have been used as a rationing device, for they prevailed during a period of high and rising interest rates when the total volume of private placement commitments fell sharply.

---

[7] These features are sometimes referred to as "equity kickers."

TABLE 2.6
Corporate Direct Placement Commitments Made by a Sample of
Life Insurance Companies

	Percent of Total Volume of Commitments					
Year	Aaa-A Quality	Baa Quality	Incentive Features*	Other†	Total (millions)	Average Coupon‡
1960	31.6%	42.8%	1.5%	23.9%	$2,271	4.63%
1961	32.0	46.6	0.6	20.7	2,702	4.34
1962	24.4	52.4	0.6	22.6	3,360	4.19
1963	26.8	50.3	0.6	22.3	3,408	4.21
1964	24.2	53.1	0.5	22.2	3,995	4.34
1965	24.4	47.4	0.5	27.7	5,127	4.51
1966	31.8	44.7	3.8	19.7	4,061	5.43
1967	31.1	46.2	6.3	16.4	4,647	5.82
1968	16.3	42.1	12.6	29.0	3,587	6.50
1969	18.1	35.8	28.0	17.9	2,646	7.71
1970	20.6	41.7	22.1	15.6	2,002	8.68
1971	28.8	50.5	8.1	12.6	4,823	7.62
1972	23.9	54.6	4.6	16.9	6,031	7.31
1973	20.9	56.8	2.7	19.6	5,356	7.74
1974	34.2	46.6	1.9	17.3	5,125	9.33
1975	46.0	39.5	0.6	13.9	8,002	9.40

Note: The sample includes companies accounting for about ⅔ of industry assets. The participating companies make their own assessments of the quality rating of the borrowers that would correspond to Moody's or Standard & Poor's categories.

* Includes convertibles and, since 1966, issues with warrants.

† Includes below-Baa straight debt, foreign issues, and mineral production issues.

‡ Average rate on new issue Aaa utilities with deferred-call provisions issued in the public market. The series indicates cycles in the bond markets, though, of course, it does not necessarily represent the *level* of coupons in the private market.

Source: Data on volume and non-yield characteristics are from American Council of Life Insurance, "Average Yields on Directly Placed Corporate Bond Authorizations." Average coupon data are from *Federal Reserve Bulletin*, Table A28.

COMMERCIAL BANK TERM LOANS TO BUSINESSES

As noted above, there are indications that commercial banks will be among the major competitors for privately placed, long-term corporate debt in the years to come. Accordingly, an analysis of the recent behavior of banks with respect to this type of credit market instrument seems appropriate.

Bank loans have always been a cyclical variable, and Table 2.7 indicates that much of this cyclical variability has arisen from fluctuations in term loans. As Tables 2.7 and 2.8 suggest, the relationship between the volume of bank term loans and total corporate borrowing tends to be inverse.[8] In 1968 and 1969, for example, term loans

---

[8] The term loan series is based on sample data, and no attempt has been made to estimate loan volume for the entire banking sector. Corporate borrowing, of course, is an economy-wide measure. Nevertheless, the figures presented in Table 2.7 should provide an indication of the directions of movement of the two series.

TABLE 2.7
Use of Bank Debt by Corporate Business (net increase in millions)

	Commercial and Industrial Loans* (Sample)			Corporate Borrowing			
	Term	Total	Percent Term	All Bank Loans	Total Borrowing†	Percent Bank Loans	Known Bank Term Loans as Percent of Total Borrowing
1968	$3,354	$ 7,324	47%	$ 9,600	$32,077	30%	11%
1969	3,258	8,349	39	11,800	35,034	33	9
1970	−431	202	—	5,600	35,781	17	—
1971	−437	2,077	—	4,400	34,917	12	—
1972	1,045	7,333	14	13,500	47,847	30	2
1973	7,829	19,018	41	30,600	64,974	51	13
1974	8,489	21,754	39	29,900	79,034	41	12
1975	−2,224	−11,312	20	−13,200	27,151	—	—

* The banks in the sample account for about 70 percent of total bank business loans.
† The borrowing includes all long-term debt such as bonds and mortgages, all short-term debt such as open market paper, and other debt items such as bank loans, which are not clearly either long-term or short-term.

Sources: Data on commercial and industrial loans are from *Federal Reserve Bulletin*, Table A23. Corporate borrowing statistics are Flow of Funds data, available from Flow of Funds section, Board of Governors of the Federal Reserve System.

represented about 10 percent of the net increase in total corporate borrowing. In those two years the gross volume of corporate bonds issued fell by about 20 percent from the 1967 level. In 1970 and 1971, on the other hand, term loans were reduced; and gross proceeds from corporate bonds rose to new peaks. Likewise, a decline in corporate borrowing in 1973 was accompanied by an increase in the ratio of term loans to total borrowing. Although the maturity structure of these term loans is unknown, their behavior strongly suggests that they are used as substitutes for corporate bonds.

The behavior of commercial banks, especially in the 1972, 1973, and early 1974 periods, also suggests that the maturity structure of these business loans might be on the longer, rather than shorter, side. During that period, banks appeared to be managing the term structure of their assets and liabilities in conformity with their presumed outlook for credit market conditions. They aggressively sought deposits, including time accounts and also large certificates of deposit (CDs) of short maturity. In turn, they acquired an unusually large volume of mortgages and, as we have seen, sharply increased their net extensions of term loans to businesses. This behavior suggests that they regarded then current conditions as representing peak interest rates and sought to maximize their returns over time by attracting short-term funds and investing them at long-term.

It is not yet clear whether commercial bank activity in term loans to business will remain as cyclical as it apparently has been. Considerable cyclicality in this market is, of course, expected depending upon such factors as the availability of funds elsewhere in the capital market, the nature of demand by businesses for debt capital, current and expected interest rates, and, importantly, the relative demand for the other kinds of loans and investments available to commercial banks.

Nevertheless, it is certainly likely that commercial banks will maintain a higher level of activity in term loans than was previously the case. Some lengthening of their asset maturities would be consistent with the new longer-term character of their liabilities. As of July 1974, almost 60 percent of the deposit liabilities of commercial banks consisted of time accounts, including large CDs. By comparison, the average proportion of commercial bank deposits represented by time accounts in the three and one half years before July 1973 was about 50 percent.[9]

---

[9] In July 1973, changes in Regulation Q permitted the use of significant rate incentives to attract "four year and longer" money from consumers.

The sums contributed by commercial banks to term business loans have been significant, as can be judged by comparing the data in Table 2.7 with those in Table 2.8. In 1973, the net increase in term

TABLE 2.8
Corporate Bond Financing through Public Offerings and
Private Placements (dollar amounts in millions)

Year	Public	Private	Total	Percent Private
1946	$ 3,019	$ 1,863	$ 4,882	38.2%
1947	2,889	2,147	5,036	42.6
1948	2,965	3,008	5,973	50.4
1949	2,437	2,453	4,890	50.2
1950	2,360	2,560	4,920	52.0
1951	2,364	3,326	5,691	58.4
1952	3,645	3,957	7,601	52.1
1953	3,856	3,228	7,083	45.6
1954	4,003	3,484	7,488	46.5
1955	4,119	3,301	7,420	44.5
1956	4,225	3,777	8,002	47.2
1957	6,118	3,839	9,957	38.6
1958	6,332	3,320	9,653	34.4
1959	3,557	3,632	7,190	50.5
1960	4,806	3,275	8,081	40.5
1961	4,700	4,720	9,420	50.1
1962	4,440	4,529	8,969	50.5
1963	4,714	6,158	10,872	56.6
1964	3,623	7,243	10,865	66.7
1965	5,570	8,150	13,720	59.4
1966	8,018	7,543	15,561	48.5
1967	14,991	6,964	21,954	31.7
1968	10,731	6,651	17,383	38.3
1969	12,735	5,613	18,348	30.6
1970	25,384	4,931	30,315	16.3
1971	24,775	7,354	32,129	22.9
1972	17,425	8,706	26,132	33.3
1973	13,244	7,802	21,049	37.1
1974	25,903	6,160	32,066	19.2
1975	32,603	10,157	42,761	23.8

Note: Components may not add to totals due to rounding.

Source: Securities and Exchange Commission data, also published in *Federal Reserve Bulletin,* Table A38.

loans at a sample of banks exceeded the gross increase in reported private placements. In 1968 and 1969, which were also periods of peak term-loan activity, the net increases in term loans represented 52 and 58 percent, respectively, of the increases in private placements.

The overlap between the bank term-loan market and the private placement market is far from perfect. Generally, the maturity structure of private placements is in the 20- to 30-year range, but shorter term placements are not uncommon. For instance, about 10 percent of the direct placement commitments (by volume) made by a major life insurance company during the past year were for maturities of 15 years or less. In the five- to ten-year maturity range, there is a significant degree of overlap between direct placements and bank term loans. Loans in this range have been attracting increasing attention from life insurance companies and commercial banks, as well as from corporate borrowers. Insurance companies thus may find their dominance of the private placement market to be subject to increasing challenges in the years to come, particularly with respect to loans in certain maturity ranges.

SUMMARY

A reasonable expectation is that lenders will continue to respond to relative yields as they did in the 1966–1975 financial markets. Having once learned to shift their acquisitions from one instrument to another in response to cyclical forces, they will be unlikely to renounce that new-found sophistication. Regulatory constraints and perhaps certain practical considerations impose some limits on their responsiveness, but within these boundaries significant flexibility is possible. As long as lenders continue this type of behavior, borrowers will have a wide range of alternatives along the maturity spectrum of debt instruments, among types of debt instruments, and between debt and equity.

The implication of this kind of fluidity among markets is that margins between types of instruments should tend to narrow toward some equilibrium level that presumably will reflect different degrees of risk and marketability among instruments. It would not be surprising if one of the margins to decline was that between direct placements and otherwise comparable public bonds.

That premium supposedly reflects the lack of marketability of private placements relative to their publicly offered counterparts. But, in a market place in which the major investor groups remain attuned to yield imbalances among instruments, opportune selling from portfolios would be expected to increase. To the extent that more lenders seek to sell private placements and more are willing to purchase seasoned issues, the penalty for lack of marketability would correspondingly decline.

This expected shifting among lenders implies that no one lender would tend to dominate a segment of the market year after year. But unless important changes occur in the liability structure of the life insurance industry, it can be expected to remain an important purchaser of corporate debt. Moreover, the advantages of a favorable risk/return position in lending to smaller or weaker credits and of forward commitments both suggest that the private placement market will continue to be a very important outlet for life insurance company investable funds.

3

Investment in Income Property Mortgages by Life Insurance Companies

By Lawrence D. Jones*

At the time of the last set of Huebner Foundation lectures dealing with life insurance company investment policies, the analysis of mortgage lending was appropriately focused upon home financing with special emphasis upon the impact of Federally underwritten loan programs. By way of contrast, an examination of life company mortgage lending in the 1970s must concentrate upon conventional income property loans. The goal of this chapter is to provide such an analysis.

The chapter begins with a brief background discussion of factors determining demand for and supply of funds in the income property mortgage market and a review of life company activity in the mortgage market over the past quarter century. Then, the core of the chapter relates the critical characteristics of income property mortgages to the investment objectives of life insurance companies in order to provide a basis for understanding, explaining, and predicting life company activity in the income property mortgage market. In the process the chapter examines life insurance company responsiveness to yield spreads, participation features, maturity and marketability characteristics, elements of default risk, and the benefits and risks associated with lending via forward commitments.

* Lawrence D. Jones is associate professor of urban land economics at the University of British Columbia.

SOME CHARACTERISTICS OF THE INCOME PROPERTY MORTGAGE MARKET

Income property loans is an imprecisely labeled catch-all category used to encompass all mortgage loans secured by improved real estate other than "homes."[1] The term derives from the presumption that a common characteristic of such properties is that their value and the security of any loans based upon such value are determined by the stream of income expected to be produced by the properties. A wide variety of residential, commercial, industrial, agricultural, and institutional structures is included in this class of properties. However, the bulk of mortgage financing on such properties is secured by apartments, office buildings, and retail stores.

Demand for Mortgage Financing

Mortgage loans are utilized for a variety of purposes including financing the construction of income properties, the acquisition of newly completed or seasoned structures, and the refinancing of existing loans secured by such improvements. Thus, the demand for financing is a function of the current and prospective activity generating the addition of new space, the rate of turnover of existing properties, and factors affecting decisions to refinance. Each of these segments of demand depends upon financing terms and the structure of the tax laws as well as real economic variables affecting the profitability of investments in various types of income properties.

Given these basic economic incentives, the amount of mortgage financing demanded is determined by the total costs of construction or acquisition of designated projects, the relative cost of debt and equity capital to investors, the relative cost of alternative forms of debt financing, and the risks associated with carrying the debt service burden. Historically, developers and many other real estate investors have perceived equity capital as being highly expensive and have been willing to accept the cash flow and earnings risks associated with leverage.[2] For the bulk of borrowers with whom life insurance company mortgage loan departments do business, this appears to continue to be an accurate characterization.[3]

---

[1] "Home mortgages" include all debt secured by one-to-four family, nonfarm residential properties.

[2] The desire of investors with limited equity funds to obtain diversification in their real property portfolios also produces a demand for debt financing.

[3] There do, of course, exist substantial equity investors in real estate; and

For various reasons, most borrowers applying to life insurance company mortgage departments do not have access to alternative credit markets, such as the bond market, to finance construction or acquisition of income properties.[4] Thus, the range of financing alternatives available to such borrowers at any point in time depends upon the cash flow position of, and competitiveness among, suppliers of mortgage money for income properties, as well as other factors determining relative yields on assets qualifying for these lenders' portfolios.[5]

Factors Affecting the Supply of Funds

Lenders look to the stream of prospective returns generated by income properties as the primary source from which debt service is covered. The adequacy of this stream of returns depends upon its projected magnitude in relation to debt service and upon its potential variability. Given a project that is initially well-designed and located for the market in question, the volatility of gross revenues depends primarily upon future competition. The vulnerability of properties to competition depends upon lease provisions, location, services, amenities, obsolescence rates, and the quality of management.

Most of these factors also enter into the determination of the net income stream available to cover debt service through their impact upon operating expenses. Lenders utilize a variety of devices in an

---

some income property markets may be dominated by individuals seeking outlets for substantial amounts of equity funds. Low rise apartments appear to be such a market. See Wallace F. Smith, *The Low Rise Speculative Apartment,* Berkeley Research Report No. 25 (Berkeley, Calif.: Center for Real Estate and Urban Economics, University of California). Equity funds are pooled through public and private syndication offerings, security issues of equity trusts, and the issues of interests in pooled real property accounts managed by insurance companies and banks. Various financial institutions, including life insurance companies, also have investment real estate in their own portfolios.

[4] This situation is substantially different from that in life company bond departments where a significant proportion of customers are likely to have public offering or bank term loan alternatives to institutional privately placed debenture issues. Grebler contends that the ability of large development firms to obtain financing outside mortgage markets represents one of the most important economies obtained from large scale operations. See Leo Grebler, *Large Scale Housing and Real Estate Firms,* UCLA Housing, Real Estate and Urban Land Studies Program Series (New York: Praeger Publishers, 1973), pp. 55–61.

[5] Financing alternatives may exist in the form of sale-leaseback arrangements where it is feasible for the "borrower" to exchange simple fee ownership for a leasehold interest. These take the form of long-term, noncancellable leases which in turn are often mortgagable.

attempt to influence the quality of tenants, lease provisions, and the identity of property management firms. The goal of these efforts is, of course, to produce a substantial, stable gross revenue stream and to minimize the effect of inflation, aging, and other factors upon the flow of net operating income.

In some cases mortgage lending is based primarily upon the credit of investor-borrowers or tenants rather than the intrinsic characteristics of the property. In general, credit-based loans are likely to be considered relatively low risk debts and to carry correspondingly low observable yields and expected returns. Similarly, loans on well-established existing structures are normally considered "safer" than loan commitments on to-be-constructed and, therefore, largely untested properties.[6]

The riskiness of such loans is also affected by risks inherent in the forward commitment process. Most commitments issued by life insurance companies which involve more than a year from commitment to delivery of funds are entered into by mortgage departments to provide permanent financing on to-be-constructed income properties.[7] Finally, within the context of prevailing market conditions, lenders and borrowers negotiate over various loan terms which affect the expected return-risk mix. These include interest, participation compensation, maturity date, amortization provisions, and prepayment rights and penalties.

INCOME PROPERTY MORTGAGE LOANS IN THE CAPITAL MARKET

Given the debt financing needs of most developers and real estate investors and the lack of feasible alternatives to mortgage lending, the income property mortgage market plays a crucial role in the financing of new development in the form of apartments, shopping centers, office buildings, hotels and motels, warehouses, etc. Since most construction lenders require that borrowers obtain a permanent

---

[6] However, lenders do frequently include contingency provisions, such as leasing requirements, which must be met before the lender is obliged to honor the full amount of the loan commitment.

[7] Using forward commitment survey data from the American Life Insurance Association, Pesando has estimated that nearly 40 percent of nonresidential mortgage loan commitments extend beyond one year. In recent years well over 90 percent of corporate bond commitments appear to have been taken down within a year. See James E. Pesando, "The Interest Sensitivity of the Flow of Funds through Life Insurance Companies: An Econometric Analysis," *Journal of Finance*, vol. 29, no. 4 (September 1974), p. 1113.

loan commitment prior to committing construction funds,[8] permanent lenders make decisions that determine whether proposed developments can go forward.

Because mortgage flow data include lending for all purposes and because equity financing is used to some extent, there is no necessary relationship between the rate of new construction and the volume of new mortgage financing. For example, over the period 1950–1975 the net volume of mortgage lending on commercial properties amounted to 90 percent of the value of new commercial construction put in place, but the rates of growth of commercial construction and of mortgage financing secured by commercial properties were only loosely related.

As the relative growth rates in Table 3.1 suggest, there has been

TABLE 3.1
Comparison of Commercial Construction Activity and Commercial Mortgage Flows

| | Current Dollars (billions) | | (3) |
Period	(1) Construction	(2) Mortgage	Column (2) ÷ Column (1) (percent)
1950–1959	$ 25.9	$ 18.4	71.0%
1960–1969°	41.6	33.4	80.3
1970–1975	79.1	80.4	101.6
1950–1975°	146.6	132.2	90.2

Note: Commercial construction is measured by the value of commercial space put in place; mortgage flows are the net change in the dollar volume of commercial mortgages outstanding.
° Excludes years 1965–1967, inclusive, due to absence of commercial construction data.
Sources: U.S. Department of Commerce, *Survey of Current Business,* various issues and Flow of Funds data, available from Flow of Funds section, Board of Governors of the Federal Reserve System.

a secular tendency for the flow of mortgage dollars to increase relative to real investment flows. This is consistent with, and presumably partially attributable to, an observable secular increase in the size of loans relative to appraised values.[9] The relatively large dollar figures for commercial construction and mortgage financing in the 1970s re

---

[8] There have been numerous reported instances where REITs waived this requirement. However, the high default rates realized on REIT construction loans during 1974–1975 have induced construction lenders once again to require permanent commitments in advance.

[9] American Council of Life Insurance sample survey data indicate that average loan-to-value ratios on life insurance company income property loans increased steadily from less than 60 percent in 1951 to about 75 percent in 1970.

(footnote continued on page 65)

TABLE 3.2
Percentage Distribution of Net Funds Raised via Various Instruments

Instrument	1952–1956	1957–1961	1962–1966	1967–1971	1972–1976
U.S. government securities	4.2%	7.9%	5.4%	9.8%	17.0%
State and local government securities	13.5	11.5	8.4	9.6	7.0
Corporate and foreign bonds	12.7	12.8	10.5	15.7	11.7
Corporate equities	8.6	8.9	4.4	8.2	4.5
Total mortgages	36.6	36.9	35.8	28.8	32.2
Consumer credit	11.6	6.8	10.7	7.3	7.1
Other bank loans	9.3	7.7	13.8	9.9	9.2
Other loans*	3.5	7.7	11.0	10.8	11.4
Total amount (billions)	$169.7	$230.6	$358.4	$582.5	$1114.2

* Other loans include various issues of open market paper, finance company loans to business, certain U.S. government and non-mortgage federal credit agency loans, and policy loans of life insurance companies.

Source: Flow of Funds data, available from Flow of Funds section, Board of Governors of the Federal Reserve System.

flect the substantial step-up in price inflation rates which occurred in that period. The implicit price deflator for gross private domestic investment in non-residential structures has increased 10 percent per annum during the 1970s compared to 3 percent per annum over the 1950–1970 period. Thus in constant dollars the value of new commercial construction put in place during 1970–1975 averaged just about the same amount per annum as the level of commercial construction activity in 1968–1969.

Mortgage borrowers must compete in the capital markets with a variety of other demands for financing. Historically, mortgage loans have accounted for a sizable share of the funds raised in U.S. capital markets. During 1950–1966 for example, net funds raised via mortgage loans substantially exceeded the sum of net amounts raised through the issuance of corporate bonds, state and local government securities, and all Treasury obligations. However, as Table 3.2 shows, mortgage financing has diminished somewhat in importance during the most recent decade.

This decline is primarily attributable to sharp increases in Treasury financing, short- and medium-term bank loans, and open-market paper. Within mortgage financing, Table 3.3 shows that only commercial properties have been able to consistently increase their share of mortgage financing during the past quarter century.

TABLE 3.3
Percentage Distribution of Net Funds Raised through Various Mortgage Instruments

Instrument	1952–1956	1957–1961	1962–1966	1967–1971	1972–1976
Home	76.1%	65.6%	60.6%	57.1%	62.9%
Multifamily	5.5	11.3	13.8	17.0	8.8
Commercial	13.3	18.4	18.5	20.5	21.0
Farm	5.1	4.8	7.1	5.5	7.3
Total amount (billions)	$62.2	$85.0	$128.4	$167.5	$358.2

Source: Flow of Funds data, available from Flow of Funds section, Board of Governors of the Federal Reserve System.

The ratio appears to have leveled off around the 75 percent level in recent years. See "Commitments of $100,000 and Over on Multifamily and Nonresidential Mortgages Made by 15 Life Insurance Companies" (Washington, D.C.: American Council of Life Insurance, quarterly).

LIFE INSURANCE COMPANIES IN THE MORTGAGE MARKET

Loan Activity of Life Insurance Companies

The importance of life insurance companies in the mortgage markets has diminished almost continuously from the early 1950s to the mid-1970s. As Table 3.4 indicates, the life insurance industry ac-

TABLE 3.4
Net Acquisitions of Various Types of Mortgage Loans by Life Insurance Companies as a Proportion of Market Activity

Period	One-to-four Family Home	Multi-family	Commercial	Farm	All Mortgages
1952–1956	20.1%	17.1%	31.6%	30.0%	22.0%
1957–1961	10.1	6.6	27.2	16.9	13.2
1962–1966	5.7	34.2	33.0	22.7	15.9
1967–1971	−5.9	22.7	28.2	4.0	6.5
1972–1976	−3.8	8.3	27.0	6.8	4.6

Source: Flow of Funds data, available from Flow of Funds section, Board of Governors of the Federal Reserve System.

counted for 22 percent of the net flow of funds into mortgages during the 1952–1956 period but less than one twentieth of the comparable flow during the most recent five-year period. The life companies' share of mortgage loan acquisitions fell especially sharply in the past decade.

This decline in mortgage lending activity suggests that mortgage loans have come to absorb a smaller share of the investable funds generated by life insurance companies. As Table 3.5 indicates, this has certainly been the case during the past decade. In order to focus upon voluntary investment decisions, the calculations in Table 3.5 eliminate funds absorbed by policy loans and relate mortgage acquisitions to total investments net of policy loans.

As a result of the pattern of mortgage acquisitions shown in Table 3.5, mortgages increased from 25.7 percent of life company financial assets in 1950 to 39.8 percent in 1966 and have subsequently declined to 30 percent. This recent decline is almost wholly attributable to life companies turning away from the home loan market. Income property loans, particularly loans secured by commercial properties, recently have absorbed a substantially larger share of life insurance company funds than was true in the 1950s.

TABLE 3.5
Allocation of Net Investable Funds by Life Insurance Companies among Selected Assets

| Period | Mortgage Loans | | | | | Corporate Issues | | Other Assets |
	1–4 Family Home	Multifamily	Commercial	Farm	Total Mortgages	Bonds	Shares	
1952–1956	38.2%	2.3%	10.5%	3.8%	54.8%	47.4%	2.4%	−4.6%
1957–1961	21.9	2.5	16.5	2.7	43.5	44.0	4.4	8.1
1962–1966	12.5	16.9	22.0	5.8	57.1	35.9	6.2	8.0
1967–1971	−13.2	15.3	22.8	0.9	25.8	38.3	22.2	13.7
1972–1976	−9.9	3.0	23.6	2.1	19.0	49.4	16.5	15.2

Note: Investable funds is defined as net acquisitions of all financial assets less net acquisitions of policy loans.

Source: Flow of Funds data, available from Flow of Funds section, Board of Governors of the Federal Reserve System.

As life insurance companies reduced their emphasis on mortgage lending, the slack thereby created in the supply of mortgage funds was absorbed by the relatively rapid growth of savings and loan associations and by the expanded activities of Federally sponsored credit agencies. These flow shifts are depicted in Table 3.6.

In evaluating responsiveness to market pressures, it is important to observe that the substantial increase in the dollar volume of mortgage financing in the 1970s has been accomplished without any of the traditional mortgage lenders increasing the share of loanable funds which they devoted to mortgage lending. Indeed, as Table 3.7 indicates, the thrift institutions actually have reduced the proportion of their investable funds allocated to mortgages.[10]

The data examined thus far does not fully indicate the role of life insurance companies in the mortgage markets. This is the case because much of the mortgage activity of institutions such as commercial banks and REITs consists of construction and development loans and other forms of short-term mortgage lending; this activity is included in the net mortgage loan acquisition data utilized in the previous tables. A more relevant measure of the importance of life companies can be obtained by focusing upon permanent lending activity.

Table 3.8 shows the percentage distribution of new commitments made to acquire long-term mortgages by type of property and lending institution for the 1973–1976 period. Even in this market, life insurers appear to have slipped to a third-place ranking behind savings and loan associations and commercial banks. However, the life insurance industry is second in financing multifamily residential units and continues to be the dominant lender in nonfarm, nonresidential mortgages as well as the leading private lender in financing agricultural properties. The role of life insurers in affecting the level and mix of new real estate development is particularly crucial because their commitment activity is concentrated on new (primarily to-be-constructed) properties. According to Table 3.9, well over 80 percent of the dollar volume of life insurance company loan commitments on

---

[10] In particular, mutual savings banks, which have broader investment power than savings and loan associations, have been gradually reducing their commitment to mortgage loans. The proportion of mortgage loans to total savings bank assets has fallen from 73.7 percent in 1964 to 60.6 percent in 1976. Corporate securities have increased from 9.2 percent to 18.3 percent of assets in the same period. The decline in savings bank mortgage activity has been focused on home loans. Thus, the response of savings banks to changes in capital market signals over the past decade has been broadly comparable to that of life insurance companies.

TABLE 3.6
Percentage Shares of Major Lenders in Net Mortgage Flows

Lender	Home		Multifamily		Commercial		Farm		Total	
	1965–1970	1971–1976	1965–1970	1971–1976	1965–1970	1971–1976	1965–1970	1971–1976	1965–1970	1971–1976
Commercial banks	16.2%	16.1%	6.2%	4.4%	32.0%	32.8%	11.0%	11.2%	17.6%	18.0%
Savings and loans	39.2	53.8	26.5	34.8	12.9	25.6	—	—	29.1	42.4
Mutual savings banks	11.9	4.2	8.2	16.6	11.2	7.5	0.6	-0.3	10.4	5.8
Life insurance companies	-1.9	-4.1	34.4	8.0	31.5	26.8	12.4	6.3	11.6	4.2
Federally sponsored credit agencies	14.4	6.2	1.2	14.4	—	—	31.9	39.7	10.5	8.1
Mortgage pools	3.2	16.0	0.2	4.9	—	—	10.0	5.6	2.5	10.9
REITs	0.6	0.1	5.0	3.2	5.9	2.7	—	—	2.4	1.0
Finance companies†	2.6	0.1	3.0	-0.5	0.9	1.6	—	—	2.1	0.4
Other	13.8	7.7	15.4	14.4	5.6	2.9	34.1	37.6	13.7	9.3
Total amount (billions)	$94.2	$256.0	$25.5	$41.1	$34.5	$85.1	$10.9	$28.7	$165.1	$410.7

† The finance company sector includes mortgage companies.

Source: Flow of Funds data, available from Flow of Funds section, Board of Governors of the Federal Reserve System.

TABLE 3.7
Proportion of Net Financial Asset Acquisitions Allocated to Various Types of Mortgage Loans at Selected Institutions

Institution	Home		Multifamily		Commercial	
	1965–1970	1971–1976	1965–1970	1971–1976	1965–1970	1971–1976
Commercial banks	7.4%	9.9%	0.8%	0.4%	5.3%	6.7%
Savings and loans	64.2	63.8	11.8	6.6	7.6	10.1
Mutual savings banks	65.9	19.1	8.5	12.1	16.3	11.4
Life insurance companies	−3.3	−9.9	16.2	3.1	19.9	21.2
Federally sponsored credit agencies	45.0	30.9	1.0	11.5	—	—
REITs	15.4	6.5	33.3	28.3	51.3	50.0
Finance companies	9.6	0.7	3.2	−0.5	0.8	3.3

Source: Flow of Funds data, available from Flow of Funds section, Board of Governors of the Federal Reserve System.

TABLE 3.8
Percentage Distribution of New Commitments to Acquire Various Types of Long-Term Mortgage Loans by Lending Institution, 1973–1976

Institution	Home	Multifamily	Commercial	Farm	Total
Commercial banks	19.2%	9.3%	23.8%	7.1%	18.3%
Mutual savings banks	9.8	15.1	7.8	*	9.2
Savings and loans	66.1	28.7	16.1	1.0	44.7
Life insurance companies	0.9	20.3	43.9	21.1	15.1
REITs	0.2	3.1	3.5	*	1.3
Pension funds†	0.6	1.2	3.3	*	1.3
Federally sponsored credit agencies ..	3.3	13.9	1.6	70.4	9.1
State and local credit agencies	*	8.3	0.0	0.3	1.0
Total amount (millions)	$90,207	$18,152	$38,869	$12,019	$159,237

* Less than 0.05%.

† Includes private and state and local government pension funds.

Source: U.S. Department of Housing and Urban Development.

TABLE 3.9
Percentage of New Commitments to Acquire
Long-Term Mortgages Accounted for by Loans
Secured by New Properties: Life Insurance
Companies versus Other Lenders: 1973–1974

Property Type	Life Insurance Companies	Other Lenders
Home	35.8%	38.8%
Multifamily	81.1	69.5
Commercial	87.3	53.2
Farm	6.4	2.7
Total	74.9	43.1

Source: U.S. Department of Housing and Urban Development.

nonfarm income properties are secured by new properties. This represents a significantly higher concentration in new properties than is characteristic of the market as a whole.

In sum, major shifts have occurred in the contribution of life insurance companies to mortgage markets and in the proportion of the companies' net investable funds devoted to the acquisition of mortgage loans. In recent years, investable funds net of policy loans have been devoted almost exclusively to corporate securities and income property mortgage loans. The distribution of funds between these alternatives and the determinants of the composition of each of these portfolios depends upon the matching of life insurance company investment objectives with various asset characteristics. The characteristics of income property mortgages which affect life company investment choices are the subject of the next section.

Investment Objectives of Life Insurance Companies

Life insurance company managers presumably design investment policies that are consistent with their ultimate objectives. In a broad sense managers can be assumed to act in their own self-interest; i.e., their objective is to maximize their own utility. Managers may, of course, derive utility in a number of ways, including pecuniary compensation and other perquisites associated with holding executive positions.[11] The ability to achieve these or other goals depends upon management's success in generating high profit rates and asset growth. Given these considerations, management has a substantial

---

[11] It is also possible that managers may derive utility from the creation of social benefits via lending or other activities.

interest in seeking portfolio return. This search for investment return must be conducted, of course, within the risk constraints imposed by stockholders, policyholders, regulators, and management's own interests.

Managers wish to avoid situations which lead to unacceptably high probabilities of poor performance. The ultimate in poor performance occurs when executives are forced out of their management positions through stockholder or regulatory action. Therefore, a reasonable assumption is that life insurance company managements select portfolios that maximize their expected utility where this utility, like that of most investors, is positively related to investment return and negatively related to investment risk. This implies that one should expect life insurance company investment choices to be responsive to changes in risk-adjusted yield spreads among asset classes.[12]

The primary investment risks faced by life companies consist of (1) risks associated with changes in future interest rate levels and asset market values and (2) risks that promised payments will not be made by debtors in accordance with contractual provisions. The first set of risks affects investment choices through the emphasis placed on marketability and maturity characteristics and through the use made of the forward commitment process.

Historically, life insurance companies issued long-term, fixed-dollar liabilities contingent upon highly predictable mortality experience. Furthermore, the industry's growth pattern resulted in substantial positive net cash inflows. The implications of these characteristics were that (1) life companies should concentrate on long-term debt investment to hedge the risk that future levels of interest rates might fall below those guaranteed on long-term insurance and pension liabilities and (2) life companies need not be constrained by marketability characteristics in selecting these assets. As a first approximation, with an explicit qualification for liabilities tied to the investment performance of equity portfolios, these implications remain valid.

However, life companies have acquired a much wider range of liabilities,[13] the growth rate of their assets has slowed, and, in the

---

[12] Observation of expected yields has been obscured in some periods by significant use of various forms of income and equity participations in income property mortgage loans and convertible features, warrants, and options on unsecured corporate debt issues.

[13] See Robert A. Rennie, "Investment Strategy for the Life Insurance Company," Chapter 1 in this volume, and *Institutional Investor Study Report of the Securities and Exchange Commission*, 92d Congress, 1st Session, House Doc. No. 92-64, Part 2, ch. 6.

past decade, they have experienced much more volatile cash flows.[14] For some companies these deviations from the traditional assumptions may have been sufficiently large to cause modifications in desired asset maturity distributions and to increase the importance of the liquidity characteristics of the portfolio.

Liquidity needs may also be met by reducing the probability of cash flow shortfalls or by establishing lines of credit. The incidence of cash flow shortages can be reduced in several ways. For instance, the companies can insist upon prepayment prohibitions or penalties on bond and mortgage loan covenants.[15] Unanticipated increases in benefit claims, operating expenses, policy loans, or cash surrenders could not generate liquidity problems were it not for the practice of committing a substantial portion of investable funds to specific assets in advance of their receipt. Consequently, cash flow problems can also be handled by altering the proportion of forecasted funds which are committed in advance.

Implementation of a conscious maturity selection policy requires the ability to predict the timing of principal repayments. In practice, this is partially achievable through selection of assets on which prepayment restrictions are available or negotiable. In periods of interest rate volatility investment earnings are also threatened by systematic antiselection in the timing of prepayments, which further reinforces the importance of bond call protection and mortgage prepayment prohibitions.

Finally, expectations regarding future levels of interest rates can be expected to affect forward commitment policies directly. Expectations with respect to future interest rates should, other things equal, depress the issuance of forward commitments if rate increases are expected and induce more forward commitments if falling interest rates are anticipated. Several investment officers interviewed in the course of this research attributed the sharp reduction in life insurance company forward commitment activity in 1974–1975 to strong infla-

---

[14] See George A. Bishop, *The Response of Life Insurance Investment to Changes in Monetary Policy, 1965–70* (New York: Life Insurance Association of America, 1971); Pesando, "The Interest Sensitivity . . ."; and J. David Cummins, *An Econometric Model of the Life Insurance Sector of the U.S. Economy* (Lexington, Mass.: D. C. Heath, Lexington Books, 1975), chap. 3.

[15] The most volatile elements of cash flow are bond calls, mortgage prepayments, and policy loan demands. Given statutory provisions that require policy loans to be offered at prescribed interest rates, life insurers can escape the policy loan drain only by changing the mix of liability characteristics over time or by lobbying for changes in the policy loan rate ceilings. As a result of recent legislative action two-thirds of the states now permit contract rates on policy loans to be 8% or higher in contrast to the 6% rate (5% in New York) which has prevailed for years.

tionary expectations. Such expectations imply that higher nominal interest rates are anticipated, inducing insurers to hold back investable funds while tending to reduce the forecasted level of future investable funds.[16] In terms of the investment mix choices, this response might be expected to cut into the companies' allocation of funds to mortgage loans on to-be-constructed income properties.

The risk that borrowers will default on interest or principal payments is a function of the credit quality of the borrowing entity and the terms of the loan in question. For secured loans, the market value of the property serving as security also affects the likelihood of default. Considerations of default risk may influence investment composition through changes in lenders' ability and willingness to incur such risk, in their evaluation of the intrinsic credit and property quality characteristics associated with an asset class, or in their ability to obtain default protection via contract provisions on certain types of debt issues.

The Impact of Investment Objectives on Income Property Mortgage Lending

Responsiveness to Changes in Yield Spreads. As demonstrated above (see Table 3.5), the proportion of life insurers' net investable funds devoted to home mortgage loans declined steadily during the 1950–1976 period. Indeed, net acquisitions of home loans have been negative during the past decade. By way of contrast, the proportion of investable funds allocated to nonfarm income property mortgages increased from 13 percent during the 1952–1956 period to 38 percent in 1967–1971.

This pattern of shifting allocations within the mortgage portfolio appears generally consistent with the pattern of yield spreads faced by life insurance companies. For example, the contract rate on conventional home mortgage loans acquired by life insurers in 1951 exceeded the average contract rate on new income property loan acquisitions by about 25 basis points. This spread deteriorated at a modest but consistent rate until the mid-1960s, when income property loans had about a 50 basis point advantage. Subsequently, the spread moved sharply to about 150 basis points in favor of income property

---

[16] Increased uncertainty with respect to future interest rates can be expected to dampen responses to changes in the expected value of future interest rates. A thorough theoretical analysis of this issue together with some empirical evidence can be found in John Lintner, Thomas Piper, and Peter Fortune, "Forward Commitment Decisions of Life Insurance Companies for Investments in Bonds and Mortgages," unpublished draft, National Bureau of Economic Research, New York, June 1974.

loans by 1970.[17] The margin in favor of income property loans has declined but remained significantly positive since 1970. Thus, assuming no major changes in the relative riskiness of the conventional home loans and income property loans acquired by life insurers, the pattern of mortgage investments suggests that life insurance companies are quite responsive to yield spreads within the mortgage portfolio.[18]

From the limited data that are available, it appears that the rate spread between newly issued corporate bonds and income property mortgages narrowed from 1950 to the mid-1960s. From 1965 to 1968 the spread between the yield on fourth quality corporate direct placements and contract rates on shopping center loans ranged between 11 and 41 basis points in favor of the latter investment.[19]

Allowing for the somewhat higher originating and servicing costs associated with mortgages and assuming that the two types fall in about the same risk class, life companies would have found these categories about equally attractive. Since 1969, yields on direct placements have become more attractive; and a shift of life company lending activity toward corporate bonds has occurred in the 1970s.[20]

The Significance of Participation Compensation. Life insurance companies have obtained compensation on income property mortgage loans in excess of contractually specified interest rates in a

---

[17] See Robert Moore Fisher and Barbara Negri Opper, "Mortgage Commitments on Income Properties: A New Series for 15 Life Insurance Companies, 1951–70," Staff Economic Study No. 79, Board of Governors of the Federal Reserve System, 1973, p. 16.

[18] Econometric estimates of yield spread sensitivity corroborate this interpretation. See especially Pesando, "The Interest Sensitivity. . . ."

[19] Corporate bond yield data are from "Average Yields on Directly Placed Corporate Bond Authorizations" (Washington, D.C.: American Council of Life Insurance, monthly). Shopping center loan yields are average contract rates on new commitments of $100,000 or more obtained from "Survey of Mortgage Commitments on Multifamily and Nonresidential Properties by 15 Life Insurance Companies" (Washington, D.C.: American Council of Life Insurance, monthly).

[20] Econometric analyses have produced mixed results in attempting to measure the responsiveness of life insurers to movements in bond-mortgage yield spreads. For example, Pesando finds evidence of substitution between nonresidential and residential mortgage commitments in response to yield spread changes, but his evidence on the yield responsiveness of the allocation of commitments between mortgages and bonds is mixed at best. See Pesando, "The Interest Sensitivity . . . ," p. 1115. Using a model of net changes in holdings of bonds and mortgages, Cummins found a significant substitution relationship between bonds and both income property and home mortgages. In his equations, commitments were taken into account through the use of distributed lags in interest rates and certain cash flow variables. See Cummins, *An Econometric Model . . .* , chap. 5.

number of ways. By far the most common form has been via participations in the income stream generated by the property securing the loan or in capital gains realized upon disposal of the property.[21] Other forms include fee ownership in the real property securing the mortgage loans, options to purchase real property or stock in developing corporations, and joint venture interests in projects being financed. Participation provisions were seldom included in loan contracts prior to 1968.[22] Their incidence spread rapidly thereafter and apparently peaked in 1970.[23] The use of participation features appears to have fallen off sharply after 1970 and to have experienced only a modest revival as interest rates rose to high levels during 1973–1974.[24]

---

[21] A survey of 56 life insurance companies near the peak of the incidence of participation activity (the first six months of 1969) revealed that contingent interest based on gross or net income was the most common participation arrangement. Among mortgage commitments with participation features, 77 percent of the dollar volume of apartment loans and 64 percent of commercial loans involved this type of provision. See Kenneth M. Wright, "Innovations in Mortgage Financing," *CLU Journal*, January 1971, p. 32.

[22] The 56-company survey reported that in 1964 only 1.8 percent of the dollar volume of new commitments for nonfarm income property mortgages included participation features. This percentage increased steadily to 7.6 percent in 1967 and then jumped to 23.9 percent in 1968 and to 56.0 percent in the first half of 1969. Wright, "Innovations . . . ," p. 31.

[23] Piper has estimated that the proportion of new income property loan commitments by life insurance companies involving income or equity participations reached 62 percent in 1969 and 70 to 75 percent during the first half of 1970. See Thomas R. Piper, "Income Participations on Mortgage Loans by Major Financial Institutions," unpublished working paper, Harvard University, February 1975, p. 2. Piper's 1969 estimate is close to that provided by the Institutional Investor Study's survey of 61 life companies. This survey indicated that in dollar terms "nearly half" of the mortgage commitments made in 1969 had contingent interest provisions and 12.4 percent had equity kickers attached. *Institutional Investor Study Report* . . . , pp. 697 and 714.

[24] The evidence with respect to 1973–1974 is very limited and mixed. On the basis of field interviews, Piper estimated that in 1973 only 5 to 10 percent of new income property commitments by life insurance companies had income or equity participation features. Piper, "Income Participations . . . ," p. 2. Chesborough found mixed responses for 1973, some companies indicating that "participations are dead" and others reporting a significant increase in the incidence of participation features in that year as compared with 1971–1972. Lowell D. Chesborough, "Do Participation Loans Pay Off?" *Real Estate Review*, Summer 1974, p. 96. A survey of an unspecified sample of commercial mortgage lenders by Roy Wenzlick Research Corp. shows that participation provisions peaked in 1970 and had declined to negligible proportions by 1973. Roy Wenzlick Research Corp., *The Real Estate Analyst Mortgage Bulletin*, September 1973. Discussions with several large companies that had been highly active in participations indicated that participations were still utilized on 20 to 40 percent of their commitments in 1974 and 1975. However, the incidence of participations has limited significance for this period in the light of the sharp reductions in new commitments which occurred.

Explanations of the existence and variable incidence of the participation phenomenon frequently emphasize inflationary expectations and the use of participations to expand the set of expected return-risk opportunities.[25] Income participations can produce returns which are reasonably responsive to inflation if included in loans secured by properties on which rentals are responsive. The responsiveness of rentals depends upon lease provisions which make rental adjustments possible (e.g., short-term leases, rent escalators, and surcharge provisions) as well as upon market conditions, demand price elasticities, and the absence of external controls.

Participation agreements potentially provide a means of increasing expected return and/or reducing default risk on a portfolio of income property loans by tying realized returns to the success of the properties involved. Participations may provide a device that permits expected return to be increased without incurring additional risk. On the other hand, an increased incidence of participations may reflect a desire to increase expected yields by accepting higher risk loans.[26]

Whether or not inflation protection and an expansion of return-risk opportunities are achieved depends on the ability of lenders to obtain participation provisions in the market and on the manner in which such provisions are structured. The evidence cited above suggests that lenders' abilities to obtain participation provisions have been quite circumscribed outside the 1969–1970 period. It seems likely that inflationary expectations were at least as strong during 1973–1974 as in 1969–1970. Interest rates were higher in the more recent period and the concept of reducing default risk via earnings sharing agreements presumably remained as valid after 1970 as it had during 1969–1970. The primary difference appears to be that the high interest rates in 1974 were approximately market clearing rates while the high rates of 1970 were apparently substantially below market clearing levels so that various forms of non-interest rate rationing performed significant capital allocation functions. Thus, while the impact of price inflation on interest rates was significantly stronger in 1974 than in 1970, real demand for investment in income producing properties was substantially softer in 1974 than in 1970.

In the 1969–1970 environment many developers appeared to resist inclusion of participation features but frequently found them a prerequisite to obtaining loans. Indeed, some lenders were reported un-

---

[25] See Wright, "Innovations . . ." and Chesborough, "Do Participation Loans. . . ."

[26] The latter possibility might be viewed as an action that is complementary to the expansion of life insurers' common stock portfolios and to increased acquisitions of lower quality corporate bonds and bonds with equity features attached.

willing to make loans unless a participation feature was included.[27] When given a choice between a participation provision (with a concession in the fixed contract rate or other terms) and a standard fixed rate loan, developers have usually chosen the standard loan.[28]

As noted above, the most common form of participation has been a share of the income generated by the property; and the form of income participation preferred by lenders is a flat percentage of gross income.[29] Supporting the proposition that participations simply reflect "tight" credit markets is the fact that gross income kickers are neither efficient inflation hedges nor effective means of reducing default risk. With respect to inflation, an "off the top" gross income kicker is capable of draining the profitability from properties. Relating extra interest to return in excess of operating expenses provides a technique for tying compensation to profitability. This device may be subject to high administrative costs, however, unless operating expenses are carefully defined.[30]

A frequently used compromise applies the additional compensation requirement to the increase in gross income above some norm specified in the loan indenture. Since expected return in dollars from income participation generally increases with time and, in amortized loans, the loan balance decreases, the contribution of participations to effective yield increases over time. In principle, this should permit a somewhat lower debt service burden on the mortgagor in the early years. However, it also makes prepayment protection necessary for the mortgagee to realize the incremental yield advantage expected from the participation provision.[31]

If substantial inflation occurs, the extra compensation portion of return will, in general, be more responsive to resulting increases in rental revenues if the participation is in terms of a percentage of gross

[27] One survey covering the first half of 1969 indicated that 25 percent of the insurers surveyed included income and equity participations in over 70 percent of their mortgage commitments. See Wright, "Innovations . . . ," p. 31.

[28] Piper, "Income Participations . . . ," p. 27.

[29] Chesborough, "Do Participation Loans . . . ," p. 98, and Piper, "Income Participations . . . ," p. 24.

[30] The decline in the popularity of income participation may be partly attributable to the administrative costs life companies found necessary to track and enforce participation provisions. Some companies apparently eliminated the practice of using income participations on loans of less than $1 million. See Chesborough, "Do Participation Loans . . . ," p. 97.

[31] There is no evidence that participation loans have more restrictive prepayment provisions that straight interest loans, however. Piper, "Income Participations . . . ," p. 30. This may reflect the fact that lenders were induced to seek strong prepayment protection on straight loans in the high interest rate period during which participations were most common.

in excess of some base rather than as a flat share of gross. However, the extra return will be much more certain in the straight gross income case.[32]

As noted above, participations can be viewed as a device to expand the return-risk opportunity set. Some observers have argued that life insurance companies utilized participations primarily to make loans which would not have qualified as fixed interest loans.[33] This might be a result of extra liberal loan terms (e.g., loan amount, or maturity or amortization provisions) or intrinsic quality defects in the credit or in the property securing the loan.

Life insurers have generally denied that the participation provisions have resulted in lower quality investments. Rather, they emphasize the trade-off between participation and the size of fixed interest coupons. Testifying in 1971, an industry representative indicated that the inclusion of a contingent interest provision generally resulted in a ½ to 1 percent reduction in the fixed interest rate portion of compensation.[34] However, Piper reports that the bulk of income participation loans are written at rates ⅛ to ½ percent below what the rate would have been without the participation.[35]

Since the participation is contingent upon future receipts and expenses, it is generally more uncertain than the portion of the fixed coupon which is given up. Consequently, the expected value of the participation must exceed the expected value of the fixed coupon sacrificed. Piper and Mundy have found that life insurers generally perceive the expected value of the participation to be worth about two to two and one-half times the portion of the fixed coupon foregone.[36] Over the expected life of the loan this implies that income

---

[32] Uncertainty here is viewed in terms of the variability of extra compensation as a function of changes in rental receipts and operating expenses, assuming all elements of debt service will be paid as due. As indicated above, a second source of uncertainty relates to the effect of the structure of the participation provision upon default probabilities. Results of simulations of participation returns using different participation provisions and various inflation assumptions are presented in Piper, "Income Participations . . . ," pp. 34–43, and Chesborough, "Do Participation Loans . . . ," pp. 99–100.

[33] This view was strongly expressed by apartment developers, who apparently found it difficult to escape participations during the 1969–1970 period. See the testimony of John A. Stastny and Donald I. Hovde in *The Banking Reform Act of 1971, Hearings before the Committee on Banking and Currency,* House of Representatives, 92d Congress, 1st Session, on HR 5700, Part 2, pp. 453–61, 463–68.

[34] See the reply by John T. Fey in *The Banking Reform Act of 1971, Hearings,* p. 528.

[35] Piper, "Income Participations. . . ."

[36] Piper, "Income Participations . . . ," p. 33, and Jefferson G. Mundy, "Par-

participations are typically worth somewhat more than 50 basis points in expected value.

Beyond the apparent interest rate concession, there is some indication that life companies have extended maturities to borrowers accepting a participation provision.[37] Little evidence exists, however, that life insurers have increased loan amounts in exchange for contingent income provisions, although additional financing is undoubtedly associated with lenders' acquisitions of equity interests.[38]

The Significance of Other Loan Terms. In addition to interest rate and participation provisions, there are other loan provisions which affect the relative attractiveness of various assets. In particular, liquidity risk, income risk, and default risk are affected by marketability, amortization, prepayment, and maturity features as well as by various restrictive provisions included in the loan indenture. In addition, each of these elements of risk exposure is affected by the terms of the forward commitment agreement.

Liquidity is available through the marketability of assets at reasonably predictable prices and through periodic payment provisions. Lacking any significant need for liquidity provisions, life insurers have been able to concentrate their investments in essentially nonmarketable private placements and income property mortgage loans. Those companies which have experienced volatile cash flows in recent years have increased the marketability of their assets primarily by purchasing publicly traded debt issues and expanding their common stock portfolios.

Bond and mortgage portfolios also provide liquidity in the form of regular sinking fund, amortization, and final maturity principal repayments. Sinking fund and amortization provisions were introduced primarily as devices to reduce the incidence of default risk by relating the debt repayment burden to the income stream generated by the investments being financed. These devices create a growing borrowers' equity interest in such investments and provide a mecha-

---

ticipation Mortgage Loans: Origins, Types and Performance" (Ph.D. diss., University of Texas, 1971).

[37] This is the most common form of concession reported by the life insurance company officers the author has interviewed. The stretching of effective maturity sometimes takes place through eliminating or reducing amortization payments for a period rather than lengthening the stated final maturity date. Also see Piper, "Income Participations . . . ," p. 31.

[38] The low incidence of cases where additional financing is traded off for a participation provision is sometimes attributed to the constraining effect of statutory loan-to-value ratios which apply to life insurance company mortgage loans. These restrictions are discussed in Chapter 14 of this book.

TABLE 3.10
Percentage Distribution of the Amount of New Income Property Mortgage Commitments by Amortization Provision: 15 Life Insurance Companies

| | Fully Amortized | | Partially Amortized | | | Total Amount Committed° (millions) |
| | Uniform Payments | Irregular Payments | Uniform Payments: Balance at Maturity | | Irregular Payments | |
Quarter			30% or Less	Over 30%		
1965.3	73.2%	14.6%	8.4%	3.9%	—%	784
1965.4	85.4	4.2	7.1	3.3	—	929
1966.1	80.4	1.8	9.0	4.1	4.7	914
1966.2	77.3	3.6	15.5	3.6	†	804
1966.3	79.2	4.0	11.5	5.3	—	532
1966.4	72.4	1.4	17.0	9.3	—	266
1967.1	81.1	2.0	11.3	5.4	0.1	441
1967.2	84.0	1.0	11.8	2.9	0.4	742
1967.3	78.7	1.3	16.0	2.9	1.1	924
1967.4	86.7	0.6	8.5	4.2	†	920
1968.1	88.9	1.0	7.9	1.7	0.5	841
1968.2	87.5	0.4	10.6	1.6	—	902
1968.3	93.1	0.1	5.5	1.3	—	737
1968.4	87.9	0.7	6.0	3.9	1.4	765
1969.1	63.6	4.1	3.9	28.2	0.1	878
1969.2	61.2	1.8	6.8	29.7	0.5	855
1969.3	63.9	1.2	3.3	31.5	0.1	794
1969.4	75.8	1.0	2.8	20.4	—	394
1970.1	53.7	6.4	1.3	38.6	—	556
1970.2	60.8	1.0	3.5	34.7	0.1	636
1970.3	48.6	0.3	—	50.6	0.4	545
1970.4	69.6	—	1.2	29.0	0.2	577

1971.1	71.0	0.1	0.2	28.6	—	731
1971.2	68.4	0.1	0.7	30.7	0.1	1,288
1971.3	57.2	8.9	2.2	31.5	0.3	1,187
1971.4	61.4	6.9	4.5	27.3	—	777
1972.1	64.3	3.8	1.7	30.2	—	1,152
1972.2	57.1	8.9	1.5	31.4	1.0	1,454
1972.3	42.4	17.7	1.5	34.7	3.8	1,291
1972.4	53.8	7.3	2.7	35.3	0.9	1,079
1973.1	60.3	15.4	0.9	23.3	0.1	1,362
1973.2	65.0	6.7	1.6	26.7	—	1,493
1973.3	63.2	7.7	2.0	24.5	2.7	1,309
1973.4	50.4	15.0	1.6	32.4	0.7	670
1974.1	57.5	0.8	0.5	41.2	—	540
1974.2	60.0	1.4	0.7	38.0	—	947
1974.3	48.7	1.1	2.6	47.5	—	789
1974.4	44.2	—	1.0	54.8	—	328
1975.1	67.4	—	0.1	32.5	—	248
1975.2	60.7	5.4	3.9	29.9	0.1	503
1975.3	55.1	5.9	7.6	30.4	1.0	409
1975.4	40.7	16.3	1.4	40.4	1.2	557
1976.1	48.0	6.7	†	36.3	9.1	534
1976.2	51.7	6.0	3.0	38.2	1.1	884
1976.3	60.4	5.3	2.3	30.8	1.2	1,159

* Excludes small amounts of commitments in some quarters for which amortization data were not available.

† Less than 0.05%.

Source: American Council of Life Insurance, "Survey of Mortgage Commitments on Multifamily and Nonresidential Properties by 15 Life Insurance Companies."

nism for identifying potential repayment problems at an earlier point in time. Such provisions also serve, however, to reduce the lumpiness in scheduled repayments and are also likely to reduce the magnitude of prepayments arising from bond refundings and mortgage loan refinancings due to the sale of secured property.

By the 1940s, fully amortized, constant monthly payment provisions were included in nearly all home loans. Amortization provisions were introduced more slowly in mortgage loans secured by income properties.[39] Nonetheless, by the early 1960s nearly ¾ of income property loans (by volume) were fully amortized. And, as Table 3.10 indicates, by 1968 about 90 percent of income property loan commitments were fully amortized.[40] However, since 1968, life insurance companies have made a substantial volume of partially amortized loans. Nearly ⅓ of the amount committed by 15 reporting companies since 1968 has involved repayment terms providing for a balloon payment at maturity of over 30 percent of the original loan amount. Balloons do not necessarily reduce the rate at which equity is built up by the mortgagor; generally, life insurers insist on shorter maturities where balloons are permitted than they would on a fully amortized loan.[41]

In this connection, it is relevant to note that the long secular trend toward longer stated maturities in income property mortgages (which was partially offset by increasing use of amortization provisions) appears to have leveled off in the late 1960s. This development is illustrated in Table 3.11. The decline since 1973 which is associated with a sharp drop in income property mortgage commitments (see Table 3.10) may reflect inflationary expectations of life insurance company investment committees.

Whether maturity policies are based on hedging income risk, inflationary expectations, desire for maturity diversification, or any other purpose, successful implementation of such policies depends

---

[39] Amortization provisions were introduced more slowly on larger loans. Data based on commitments made by 15 life insurers show, for example, that 80 percent of income property loans under $100,000 were fully amortized in 1951 but only 40 percent of loans in excess of $2 million were fully amortized. These data are from "Commitments on Multifamily and Nonresidential Mortgages Made by 15 Life Insurance Companies," collected for the National Bureau of Economic Research study of interest rates.

[40] See American Council of Life Insurance, "Survey of Mortgage Commitments on Multifamily and Nonresidential Properties by 15 Life Insurance Companies."

[41] Frequently, balloons result from calculating the mortgage payment on the assumption of an amortization period that is longer than the term, e.g., setting the mortgage payment on a 20-year loan equal to what the mortgage payment would be, *ceteris paribus,* on a fully amortized 25-year loan.

TABLE 3.11
Selected Characteristics of Income Property Mortgage Loan Commitments
Made by 15 Life Insurance Companies

Year	Debt Coverage Ratio[*]	Maturity (years/months)	Loan/Value Ratio (percent)	Average Loan (thousands)
1951	1.45	15/3	58.2%	$ 386
1952	1.47	15/6	57.2	393
1953	1.44	15/11	60.6	463
1954	1.54	16/3	60.7	584
1955	1.57	16/4	61.4	501
1956	1.54	16/2	61.5	489
1957	1.45	16/2	62.6	633
1958	1.52	17/0	62.3	550
1959	1.49	17/6	62.7	584
1960	1.53	17/9	63.3	522
1961	1.55	18/4	63.8	667
1962	1.51	18/11	64.9	735
1963	1.47	19/6	66.0	800
1964	1.48	19/11	67.7	772
1965	1.43	20/2	69.1	843
1966	1.36	20/5	70.0	900
1967	1.33	21/2	71.0	1,111
1968	1.30	22/11	73.6	1,263
1969	1.29	21/8	73.3	1,633
1970	1.32	22/8	74.7	2,567
1971	1.29	22/10	74.9	2,393
1972	1.29	23/3	75.2	2,339
1973	1.29	23/3	74.3	2,259
1974	1.29	21/3	74.3	2,232
1975	1.33	21/9	73.8	2,866
1976†	1.30	21/10	73.6	3,372

[*] The debt coverage ratio is computed by the ACLI only for fully amortized, level payment loans. Data in the other three columns cover all loan commitments surveyed.

Source: American Council of Life Insurance, "Survey of Mortgage Commitments on Multifamily and Nonresidential Properties by 15 Life Insurance Companies."

upon being able to predict the timing of principal repayments. The major obstacle to predicting repayments accurately are prepayments. As indicated above, prepayments can also frustrate the realization of anticipated returns from variable interest rate loans and loans with participation features. Furthermore, from a lender's perspective, prepayments are systematically adverse in their cyclical timing. Consequently, other things equal, life insurers prefer assets with low prepayment rates; and this is achieved through prohibiting prepayments or levying stiff penalties on prepaid amounts.

Although life companies have long insisted on substantial call protection on directly placed bonds, prepayment protection was somewhat slower to develop in the income property mortgage loan market.

In the early 1950s it appears that less than ⅓ of income property loan commitments included any prepayment prohibition provision.[42] However, in recent years about ¾ of the amount committed on income property loans has been closed to prepayment for nine or more years. Substantial penalty fees apply to prepayment on much of the remaining loan commitments.[43] Consequently, it appears that life insurance companies have been able to obtain prepayment protection on mortgage loans comparable to that available on privately placed bonds.

In general, loan terms affect default experience through their influence upon the size of periodic debt service payments and via their impact upon the rate at which mortgagors build up equity in properties securing loans. Large loans relative to property values, high interest rates, income participation features, and short maturities tend to increase the probability that debt service payments may not be covered by net operating income at some point in the future. While short maturities and full amortization add to the debt service burden, they also contribute to the accumulation of mortgagors' equity. This is especially important where the mortgagor assumes no liability for loan repayment beyond the pledged property.

As noted above, in recent years life insurance companies have written numerous partially amortized income property loans. Also, as Table 3.11 indicates, over a longer period of time lenders became more liberal with respect to loan amounts and maturities while permitting the ratio of projected net operating income to debt service to decline. This suggests that unless underwriting capabilities improved or offsetting indenture protections were added, loan quality must have deteriorated over time.

It is difficult to assess the ability of appraisers to estimate future income streams and property values. However, contingency provisions have become increasingly common in the loan commitments and indentures negotiated by life insurance companies. These provisions are designed to reduce the companies' exposure to delinquency or foreclosure and to reduce the probability of losses associated with such events. Contingencies written into forward commitments on to-be-constructed properties include provisions specifying the level

---

[42] In addition, about half the loans that did include such a provision prohibited prepayment only during the first year of the loan. See Royal Shipp, "The Structure of the Mortgage Market for Income-Property Mortgage Loans," in *Essays on Interest Rates*, ed. Jack M. Guttentag and Phillip Cagan, 2 vols. (New York: National Bureau of Economic Research, 1969), vol. 1, p. 93.

[43] American Council of Life Insurance, "Survey of Mortgage Commitments on Multifamily and Nonresidential Properties by 15 Life Insurance Companies."

and quality of tenants. These agreements also protect against the failure of contractors to meet design, materials, or other specifications, including the construction timetable set forth in the commitment agreement. Failure to comply with any of these provisions may free the lender fully or partially from the obligation to deliver the loan amount.[44]

Life companies have attempted to obtain protection against operating expense increases by insisting that long-term leases include adequate rental escalator clauses, that merchants' associations be formed, and that property management firms meet with lender approval. To the extent lenders and equity investors are attempting to reduce risk by shifting risk exposure to tenants, the effectiveness of such devices is vitiated in soft markets. Lender attitudes toward the relative risk associated with lending on various sorts of income properties are undoubtedly being reformulated as a result of recent delinquency and foreclosure experience.

Default and Foreclosure Experience

Most life insurance company income property mortgage loans are secured by apartments, office buildings, or retail stores.[45] As Table 3.12 shows, about 78 percent of the income property loan commitments made by 15 life major insurance companies during the period 1969–1975 were accounted for by these three types of property. Most of the remaining loan commitments consisted of loans on hotels and motels, warehouses, and institutional properties.

Normally, defaults occur on income property loans when revenue net of operating expenses is inadequate to cover debt service. The most common threat to projected rental income is competition, and one key factor affecting the sensitivity of rental income to competition is the turnover rate of tenants. On this basis, hotels and motels are especially vulnerable. This is reflected in the relatively small loans lenders are willing to make on these properties.[46]

---

[44] Frequently, the commitment provides for split-level financing on which a floor amount is promised when occupancy or other specified contingencies are not realized. The floor amount is typically 20 to 40 percent less than the full loan amount.

[45] Most stores are included in shopping centers in which the entire center, or a large portion thereof, constitutes property securing a single mortgage loan. See Table 3.12.

[46] The capitalization rates and debt coverage ratios applied by lenders to hotels and motels are higher than those for other types of properties. For example, for commitments made during 1976 the overall capitalization rate was 10.3 percent; but the capitalization rate on hotel and motel loans was 11.7 percent. The

TABLE 3.12

Distribution of Income Property Mortgage Loan Commitments by Property Type for 15 Life Insurance Companies: 1969–1975

Property Type	Number of Loans	Total Amount Committed (millions)	Percentage Distribution by Loan Amount
Conventional elevator apartment	479	$ 1,543.0	6.6%
Conventional nonelevator apartment	2,516	4,916.7	21.0
FHA elevator apartment	25	75.2	0.3
FHA nonelevator apartment	77	111.9	0.5
NHA elevator apartment	30	94.7	0.4
NHA nonelevator apartment	22	42.7	0.2
Retail—less than five stores	308	438.2	1.9
Shopping center— five or more stores	910	3,594.0	15.4
Supermarket	58	28.4	0.1
Department store	110	276.9	1.2
Automobile sales and service	20	38.5	0.2
Other sales and service	52	28.6	0.1
Office building	1,712	6,582.8	28.2
Medical office building	245	353.4	1.5
Post office	3	0.8	°
Parking garage	22	56.2	0.2
Restaurant	94	31.9	0.1
Commercial warehouse	1,418	1,030.6	4.4
Truck terminal	14	9.6	°
Service station	1	0.3	°
Other commercial	67	99.5	0.4
Religious	12	9.7	°
Educational	21	36.5	0.2
Hospital and institutional	96	415.6	1.8
Social and recreational	43	58.0	0.3
Nursing homes	143	190.2	0.8
Industrial warehouse	1,047	899.3	3.9
Manufacturing plant	423	298.2	1.3
Other industrial	58	94.6	0.4
Hotel	61	739.0	3.2
Motel	282	719.4	3.1
Multiple property complex	31	558.7	2.4
Public utility	1	11.0	0.1
Total	10,401	23,384.1	100.0

° Less than 0.05%.

Source: American Council of Life Insurance, "Survey of Mortgage Commitments on Multifamily and Nonresidential Properties by 15 Life Insurance Companies."

By way of contrast, relatively long leases and the expense associated with relocating tend to keep turnover rates quite low in most high-rise center city office buildings.[47] However, the durability of office buildings, the long gestation period of large new buildings, and the impact of custom buildings, especially those sponsored by tax-exempt entities, upon the speculative office building market continually provide a threat that a substantial oversupply will develop in major office-oriented cities. Indeed, as Table 3.13 indicates, an excess supply of office space did develop in a majority of downtown office markets during the first half of the 1970s.

Because of the relative immobility of office tenants, soft markets frequently have their greatest initial impact upon new space coming onto the market. High vacancy rates depress rental scales gradually throughout the market and rents become inadequate to cover debt service in a nonnegligible number of buildings. In this situation, occupancy requirements and split-level financing provisions serve to limit the mortgagee's exposure and, given life companies' staying power, make successful workouts of foreclosures possible.

The quality of major shopping center loans frequently rests primarily on the credit of the key tenants. Life insurance companies generally have attempted to ensure that the key tenants were committed to operating specified lines of business in the center for a period of time approximating the maturity of the mortgage loan. Risks associated with rising operating expenses are frequently shifted to tenants via absolute net leases. At the same time, both equity investors and mortgagees often share in tenants' success in attracting customers via rent overages based on sales and income participations. These provisions make tenants vulnerable to rising rents and operating expenses. Rapidly increasing energy costs, the dependence of customers on automobiles, rising land costs, and restrictive land use criteria have all contributed to a substantial slowdown in shopping center construction and to the impairment of some retailers' profitability.

As with office buildings and shopping centers, loan commitments on to-be-constructed apartments are frequently contingent upon

---

average debt coverage ratio on hotel and motel loans was 1.52 against 1.30 for all commitments.

[47] Data from the Building Owners and Managers Institute International semi-annual office building survey for recent years suggest that turnover rates are less than 5 percent per annum. This is consistent with earlier estimates presented in Robert M. Fisher, "The Boom in Office Buildings," Urban Land Institute, Technical Bulletin No. 58 (1967).

TABLE 3.13
Office Building Occupancy Rates by Geographic Regions and Cities

Region and City	Occupancy Rate* May 1970	October 1974
New England and Middle Atlantic	97.7%	85.1%
Baltimore	92.2	95.6
Boston	98.4	92.9
New York	99.7	78.8
Philadelphia	97.3	86.6
Pittsburgh	95.6	85.2
North Central	94.9	86.8
Chicago	96.4	85.2
Cleveland	91.6	90.5
Detroit	94.4	93.9
Indianapolis	92.4	91.7
Midwest Northern	90.5	85.4
Des Moines	92.1	88.6
Duluth	89.6	88.8
Milwaukee	93.2	81.4
Minneapolis	94.0	89.5
Omaha	83.3	84.8
St. Louis	84.6	84.3
Southern	88.0	86.5
Atlanta	77.0	91.0
New Orleans	95.7	86.6
Southwest	95.8	83.8
Dallas	95.8	81.0
Denver	97.4	84.1
Houston	95.6	89.6
Tulsa	92.2	94.5
Pacific Northwest	90.5	88.9
Portland	90.7	89.6
Seattle	90.9	89.4
Pacific Southwest	90.2	86.0
Los Angeles	89.5	79.0
Oakland	90.6	82.9
Phoenix	90.5	90.9
Salt Lake City	90.8	85.9
San Francisco	90.2	92.0
Canada	94.7	97.7
Montreal	93.5	98.7
Vancouver	98.6	97.9
Grand total	94.1	86.4

* Proportion of competitive rentable area occupied.

Source: Building Owners and Managers Institute International, "Semi-Annual Occupancy Surveys."

achievement of specified occupancy rates. However, lenders are unable to influence the identity of tenants or to depend upon the credit of tenants in the way they do in evaluating office building and shopping center loans. Therefore, evaluation is much more dependent upon fundamental housing analysis, focused upon total housing demand in the market and the mix of demand by housing unit characteristics, including rental versus ownership tastes.

Apartments appear to have been especially vulnerable to rising operating expenses and construction costs. Consequently, life insurance companies report that even many well-occupied projects have experienced difficulty in generating enough net operating income to cover debt service. In spite of the mobility of tenants and the existence of relatively short leases, a significant proportion of troubled apartment loans is reported to be secured by recently constructed units. This is largely attributable to the high construction and financing costs of such units relative to those of older competitor buildings.

The vulnerability of apartment loans is indicated by the delinquency experience of life insurance companies, which is reported in Table 3.14. In 11 of the 12 years 1965–1976, the delinquency rate on conventional apartment loans exceeded that on nonresidential property loans. The effects of overbuilding and rising operating expenses have been reflected in rising delinquency rates on income properties during the 1970s.[48] As Table 3.15 shows, rising delinquency rates have resulted in a significant increase in foreclosure rates on apartment loans relative to foreclosures of loans secured by nonresidential properties. Because life insurance companies often forebear delinquency for a period of time or modify loan terms to avoid foreclosure,[49] observed foreclosure rates are not a very good measure of the extent of losses realized by mortgagees.[50]

---

[48] The apparent lack of comparable increases in delinquent loans on one-to-four family residential units reflects the seasoned character of these portfolios. The incidence of delinquency peaks during the third or fourth year of loan life. Due to their inactivity in this market, life insurers have had few young loans in their portfolios in recent years.

[49] Data on the incidence of contract modifications in recent years is not available. Lenders report that temporary forebearance of interest due or stretching out of amortization payments is not unusual. Data from 24 life insurance companies indicate that over 1/3 of the loans made during the 1920s were modified one or more times. Most of these modifications involved extensions of maturity, but interest rate reductions were also granted in about 1/2 of the cases. Added funds were supplied or a portion of principal forgiven in 1/6 and 1/10 of the cases, respectively. See R. J. Saulnier, *Urban Mortgage Lending by Life Insurance Companies* (New York: National Bureau of Economic Research, 1950), p. 48.

[50] Foreclosure frequently is used as a solution to delinquencies for relatively

TABLE 3.14
Loan Delinquency Experience of Life Insurance Companies

Mortgage Instrument	Delinquency Rate*											
	1965	1966	1967	1968	1969	1970	1971	1972	1973	1974	1975	1976†
1–4 Family												
FHA	1.25%	1.15%	1.00%	0.88%	0.97%	1.20%	1.25%	1.48%	1.45%	1.50%	1.42%	1.23%
VA	1.29	1.15	0.98	0.88	0.87	0.95	1.00	1.08	0.96	1.12	1.29	1.13
Conventional	0.66	0.66	0.56	0.41	0.46	0.60	0.62	0.68	0.67	0.76	0.99	1.10
Multifamily												
FHA	5.14	3.58	4.21	1.13	1.04	1.86	3.57	3.35	4.35	2.43	2.61	3.62
Conventional	0.88	0.93	1.04	0.89	0.71	0.95	0.73	1.31	2.54	4.46	6.22	6.11
Nonresidential												
Conventional	0.38	0.56	0.49	0.41	0.30	0.70	0.82	0.95	1.23	2.33	3.52	4.13

Note: Delinquent loans are mortgages with two or more monthly interest payments past due. These data are reported by life companies accounting for about 84 percent of mortgages held by U.S. life companies.

* Delinquent loans as a percentage of the total amount of loans outstanding at year-end.

† 1976 figures are based on data for the end of June.

Source: American Council of Life Insurance, "Semiannual Survey of Mortgage Loan Delinquencies and Foreclosures."

TABLE 3.15
Foreclosure Rates on Nonfarm Conventional Mortgage Loans Held by Life Insurance

Year	Home		Multifamily		Commercial		Total	
	By No.	By Amount	By No.	By Amount	By No.	By Amount	By No.	By Amount
1965	0.06%	0.08%	0.21%	0.39%	0.11%	0.08%	0.07%	0.14%
1966	0.06	0.08	0.27	0.36	0.11	0.09	0.07	0.15
1967	0.05	0.07	0.15	0.31	0.14	0.12	0.06	0.14
1968	0.03	0.04	0.10	0.14	0.19	0.20	0.04	0.14
1969	0.02	0.02	0.13	0.15	0.11	0.18	0.03	0.13
1970	0.02	0.03	0.10	0.27	0.10	0.13	0.03	0.14
1971	0.02	0.03	0.03	0.19	0.14	0.15	0.03	0.14
1972	0.03	0.04	0.18	0.29	0.15	0.20	0.04	0.20
1973	0.02	0.03	0.30	0.53	0.16	0.17	0.03	0.26
1974	0.01	0.01	0.31	0.74	0.19	0.22	0.04	0.35
1975	0.03	0.07	0.70	1.64	0.45	0.78	0.10	0.96

Note: Foreclosure rates represent the ratio of total loans foreclosed during the year to total holdings at the beginning of the year stated as a percentage. These data cover companies which account for about 80 percent of the mortgages held by the U.S. life insurance industry.

Source: American Council of Life Insurance, "Semiannual Survey of Mortgage Loan Delinquencies and Foreclosures."

Recent Behavior of Mortgage Commitments

A frequent assumption is that the ability of life insurance companies to change, and especially to reduce, the level of mortgage lending activity is constrained by the need to maintain origination and search facilities and personnel in the form of employed staff and agents.[51] The extent to which this is the case is presumed to distinguish mortgage lending from corporate security investments and to explain why econometric estimates of asset substitutability find much less responsiveness to yield spreads in allocations between bonds and mortgages than are found within either of these sectors.

The rapid departure of life companies from the home loan market in the mid-1960s should have raised questions about whether the severity of this constraint has been exaggerated. Recently, using data from 1965–1971, Lintner, Piper, and Fortune have found some evidence of a ratchet effect in the adjustment of one-to-four family and multifamily residential loans which they attribute to organizational constraints in the mortgage origination function.[52] More recently, however, life companies have not only largely deserted the home mortgage market but also have severely cut back on apartment loan commitments and substantially reduced their new commitment activity in loans secured by nonresidential income properties.[53]

Since the organizational constraint hypothesis has some a priori plausibility, a reasonable hypothesis seems to be that a reduction in commitments of the magnitude indicated in Table 3.16 must be due primarily to a substantial reduction in the demand for funds. The

---

strong loans. Thus, there is not much relation between foreclosure rates and loss rates. Life insurance companies had substantially higher foreclosure rates than other types of financial institutions in the 1930s but much lower loss rates. See Carl F. Behrens, *Commercial Bank Activities in Urban Mortgage Financing* (New York: National Bureau of Economic Research, 1952), p. 11, and J. E. Morton, *Urban Mortgage Lending: Comparative Markets and Experience* (New York: National Bureau of Economic Research, 1956), p. 110. Losses associated with foreclosure are also affected by variations in statutory requirements. For some recent evidence pertaining to conventional home loans see Touche Ross & Co., "The Costs of Mortgage Loans Foreclosures: Case Studies of Six Savings and Loan Associations," prepared for the Federal Home Loan Bank Board, April 1975.

[51] This is a position the author has previously taken. See L. D. Jones, *Investment Policies of Life Insurance Companies* (Boston: Division of Research, Graduate School of Business Administration, Harvard University, 1968), pp. 417–19, 452–53.

[52] Lintner, Piper, and Fortune, "Forward Commitment Decisions . . . ," pp. 241–42.

[53] One officer of a major life company with a large internal income property mortgage loan staff reported in October 1975 that their mortgage department had not made a single new income property loan commitment since August 1974.

TABLE 3.16

New Commitments for Long-Term Income Property Mortgage Loans
(millions of dollars)

Year	Life Companies		Other Lenders	
	Multi-family	Nonresi-dential°	Multi-family	Nonresi-dential°
1971	$2,588	$6,111	$ 9,470	$10,876
1972	3,599	8,237	12,414	14,130
1973	2,712	9,726	8,037	12,051
1974	864	6,025	5,159	7,841
1975	22	430	386	809
1976	96	863	865	1,125
1975 commitments as a percentage of the previous annual peak	0.6%	4.4%	3.1%	5.7%

° Excludes loans on farm properties.

Source: U.S. Department of Housing and Urban Development.

preceding discussion of delinquency experience suggests that enough saturation of apartment, office building, retail store, and hotel markets occurred to make this a credible hypothesis. A substantial softening of demand ought to be reflected in declining yields on income property mortgages relative to yields on corporate bonds. Table 3.17 does show a sharp widening in yields in favor of directly placed corporate bonds in 1974 after several years in which the spread only drifted gradually in favor of bonds.[54] Also consistent with the demand reduction hypothesis is the sharp reduction in new commitments made by other lenders (see Table 3.16).

The radical cutback of apartment loan commitments by life insurance companies in 1974 and 1975 suggests, however, that more was involved than a slackening of the demand for funds. In addition to the lack of opportunities and relatively unattractive yields available on income property loans due to the decline in demand, life insurers may have reduced new commitments because of inflationary expectations, the relatively high level of outstanding commitments which had been accumulated, and recent delinquency experience. The author's interviews suggest that as of 1974 many life insurance company investment officers and finance committees anticipated increases in

[54] Interest rates on income property loans (especially apartment loans) also failed to increase as much as bond yields in the 1969–1970 "tight money" period. This could partly reflect the substitution of contingent interest and other participation provisions for higher contract interest rates. Corporate bonds with warrants, convertible features, or other equity kickers are excluded from the corporate bond yield series.

TABLE 3.17
Yields on Corporate Bond and Income Property Mortgage Commitments Made by Life Insurance Companies

	(1)	(2)	(3)	(4)	(5)	(6)	(7)
				Conven-		Basis Points	
Quarter	Corporate Bonds	Commercial Retail	Office Buildings	tional Apart- ments	Col(1)–Col(2)	Col(1)–Col(3)	Col(1)–Col(4)
1965.3	5.49%	5.76%	5.76%	5.94%	−27	−27	−45
1965.4	5.60	5.77	5.82	5.98	−17	−22	−38
1966.1	5.83	5.91	5.98	6.12	− 8	−15	−29
1966.2	6.09	6.27	6.10	6.34	−18	− 1	−25
1966.3	6.41	6.60	6.38	6.79	−19	3	−38
1966.4	6.64	6.83	6.67	7.16	−19	− 3	−52
1967.1	6.63	6.82	6.61	6.90	−19	2	−27
1967.2	6.50	6.63	6.74	6.83	−13	−24	−33
1967.3	6.73	6.73	6.72	7.02	0	1	−29
1967.4	6.74	6.98	6.82	7.21	−24	− 8	−47
1968.1	7.20	7.32	7.32	7.49	−12	−12	−29
1968.2	7.40	7.52	7.51	7.65	−12	−11	−25
1968.3	7.62	7.80	7.83	7.91	−18	−21	−29
1968.4	7.67	7.75	7.83	7.91	− 8	−16	−24
1969.1	7.95	8.03	7.93	8.12	− 8	2	−17
1969.2	8.46	8.31	8.38	8.56	15	8	−10
1969.3	9.21	9.11	8.92	9.00	10	29	21
1969.4	9.37	9.52	8.94	9.33	−15	43	4
1970.1	10.08	9.97	9.60	9.58	11	48	50
1970.2	10.02	10.22	9.88	9.75	−20	14	27
1970.3	10.34	10.12	9.96	9.80	22	38	54
1970.4	10.34	10.16	10.01	9.85	18	33	49

1971.1	9.04	9.37	9.32	9.19	−33	−28	−15
1971.2	8.99	8.91	8.71	8.81	8	28	18
1971.3	9.20	9.01	8.92	9.02	19	28	18
1971.4	8.76	8.80	8.78	8.96	−4	−2	−20
1972.1	8.49	8.36	8.37	8.59	13	12	−10
1972.2	8.47	8.32	8.29	8.50	15	18	−3
1972.3	8.48	8.37	8.46	8.47	11	2	1
1972.4	8.36	8.42	8.59	8.56	−6	−23	−20
1973.1	8.36	8.35	8.39	8.54	1	−3	−18
1973.2	8.34	8.48	8.47	8.56	−14	−13	−22
1973.3	8.77	8.69	8.71	8.82	8	6	−5
1973.4	8.96	8.95	8.88	9.05	1	8	9
1974.1	9.05	8.80	8.88	8.97	25	17	8
1974.2	9.56	9.14	9.03	9.02	42	53	54
1974.3	10.48	9.74	9.74	9.76	74	74	72
1974.4	10.99	10.36	10.13	10.12	63	86	87
1975.1	10.61	9.90	10.07	10.09	71	54	52
1975.2	10.74	9.90	9.86	9.97	84	88	77
1975.3	10.85	10.03	10.00	10.15	82	85	70
1975.4	10.75	9.90	10.04	10.12	85	71	63
1976.1	10.21	9.92	9.90	9.92	29	31	29
1976.2	9.97	9.66	9.75	9.73	31	22	24
1976.3	10.01	9.53	9.59	9.70	48	42	31
1976.4	9.47	9.47	9.58	9.62	0	−11	15

Note: Corporate bond yields are those on fourth quality direct placements. Mortgage yields are contract rates. Each series represent dollar weighted averages of loans reported. Bond yields are for issues of U.S. corporations and mortgage yields are restricted to loans secured by properties located in the U.S.

Source: American Council of Life Insurance, "Average Yields on Directly Placed Corporate Bond Authorizations" and "Survey of Mortgage Commitments on Multifamily and Nonresidential Properties by 15 Life Insurance Companies."

nominal interest rates over the next two or three years due to a monetary/fiscal policy mix which would tend to generate increased inflation. Such expectations tend to dampen new commitment activity because of the negative impact of higher interest rates on cash flows through life companies and, unless forward commitment rates adjust, because future rates are expected to be higher than current rates available on commitments for future delivery. As Table 3.18 shows, the flow of investable funds available to life companies did fall in 1974.[55] This decline may well have been extrapolated by life companies into the future,[56] even though, as Table 3.18 shows, such funds forecasts, and the interest rate forecasts on which they were based proved to be highly inaccurate.

If inflationary expectations were indeed affecting life insurers' forward commitment policies, then one would expect to see the companies attempting to reduce the stock of forward commitments relative to the anticipated flow of investable funds. Any attempt to reduce the stock of forward commitments would necessarily have an accelerated impact upon the rate at which new commitments are made. Comparing Tables 3.16 and 3.18, we see that it took a 68 percent cut in new commitments on multifamily residential units during 1974 to accomplish a 53 percent reduction in the stock of commitments and a 38 percent cut in new commitment activity on nonresidential properties to produce an 18 percent reduction in the stock of this category of outstanding commitments.[57]

As Table 3.19 shows, life companies did reduce the ratio of the forward commitment stock to investable funds from 123 to 75 percent between the first quarters of 1970 and 1975. However the ratio of nonresidential mortgage loan commitments to investable funds did not decline until 1975 (see Table 3.18). This presumably reflects both the fact that life companies did not cut back the rate of new commit-

---

[55] About $1.3 billion of the $5.0 billion decline in investable funds between 1973 and 1974 was attributable to reductions in mortgage prepayments and bond calls and to increases in policy loans. All of these factors are adversely affected by higher interest rates. However, about $3.2 billion of the cash flow short-fall reflected reduced sales of corporate bonds and common stocks. Bond sales may have been inhibited by high interest rates since, except where the bond credit is considered to be impaired, market losses are recognized in statement values only when realized. This inhibition could have been especially significant in 1974 since realized losses together with credit losses exceeded the amount chargeable to the mandatory securities valuation reserve for many companies and necessitated charges against surplus.

[56] Evidence that there is a strong extrapolative element in life companies' cash flow forecasts is provided by Pesando, "The Interest Sensitivity. . . ."

[57] Even more dramatically, a 93 percent reduction in new loan commitments on nonresidential properties in 1975 yielded a 20 percent reduction in the stock.

TABLE 3.18
Outstanding Long-Term Income Property Loan Commitments and Total Investable Funds of Life Insurance Companies

	(1)	(2)	(3)	(4)	(5)	(6)
	Year-End Commitments					
	Multifamily	Nonresidential	Investable Funds	Col. (1) ÷ Col. (3)	Col. (2) ÷ Col. (3)	Col. (1) + Col. (2) ÷ Col. (3)
Year						
1970	$2,666	$ 5,678	$16,590	16.1%	34.2%	50.3%
1971	3,030	6,907	25,280	12.0	27.3	39.3
1972	4,203	8,994	30,820	13.6	29.2	42.8
1973	3,854	11,192	31,000	12.4	36.1	48.5
1974	1,797	9,216	25,980	6.9	35.5	42.4
1975	691	7,353	33,500	2.1	21.9	24.0
1976	852	8,359	46,200	1.8	18.1	19.9

Note: Investable funds is the gross flow of funds available for investment net of amounts absorbed by policy loans. Nonresidential excludes loans on farm properties.

Source: Commitment data are from U.S. Department of Housing and Urban Development. Col. (3) is from American Council of Life Insurance, "Cash Flow for Investment Survey."

TABLE 3.19

Relationship of Outstanding Life Insurance Company Commitments to
Investable Funds

End of Quarter	(1) Outstanding Commitments (millions)	(2) Annual Investable Funds° (millions)	(3) Ratio: Col. (1) to Col. (2) (percent)
1970.1	$12,962	$10,577	123%
1970.2	12,536	10,657	118
1970.3	12,484	11,481	109
1970.4	11,391	11,936	95
1971.1	11,728	14,049	84
1971.2	12,763	14,908	86
1971.3	13,561	15,716	86
1971.4	13,286	16,903	79
1972.1	14,565	18,274	80
1972.2	16,603	18,886	88
1972.3	17,512	20,285	86
1972.4	15,623	20,247	77
1973.1	17,991	22,228	81
1973.2	19,806	21,082	94
1973.3	20,085	20,682	97
1973.4	17,721	19,717	90
1974.1	17,118	19,084	90
1974.2	17,875	18,304	98
1974.3	17,580	18,575	95
1974.4	15,739	18,245	86
1975.1	14,033	18,817	75
1975.2	14,760	20,592	72
1975.3	15,282	21,195	72
1975.4	14,215	23,452	61
1976.1	14,381	25,915	55
1976.2	16,648	27,301	61
1976.3	17,381	28,498	61
1976.4	16,103	29,904	54

Note: Data are for companies that report both commitment and cash flow information to the ACLI. The dollar figures are somewhat distorted because one company was dropped after 1973. The remaining companies accounted for 76 percent of U.S. life insurance company assets at year-end 1974. Commitment data are for all assets.

° Investable funds are defined as cash flow available for investment net of policy loans and separate account inflows. Annual funds represent actual cash flow for the quarter indicated and the previous quarter plus company forecasts for the next two quarters.

Source: American Council of Life Insurance, "Forward Commitment Survey" and "Cash Flow for Investment Survey."

ments on these loans as fast as they did on other types of assets and the fact that a disproportionate amount of long commitments are found in the nonresidential mortgage loan class.

Strong inflationary expectations should, however, not only lead to a reduction in forward commitments but should inhibit the making

TABLE 3.20

Distribution of Outstanding Loan Commitments of Life
Insurance Companies by Length of Time Remaining
to Expected Takedown

End of Quarter	Time until Expected Takedown		
	6 Months or Less	7–12 Months	More than 12 Months
1970.1	34.3%	26.6%	39.1%
1970.2	31.8	25.6	42.6
1970.3	38.2	20.9	40.9
1970.4	34.9	23.4	41.7
1971.1	36.2	23.5	40.3
1971.2	39.2	21.8	39.0
1971.3	40.0	20.4	39.6
1971.4	39.3	23.9	36.8
1972.1	40.9	23.2	35.9
1972.2	44.1	19.1	36.8
1972.3	42.6	18.9	38.5
1972.4	36.9	24.7	38.4
1973.1	41.6	22.3	36.1
1973.2	44.9	17.9	37.2
1973.3	42.1	19.6	38.3
1973.4	40.1	24.2	35.7
1974.1	40.8	24.2	35.0
1974.2	41.2	25.6	33.2
1974.3	44.8	24.7	30.5
1974.4	48.2	24.2	27.6
1975.1	47.2	24.2	28.6
1975.2	46.9	24.2	28.9
1975.3	52.0	20.4	27.6
1975.4	50.2	21.2	28.6
1976.1	51.4	22.9	25.7
1976.2	55.0	16.6	28.4
1976.3	54.5	19.2	26.3
1976.4	49.8	21.9	28.3

Source: American Council of Life Insurance, "Forward Commitment Survey." Data are for companies reporting both commitment and
cash flow data.

of long forward commitments. Unfortunately, data are not available
on the distribution of new commitments by length of time to anticipated takedown. However, Table 3.20 shows the changes which have
taken place in the distribution of the stock of outstanding commitments by time remaining to expected takedown. Of course, some
time is required before changes in the characteristics of new commitments are reflected in observable changes in those of outstanding
commitments. Nonetheless, a clear increase did occur in the pro-

portion of commitments due for delivery within six months and a substantial reduction in commitments with more than 12 months remaining to takedown.[58]

Finally, loan delinquency experience undoubtedly had an adverse effect on life companies' willingness to lend on apartment projects in particular. It seems likely that somewhat more stringent underwriting standards will evolve from this experience. In addition to closer scrutiny of property income and expense estimates, life insurers are likely to opt for shorter maturities, stronger amortization provisions, and, to accommodate these standards within debt service coverage rules, somewhat smaller loans in relation to value. In any case, the experience of the past few years indicates that life insurance companies possess considerable flexibility in adjusting their mortgage loan activity.

SUMMARY AND CONCLUSIONS

This paper has examined the role of income property mortgage loans in life insurance company portfolios and the concomitant role of life companies in the income property loan market. At the center of the analysis is the question of whether fluctuations in the amount of income property financing are caused primarily by shifts in the demand for such financing or by changes in the supply of funds to such markets. Demand for financing derives from current and prospective activity generating the addition of new space, the rate of turnover of existing properties, and factors affecting decisions to refinance. Financing terms and the structure of tax laws impact upon the relative profitability of equity investments in income properties along with real economic variables.

Most borrowers applying to mortgage loan departments of life insurance companies are limited in their ability to assess alternative credit markets. Furthermore, life companies play a crucial role in affecting the level and mix of new real estate development because they specialize in the permanent financing of to-be-constructed properties. Normally, construction lenders insist upon permanent loan

---

[58] For a temporary period this pattern would result from a cutback in forward commitments which was neutral in terms of the distribution of new commitments by time lag to delivery. However, the distribution of the commitment stock by delivery lag would soon return to its original distribution. The shifts shown in Table 3.20 appear to be too pronounced and too enduring to be explained by a distributionally neutral reduction in new commitments. Therefore, it seems quite certain that lengthy commitments were reduced disproportionately.

commitments as a precondition for a construction loan commitment. The dominance of life companies in this financing specialty together with the lack of credit alternatives available to many developers places the focus upon determinants of the supply of funds from life companies as a critical variable in explaining income property financing and construction activity.

Although there are some structural changes that likely affected the cost competitiveness of life companies in the home mortgage business, the withdrawal of life insurance companies from this market in the last decade can be explained largely as a response to changing yield spreads as opposed to shifts in the life company supply schedule of funds. This chapter suggests that, to some extent, variations in the amount of income property financing done by life companies over the past quarter century also reflect responses to changing yield spreads. However, in this market there is more reason to suspect that shifts in the supply of funds schedules also have been significant.

Of particular interest is evidence of an increasing reluctance on the part of life insurers to make extended forward commitments. This reluctance may result particularly from greater volatility in interest rates and heightened inflationary expectations. These factors impair life companies' ability to forecast future cash flows and increase the perceived interest rate risk associated with entering into long-term commitments. The impact of a reduced willingness to make forward commitments is not spread uniformly across assets but falls most significantly upon income property mortgage lending. Maintenance of life companies' role in this market may depend upon the development of more effective devices for hedging interest rate risk in income property loan commitments.

Interest rate risk, liquidity needs, and default experience also impact upon the underwriting standards utilized in making income property mortgage loan decisions. For example, considerations deriving from all these factors have combined to create a preference on the part of life companies for substantially shorter loan maturities. The structuring of income and equity participation provisions are also viewed as responses to risk perceptions arising from default and inflation concerns. However, the ability of life companies to structure desired participation provisions apparently has been severely constrained by competition from other mortgage suppliers.

4

Modern Portfolio Theory and the Common Stock Investment Process

By James L. Farrell, Jr.*

Although modern portfolio theory has been discussed in the academic community for some time, it is relatively untested by institutional investors, particularly life insurance companies. The College Retirement Equities Fund (CREF) has recently begun to integrate portfolio theory into its investment process. Thus, a discussion of the use of portfolio theory at CREF is not only timely but may prove valuable to other institutions that are considering the adoption of this methodology. This chapter presents such a discussion.

Before proceeding with the analysis, it may be helpful to provide some background on CREF. The fund is affiliated with Teachers Insurance and Annuity Association (TIAA). Both TIAA and CREF are non-profit educational corporations with the primary goal of providing pension plans for employees of colleges and universities.

CREF was the first variable annuity fund, having been established in 1952. Its portfolio, which aggregates some $3 billion, ranks in size with some of the larger bank trust departments and probably exceeds any single mutual fund. By virtue of its size as well as the fact that close to 200 different common stock issues are held, the portfolio is fairly broadly diversified. CREF has grown rapidly since its inception and continues to grow with net cash flow of $417 million in 1974, $461 million in 1975, and $505 million in 1976. Most experts would

---

* James L. Farrell, Jr., is investment officer of the College Retirement Equities Fund.

characterize CREF as a large and rapidly growing institutional investor with a fairly long experience in common stocks.

MODERN PORTFOLIO THEORY

In order to better understand the aspects of modern portfolio theory that are relevant to operating a portfolio of common stocks, it is useful to review some essential elements of that theory. Modern portfolio theory begins by asserting that the total risk of an individual common stock can be considered to be composed of two components, *systematic risk* and *specific risk;* i.e., total risk = systematic risk + specific risk. Systematic risk is perfectly correlated with movements in the general market while specific risk is uncorrelated with the market.

For an individual security, systematic risk accounts for approximately 30 percent of the total risk. Specific risk, which accounts for the remainder, depends on factors unique to the company, such as new technical developments, quality of management, or special market situations. The fact that specific risk depends on factors unique to the company indicates that this risk is uncorrelated from one company to another.

Because specific risk is presumed independent from one security to another, adding securities to a portfolio (diversification) reduces specific risk. In a large, diversified portfolio, specific risk tends to cancel out, leaving systematic risk as the dominant component, accounting for perhaps 90 percent or more of the total risk. Correspondingly, variations in the return of a large portfolio of common stocks are largely explained by variations in the general market. A quantitative measure of the systematic risk or sensitivity to variations in the general market—whether for a portfolio or individual security—is provided by the *beta* of the portfolio or individual security.

The meaning of beta can be illustrated by reference to the scatter diagram shown in Figure 4.1. The vertical axis in the figure refers to the rate of return on the CREF portfolio of common stocks, while the horizontal axis refers to the rate of return for the Standard & Poor's 500 Stock Index (S&P 500), representing the rate of return for the market. Quarterly returns have been calculated for both CREF and the S&P 500 for the period 1957–1974. The Xs on the diagram represent the 72 quarterly pairs of points for this period.

A least-squares line has been fitted to the plotted points. This regression equation is known as the *market model,* and its specification is indicated in the lower right-hand portion of the diagram. The

FIGURE 4.1
The Relationship between the Market Rate of Return and the Rate of Return
on the CREF Portfolio

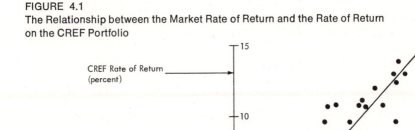

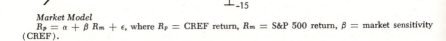

Market Model
$R_p = \alpha + \beta R_m + \epsilon$, where R_p = CREF return, R_m = S&P 500 return, β = market sensitivity (CREF).

slope of the line fitted to the plotted points is a measure of the sensitivity of the CREF portfolio to variations in the general market. It corresponds to the beta (β) shown in the market model equation and gives the expected increase in portfolio return for a 1 percent increase in market return.

In this case, the beta (slope of the line) is 1.1 and compares to a beta value of 1.0 for a fund constructed to be exactly like the S&P 500. In other words, CREF is about 10 percent more sensitive to market movements than a fund invested to duplicate the S&P 500. When the market goes up by, say, 10 percent, CREF would be expected to increase by 11 percent. Conversely, when the market declines by 10 percent, CREF would be expected to decline by 11 percent. A portfolio or security with a beta greater than 1.0 might be termed "aggressive" relative to the market, while a portfolio or security with a beta less than 1.0 might be termed "conservative" with respect to the market.

APPLICATIONS OF PORTFOLIO THEORY

With the preceding discussion of modern portfolio theory as background, it is now possible to indicate the ways in which this theory can be applied in the investment process of a large common stock fund like CREF. Essentially, modern portfolio theory affects three phases of the investment process. Before examining each of these areas in detail, a broad overview is provided of the applicability of portfolio theory in each instance.

First, the theory emphasizes that the relevant component of risk for an individual security is the systematic risk and provides a quantitative measure of this risk in the form of the beta of the security. The use of this measure facilitates the selection of a portfolio with an overall risk (beta) level which is consistent with long-range fund objectives. Correspondingly, it provides a means for controlling changes in the risk level of the portfolio when market conditions appear to warrant such changes.

A corollary to this is the use of portfolio analysis as a means of controlling the purchase and sales program. CREF has an annual cash flow exceeding $400 million that must be invested (added to the portfolio) over the course of the year. There is a need to ensure that the kinds of securities being added to the portfolio are not going to change the risk level of the portfolio in a way that is inconsistent with the objectives of the fund. There is similar need to control the sales program to ensure against unintended changes in the portfolio beta.

Secondly, the fact that variations in the return of large portfolios can be substantially explained by variations in the general market emphasizes the importance of properly assessing the relative attractiveness of the overall stock market. This is a difficult task but one that is probably not impossible. At any rate, it is possible to assess the relative attractiveness of the market, at least in terms of identifying periods of extreme over- and under-valuation. CREF has been developing techniques for this purpose for some time and has been actively using them since 1974. The experience to date has been favorable.

Finally, availability of a quantitative measure of risk, i.e., beta, allows those in the investment organization (analysts, portfolio managers, etc.) to assess more precisely the relative attractiveness of individual stocks. High risk stocks are expected to offer high returns by virtue of their risk level; the question is whether they are offering returns more or less than proportional to their risk. Conversely, low risk stocks are expected to offer lower returns by virtue of a lower risk level; and again the question is whether they are offering returns more or less than proportional to their risk. Beta measurement can be utilized to answer questions of this nature.

Portfolio Risk Level (Beta)

In order to determine the risk level (beta) of a portfolio at any given time, a cross-sectional beta for the portfolio is computed. To accomplish this, a beta estimate must be obtained for each of the securities in the portfolio; the standard procedure is to regress the monthly returns of the security against the return of the S&P 500 for the last five years and to use the calculated slope coefficient as an estimate of the security's beta. Each beta so obtained is then weighted by the proportion that its stock represents in the portfolio, and the weighted values are summed to obtain the cross-sectional beta for the portfolio.

Table 4.1 illustrates the calculation of a cross-sectional beta for a hypothetical portfolio of 15 representative securities. The first column shows the weighting of each security in the portfolio while the second shows the beta of the stock. The third column shows the weighting factor for each stock (beta times portfolio weight). The total of this column is the cross-sectional beta of the portfolio. Note that this hypothetical portfolio has a beta of 1.1 or a market sensitivity 10 percent greater than that of a portfolio constructed to be exactly like the S&P 500. If 1.1 were consistent with the risk (beta) objective of the fund, no change would be suggested in weighting the securities or types of securities in the portfolio.

On the other hand, if the calculated beta were too high, the appropriate course of action would be to reweight the portfolio holdings, i.e., to increase the weightings of low beta stocks and decrease the weights of high beta stocks. Alternatively, high beta stocks could be replaced with low beta stocks. Conversely, if the calculated beta were lower than desirable for portfolio objectives, the suggested action would be to reweight toward higher beta stocks or to remove low beta stocks and add high beta stocks. In either case, cash or

TABLE 4.1
Computation of the Cross-Sectional Portfolio Beta

Company	Proportion of Portfolio	Beta	Weighting
American Home Products	0.07	0.84	0.06
Broadway Hale	0.06	1.24	0.07
Crown Zellerbach	0.08	1.26	0.10
Eastman Kodak	0.09	0.83	0.07
Emerson Electric	0.07	1.23	0.09
First Charter Financial	0.06	1.32	0.08
Florida Power and Light	0.04	0.70	0.03
General Electric	0.04	1.05	0.04
Gulf Oil	0.04	0.80	0.03
IBM	0.09	1.13	0.10
International Paper	0.05	1.01	0.05
MGIC	0.09	1.92	0.17
Ryder System	0.08	1.31	0.10
Southern California Edison	0.06	0.95	0.06
Standard Oil New Jersey	0.08	0.58	0.05
	1.00		1.10

short-term "risk-free" securities such as Treasury bills or commercial paper could be added or subtracted to alter the beta of the portfolio. Since these instruments have betas of zero (by virtue of being risk-free), adding them would decrease the beta, while their subtraction would increase the beta of the portfolio.

The use of cash or short-term securities to alter the portfolio beta is a highly restricted alternative for CREF. The fund is advertised to its participants as providing an all-equity variable annuity option. A companion organization, Teachers Insurance and Annuity Association (TIAA), provides a fixed income option for the participants. The philosophy is to allow participants in the TIAA–CREF plan to make their own decisions with respect to allocating funds between equities (CREF) and fixed income investments (TIAA).

CREF uses the method described above to develop a cross-sectional beta for its portfolio. It also calculates a cross-sectional beta for the purchase and sales programs. These betas are calculated in the same way as for the overall portfolio except that the securities and weightings in each program (purchase and sales) represent projected intentions rather than actual holdings. These calculations (for total portfolio and purchase and sales programs) are now made each month and are provided to the finance committee as a means of monitoring the risk posture of the fund on a regular basis.

Table 4.2 shows the type of report that is submitted to the finance

TABLE 4.2
Portfolio Structure of CREF (June 30, 1975)

| | S&P 500 | CREF | CREF versus S&P | CREF Program | | CREF Projected |
				Purchases	Sales	
Market value (millions)		$3,088		$359	$48	$3,399
Risk characteristics (beta):						
Equity portfolio	1.00	1.10		1.11	1.21	1.10
Risk sectors						
1. 0–0.93	52%	25%	−27%	27%	0%	25%
2. 0.94–1.08	20	20	0	14	19	19
3. 1.09–1.23	13	23	+10	14	48	22
4. 1.24–1.43	11	20	+ 9	43	8	23
5. 1.44 and over	4	12	+ 8	2	25	11
	100%	100%		100%	100%	100%
Cash and equivalents	—	2%				2%
Total portfolio	1.00	1.08				1.08

committee for use in monitoring the risk exposure of the fund.[1] The first row of the report shows the size of the portfolio as of June 30, 1975 (approximately $3 billion), as well as the projected size of the purchase and sales programs. Note that the sales program is relatively insignificant when compared to the purchase program. The second row shows the cross-sectional beta of the equities in the portfolio. CREF's beta was 1.1, compared to a beta of 1.0 for the S&P 500.

The middle rows of the report show the weighting of the CREF portfolio in five beta sectors (from the lowest beta stocks to the highest) as well as the weighting of the S&P 500 in these same five sectors. This allows one to determine whether the fund has an unusual concentration (relative to the S&P 500) in any particular beta sector that might lead to unexpectedly adverse performance. It is noteworthy that CREF has a higher proportion of its portfolio in high beta stocks and a lower proportion in low beta stocks than the S&P 500. This is, of course, the sort of distribution that would be expected for a fund with an overall beta greater than 1.0.

The table also shows the weighted beta of the purchase and sales programs. On June 30, 1975, the purchase program had a weighted beta of 1.11 while the sales program had a weighted beta of 1.21. Weighting the purchase and sales program with the current portfolio results in virtually no change in the cross-sectional beta of the equities in the portfolio.

It is useful at this point to emphasize that the importance of making this calculation is to determine whether the current purchase and sales program is consistent with the outlook for the general market. For example, a forecast of a rising market would suggest increasing the current portfolio beta level and require a purchase program heavily weighted with high beta stocks and a sales program heavily weighted with low beta stocks. On the other hand, a forecast of a declining market would suggest decreasing the current portfolio beta level. A projection of no change in the portfolio beta, as shown in Table 4.2, implies a neutral outlook for the market.

The next-to-last row of Table 4.2 shows the CREF position in risk-free assets. This percentage can vary between 0 and 5 percent, with the lower limit due to legal restrictions against fund borrowing and the upper limit a policy constraint. As noted before, CREF advertises itself as a virtually all-equity variable annuity. Also recall that since cash and short-term securities have betas of zero, an increase in this category reduces the portfolio beta while a decrease increases

---

[1] Table 4.2 is actually the first report of this nature to be submitted.

the beta. CREF's 2 percent cash position on June 30, 1975, resulted in a total portfolio beta of 1.08, which is less than the 1.10 beta of the equities alone.

Evaluation of Overall Market

As the preceding discussion suggests, an evaluation of the relative attractiveness of the overall market has a great deal of significance in determining how a portfolio is to be structured. CREF uses essentially two types of indicators in an attempt to assess the relative attractiveness of the market—valuation indicators and economic indicators. The latter can be subdivided into business cycle, monetary and credit, and long-term economic indicators. The following paragraphs provide a fairly detailed description of one of the indicators as well as some general comments on the others.

The indicator that CREF uses to assess the relative attractiveness of the general market is most properly classified as a valuation indicator. It is derived by the Wells Fargo Bank investment department and provided to CREF for a fee. The indicator is known as the Wells Fargo market line and is described by the bank as "a device for showing the relationship in the market between the expected return and risk for stocks at a given time." The line is purported to be the empirical counterpart of the theoretical security market line described by Sharpe and other portfolio theorists.[2]

To derive the market line, Wells Fargo monitors a universe of some 300 stocks, consisting primarily of large and well-known companies. They first derive an estimated (or expected) return for each of the stocks in the universe. The beta value for each of the stocks is also calculated to develop a measure of the market risk of the stock. This procedure provides 300 different risk-return pairs.

A hypothetical market line is presented in Figure 4.2. The vertical axis represents expected return while the horizontal axis shows risk as measured by beta. The risk-return values for each of the 300 stocks can be plotted on such a diagram. Figure 4.2 shows some hypotheti-

---

[2] The theoretical underpinnings for the market line were first developed and described in William Sharpe, "Capital Asset Prices: A Theory of Market Equilibrium under Conditions of Risk," *Journal of Finance* (September 1964), pp. 425–42. Other sources that provide an especially lucid and yet comprehensive description of the market line are James Lorie and M. T. Hamilton, *The Stock Market: Theories and Evidence* (Homewood, Ill.: Richard D. Irwin, 1973), chaps. 10 and 11; F. Modigliani and G. A. Pogue, "An Introduction to Risk and Return," *Financial Analysts Journal* (May–June 1974); and O. A. Vasicek and J. A. McQuown, "The Efficient Market Model," *Financial Analysts Journal* (September–October 1972).

FIGURE 4.2
Risk-Return Diagram for Hypothetical Stocks

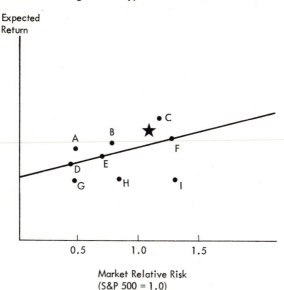

Market Relative Risk
(S&P 500 = 1.0)

cal plots to illustrate the procedure. A line can be fitted to the points, as was done in the case of these hypothetical plots. This fitted line is known as the market line.

Figure 4.3 shows the actual Wells Fargo market line at various dates during the period 1972 through 1975. The line for June 1972 reflects the peak of the 1971–1972 bull market, while that for September 1974 reflects the bottom of the 1973–1974 bear market. The other two lines represent the market situation at more recent dates. The level of a line reflects the general attractiveness or unattractiveness of stocks based on expected returns. The slope reflects the risk-return relationship in the market and allows the analyst to assess the relative attractiveness of high versus low risk stocks.

The expected returns offered by a portfolio of stocks with a beta level of 1.0 at each of the four dates represented by the lines are presented in the accompanying table. The stock returns can be read from the vertical axis in the figure at the intersection of the market lines and a vertical line emanating from a beta level of 1.0 on the horizontal axis. It is noteworthy that stocks were offering 9 percent returns at the June 1972 market peak compared to 15.7 percent at the market trough of September 1974.

It is useful to relate these absolute returns to the returns on risk-

FIGURE 4.3
Actual Market Lines, Including the Historical High and Low between 1970 and 1975

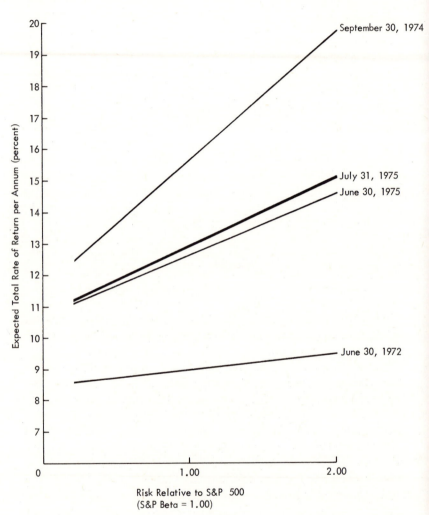

free securities, which can be represented by short-term Treasury bill rates. It is thereby possible to derive an expected risk premium for stocks and relate it to the risk premium provided by stocks over longer periods. As a benchmark, over the 1926–1973 period (the most extended period for which the data are available) stocks provided a return of 9.3 percent, while Treasury bills provided a return of 2.2

Date	Expected Return on Stocks*	Treasury Bill Rate	Risk Premium
June 6, 1972	9.0%	4.0%	5.0%
September 9, 1974	15.7	8.0	7.7
June 6, 1975	12.5	5.3	7.2
July 7, 1975	12.9	6.5	6.4

* This return is that expected on a portfolio of stocks with a beta of 1.0, i.e., a portfolio equivalent to the S&P 500.

percent.[3] Stocks thus provided a premium over risk-free assets (Treasury bills) of about 7 percent during the period 1926–1973.

In addition, it appears that Treasury bill rates and rates of inflation are highly correlated. For example, over the 1926–1973 period, inflation averaged 1.7 percent and Treasury bill rates averaged 2.2 percent. Recent research tends to confirm this by indicating that Treasury bill rates may in fact be good predictors of inflation.[4] To the extent that this is true, one could also look upon risk premium analysis as a means of adjusting the nominal return on stocks for inflation. In other words, the risk premium of 7 percent on stocks over the 1926–1973 period was also approximately in line with the real return on stocks (nominal return of 9 percent less inflation of about 2 percent).

As shown above, at the June 1972 market high the risk premium for stocks relative to Treasury bills was 5 percent. This premium was low in terms of the longer-term average of 7 percent. One might also have forecast at the time that the premium would narrow still further due to inflationary forces and an anticipated increase in the Treasury bill rate. Stocks thus would have appeared unattractive on the basis of this analysis and in fact proved to be so, as witnessed by the severe bear market of 1973–1974.

On the other hand, at the September 1974 market trough the risk premium was approximately 8 percent, as the expected return for stocks was 15.7 percent and the Treasury bill rate was 8 percent. This was higher than the longer-term average of 7 percent. At the same time, it was apparent that inflationary forces were abating and that Treasury bill rates were likely to decline. Thus, one might have pre-

[3] Roger G. Ibbotson and Rex A. Sinquefield, "Stocks, Bonds, Bills, and Inflation: Year-by-Year Historical Returns (1926–1974)," *Journal of Business,* vol. 49, no. 1 (January 1976), pp. 11–47.

[4] Eugene Fama, "Short-Term Interest Rates as Predictors of Inflation," *American Economic Review,* vol. 65, no. 3 (June 1975), pp. 269–82.

dicted that the risk premium would increase; and the market situation would have appeared quite attractive.

As noted above, however, CREF uses several indicators in assessing the relative attractiveness of the market. Two other indicators that have been helpful in relating current valuation levels to broad historical patterns are the dividend yield on the Dow Jones Industrial Average (DJIA) and the price to book value ratio for the Standard & Poor's 425 Stock Index (S&P 425). Both indicators confirmed the relative attractiveness of stocks in the fourth quarter of 1974 with the DJIA showing a historically high yield of 6.5 percent and the S&P 425 book value ratio at an especially depressed level (approximately 1.0).

In addition, the economic indicators all appeared to be favorably positioned for a market advance in the fourth quarter of 1974. For example, the rate of change of corporate profits, which is one of the major business cycle indicators, was projected to show an upturn by mid-1975—an event which the market usually anticipates by two to three quarters.[5] Also, the expectation that the growth in the real money supply would reverse its negative trend provided an indication that money and credit conditions would probably improve. Finally, the GNP gap, which is a useful longer-term economic indicator,[6] was unusually wide, creating a favorable environment for relatively lower inflationary pressures in the next period of economic expansion.

In sum, the outlook for stocks in general appeared quite favorable in the fourth quarter of 1974. Correspondingly, the steep upward slope of the Wells Fargo market line in September 1974 (see Figure 4.2) suggested that high risk stocks were quite attractive relative to low risk stocks. As high risk stocks are expected to show the most extensive increases in a rising market, the strategy under these circumstances would be to increase the beta of the portfolio by increasing the weighting in high beta stocks. High risk stocks, in fact, did show above-average performance in the subsequent market rise, as indicated by the downward rotation of the line to June 1975.

Restructuring the portfolio to take advantage of a market forecast thus appears to be a promising approach. Ideally, a forecast of a de-

---

[5] The Boston Company Research and Technology Department, Boston, Massachusetts, is the source of many of these economic indicators. In the fourth quarter of 1974, this organization was projecting an upturn in corporate profits by mid-1975.

[6] The GNP gap is defined as the difference between potential and actual GNP. Potential GNP is an estimate of the production capability of the nation with relatively full utilization of its productive resources and existing technology.

clining market would suggest reducing the beta of the portfolio to below 1.0 to ensure a lesser decine than the market and thus a relatively better performance for the portfolio. On the other hand, forecasts of rising markets would suggest increasing the beta of the portfolio to well above 1.0, again to ensure outperforming the market. Specifically, this would imply that the beta of a portfolio should vary between, say, 0.8 with a forecast of a declining market and 1.2 with a forecast of a rising market.

There are, however, substantial practical problems associated with varying the beta of a portfolio of any significant size over such a wide range (40 percentage points). First, changes of even 5 percentage points in the beta of a large portfolio would entail sizeable purchase and sales programs. These programs could take a substantial period of time during which the market outlook could change. Second, market forecasts are, by nature, estimates of the probability of events occurring and even the best forecasts are likely to be incorrect at times. It thus seems prudent to keep the variation in the portfolio beta within fairly tight limits around a beta level that has been established as appropriate for longer-range portfolio objectives. Presuming, for example, that the current CREF portfolio beta of approximately 1.1 is the appropriate longer-range level, the suggested range for variation around that level might be from a maximum of 1.15 to 1.20 to a minimum of 1.00 to 1.05.

Appraising Individual Stocks

The Wells Fargo market line provides an explicit framework for appraising the relative attractiveness of individual stocks. In other words, it provides the benchmark for assessing whether stocks are offering returns more or less than proportionate to their risk (beta). Figure 4.2 on p. 113 shows a risk-return diagram with some hypothetical stock plots and a market line fitted to these risk-return plots. Note that the line shows an upward slope indicating that stocks with high market risk (high beta values) should offer higher returns than stocks with low market risk (low beta values). This is of course the expected relationship; and experience to date with the line bears this out; i.e., while the level and degree of the slope of the line may vary over time, it has always shown an upward slope.

In the market line context, stocks that plot above the line are presumably undervalued (attractive) because they offer a higher return than stocks of similar risk. Stocks A, B, and C in Figure 4.2 are undervalued relative to their beta class. On the other hand, a stock is presumably overvalued (unattractive) when it is expected to produce a lower return than issues of comparable risk. Stocks G, H, and I in the figure are overvalued relative to their beta class. Stocks D, E, and F plot on the line and are thus appropriately valued in the context of the market line. Finally, note that issues A, D, and G, occupying approximately the same vertical position at the left end of the relative risk spectrum, are low risk stocks, while issues C, F, and I are high risk stocks, occupying positions at the right end of the range.

Ideally, the optimal policy for a fund, at any given risk level, would be to hold only stocks that were offering returns greater than others of equivalent risk. In other words, the optimal policy would be to hold only stocks that plotted above the line. In practice, however, there are several considerations that would constrain an investor from holding only stocks plotting above the line.

First, estimated risk and return values for individual stocks are subject to much greater error than in the case of a full portfolio where errors of individual estimates tend to offset one another. In effect, there is less confidence in some estimates than others and there is a resultant need to make some sort of ad hoc adjustment in many cases. Secondly, there are diversification considerations. For example, there may be periods when particular classes of securities such as utilities or oils appear particularly attractive, but overweighting in these could expose a portfolio to undesired industry risk. Correspondingly, many of the companies that appear particularly attractive could be small illiquid companies that may be difficult to position in a portfolio. Finally, this is a relatively untested method. It appears to have promise at least on the basis of preliminary tests, but the lack of more thorough testing argues for caution, at least in the early stages of implementation.

Currently, CREF is using this technique in conjunction with the more traditional methods of individual stock analysis to identify and hold what appear to be the relatively most promising opportunities. On the basis of limited experience, it appears that there are sufficient individual opportunities available to permit the construction of a portfolio that offers a somewhat greater return than would be anticipated at a given level of risk. In other words, it appears possible to construct a portfolio at a given beta level that plots above the market line. Such a portfolio is illustrated by the star in Figure 4.2. However, it is important to note that *expected* returns are being considered; there is no guarantee that above-average returns would be realized in practice.

SUMMARY AND CONCLUSION

As noted above, CREF is currently implementing some aspects of modern portfolio theory as an aid in improving its investment process. This implementation is expected to impact the operation in three major respects.

First, the beta coefficient provides a quantitative measure of the relevant risk of individual securities and hence allows the investor to determine how the mix of securities in the portfolio affects the overall risk of the fund. Systematic and continued analysis of this aspect of the investment process will allow CREF to control more closely the overall risk of the portfolio to ensure consistency with overall fund objectives.

In addition, portfolio theory emphasizes the importance of general market trends in determining the performance of large portfolios. CREF recognizes this and has endeavored to develop techniques for monitoring the relative attractiveness of the market. To the extent that these techniques are successful in identifying extremes of over- and under-valuation in the market and to the extent that the fund takes the appropriate action to reorient the risk posture of its portfolio, some incremental performance benefits should accrue.

Finally, modern portfolio theory provides a benchmark for evaluating the relative attractiveness of returns offered by individual stocks across the risk spectrum. CREF is currently combining this benchmark, as represented by the Wells Fargo market line, with more traditional techniques to identify the most promising individual stock opportunities. If this approach is in fact successful in identifying promising opportunities, it should result in additional performance benefits.

In short, modern portfolio theory should provide CREF with a better means of controlling the risk exposure of its portfolio to meet fund objectives. To the extent that CREF can successfully identify extremes of over- and under-valuation in the market as well as promising individual stock opportunities, portfolio theory should also be an aid in earning excess returns in a market that is highly but not perfectly efficient.

5

The Geometric Mean Strategy and Common Stock Investment Management

By Henry A. Latané* and William E. Avera†

This chapter describes a portfolio selection model based on the geometric mean strategy. Although less general than the mean-variance approach which dominates the academic literature, this model seems particularly applicable to life insurance company portfolio management. By sacrificing generality, the model gains a simple and specific decision rule which may be applied myopically period after period. Under seemingly reasonable assumptions about the investment opportunities faced by the company, the geometric mean strategy leads to the maximization of the chance that the portfolio will realize a higher growth rate in capital than would have been realized had the company followed a significantly different sequence of decisions. In addition, assuming that the company is efficient in specifying the probability distributions associated with asset returns, the strategy leads to a steadily diminishing probability that the portfolio will fail to realize the rate of growth assumed by actuaries in rating the company's policies.

The chapter begins with a discussion of the role of quantitative portfolio selection models in the process of investment management. This first section presents the conceptual framework of modern port-

---

* Henry A. Latané is Willis Professor of Investment Banking at the University of North Carolina, Chapel Hill.

† William E. Avera is assistant professor of finance at the University of Texas, Austin.

folio theory followed by an analysis of the appropriate criteria in choosing a portfolio model for use in a particular investment environment. This section also explores practical investment management techniques which flow from a theoretical portfolio selection model.

The second section focuses on the unique characteristics of investment management within the context of the life insurance industry. In identifying the particular requirements for a portfolio selection model in this industry, the authors are led to propose the *maximum chance subgoal* as an operational characterization of the investment objective in life insurance companies. This subgoal presumes that, subject to legal constraints, managers attempt to maximize the chance that after a number of years the capital growth of the company's funds will have exceeded both the actuarially assumed rate and the growth rate available through any other asset management strategy.

The maximum chance subgoal leads directly to the geometric mean strategy, which is the subject of the third section. A mathematical statement of the model is given and its ability to achieve the maximum chance subgoal demonstrated. Also included is a brief historical sketch of the strategy's development and a review of some of the controversies surrounding the strategy.

Crucial to the attractiveness of the geometric mean strategy is its ability to achieve the maximum chance objective within a time frame considered reasonable by managers. The fourth section attempts to shed some light on the timing issue by developing the analytical relationship between the probability of realizing a given growth rate of capital and the number of investment periods. In order to derive the analytical formulas, it is necessary to assume that portfolio returns are independently and identically distributed. While this is a common assumption, it may not be completely acceptable. In order to obtain an indication of the behavior of the probabilities in the absence of this assumption, an empirical experiment was conducted, the results of which are presented in this section. Section five examines some of the techniques for implementing the strategy.

PORTFOLIO MODELS AND INVESTMENT MANAGEMENT

This section has two themes: (1) although abstract and quantitative, portfolio models are useful in practical portfolio management; and (2) there is no universal "best" portfolio model, there is only the portfolio model which is most fruitful in a particular application. In advancing these two themes, the section sets the stage for choosing the model which is likely to be most effective in the context of the life insurance industry.

The Framework of Modern Portfolio Theory

If future asset returns were known, choosing a portfolio would be simple. The best portfolio would be that which produces the highest terminal wealth. In reality, asset returns are uncertain and vary with a host of stochastic events, some of which impact on particular firms and industries while others cut across the entire economy. As a result, the portfolios which can be constructed from a set of assets offer a variety of probability distributions over future returns. The fundamental goal of investment management is to build the portfolio having the probability distribution most consistent with the preferences and constraints of the portfolio's owner(s).

Modern portfolio theory breaks the process of building an optimal portfolio into two steps. The first step is to estimate future asset returns under each possible combination of relevant future events. This step corresponds to the traditional role of security analysis. The full statement of asset returns in each state of nature and of the probabilities associated with the states of nature is termed the *payoff matrix*. Given a fully articulated payoff matrix, the next step is to combine the assets in such a way that the resulting probability distribution of portfolio returns maximizes the investor's objective function. A portfolio selection model is a mathematical statement of the process followed in generating the optimal portfolio.

The reduction of portfolio selection to a set of mathematical statements has tremendous advantages, both direct and indirect. Among the key direct advantages of mathematical modeling is the simplification of investment decision making. Even from a limited set of assets, an enormous number of portfolios can be generated by varying the assets included and their relative weightings. It is clearly unworkable to test each feasible portfolio against the preferences and constraints of the investing institution in order to determine the most desirable investment mix. By expressing the preferences and constraints in the proper form, a portfolio selection model permits the speed and accuracy of the computer to be mobilized in the search for the optimal portfolio.

Mathematical optimization can assist in the search for the best portfolio in either of two ways. It can narrow the set of feasible portfolios to a more manageable subset, or it can determine the single best portfolio. The classic contribution of Markowitz is an example of the former approach, as the feasible set of candidate portfolios is reduced to an efficient set by eliminating portfolios which are dominated.[1] The portfolio selection model presented in this chapter is of the latter variety since it implies that one particular portfolio is superior to all others.

The technology of mathematical programming has been developing rapidly. The employment of portfolio selection models makes available to investment managers some of the analytical techniques which have proven so powerful in other management disciplines. For example, sensitivity analysis can be used to estimate the impact on investment decisions of slight alterations in the payoff matrix, objective function, or constraint set. Such an analysis might lead to a prediction of the changes in portfolio composition which would result if regulatory authorities were to alter the restrictions on the assets which an insurance company may hold.

The authors' enthusiasm for portfolio selection models should not be interpreted as a belief that the computer can solve all of the problems of investment management in life insurance companies. The first step in portfolio building—filling out the payoff matrix—is a task of enormous difficulty. Indeed, estimating future returns and associated probabilities is where most of the effort of life insurance investment departments is (and probably should be) directed.

The focus on portfolio selection models is justified because such models enable the investor to make the best possible use of the information gathered through security analysis. To ignore the potential improvement in investment decisions available through the use of portfolio selection models (even though the contribution might be slight relative to the benefits of knowing a little more about the future) is to sacrifice an advantage in an arena where the competition is fierce and the advantages scarce.

Other Applications of Portfolio Models

An insurance company need not use a portfolio model in the actual selection of assets for purchase and sale in order to benefit from the analytical framework the model provides. There are a number of indirect spinoffs from portfolio theory to practical investment management. Four such areas have been identified: (1) setting management goals, (2) defining the inputs required from security analysis,

---

[1] Harry M. Markowitz, "Portfolio Selection," *Journal of Finance*, vol. 7, no. 1 (March 1952), pp. 77–91.

(3) establishing a feedback and control mechanism for the investment process, and (4) providing insights into the behavior of security markets.

Integral to a portfolio selection model is a mathematical representation of the objectives of the investor and the constraints under which the portfolio is being managed. The precision required by the model forces the investor to formulate these objectives and constraints in a clear-cut manner. Key variables must be identified and expressed in quantitative terms, e.g., trade-offs between risk and return must be made explicit both in the definition of the terms and their functional relationship.

If an investing institution (or individual) can find a portfolio selection model which seems appropriate to its situation, then the model can provide a pattern for establishing goals for investment activities. The structure of the portfolio model will force upon the setting of goals the logical discipline and clarity inherent in mathematics. This is not to say that the goals necessarily will be "better," but they will be explicit and logically connected and therefore more operational.

The structure of a portfolio selection model is also useful in defining the inputs from security analysis. In specifying the process of selecting the optimal portfolio from a set of securities, the model identifies the particular information which is used to discriminate between attractive and unattractive investment opportunities. Since the model requires quantitative inputs, the estimates must be in a precise numerical form.

As with setting goals, adding precision to an analyst's estimates does not necessarily make his estimates "better" in the sense of predicting the future. However, the precision does improve the usefulness of the analyst's output for comparing large numbers of investment opportunities. In making his judgments explicit, they can be compared to those of other analysts and to subsequent events. Conceivably, the institution could adjust for any consistent bias which is observed in the analyst's estimates of key variables.

The suggestion that analysts' estimates be made precise in no way contradicts the view that a large subjective input enters into the process of estimation. The formation of human judgment may well be too complex to reduce to equations, but the outcome of the analytical process is employed more effectively when expressed with precision and in terms consistent with a portfolio selection model.

The third indirect use of a portfolio selection model is in designing systems to monitor and control the investment process. Since the portfolio model rigorously prescribes the properties of optimal portfolios, it leads naturally to a set of parameters which may be used to judge the output of the investment process. With the relevant parameters identified, management can establish control limits on the parameters and initiate corrective action when performance drifts beyond allowable tolerances.

The structure of a portfolio selection model also suggests techniques for comparing the performance of portfolios having different risk and return characteristics since many models imply a particular trade-off function between risk and return. Such techniques may be used in comparing the performance of a particular portfolio to the market index even though the portfolio differs in riskiness from the market average. Techniques of risk-adjusted performance measurement using the mean-variance framework have been extensively employed both in the academic literature and in practice.[2] The geometric mean strategy model presented in this paper leads directly to a number of techniques for performance evaluation and comparison.

The final spin-off from portfolio selection models is the insight into the behavior of securities markets which accompanies the use of positive models of investor behavior. A *positive* model attempts to describe observed events with simplicity and accuracy, while a *normative* model (such as the geometric mean strategy presented below) attempts to lend guidance which improves decisions. In describing the portfolio selection process, a positive model leads to certain necessary conditions for securities market equilibrium. These conditions in turn imply a particular structure of security prices and portfolio returns. The positive model permits one to trace the impact on prices and returns of various changes in market conditions. The capital asset pricing model is a very useful positive view of securities market equilibrium stemming from the mean-variance approach to portfolio selection.[3] The positive implications of the geometric mean strategy are yet to be fully articulated.

Choosing a Portfolio Model

A portfolio model is an analytical tool which reduces a very complex choice to mathematical statements by focusing on a few strategic variables. In the drive for simplicity, a model necessarily ignores many aspects of the problem which it is designed to solve. The par-

---

[2] Peter Williamson, *Investments: New Analytic Techniques* (New York: Praeger Publishers, 1970), chap. 3.

[3] William F. Sharpe, "Capital Asset Prices: A Theory of Market Equilibrium under Conditions of Risk," *Journal of Finance*, vol. 19, no. 3 (September 1964), pp. 425–42.

ticular aspects ignored and the degree of simplification vary with different models, but all share the general feature of trading off reality for simplicity and mathematical tractability.

No universal "best" model exists since all involve differing levels of sacrifice of reality and must ignore (assume away) some elements of the decision. However, in each application, there is a model which involves the optimal trade-off between reality and simplicity and which focuses on the variables of most interest and availability to users of the model. Thus, a portfolio model which serves very well in one case may be completely inappropriate in another. In this section, criteria are set forth which may facilitate the choice of the best portfolio model for particular applications.

A portfolio model may have a single period horizon and focus on the choice of a portfolio to be held over one increment of time, or it may be multiperiod and focus on the sequential choice of a series of portfolios through a number of periods. Single period models are simpler; but where the sequential aspect of decisions is crucial, a multiperiod model may be more appropriate. In the next section, it is argued that the sequential nature of the life insurance company investment process is of prime importance so that consideration should be restricted to multiperiod models.

Portfolio models also differ in their assumptions about the preferences of the investor(s) for whom the portfolio is managed. Most models presume that a rational investor involved in the process of choosing a sequence of portfolios through time has a clearly defined goal—maximize terminal wealth. In a stochastic world, it is impossible to determine ex ante which sequence of portfolio choices will realize the highest terminal value ex post. Therefore, the investor must make his decisions based on a subgoal which allows him to order the probability distributions of terminal wealth implied by alternative strategies. The transformation the investor uses to order the alternative distributions of terminal outcomes is the subgoal.

Decision theory as a branch of statistics, psychology, and economics has developed a number of alternative methods to specify the subgoal transformation. In dealing with a multiperiod decision process the criteria for selecting the best subgoal transformation are:

1. It must be robust in expressing decision-maker preferences.
2. It must generate a decision rule for each stage of the multiperiod process.
3. The decision rule for each stage should use only the information set available at that point in time.

4. To be termed rational, the decision rule at each stage should use all information available at that point in time.

The selection of the appropriate subgoal transformation depends upon the purpose of the analysis. If one is attempting to describe abstractly and formally the decision process, a very general and implicit specification is used. If the purpose is to provide guidance for practical decisions, a more specific and closed-form specification is indicated.

In most modern treatments of portfolio theory, a utility transformation of the von Neumann–Morgenstern type is used with terminal wealth as the argument in the utility function. While this transformation has proved to be a powerful theoretical tool, it is perhaps not the best approach to the multiperiod portfolio selection problem. This paper suggests an alternative specification of the subgoal not because expected utility of wealth is "wrong" but because it is usually not the best method for obtaining a specific strategy to be followed in a practical multiperiod portfolio choice environment.

There are potential costs involved in adopting a specific subgoal like the maximum chance approach suggested below. For example, this subgoal may not be consistent with the preferences of all multiperiod portfolio investors. Also, the subgoal is tailored to the particular characteristics of multiperiod portfolio choice and thus may not be applicable to other multiperiod decision problems unless they are nearly equivalent to portfolio selection.

Nevertheless, the maximum chance subgoal is probably an excellent choice in a multiperiod context. This is the case because there are three characteristics of the multiperiod portfolio problem which severely limit the operationality of subgoals other than the maximum chance subgoal. First, estimates of portfolio opportunities beyond the immediate period are tenuous. Thus, the subgoal should imply completely myopic decision rules; i.e., it should permit each period's decisions to be made independently of future opportunities.

Second, the terminal horizon is not fixed. For most individual and institutional portfolios, the exact terminal date is itself stochastic. The subgoal should not dictate a change in strategy when the horizon changes. And, third, most portfolios experience anticipated and unanticipated withdrawals unrelated to investment performance. The subgoal should allow specification of a portfolio policy net of these additions and withdrawals which is not dependent upon the external factors which control these cash flows. Otherwise, analysis of the portfolio decision would be impossible without bringing in the entire consumption/investment decision of the economic unit.

These characteristics impose severe restrictions on many subgoals which perform quite well in other environments such as in single period portfolio selection. However, they do not seriously limit the usefulness of the maximum chance subgoal. Given that this subgoal is able to generate a strategy which meets the requirements for an operational model of multiperiod portfolio choice, one must next inquire as to whether it fits investor preferences. In order to answer this question for life insurance companies, one must consider the environment in which they operate.

LIFE INSURANCE COMPANY INVESTMENT POLICIES AND THE MAXIMUM CHANCE SUBGOAL

This section examines the unique aspects of the investment problem faced by life insurance companies and argues that the maximum chance subgoal is a reasonable characterization of management objectives in the industry. The investment policies of insurance companies are strictly regulated by state authorities. It is clearly beyond the scope of this chapter to deal with these regulations and their full impact on investment strategy. Thus, the objectives of management are examined under the assumption that any strategy undertaken can be designed so as to comply with all constraints on investment decisions imposed by external organizations.

Although there has been some controversy with regard to the matter, it is probably reasonable to characterize the ultimate objective of a stock life insurance company as profit maximization and that of a mutual company as providing insurance to its policyholders at the lowest possible cost.[4] Leaving aside the intricacies of rate setting in a competitive environment, these objectives translate into maximizing the asset share (before policyholder dividends) on each block of policies issued.[5] That is, given the premium rate and the fact that the policies have already been sold, the company hopes to outperform the interest and expense assumptions inherent in the premiums by as wide a margin as possible.[6] In terms of investment objectives, this

---

[4] This refers to profit maximization in the classic economic sense and is not intended to imply that stock life insurance companies have a callous attitude toward their policyholders.

[5] A block of policies can be defined as a group of policies of similar type issued to persons in the same age bracket at a particular time.

[6] Mortality has not been mentioned because of the assumption that the policies have already been issued, i.e., that underwriting has already taken place.

means that the company wants to do at least as well as the assumed interest rate and would like to do substantially better.

In an uncertain world, no investment strategy is available which will guarantee a return in excess of the actuarial rate and at the same time maximize the funds available from investment operations.[7] Insurance managers must opt for some subgoal which most nearly represents their preferences. The maximum chance subgoal would seem a likely candidate. It implies that the company wishes to maximize the chance that when the value of the portfolio is called upon to fund liabilities, the realized growth rate would have been as high as possible. This means both that the growth rate has the greatest possibility of exceeding the actuarial rate and that it has the greatest probability of surpassing the growth available from any other investment strategy.

Furthermore, as the bulk of liabilities under most policy blocks is not discharged until a number of years after policy issue, it would be desirable for the probability to increase with the number of periods over which the funds are managed. That is, an interest rate shortfall is much more serious as the policy block matures than it is in the first few years after policy issue; and an investment strategy which maximizes the probability of meeting the peak reserve demands of the policy block is to be preferred.

Thus, according to this interpretation of the life insurance company investment problem, the maximum chance subgoal seems to have definite appeal. The attractive feature of the geometric mean strategy in fulfilling the maximum chance subgoal is that the probability of exceeding the assumed interest rate increases with the number of cumulative periods the strategy is followed. Hence, a persuasive justification for the geometric mean strategy presented in the next section is that the longer the time that elapses between policy issue and maturity, the more likely that the reserve interest rate will be attained and the excess of capital value above insurance liability will be maximized. The ability of a company actually to achieve the subgoal depends upon whether its payoff matrices accurately repre-

[7] Since the future date of cash outflows is not known with certainty, a strategy of purchasing securities with certain coupons and payment at maturity, e.g., U.S. government bonds, does not assure the attainment of the actuarial rate in a cash sense. If outflows occur before maturity, the resale value of the bond will depend upon prevailing interest rates. If outflows occur after maturity, realized capital growth depends upon reinvestment rates for the principal. Even if the maturity date exactly corresponds to the cash outflow date, the reinvestment rate of coupons will have an impact on the realized compound growth rate of capital.

sent investment opportunities and whether the underlying stochastic assumptions of the geometric mean strategy are met.

THE GEOMETRIC MEAN STRATEGY

This section introduces the multiperiod portfolio model which seems most operational in the life insurance company investment environment. The discussion begins with a brief review of the historical development of the model and a synopsis of some of the academic controversy surrounding its justification. Next, a simple version of the model is presented in which portfolio returns are assumed to be independently and identically distributed through time. The ability of the geometric mean strategy to fulfill the maximum chance subgoal is demonstrated by developing expressions for the probability that a portfolio will realize a given growth rate. These expressions lead directly to the result that the sequence of portfolios having the highest geometric mean maximizes the probability of exceeding alternative strategies and a fixed actuarial rate.

Both the model and the expressions for probabilities could be presented using a more general specification of the stochastic nature of sequential portfolio returns, but the resulting mathematical expressions and statistical arguments would be much more complex. A simplified presentation has been adopted here to communicate the basic structure of the geometric mean strategy. References to more general proofs are provided in the footnotes.

History of the Strategy

The geometric mean strategy is a rule for making repetitive and cumulative choices under uncertainty in which the geometric mean of the probability distribution of payoffs is maximized. This strategy has been applied to a wide range of choice situations including gambling[8] and the selection of optimal communications systems.[9] The strategy was applied explicitly to the problem of portfolio selection by Latané.[10]

Recently the geometric mean strategy has attracted increasing attention in the literature of finance and economics. Due to its myopic

---

[8] Leo Brienan, "Optimal Gambling Systems for Favorable Games," in *Proceedings of the Fourth Berkeley Symposium on Mathematics and Probability*, ed. Jerzy Neyman (Berkeley: University of California Press, 1961) vol. 1, pp. 65–78.

[9] John L. Kelly, "A New Interpretation of Information Rate," *Bell System Technical Journal* (August 1956), pp. 917–26.

[10] Henry A. Latané, "Criteria for Choice among Risky Ventures," *Journal of Political Economy*, vol. 38 (April 1959), pp. 145–55.

property and other advantages in sequential decision analysis, the geometric mean strategy has formed the basis for both positive and normative models of multiperiod portfolio selection.[11] The generic term for portfolio selection models predicated on the geometric mean strategy has become *growth-optimal* since the strategy leads to maximizing the expected continuously compounded growth rate of invested capital.

In their early application of the geometric mean strategy, Kelly and Brienan argue that a decision maker would adopt the strategy because asymptotically it almost certainly leads to a higher terminal value than any alternative sequence of decisions. This argument is not sufficient motivation for a multiperiod portfolio model on both practical and theoretical grounds. Real world portfolio owners might have distant but not infinite horizons. A pragmatic motivation for the growth-optimal strategy should deal with horizons which would seem reasonable to portfolio managers.

Samuelson has argued that the asymptotic property of the geometric mean strategy does not imply its general optimality in terms of utility theory even for investors whose horizons are infinite.[12] Only those investors whose preferences are characterized by the log utility function would consistently follow the strategy. In the theoretical literature, there have been a number of interesting papers dealing with various aspects of the utility issue.

It is not the purpose of this chapter to join the theoretical controversy over the justification of the geometric mean strategy within the context of utility theory. If the reader accepts the maximum chance subgoal as an appropriate characterization of life insurance investment management objectives, then one can justify the geometric mean strategy by demonstrating that it fulfills that subgoal.

The Model

Define some interval of time to be a "period." Over each period a portfolio realizes a *holding period return, H_t*. The holding period re-

---

[11] Nils Hakansson, "Multi-Period Mean-Variance Analysis: Toward a General Theory of Portfolio Choice," *Journal of Finance*, vol. 26 (September 1971), pp. 857–84. Richard Roll, "Evidence of the 'Growth-Optimum' Model," *Journal of Finance* (June 1973), pp. 551–66.

[12] Samuelson incorrectly includes Latané among those who claim the asymptotic property would cause all rational investors to pursue the strategy. In the 1959 article, note 3 begins, "For certain utility functions and for certain repeated gambles, no amount of repetition justifies the rule that the gamble which is almost sure to bring the greatest wealth is the preferable one." Latané, "Criteria for Choice . . . ," p. 145.

turn is calculated by dividing the end of period value of the portfolio plus any cash flows through dividends and interest by the beginning of period portfolio value. All holding period returns are assumed to be equal to or greater than zero; i.e., at no time can the portfolio have a negative value at the end of a holding period.

The *geometric average return* to a portfolio is computed as follows:[13]

$$G = (\prod_{t=1}^{T} H_t)^{\frac{1}{T}} \tag{5.1}$$

Often $G-1$ is referred to as the *compound average yield*. Since the set of H_t is restricted to non-negative values, the natural logarithm of both sides of (5.1) may be obtained:

$$\ln G = \frac{1}{T} \sum_{t=1}^{T} \ln H_t = g_t \tag{5.2}$$

The logarithm of the geometric average is the continuous rate of growth of portfolio capital. The realized growth rate over a T-period horizon will be denoted g_T.

Assume that the holding period return for each period is drawn from the same distribution and that the outcome of previous periods has no effect on the distribution associated with any particular period. If the generating distribution is represented as a discrete payoff matrix with M states of nature, the expected natural logarithm of holding period return is defined as follows:

$$E(\ln H_t) = \sum_{i=1}^{M} (\ln H_i) p_i = \gamma, \text{ for all } t \epsilon T \tag{5.3}$$

where $p_i =$ the probability of occurrence of the ith state of nature. The expected value of log holding period returns is denoted by γ and is termed the *growth parameter* of the distribution.

The relationship between the growth parameter and the geometric mean can be seen by writing the definition of the geometric mean and taking logs.

$$\Gamma = \prod_{i=1}^{M} H_i^{p_i}$$

$$\ln \Gamma = \sum_{i=1}^{M} (\ln H_i) p_i = \gamma \tag{5.4}$$

---

[13] The term "average" is used to indicate a function of realized values. Functions of realized returns are denoted with Roman letters. Parameters of the holding period return distribution are indicated with Greek letters.

Thus, the geometric mean is the antilog of the growth parameter.

Since the log function is monotonic, when an investor maximizes the geometric mean of his portfolio, he is maximizing the growth parameter. The effect of maximizing this growth parameter is to maximize the expected continuously compounded growth rate of capital. This can be seen by substituting (5.3) into (5.2) and taking the expected value of the resulting expression.

$$E(g_T) = E\left(\frac{1}{T} \sum_{t=1}^{T} \ln H_t\right) = \frac{1}{T}(T\gamma) = \gamma \qquad (5.5)$$

Apart from maximizing the expected continuously compounded growth rate of capital, the geometric mean strategy asymptotically leads to a higher terminal wealth than available through any significantly different sequence of decisions. This property can be demonstrated in a number of ways, but the most straightforward is by appeal to the law of large numbers. As the number of investment periods becomes very large, the relative frequency of occurrence of each state of nature will approach its probability. This implies that the sequence of portfolios with the highest geometric mean will approach the highest terminal growth rate; i.e., $g_T \to \gamma$ as $T \to \infty$. Given a fixed initial wealth, the portfolio with the highest growth rate yields the highest terminal wealth. Thus, an investor who followed the geometric mean strategy through a nearly infinite number of periods would almost certainly end up with more wealth than another investor who started with the same capital and faced the same investment opportunities but followed a significantly different strategy.

The Probability of a Portfolio Realizing a Given Growth Rate

This subsection derives explicit expressions for the probability of one portfolio sequence producing a greater terminal wealth than an alternative sequence under the assumption that returns are distributed lognormally and independently through time (that is, the log of returns—portfolio growth rates—are normally distributed). By appeal to the central limit theorem, these expressions approximate probability of return distributions of any shape which are independently distributed, with the approximation becoming more precise as the number of periods increases.

Recall that γ, the growth parameter, is the mean of the single period log distribution. Let σ^2 be the variance of that distribution. Using the tabulated integrals for the standard normal distribution, we can make probability statements about portfolio growth rates, given a specification of the growth parameter and its variance. The types of statements that can be made and the mathematical form of the test statistics are analogous to the statements made about sample means in sampling theory since the realized growth rate is the arithmetic average of the independently drawn single period log returns.

Consider the probability that the realized portfolio growth rate will exceed some fixed value r. The probability is the integral of the normal distribution of growth rates from r to plus infinity; i.e.,

$$
\begin{aligned}
P(g_T > r) &= P\left(\frac{g_T - \gamma}{\frac{\sigma}{T^{\frac{1}{2}}}} > \frac{r - \gamma}{\frac{\sigma}{T^{\frac{1}{2}}}}\right) \\
&= P\left(z > \frac{r - \gamma}{\frac{\sigma}{T^{\frac{1}{2}}}}\right) \\
&= P\left(-z < \frac{\gamma - r}{\frac{\sigma}{T^{\frac{1}{2}}}}\right) \\
&= N(Z)
\end{aligned}
\tag{5.6}
$$

where N = the standard normal distribution function, and $Z = (\gamma - r)\frac{T^{\frac{1}{2}}}{\sigma}$.

As Z increases, the probability of the portfolio realizing a return greater than or equal to r increases. The partial derivatives of the Z transformation are: $\partial Z/\partial \gamma > 0$, $\partial Z/\partial T > 0$, and $\partial Z/\partial \sigma < 0$. Thus, the probability of exceeding r is directly related to the growth parameter and to the number of periods in the horizon and inversely related to the standard deviation of the single period holding return.

From Equation (5.6) it is clear how increasing the number of holding periods impacts upon the probability of surpassing some fixed growth rate, e.g., the actuarial rate. If the growth parameter of the portfolio is greater than the fixed growth rate, then some number of periods exists which will assure dominance at a specified probability level. As T approaches infinity, the probability of dominance will approach one.

The probability that one portfolio sequence will yield a higher terminal wealth than another after a given number of periods can be derived in a similar manner. This case is analogous to the sampling theory problem of testing the difference of two means. Since security returns move together, the variance of the difference in two growth rates involves a covariance term. Specifically, this variance is derived as follows:

$$\text{Var}(g_T{}^A - g_T{}^B) = \frac{1}{T}(\sigma_A{}^2 + \sigma_B{}^2 - 2\text{COV}_{AB}) \qquad (5.7)$$

where

$g_T{}^A, g_T{}^B$ = the realized multiperiod growth rates of portfolio sequences A and B,

$\sigma_A{}^2, \sigma_B{}^2$ = the variances of the single period log return distributions of portfolio sequences A and B; and

COV_{AB} = the covariance between the single period log returns for portfolio sequences A and B.

Using this statement of variance, the Z transformation, and an integral table for the standard normal distribution, we can compute the probability that the growth rate of portfolio sequence A will exceed that of B:

$$P(g_T{}^A - g_T{}^B > 0) = N(Z) \qquad (5.8)$$

where

$$Z = \frac{(\gamma_A - \gamma_B)T^{\frac{1}{2}}}{(\sigma_A{}^2 + \sigma_B{}^2 - 2\text{COV}_{AB})^{\frac{1}{2}}}$$

To the extent that the normal approximation fits the return distributions, Equation (5.8) reveals four important relationships when comparing the realized multiperiod growth rates of two portfolio sequences with $\gamma_A > \gamma_B$:

1. It is always more than 50 percent probable that the realized growth rate of the portfolio sequence with the highest geometric mean will exceed that generated by a portfolio sequence with a lower geometric mean.
2. The probability always increases with the number of investment periods.
3. With a given horizon, the divisor is smaller and hence the probability is larger when the covariance between the portfolios is larger.
4. By rewriting the covariance as the correlation coefficient times the standard deviations (i.e., $\text{COV}_{AB} = r_{AB}\sigma_A\sigma_B$, where $r_{AB} =$ the correlation coefficient), the effect of the variances is seen to be a function of the correlation coefficient. When the portfolio sequences are perfectly correlated ($r_{AB} = 1$), the denominator of (5.8) becomes ($\sigma_A - \sigma_B$). Thus, the probability depends not

on the size of the individual standard deviations but on their difference.

The precision of the central limit theorem assumption in characterizing the distribution of sample means depends upon the shape of the underlying distribution. In dealing with highly skewed distributions, a fairly large sample size may be needed in order for the probabilities derived through the normal approximation to characterize terminal distributions.[14]

EMPIRICAL EVIDENCE ON THE MAXIMUM CHANCE SUBGOAL

Regardless of its intuitive appeal and operational simplicity, no insurance company portfolio manager will adopt the geometric mean strategy unless he can be convinced that it fulfills the maximum chance subgoal when applied to actual security returns over a horizon he considers reasonable. The purpose of this section is to provide some evidence in this regard gleaned from an experiment using historical common stock returns.

The preceding section relied on the law of large numbers to show that as the number of returns drawn from an identically and independently distributed return distribution approaches infinity, the realized portfolio growth rate approaches the growth parameter. This asymptotic property can be cast in terms of paired portfolio comparisons in the following way: Given that the growth parameter of A exceeds that of B, then the probability of the realized growth rate of A exceeding that of B will approach one as the number of periods approaches infinity. In symbols this statement becomes

$$P(g_{T^A} > g_{T^B} \mid \gamma^A > \gamma^B) \to 1 \text{ as } T \to \infty \tag{5.9}$$

When γ^A is significantly larger than γ^B, the power of the geometric mean strategy in fulfilling the maximum chance subgoal depends on the approach path of the probability to unity as the number of periods increases. If the probability approaches close to one in a few periods, then the strategy is more attractive than if the probability remains far from one when the horizon is very distant.

The experiment to test the path of probabilities through time

---

[14] A more thorough discussion of the sampling properties of the geometric mean strategy can be found in William E. Avera, "The Geometric Mean Strategy as a Theory of Multiperiod Portfolio Selection" (Ph.D. diss., University of North Carolina at Chapel Hill, 1972).

should not impose a priori assumptions about the shape of return distributions or their stochastic structure through time. Once such assumptions are made, the path of probabilities through time derived analytically above would apply exactly. A simulation test would be a computer time-intensive method to confirm the consistency of the analytical derivation. The experiment in this section is an attempt to approach the ex post data with a minimum of a priori restrictions.

Of necessity, the experiment makes one assumption, which, although very common in tests using ex post market data, is arbitrary. The realized growth rate over a large number of periods is assumed to be equal to the growth parameter for any subset of periods. This assumption is similar to assuming that the mean and standard deviation of returns over some historical horizon are equal to the ex ante expected value and standard deviation that investors used in constructing portfolios in any single period. The assumption is also utilized in most tests of the capital asset pricing model.

To conduct the experiment, 400 randomly selected stocks were ranked on the basis of their realized compound growth rates over 366 months from January 1936 through June 1966.[15] Sixteen portfolios were formed by combining groups of 25 stocks in descending order of growth rate. Thus, portfolio no. 1 contained the 25 stocks with the highest realized growth rates while no. 16 contained those with the lowest. The aggregate portfolio of all 400 stocks will be termed the "market." The parameters of the portfolio distributions are shown in Table 5.1.

The portfolios were then paired in a manner designed to give examples of paired portfolios having long-term growth rates which differed considerably in value and cases of portfolios with growth parameters very close in value. Portfolio no. 1 was paired with no. 16, no. 2 with no. 15, etc. In addition, portfolios no. 1 and no 16 were paired with the market, giving a grand total of ten pairs.[16]

In order to compare the relative performance of the portfolio pairs as the horizon changed, all possible horizons of 1, 3, 12, 24, 60, and 120 months were extracted from the 366 months of data. Since preserving the structure of returns was important to the realism of the test, each horizon was made up only of contiguous months. Thus, the

---

[15] The data were obtained from tapes available from the Center for Research on Security Prices at the University of Chicago.

[16] As discussed below, because of the interactions of individual security returns, the portfolio composed of securities having the lowest geometric means may not itself have the lowest geometric mean. Such is the case for portfolio no. 16.

TABLE 5.1

Performance Parameters for 16 Hypothetical Common Stock Portfolios Based on Actual Market Performance from January 1936 to June 1966

Portfolio Number	Geometric Mean Return	Standard Deviation	Beta	Alpha	R^2
1	0.0173	0.068	1.111	0.005	0.946
2	0.0147	0.063	1.037	0.003	0.938
3	0.0135	0.058	0.945	0.003	0.937
4	0.0131	0.065	1.076	0.001	0.956
5	0.0122	0.055	0.901	0.002	0.932
6	0.0113	0.060	0.988	0.001	0.952
7	0.0108	0.047	0.764	0.003	0.902
8	0.0110	0.063	1.044	−0.000	0.953
9	0.0107	0.063	1.052	−0.001	0.960
10	0.0097	0.051	0.844	0.001	0.940
11	0.0094	0.061	1.019	−0.002	0.958
12	0.0090	0.053	0.868	−0.000	0.933
13	0.0088	0.059	0.980	−0.002	0.953
14	0.0085	0.060	0.981	−0.002	0.929
15	0.0076	0.059	0.967	−0.003	0.941
16	0.0078	0.066	1.055	−0.004	0.903
Market	0.0108	0.059			

Note: The "market" portfolio consists of a sample of 400 stocks. The 16 portfolios were formed by combining groups of 25 stocks in descending order of growth rate. Thus, portfolio no. 1 contains the 25 stocks with the highest realized growth rates, while portfolio no. 16 contains those with the lowest. Beta, alpha, and R^2 are based on the market line regression equation: $R_{it} = a + \beta R_{Mt}$, where R_{it} and R_{Mt} are the rates of return on the ith portfolio and the market, respectively, in period t.

Source: Data available from the Center for Research on Security Prices of the University of Chicago.

size of the population of horizons varied from 366 with one month to 246 with 120 months. The results of the 60 paired comparisons (ten pairs with six time horizons for each) are presented in Table 5.2. The term *adverse dominance* is used to indicate cases in which the portfolio with the lower assumed growth parameter produced the higher terminal wealth.

The results of the experiment essentially speak for themselves. When the portfolios differed greatly in growth rates, the probability of the higher growth rate portfolio yielding more terminal wealth increased rapidly with the horizon. Portfolio pairs with slight differences in growth rates also showed increasing probability with the horizon, but the changes were less dramatic.

One of the more interesting results is that the probability of portfolio no. 1 exceeding the market portfolio is on the same order of magnitude as that of portfolio no. 1 exceeding portfolio no. 16, which is characterized by a significantly lower average growth rate. On the other hand, the probability of the market exceeding portfolio no. 16

TABLE 5.2
Relative Frequency of Adverse Dominance among Selected Pairings of the Hypothetical Portfolios

Portfolio Comparisons	Number of Periods (T)						$g_T^A - g_T^B$	Var_{AB}*	R_{ab}†
	1	3	12	24	60	120			
1–16	0.306	0.255	0.107	0.041	0.000	0.000	0.0096	0.031	0.89
2–15	0.393	0.321	0.158	0.111	0.000	0.000	0.0071	0.025	0.92
3–14	0.393	0.358	0.270	0.213	0.000	0.000	0.0050	0.024	0.92
4–13	0.393	0.335	0.178	0.073	0.000	0.000	0.0042	0.020	0.95
5–12	0.424	0.368	0.318	0.178	0.094	0.000	0.0032	0.019	0.94
6–11	0.434	0.379	0.321	0.309	0.124	0.000	0.0020	0.019	0.95
7–10	0.481	0.464	0.397	0.335	0.329	0.247	0.0012	0.018	0.94
8–9	0.516	0.505	0.499	0.455	0.469	0.287	0.0003	0.018	0.96
1–mkt.	0.320	0.269	0.070	0.003	0.000	0.000	0.0065	0.018	0.97
16–mkt.	0.623	0.673	0.690	0.767	1.000	1.000	−0.0031	0.021	0.95

Note: Adverse dominance occurs when the portfolio with the lower growth parameter produces the higher terminal wealth. The entries in the number of periods columns are the proportions of the trials in which adverse dominance occurred for the various portfolio pairings and time horizons.

*$\mathrm{Var}_{AB} = \sigma_A^2 + \sigma_B^2 - 2\mathrm{COV}_{AB}$.

†R_{ab} = the bivariate correlation between the returns on portfolios A and B.

is on the same approximate time path as the probability of portfolio no. 1 exceeding no. 16. This phenomenon is expected given the analytic model presented above since the correlation of the portfolios with the market is higher than the intercorrelation between the portfolios.

Table 5.3 presents a direct test of the analytic model by comparing

TABLE 5.3
Comparison of the Relative Frequencies of Adverse Dominance Predicted by the Analytical Model with Those Observed in the Hypothetical Portfolios

Z Value	Number of Observations	Adverse Relative Frequency	
		Normal[*]	Observed
Over 1.6	3,053	0.017	0.000
1.0–1.6	2,943	0.110	0.082
0.50–1.0	3,388	0.245	0.232
0.25–0.5	3,559	0.360	0.339
Less than 0.25	4,895	0.452	0.439
Negative[†]	1,982	0.723	0.774

[*] Based on Equation (5.8).

[†] A negative Z value was observed when portfolio no. 16 was paired with the market portfolio.

the observed adverse relative frequency (the number of times the portfolio with the lower geometric mean realized a higher growth rate) with that computed on the basis of the assumption that portfolio growth rates are distributed normally. This table indicates that for most Z value levels, the normal assumption yields conservative estimates of the relative frequency of adverse dominance.

IMPLEMENTING THE STRATEGY

This section outlines the procedures a life insurance company might follow in implementing the geometric mean strategy. The specifics of the techniques mentioned may be found in the sources indicated by the footnotes.

The process begins with the selection of a "buy list" of securities which are likely candidates for inclusion in the portfolio. To be on the buy list the security must meet all the constraints placed upon portfolio holdings by regulatory authorities as well as by internal management policies. These constraints include quality, marketability, size of issue, maturity, indenture provisions, and so forth. In addition, issues judged by security analysts to have poor prospects are deleted from the buy list.

The next step is to determine a set of economic and securities market scenarios during the coming period—each of which implies a particular pattern of security returns. These scenarios could range from a simple good year/bad year dichotomy to detailed combinations of inflation, interest rates, fiscal policy, and Federal Reserve actions. The number and detail of these "states of nature" depends upon the manager's judgment of the trade-off between the extra cost and benefits of the increased precision stemming from a more complete specification of the future investment environment.[17] Due to the convenient myopic property of the geometric mean strategy (discussed above) the manager need only be concerned about defining possible states of nature for the coming period. While this is by no means easy, it is simpler than specifying possible economic and market events for the entire investment horizon.

The next step is to estimate payoffs in a matrix format. Each of the columns of the matrix represents one of the possible states of nature over the coming investment period. Each of the rows corresponds to one of the securities on the buy list. In each cell of the matrix the manager fills in the return which he predicts will accrue to a security (row) given that a particular state of nature (column) occurs. In assigning the returns to each security in each state of nature the manager must mobilize the inputs of his security analysts and external investment advisors.

To each state of nature the manager assigns a probability representing his judgment of the relative likelihood that the state will occur. Since the states defined by the manager should span all possible future environments (at least as currently foreseen) the probabilities must total to unity. The probabilities are added to the payoff matrix at the bottom of the column of returns corresponding to each state of nature. Table 5.4 illustrates the payoff matrix.

Given a fully articulated payoff matrix, there are two possible routes to selecting the portfolio having the highest geometric mean. The complete route would be to apply a mathematical optimization program directly to the matrix. If the matrix is very large (having many states of nature), this procedure may be expensive in terms of computer time. The short-cut route, which has been shown to yield portfolios very close to optimal, is to reduce the rows of the payoff matrix to summary statistics. The next several paragraphs discuss these routes to finding geometric mean optimal portfolios.

---

[17] For a complete discussion of states of nature, see Henry A. Latané, Donald L. Tuttle, and Charles P. Jones, *Security Analysis and Portfolio Management* (New York: The Ronald Press, 1975).

TABLE 5.4
Illustrative Payoff Matrix

Securities	States of Nature					
	1	2	.	.	.	M
1	H_{11}	H_{12}	.	.	.	H_{1m}
2	H_{21}	H_{22}	.	.	.	H_{2m}
.	.	.	.	.	.	.
.	.	.	.	.	.	.
.	.	.	.	.	.	.
N	H_{n1}	H_{n2}				H_{nm}
Probabilities	P_1	P_2	.	.	.	P_m

Note: State 1 might have a description like ". . . over 10 percent inflation, 14 percent AAA bond rate, below 800 on Dow Jones Industrial Averages, over 9 percent unemployment, etc." Security 1 might be "ATT common stock." Holding period return H_{21} would be a number like 0.86. The probabilities would be numbers between 0 and 1, the sum of which is exactly one.

The portfolio optimization problem in the geometric mean strategy has a straightforward specification. Let the variable w_i represent the proportion of portfolio net worth allocated to asset i. Thus, a value of 0.05 would mean that 5 percent of the portfolio value is invested in the security. If there are N securities on the buy list, then a portfolio chosen from the buy list can be defined by a vector of w_i's with N entries. Since short-selling is generally prohibited, the value of each w_i must be greater than zero. State investment regulations establish an upper limit on the w_i's, and management may choose to impose more stringent limits of its own in order to restrict further the exposure arising from any one security. And, finally, since the full value of the portfolio is invested (cash being one of the securities on the buy list) the sum of the w_i must be unity.

The geometric mean of a portfolio drawn from the N securities in the payoff matrix is defined using Equation (5.4) above:

$$\Gamma = \mathop{\pi}_{j=1}^{M} \left(\sum_{i=1}^{N} w_i H_{ij} \right)^{p_j} \qquad (5.10)$$

The goal of the manager is to choose the values of w_i which maximize this expression subject to the constraints on their values. These constraints are as follows:

$$\sum_{j=1}^{N} w_i = 1 \qquad (5.11)$$

$$0 \leq w_i \leq k$$

with k being the maximum percentage of portfolio value that may be held in a particular security.

The most efficient technique for maximizing (5.10) subject to (5.11) depends upon the number of securities and states of nature. Very small problems can be solved with calculus, e.g., two securities and two states of nature. Complete enumeration is feasible for slightly larger problems. The general case of many securities and many states of nature can be handled with an algorithm utilizing the Kuhn-Tucker conditions.[18]

Fortunately, the short-cut methods based on statistics drawn from the payoff matrix have proved to be reasonably efficient in selecting portfolios which are nearly optimal. At first blush, one might think the most useful statistic would be the geometric mean of the individual securities. This is not the case because the geometric mean of the portfolio is determined in part by the interaction of the component security returns. Depending on the nature of the interactions, the portfolio composed of the securities having the highest geometric mean may not itself have a higher geometric mean than a portfolio made up of a different set of securities. The empirical experiment reported above provides an illustration. Portfolio no. 16 is constructed from the 25 stocks having the lowest geometric mean; yet the resulting portfolio geometric mean is greater than that for portfolio no. 15.

An approach which takes into account the interactions of component securities has been developed by Latané and Tuttle.[19] For the method to be effective two conditions must be valid. First, the portfolio must be highly diversified such that the main element of interaction comes through each security's covariance with the general market (commonly termed the *beta* effect). Second, the portfolio manager must have available some risk-free opportunity which will provide a known yield over the holding period, e.g., U.S. government securities. Given these conditions, a statistic called the *pure risk yield* can be calculated for each security. The portfolio composed of the securities with the highest pure risk yield in combination with the risk-free government securities will in general have the highest available geometric mean.

Mathematically, the pure risk yield is defined as:

$$PRY = \frac{E(H_i) - R_F}{\beta_i \sigma_I} \tag{5.12}$$

---

[18] See Steven F. Maier, David Peterson, and James VanderWeide, "A Monte Carlo Investigation of Characteristics of Optimal Geometric Mean Portfolios," unpublished working paper, Duke University.

[19] Henry A. Latané and Donald L. Tuttle, *Security Analysis and Portfolio Management* (New York: The Ronald Press, 1970), chap. 25.

where

$E(H_i)$ = the expected holding period return of the security,

R_F = the known return on the risk-free asset,

β_i = the beta of the security, and

σ_I = the standard deviation of the index of total market return.

The method of calculating the statistics is as follows:

$$E(H_i) = \sum_{j=1}^{M} (H_{ij})p_j \tag{5.13}$$

$$\beta_i = \frac{\sum_{j=1}^{M} [(H_{ij} - E(H_i))][H_I - E(H_I]p_j}{\sum_{j=1}^{M} [H_{Ij} - E(H_I)]^2 p_j} \tag{5.14}$$

$$\sigma_I^2 = \sum_{j=1}^{M} [H_{Ij} - E(H_I)]^2 p_j \tag{5.15}$$

where I denotes a market variable, i stands for an individual security, and j represents a state of nature.

Operationally, management decides on how many issues it wants to have in the portfolio, having due regard for the diversification assumption underlying pure risk yield. The portfolio is constituted by selecting that number of securities having the highest pure risk yield. In general, the number of securities required for diversification will be such that the relative weightings are of no great importance if they are near to each other in magnitude (since a portfolio composed of many issues would not be diversified if the position in any one issue was so large as to dominate portfolio return). The proper proportion of net assets to commit to the risk-free security is computed approximately as follows:

$$\text{risk-free weight} = 1 - \frac{E(H_p) - R_F}{\sigma_p^2} \tag{5.16}$$

where

$E(H_p)$ = the expected return of the package of securities having the highest pure risk yield,

R_F = the risk-free rate, and

σ_p^2 = the variance of return of the package of securities with the highest pure risk yield.

In practice, the two methods of obtaining geometric mean portfolios are complementary. The statistic approach can be used to narrow the buy list to those securities having the highest pure risk yield and to government securities. From this reduced list, adjustments may be performed using direct optimization to determine if some slight change in the portfolio selected through the short-cut method would result in a higher geometric mean. Thus, the statistic approach brings the portfolio to the neighborhood of optimality; and the full payoff matrix is consulted for purposes of fine-tuning.

SUMMARY AND SUGGESTIONS FOR FURTHER RESEARCH

The crux of this paper is that mathematical models of portfolio selection have an important role to play in investment management and that the geometric mean strategy represents a pragmatic model which is especially suited for use in the life insurance industry. The paper focuses on the uses of portfolio theory and the justification of the geometric mean strategy through the maximum chance subgoal. Both analytical and empirical evidence was developed that, subject to the accuracy of the probability estimates used and the validity of assumptions about the stochastic structure of portfolio returns, the geometric mean strategy leads to the maximization of the probability that the realized capital growth will exceed both the actuarial rate and the growth available from any significantly different sequence of investment decisions.

The paper did not concentrate on rigorously demonstrating the properties of the geometric mean strategy under general statistical assumptions or on the details of the techniques for generating geometric mean optimal portfolios since these subjects are well covered in references indicated in the footnotes. A number of issues concerning the implementation of the geometric mean strategy in the insurance company context deserve further examination. Among the more trenchant issues are: (1) how is the outcome of the strategy affected when the underlying payoff matrices of security returns misrepresent reality; and (2) what is the effect of integrating taxes, transactions costs, and the maturity structure of fixed income investments?

The unresolved issues are important. Nevertheless, even at the current state of development, the geometric mean strategy offers useful guidance to investment managers in the insurance industry. As a simple and mathematically tractable decision rule in a multiperiod framework, the model serves well many of the functions of portfolio selection models outlined above. Further research should enhance the practical appeal and usefulness of the geometric mean approach to modeling portfolio selection in life insurance companies.

6

Equity Real Estate Investments of Life Insurance Companies

By Howard H. Stevenson*

Equity real estate investments of life insurance companies have generated discussion in the trade press which is far out of proportion to their actual economic importance. However, in many cases these investments have provided the opportunity for significant returns to the insurance companies which have made them. These returns have been achieved without significantly higher risk exposure than with high loan-to-cost mortgages. This chapter examines four principal areas: (1) the importance to the real estate industry and life insurance companies of equity real estate investments, (2) the reasoning underlying real estate equity investment by life insurance companies, (3) current economic, social, and legal pressures affecting investment policies, and (4) an outlook for the future.

THE ROLE OF LIFE INSURANCE COMPANIES IN THE REAL ESTATE MARKET

The declining importance of life insurance companies as sources of funds in the U.S. money and capital markets has affected their participation in the real estate sector.[1] Nevertheless, the companies

* Howard H. Stevenson is associate professor of business administration at Harvard University.

[1] The overall decline in the role of life insurers is documented in J. David Cummins and Steven N. Weisbart, "The Role of Insurance in the United States Economy," *CPCU Annals,* vol. 29, no. 2 (June 1976), pp. 123–40.

continue to represent one of the major sources of funds for that sector. This development is exemplified by the relationship between the funds supplied by life insurers to the real estate market and the value of private investment in new structures. As shown in Table 6.1,

TABLE 6.1
Life Insurance Companies as Sources of Real Estate Funds

| Year | Value of New Private Construction (billions) | Insurance Company Acquisitions | | Percent* |
		Mortgages (billions)	Real Estate (billions)	
1955	$ 34.8	$ 6.614	$0.371	20.1%
1965	51.7	11.137	0.448	22.4
1970	66.8	7.181	0.859	12.0
1971	80.1	7.573	1.035	10.7
1972	93.9	8.696	0.976	10.3
1973	105.4	11.463	1.177	12.0
1974	100.2	11.339	1.294	12.6
1975	93.0	9.595	2.115	12.6

* Insurance company mortgage and real estate acquisitions as a percent of the value of new construction put in place.

Source: The value of new construction put in place is from the *Statistical Abstract of the U.S.: 1976,* while the life insurance company data are from the *Life Insurance Fact Book—1976.*

the life insurance industry's mortgage and real estate investments amounted to 20.1 percent of the value of private construction put in place in 1955. The aggregate participation of the life insurance industry in the financing of new construction decreased in importance, however, as the percentage declined to 10.3 percent by 1972. Thereafter, the industry's relative contribution increased slightly, reaching 12.6 percent in 1974 and 1975. Thus, although the absolute amount invested by life insurers in the real estate markets has increased, their participation has declined somewhat in importance relative to that of other financial institutions.[2]

As shown in Chapter 3, mortgages have represented a declining share of the net asset acquisitions of life insurance companies, especially during the past ten years.[3] Equity real estate acquisitions, on the other hand, declined somewhat in relative terms during the 1960s but rebounded in the early 1970s to a level roughly equivalent to that achieved during the 1950s. A possible trend toward a more prominent

---

[2] The sources of mortgage funds after 1965 are presented in Chapter 3, Table 3.6.

[3] *Supra,* p. 67.

TABLE 6.2
Equity Real Estate Investments as a Percentage of Net Investable
Funds of Life Insurance Companies

Period	Net Equity Real Estate Purchases (millions)	Net Investable Funds (millions)	Real Estate as Percent of Total
1950–1954	$ 853	$19,752	4.3%
1955–1959	1,353	27,673	4.9
1960–1964	877	33,298	2.6
1965–1969	1,384	41,053	3.4
1970–1974	2,419	57,104	4.2
1975	1,290	24,350	5.3

Note: Net investable funds are defined as net acquisitions of financial assets less net policy loans.

Source: *Life Insurance Fact Book,* various years.

role for equity real estate investments is evidenced by the fact that acquisitions in 1975 were more than 50 percent as large as those during the entire five-year period 1970–1974. These developments are shown in Table 6.2. As a percentage of the total asset holdings of life insurance companies, real estate has remained virtually constant at about 3 percent during the past two decades.[4] However, at the end of 1975 real estate holdings stood at 3.3 percent of the total, the highest level in at least 25 years.

It is probably too soon to tell whether the increased life insurance company activity in the equity real estate investment field is merely transitory or whether it represents a more permanent shift in company investment behavior. However, little doubt exists that considerable change has occurred in the outlook of the life insurance companies with regard to equity holdings in real estate. The remainder of this chapter discusses some of the forces which have contributed to these changing attitudes.

THE RATIONALE UNDERLYING REAL ESTATE EQUITY INVESTMENTS

Types of Real Estate Investments

Real estate equity investments can be structured in a variety of ways. In general, they can be placed on a continuum with respect to

---

[4] *Life Insurance Fact Book—1976* (New York: American Council of Life Insurance, 1976), p. 64.

the managerial input necessary. The accompanying diagram illustrates this continuum:

Increasing Managerial Involvement

The continuum bears some but not a complete relationship to the risk spectrum of properties. It is readily apparent that differing properties and differing deal structures affect the risk level of the equity investment in a substantial way. The aggregate data reported for equity investments encompass all types of investments, including home office facilities. It is dangerous, therefore, to speak categorically about the issue of life insurance company equity investments.

As an illustration of the complexity of the problem, the real estate equity portfolio of one major insurance company is presented in Table 6.3. Although this portfolio should not be considered typical, it

TABLE 6.3
Real Estate Equity Holdings of a Large Life Insurance Company

Type of Investment	Amount Held (millions)	Percent of Total
Home office facilities	$ 15	11.5%
Development projects	20	15.3
Residential housing projects	19	14.5
Warehouse and industrial properties	15	11.5
Sale and leasebacks with market rate renewal provisions	35	26.7
Sale and leasebacks with below market purchase and/or renewal options	20	15.3
Land leases	7	5.3
Total	$131	

Note: Percentages do not add to 100 due to rounding.

does illustrate the difficulty which arises in attempts to categorize equity real estate investments. Each of these investments involves different management problems and different opportunities and risks.

This breadth of investments is not uncommon. A survey of 48 insurance companies conducted in 1972 by McKinsey & Co. showed participation in a wide range of projects. Some of the key results of this survey are presented in Figure 6.1. According to the figure, a

FIGURE 6.1

Life Insurance Company Participation in Real Estate Development Projects

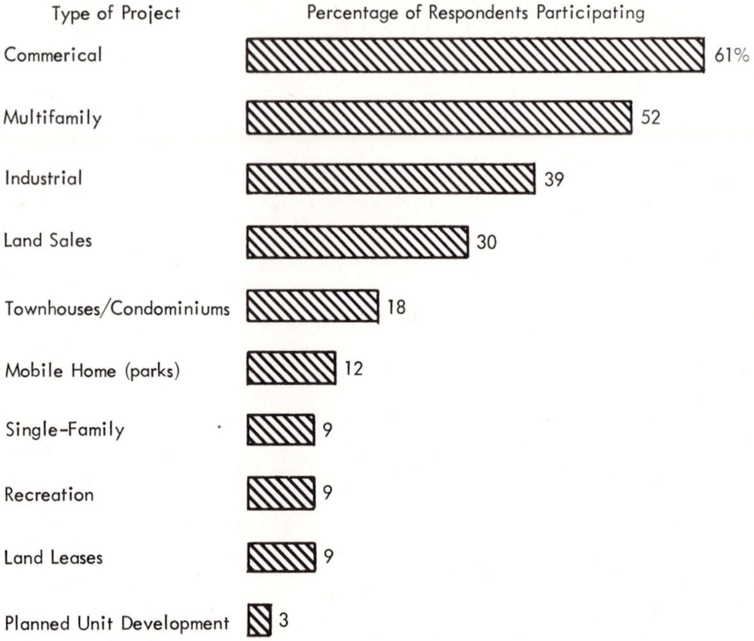

Type of Project	Percentage of Respondents Participating
Commerical	61%
Multifamily	52
Industrial	39
Land Sales	30
Townhouses/Condominiums	18
Mobile Home (parks)	12
Single-Family	9
Recreation	9
Land Leases	9
Planned Unit Development	3

Source: Peter Braun, *The Future of Insurance Companies in Real Estate Development* (New York: McKinsey & Co., 1972).

majority of the respondents participated in commercial and multi-family projects, while 30 percent or more were involved in land sales and industrial developments. Smaller numbers of respondents were involved in townhouse and condominium developments, mobile home parks, land leases, and other activities.

The McKinsey survey also showed that involvement in equity interests takes place through a wide variety of legal forms. The following methods of participation are utilized:[5]

Form of Participation	Percentage of Respondents Using Forms
Single project joint venture	88%
Profit participation on loan	73
Minority ownership of development corporation	33
Majority ownership of development corporation	24

[5] Peter Braun, *The Future of Insurance Companies in Real Estate Development* (New York: McKinsey & Co., 1972), p. 9.

The nature of the form of ownership often significantly affects the financial reporting requirements, the degree of management intervention, and the willingness of other investors to provide assistance when problems arise. The diversity of ownership terms can itself hamper the ability of life insurance companies to manage their investments.

Characteristics of Real Estate Equity Investments

Real estate equity investments have certain characteristics which distinguish them from other types of equity investments. Fundamentally, these relate to the characteristics of the real estate product itself. Some of the most important of these characteristics are the following:

Physical	Immovable
	Unique or Rarely Repeated
	Long Product Life
	Complex, Large Size
	Multiple Markets
	Locally Regulated
Financial	Capital Intensive
	Pricing Unique to Particular Circumstances (Location, Time, Market Conditions)
	Federally Influenced
Human	Politically Visible—Multiple Levels of Regulation
	Multifunctional Skills Required
	Transaction-Oriented, Requiring Negotiation
	Easy Entry

As noted below, the importance of some of these product characteristics has been increased by the observable trends of the past five years. The characteristics require that management understand the dynamics affecting the investment components.

The Components of the Investment Decision Process

Real estate equity investment decisions must take into account the characteristics identified above. Each equity investment decision must reflect an evaluation of the interaction of the physical, the financial, and the human components of the product. These components are affected by trends and cycles such as the following:

Consumerism
Environmental Concern
No-Growth Pressures
Rising Cost of Capital
Inflating Operating Expenses
Capital Market Pressures
Cyclical Economic Environments
Increasing Public Sector Involvement

These factors have affected some of the basic assumptions upon which earlier real estate investments were based and have influenced both the market value and the current viability of prior investments.

As previously noted, every real estate investment decision ultimately involves three components: the property, the financial deal, and the people. The term *property* refers to the product and its market, while *deal* refers to the financial investments and their returns. In this context, *people* means the participants in the transaction. As illustrated in the accompanying diagram, it is only when the three elements interface and are in balance that a project or transaction should proceed. Understanding the interactive nature of the problem is the key to a prudent and remunerative equity investment.

It is to be noted that only small portions of the circles actually intersect. Among all of the possible projects, many must be analyzed in order to determine those which are ultimately feasible. Differing estimates of value, different access to capital, and differing personal or organizational objectives all contribute to the complexity of the analytical process.

There are some real estate investments within insurance company portfolios in which there is no need to base the transaction upon all three elements. For example, even today, a traditional long-term, net lease to General Motors is dependent only on the deal and the involved parties. More and more, however, the real estate investor in both equity and debt instruments must be concernd about the totality of the project.

With the rapid changes occurring in monetary policies and, therefore, in the financial health of various organizations, more attention is being devoted to an understanding of all aspects of each project. Once stable assumptions may be undermined by changes. The best analysis of an equity investment is an inductive process leading to a comprehensive strategy. Such a process is designed to do the following:

1. To identify the critical elements of the problem and the relationships among them.
2. To ask questions that will lead to more informed decision making.
3. To facilitate consistent implementation of the decision-making procedures.
4. To assist in the recognition of change and the understanding of its significance.
5. To permit constant evaluation and reformulation of the investment and its management based upon these changes.

Such an analytical methodology is based upon a series of questions relating to the property, the deal, and the people. Table 6.4 presents one such set of key questions.

It is clear that the answer to each of the questions listed in the table involves more than the kind of analysis which can simply be summed up to a single numerical result. The individual answers involve judgment and the weighing of conflicting information. Considering the individual questions, it is clear that the interchange of views among talented functional specialists is required in order to obtain meaningful answers for complex projects. One need only consider those judgments which go into deciding the use of a particular land parcel to appreciate the complexity of the analytical process. True equity investment in real estate is management intensive. For this reason, many of the life insurance equity investments have been structured with deals which reduce the management involvement.

Legal Considerations

In a few specific instances, legal constraints may limit the investment of life insurance companies in real estate equities. In general, however, investments to date fall far short of the legally allowed limits. New York law currently permits insurance companies to invest up to 10 percent of their admitted assets in real estate. Companies are

TABLE 6.4
Conceptual Framework for Real Estate Equity Investment Analysis

PROPERTY	DEAL	PEOPLE
What are the present and potential uses for the property considering?	What are the sources of funds?	Who are the people involved and affected?
Physical conditions Locational characteristics Market implications of demand, competition, and comparable projects Regulatory controls and conditions of use	Adequacy Reliability Timing Cost	What are their objectives? How do they interrelate?
	In what legal form will the property be held?	What are their resources?
What are the cash operating projections over time?	What are the income tax consequences?	Skills Experience Contacts Finances Organizational capabilities Time horizons
What does one need to know? How accurate are the numbers?	What are the financial benefits, for whom, and when realized?	
What are the capital costs?	Cash flow from operations Income taxes Capital appreciation	How much of each resource will they commit and for how long?
When will they be paid? How does the capitalized value of one income stream relate to the capital cost?	How do the values of these returns compare with the investment?	
	Amount Timing Risk	

STRATEGY FOR IMPLEMENTATION

What are the key decisions which must be made?

Price, terms, contractual conditions
Negotiating tactics
Organizational and operational policies

On what key assumptions does the transaction rest?

The Environment
The Property
The Deal
The People

permitted to invest an additional 10 percent to provide housing "for persons of low and moderate income and to assist in relieving the housing situation."[6] The laws of other states impose similar restrictions.[7]

---

[6] Sec. 81 and sec. 84, New York Insurance Code.

[7] Lawrence D. Jones, *Investment Policies of Life Insurance Companies* (Boston: Division of Research, Graduate School of Business Administration, Harvard University, 1968), p. 92.

Effect of Equity Investment Definition. One of the impacts of the legislative rules and regulations has been the lack of differentiation among the risk levels associated with various types of real estate equity investments. Because of the definitional problems, certain very secure investments may be precluded. In many cases, there is considerably greater cash flow coverage of an equity investment than there is of mortgage debt. The accompanying example illustrates this point:

Mortgage
Net operating income	$ 1,000,000
Debt service	750,000
Before tax cash flow	250,000
Loan	7,500,000
Value	10,000,000
Coverage ratio	1.33

Unsubordinated ground lease
Net operating income	$ 1,000,000
Lease payment	150,000
Leasehold mortgage payment	750,000
Before tax cash flow	100,000
Leasehold coverage ratio	6.67

Thus, the rules do not reflect differential risk. They reflect categorical assessments relating to form of ownership rather than economic risk/reward considerations inherent in the property and the financial returns.

Even in situations where the risk/reward ratio is less obvious than the above, there are serious problems of evaluating risks. In many cases, the so-called safe first mortgage investments represent 95 percent or more of cost. They are deemed safe since the required debt service represents only 75 percent of net operating income. A marginal investment of an additional 5 to 15 percent would purchase the totality of the flows. Such equity investments are deemed risky simply because of the potential variability, not because there is a significantly greater inherent probability that income will not be earned nor principal repaid. The confusion of form of ownership with economic risk is one of the most fundamental errors in the economic analysis of real property equity investments.

Valuation. Valuation rules also affect the benefits to be derived from real estate equity ownership. Most states require systematic writedown of equity values at a rate which exceeds either tax-based or true economic depreciation. Such "conservative" rules impose a penalty upon real estate equity ownership. There are proposals such as one made recently in Massachusetts to allow additional flexibility in the book value writedowns. Life insurance companies would not be forced to depreciate properties for book purposes at an unrealistically rapid rate. Proponents of such changes argue that they would cause the balance sheet valuations to reflect economic substance more accurately. As noted below, the impact of valuation procedures on reported earnings results is an important drawback to equity real estate investment.

Taxation. A final legal consideration in real property equity ownership is that of taxation. The history of the Federal income tax rate of life insurance companies has been highly variable.[8] Until 1959, the willingness of life insurance companies to make real estate equity investments was adversely affected by the companies' low effective marginal tax rate. The Life Insurance Company Income Tax Act of 1959 was designed to alter this situation by imposing the standard corporate tax rate on an amount which is essentially a function of underwriting and loading gains and the company's share of net investment income.[9]

The impact of the 1959 legislation has been to raise the consciousness of the life insurance companies regarding Federal taxation. Each company is subject to a different degree of taxability based upon its operating history. The net effect, however, is that although rates have been raised, life insurance companies still calculate taxes at rates substantially below the standard corporate rate. Consequently, the economic value of tax shelters for insurance companies is less than for an individual or corporation taxed at a higher rate. Thus, the life insurance companies may be competing at a slight disadvantage for properties in which tax shelter considerations are paramount.

Economic Considerations

The traditional economic bases underlying real estate equity investment have been the return available, fulfillment of social purposes, and the operational needs of the institution. Each of these has led to equity real estate investment decisions, and each has brought about investment in different kinds of properties with differing deal structures.

Expectations of High Return. The fundamental motivation un-

---

[8] Ibid., p. 145.

[9] Dan M. McGill, *Life Insurance,* rev. ed. (Homewood, Ill.: Richard D. Irwin, 1967), p. 912.

derlying equity investment in real estate has been a search for higher return. The belief developed that real estate owners had achieved substantial returns due to the willingness of the insurance industry and other groups to provide high loan-to-cost ratio financing. The belief that the returns were substantial was confirmed by at least three published studies. David, Hayes and Harlan, and Wendt and Wong all cite high achieved returns in the field.[10] Returns such as those cited by David in the 21 to 29 percent range attracted the interest of portfolio managers seeking additional return. Private studies by individual life insurance companies reportedly verified the substantial additional return available through equity investment.

The search for additional return was related to three different types of investments. The first type, the sale and leaseback, has been in use since the initial liberalization of the laws regarding insurance company equity holdings. When New York State first authorized investment in commercial and industrial property in 1946, the insurance companies began to use this financing technique. Under this procedure, a property owner sells the property to an insurance company and leases it back with a lease which would both amortize the purchase price and pay a return.

This so-called old style sale and leaseback has two key characteristics. First, it is a credit transaction allowing a high loan-to-value ratio loan to a particularly creditworthy client. The equity nature of the investment circumvents legal loan-to-value restrictions and allows receipt of additional interest over and above what a mortgage on the same property to the same owner would allow. Secondly, the residual value of the property tends to remain with the original owner or lessee, either through bargain repurchase options or bargain rents upon lease renewal. This type of real estate equity transaction is based upon credit with little concern for the underlying real estate. The nominal owner, the insurance company, gives up most of the benefits of ownership in favor of security.

The second type of transaction is the equity participation (equity kicker). Such features have been written into many income property mortgages as a means of permitting the lender to gain some of the benefits of the value being created by the mortgage transaction. The

---

[10] Phillip David, "An Analysis of Returns and Risks Provided by Major Types of Investment and Their Efficient Combinations" (Ph.D. diss., Harvard University, 1963); Samuel L. Hayes, III, and Leonard M. Harlan, "Real Estate as a Corporate Investment," *Harvard Business Review* (July–August 1967); and P. F. Wendt and S. N. Wong, "Investment Performance: Common Stocks versus Apartment Houses," *Journal of Finance* (December 1975).

lender writes a normal mortgage but receives additional interest, which is a function of gross rent, net income, or other defined measures. Such features also provide a means for lowering the capitalization rate in order to maintain economic feasibility. Equity kickers became important in the latter half of the 1960s, peaked in 1970, and have fallen off sharply in more recent periods.[11]

The problems of such loans have been thoroughly researched in works by Mundy and Piper.[12] In general, they conclude that these "equity investments" are primarily adjuncts to mortgage lending with the additional return treated as a bonus available because of unusual market conditions. During the equity kicker boom periods, the expectation was that such features would boost returns from 50 to 150 basis points over similar non-participatory loans.

The third form of equity investment is the true equity real estate investment in which the insurance company becomes either the sole owner or a joint venture partner. This type of equity investment is discussed in more detail below. Generally, however, the results have not lived up to the hopes and expectations which were established at the outset of the equity investment programs. The reasons are manifold and in many cases external to the management and operational strategies of the life insurance companies involved.

Socially Oriented Investments. During the post-World War II period, the major life insurance companies occasionally have been confronted with political suggestions that they make real estate investments to support social purposes. As noted above, the insurance laws of several states treat housing as a special class of real estate equity investment in order to attract life insurance funds to the housing market. In spite of these incentives, housing has never represented a very large proportion of the investments of life insurance companies.[13]

A variety of reasons for this situation have been cited. Even though explicit statutory authority for such investment exists, significant housing investment activity is unlikely to be undertaken in the absence of specific legislative requirements. The reasons cited are manifold, but they are largely unrelated to the prospective return. Life insurance companies have found housing investments unat-

---

[11] *Supra*, Chapter 3, p. 77.

[12] Jefferson G. Mundy, "Participation Mortgage Loans: Origins, Types and Performance" (Ph.D. diss., University of Texas, 1971); and Thomas B. Piper, "Income Participations on Mortgage Loans by Major Financial Institutions," unpublished working paper, Harvard University, February 1975.

[13] Jones, *Investment Policies*, p. 118.

tractive for two primary reasons. First, residential properties are extremely management intensive—a characteristic which is avoided by many insurance company decision makers. Secondly, the institutional owner is perceived to be politically vulnerable.

A second instance of socially based real estate investment resulted from the concern for the central cities in the late 1960s. Proposals were seriously advanced in Congress that a fixed portion of life insurance company assets be invested in central city locations. Some companies responded voluntarily with highly publicized commitments in order to fend off proposed legislative action. Others participated willingly as part of urban renewal ventures providing for headquarters and branch location space. In general, however, there is little evidence that this "socially responsible" investment policy movement had a dramatic effect on the equity investment posture. Aside from home office facilities, most central city equity investments came about largely as a result of debt infusions.

Operational Needs of the Company. The companies' own operational facilities have always represented a significant component of their real estate equity investment portfolios. In the early period of regulation, the development of assets for the company's own use was deemed by regulators to be a potential loophole which might permit unbridled speculation. Such fears have proven unfounded. Historically, company facilities have accounted for approximately 20 to 30 percent of the real estate equity holdings of life insurance companies.[14] As of 1975, 22 percent of life insurers' real estate equity investments were in home and branch office facilities.[15]

Some regulatory and political bodies have expressed concern about the "edifice complex" regarding company-used facilities. As with banks and other financial institutions, there is a long history showing that companies are extremely competitive with respect to visible investment in facilities.[16] Home and regional offices proliferate. Such

---

[14] Ibid.

[15] *Life Insurance Fact Book—1976*, p. 80.

[16] In a recent survey of the factors affecting the locational decision for regional home office facilities of major insurers, 25 percent of the responding companies rated the visibility of the office facility as "very important" when deciding on a site while 75 percent rated this factor "somewhat important." None of the respondents indicated that visibility was "not important." However, visibility was outranked by the quality of the clerical labor market and the "projected economic growth and development of the locality" as a determining factor in the site selection process. J. David Cummins and Douglas G. Olson, "Insurance Administrative Facilities in the District of Columbia: Attraction, Retention, and Impact" (Report presented to the Department of Insurance, Government of the District of Columbia, March 18, 1973), pp. 124–25.

investments have in many cases served extremely valuable social purposes in maintaining or restoring the vitality of downtown areas such as Hartford and Boston and in anchoring other larger scale renewal such as Chicago's. They have in many cases been at extraordinarily high cost when measured in terms of competitive speculative space. Such costs may be justified on the basis of long-term investment value, company image, or simply unanticipated cost overruns. The impact upon sales and hiring capacity is largely unmeasured.

Summary

The fundamental rationale for real estate equity investments is based upon a series of strategic decisions. Over the past two decades, there has been increasing understanding of the need to balance the "property," "deal," and "people" aspects of an investment. However, the basic motivations remain the same—increased investment income, visibility, socially responsible civic performance, and the organization's own needs. As shown below, these objectives have often been frustrated by uncontrollable events and organizational difficulties.

PRESSURES AFFECTING LIFE INSURANCE COMPANIES' REAL ESTATE EQUITY INVESTMENTS

As noted previously, the environment in which real estate equity investment decisions are being made is changing rapidly. Such changes are affecting the relative balance of risk and reward available from debt and equity investments. Given the importance of the real estate industry to the investment posture of the life insurance companies and the importance of the life insurance companies' investments to the real estate industry, some adaptations seem likely to occur. This section reviews some of the critical changes which are occurring and some of the tentative responses identified. The changes have been both internal and external to the life insurance industry.

External Pressures

Pressures beyond the control or influence of life insurance company management have significantly affected the structure and returns of the companies' real estate investments. These changes can be categorized into three primary areas—economic, product, and competition.

Economic Pressures. The post-World War II decades have witnessed two major phases—a 23-year period of unparalleled stability and growth and the post-1968 period of rapid change and turmoil. The latter period has caused particular concern because of its fluctuating monetary policies, inflation, and erratic interest rates.

Fluctuating monetary policies have had a two-fold impact upon the real estate equity investment policies of life insurance companies. First, there is some evidence that the companies have become less willing to make the long-term commitments required in both the real estate mortgage and equity markets. The accompanying tabulation shows the recent history of short-term investments as a percentage of total insurance company investment acquisitions:[17]

Year	Percent Short-Term
1970	61.7%
1971	59.5
1972	62.2
1973	67.2
1974	69.7
1975	67.9

Such behavior is consistent with the need to generate additional liquidity in order to meet high policy loan demands. These demands have reached levels not seen since the depression years. In addition, this phenomenon is responding to unprecedented short-term interest rates, which have provided as much as a 250 basis point positive spread over long mortgage rates and a 100 point spread over expected initial yields on equity investments.

The second effect of the shifting monetary policies has been a growth in the need for funds in the real estate business. This need has not been met by the life insurance companies, since in most cases they have been affected in the same cyclical fashion as other financial intermediaries. Such demands, however, have provided opportunities for shifting the balance among equity and debt real estate investments.

One vice president of real estate for a major life insurance company has noted that "unusual conditions provide unusual opportunity." Even though the absolute dollar investments of his company reflected the changing monetary fortunes of the economy, he shifted the equity/debt mix to improve the company's yields. Table 6.5

---

[17] *Life Insurance Fact Book—1976*, p. 69.

TABLE 6.5
Equity and Mortgage Real Estate Commitments of a
Major Life Insurance Company

Year	Ratio of Equity to Mortgage Commitments	Index of Total Value of Real Estate Commitments
1968	0.34	100
1969	0.48	100
1970	0.18	25
1971	0.07	111
1972	0.22	153
1973	0.11	165
1974	0.54	92
1975	0.59	136
1976	0.09	451

Source: Data supplied to the author. The company has requested anonymity.

shows this shifting balance for nine recent years. The table reveals that when money was readily available or extremely tight, equity commitments were not made. In periods of moderate shortage, however, the conditions were such that both funds and competitive opportunities were available.

The second external economic pressure which has affected real estate equity investment decisions has been the recent incidence of inflationary price increases in construction and operating costs. These have resulted in concern both for the initial construction economics of a project and for the long-run viability of projects underwritten either from a debt or an equity position. The life insurance industry's traditional role as a long-term lender or a purchaser of completed projects has mitigated some of the risks. However, the magnitude of recent inflationary pressures has seriously affected the entire development and ownership role. Figure 6.2 illustrates the problem. The figure shows the relationship between the owner's internal rate of return on investment and the cost per square foot of a building. Note the drastic impact of rising costs, even though financing is assumed to be equal to 90 percent of total cost.

Another major concern is the impact of continued high rates of inflation on the ability of the ultimate consumer to afford the cost increases, which must be passed along either through escalation clauses or price increases. If the landlord must bear the cost increases, the property becomes uneconomic. If they are borne by the tenant, they may impair the tenant's economic position. As Table 6.6 shows, the impact of continued cost escalation over a sustained period can be

FIGURE 6.2
Relationship of Return on Investment to Total Cost per Square Foot

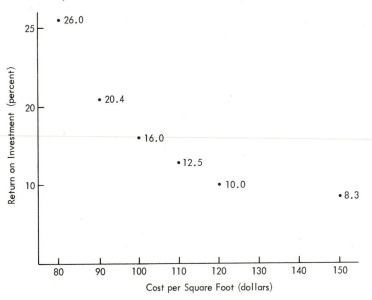

Note: The following assumptions have been made to derive the curve shown in the figure: rentals = $13 per square foot, rental increase = 3 percent per annum, expenses = $3.25 per square foot, expense increase = 6 percent per annum, interest expense = 9 percent, term of loan = 360 months, depreciable life = 45 years, rate of depreciation = 150 percent declining balance, total cost = $100 per square foot, loan-to-cost ratio = 90 percent, sales price = $200 per square foot, time of sale = 50 years, and tax rate = 50 percent of net taxable income.

very large in relationship to the initial contract rent of a project. In this case, the initial rent is $8 per square foot. If inflation is 6 percent per annum and inflation-induced cost increases are passed along to the tenant, his rent would increase by 66 percent in 20 years. If the inflation rate is 9 percent, the rent increase would be 138 percent in 20 years and 16 percent in the first 5 years. Double-digit inflation, of course, would lead to even larger rent increases.

Interest rate changes have also undermined the economic viability of the projects and increased the need for equity. The combination of increased construction costs and higher interest rates has reduced the number of feasible projects substantially. Table 6.7 shows the impact upon rentals of these two factors. The increase in interest rates also affects the capitalization rates used to value buildings and thus creates pressure for additional equity infusions. Table 6.8 illustrates the impact of increasing capitalization rates.

TABLE 6.6
Incremental Cost to Tenant of Inflation-Induced Increases in
Operating Expenses

Rate of Expense	Incremental Cost of Escalation after			
Escalation	5 Years	10 Years	15 Years	20 Years
3%	$0.38	$0.83	$ 1.34	$ 1.93
6	0.81	1.90	3.35	5.30
9	1.29	3.28	6.34	11.05
12	1.83	5.05	10.74	20.75
15	2.43	7.31	17.13	36.88

Note: The figures in the table are based on initial operating expenses of $2.40 per square foot. The initial rent for the project is assumed to be $8 per square foot.

TABLE 6.7
Rental Rates Required to Cover Capital Charges

Building Cost	Rental Rate If Interest Rate Is		
per Square Foot	5.0%	7.5%	10.0%
$ 40	$2.58	$3.36	$ 4.21
60	3.87	5.03	6.32
80	5.15	6.71	8.42
100	6.44	8.39	10.53

Note: The figures in the table are derived on the assumption of 30-year level payments. Rental rates are in dollars per square foot.

TABLE 6.8
Effect of the Capitalization Rate on the Equity Requirement for a
Building Which Costs $36 Million

Capitalization Rate	Net Operating Income Stream	Value	75% Loan	Equity Required
8%	$4.0	$50.0	$37.0	(1.5)
10	4.0	40.0	30.0	6.0
12	4.0	33.3	25.0	11.0

Note: All dollar values are in millions.

The overall effect of the economic changes occurring in the industry apparently has been to increase the life insurance company management's perception of risk. Certainly, there has been additional economic risk created, but new opportunities also have arisen.

Product Pressures. Many of the life insurance companies which chose to undertake "new style" real estate equity investments entered into ventures where their financial strength allowed them to achieve a competitive advantage. Such ventures were often typified both by their large scale and by their long time horizons. The arguments underlying the choice of such projects were manifold. Among those most often used were that the competitive pressures would be less, the company's negotiating strength would be greater, its staying power could guarantee success, and the project would itself create a positive public image and generate wide-ranging value increases.

The choice of the large-scale project has had drastic and in many cases negative effects upon the success of such investments. Many of the trends identified earlier have mitigated against the success of such projects. Consumerism, environmentalism, no-growth pressures, and increasing public sector involvement have reduced management flexibility with regard to working out the problems that have arisen. In fact, they have created problems where none previously existed. In many cases, the long time horizons of the projects have left the ventures exposed to inflationary and political pressures over an extended period.

A second and more subtle effect of long time horizons is the compounding effect on required net income as capital return objectives have risen. In order to achieve high rates of return, starting in the future, the actual cash returns on present dollars invested must be very high. Table 6.9 shows the net income which must be received

TABLE 6.9
Annual Net Income Required for 60 Years to Earn a Specified Rate of Return on an Investment of $1 Million

Desired Rate of Return	Income Required If Return Begins in			
	0 Years	3 Years	6 Years	9 Years
5.0%	$ 52,828	$ 61,155	$ 70,795	$ 81,954
7.5	75,991	94,404	117,278	145,694
10.0	100,330	133,539	177,740	236,572
12.5	125,107	178,130	253,627	361,121
15.0	150,034	228,183	347,038	527,802

Note: The returns are assumed to begin at the specified durations and to continue for 60 years thereafter.

annually for 60 years, starting a given number of years in the future, in order to provide the specified rate of return on $1 million invested currently. As the time horizon lengthens and rates of return increase, there are dramatic effects on the required net income. For example, increasing the desired rate of return from 10 to 12.5 percent for a three-year time horizon leads to a 33 percent increase in the net income requirement. Even without drastic shifts in the economic environment, the risk factor involved in long-term development is quite substantial.

The response of many life insurance companies has been to retrench from major project development joint ventures. They have tended to learn from some bitter experiences such as Connecticut General's writeoff of a substantial investment in the new town of Columbia, Maryland. The preferred project now appears to be more simple, easily analyzed, and consumer-oriented.

Competitive Pressures. Two major competitive factors emerged in the early years of the 1970s. Significant pressure on the insurance companies to provide long-term residential mortgages was relieved by the creation of the Government National Mortgage Association (Ginnie Mae), the Federal National Mortgage Association (Fannie Mae), and state housing finance agency mortgage markets. Although these governmental agencies do not serve identical functions, they provide another means of access to the long-term capital markets by those engaged in the residential housing markets.

The other significant factor in the real estate capital market was the emergence of the Real Estate Investment Trust (REIT) industry.[18] Some of the major life insurance companies sponsored long-term–oriented REITs. These trusts provided direct access to the equity market for the insurance company management teams. They provided a cooperative/competitive source of investment funds and enabled the sponsoring insurance companies to extend their range of activities.

Most importantly, however, the emergence of the REITs had a negative effect on the underwriting standards applied to new project development. During the period 1969–1972, almost $21 billion dollars was put into the REIT industry through equity investment and debt capital. During this period, the principal objective of many of the trusts was to expand their asset bases. In order to do this quickly, the management of the trusts sought out construction loans without requiring the existence of take-out permanent financing. Although this was profitable in the short-term, many of the projects so financed could not meet the more stringent underwriting tests applied by the long-term lenders such as life insurance companies.

In the parlance of the analytical scheme discussed earlier, for these REITs the deal was everything. Little attention was paid to the long-run viability of the projects. Such "stupid" competition induced a competitive response on the part of many banks. The result was mas-

---

[18] REITs are discussed in more detail in Chapter 7.

sive overbuilding. The overbuilding in some areas was on such a scale that it affected both new construction and the existing seasoned properties.

Thus, the combination of fluctuating monetary conditions, changing interest rates, the product choice, and the disastrous competitive situation have created an unstable environment for the equity real estate investor. As noted in the next section, such an environment is hardly conducive to increased investment activity on the part of an industry with a long history of fiduciary conservatism.

Internal Pressures

At the same time that the external environment was changing the investment posture of insurance companies, there were some internal forces at work as well. These were perhaps more simple but nonetheless have served to reduce the emphasis which might otherwise have been placed upon equity real estate investment. The two primary areas of concern were the economic measurement system used by the companies and the managerial requirements of real estate equity investment. Of specific concern to certain life insurance companies as well was the broadening of the services which the companies were attempting to offer. Term insurance, pension fund management, and variable annuities all posed new requirements.

Performance Measures. When investing in equity real estate, life insurance companies face the same problems as public real estate companies. Due to accounting conventions and valuation practices, the reported earnings performance of equity investments suffers by comparison with the available alternatives. In many cases, the discounted present values of the cash flow streams for real estate equities have been superior to those of other potential investments. In the early years, however, a real estate equity investment shows low accounting returns compared to the easily measurable performance of the stock market. Charges for depreciation reduce reported earnings even though they improve the cash flow situation.

As the investment performance of life insurance companies has come under increasing public scrutiny, management has been less willing to suffer short-term penalties for the potential of greater future benefits. When equity investments have been made, there has been a tendency to structure them with competitive base rate features. Examples of such "modern equity investments" include the subordinated land lease, the short-term sale and leaseback, the mortgage-based joint venture, and in some unfortunate cases the subordinated financing of development companies. The common characteristic of these "modern" techniques is a competitive coupon rate. Very little is sacrificed to obtain long-term or residual benefits. In spite of inflationary fears, competitive pressures have induced more short-term responses.

Those institutions which have taken the longer point of view have not necessarily been rewarded for their perceptive outlook. When life insurance companies have become involved in true joint ventures, they have in many cases suffered from the same serious rigors of the market which have affected the majority of other independent developers. The period 1970–1975 has not been particularly rewarding to institutions which have attempted to parlay a long time horizon into a long-term, large-scale return. Lack of stable monetary conditions, overbuilding by "stupid" competition, and inflationary ravages have not respected good intentions and good strategies.

An additional aspect of the economic performance of real estate equities is that foreclosed properties from the mortgage portfolios are often put into the equity portfolio at cost. Any losses then accrue to the equity portfolio, further heightening equity real estate risk perceptions even though the actual loss occurred in the mortgage underwriting or management process.

Management Considerations. As noted previously, the management of equity real estate investments is not a single, undifferentiated problem. Different types of investments require very different levels of management involvement. One of the most critical strategic decisions regarding equity real estate investment is the level of management involvement which will be tolerated. Among the most critical factors to be considered with respect to the management problems are the form of the organization involved and the capacity to develop and retain skilled management.

The decision with respect to the form of organization has two dimensions—the activities to be undertaken and the corporate or legal form in which those functions are to be carried out. The first decision is the more critical since it represents a strategic choice as to the product/market strategy for the firm's entry into the real estate equity investment business. Some firms have taken the position that even a $200 million portfolio imposes major constraints. Starting with the need to be geographically diversified, they find that insufficient concentration exists to justify development of on-site management expertise. Based upon this judgment, the choice is made to restrict investment to properties which are not management intensive. Thus, only properties with relatively long leases and minimal maintenance requirements are deemed to be acceptable investment possibilities. In a few cases, a quasi-equity joint venture position has been taken by such firms, but with the expectation that all management input will come from the joint venture partner.

When the companies have sought to be actively involved in the development process, a wider variety of approaches has been used. As indicated in Figure 6.3, consolidated and unconsolidated subsid-

FIGURE 6.3
Approaches Used to Organize Real Estate Development Activities

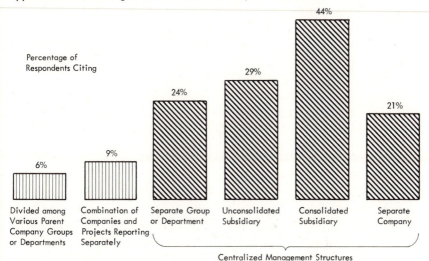

Source: Peter Braun, *The Future of Insurance Companies in Real Estate Development* (New York: McKinsey & Co., 1972).

iaries, separate groups or departments, and separate companies are among the more common devices that have been adopted. To date, little research has been reported on the comparative results of these various approaches to the management of the development activities within life insurance companies.

Acquiring and retaining skilled management in real estate equity investment has been a critical problem during the last five years. The emergence of the REIT industry and the publicly held real estate development companies during the last half of the 1960s was a major factor in the employment market. The life insurance companies were a readily identifiable target for management recruiters. Although one senior executive has commented that "we didn't lose many we wanted to keep," the problem of turnover was deemed by some to be significant.

Turnover has been more frequent among project and middle management than at the top management level. Seventy-four percent of the companies responding to the McKinsey survey indicated that top management turnover was "low," while 58 and 57 percent, respectively, said that turnover rates among middle and project management were low.[19] "High" turnover among top management was reported by 17 percent of the companies, but at the project and middle management levels 24 and 21 percent, respectively, indicated that turnover was high.[20]

The problem was especially critical for those firms which had taken an active posture in the development field. Among firms that had set up development companies, the turnover problem was exacerbated. According to the McKinsey report, 75 percent of the respondents which reported high top management turnover had established a development company, while the majority of those reporting low top management turnover did not have a development company. This pattern was repeated at the middle and project management levels.[21]

Overall, managers experienced mixed feelings following the periods of buoyant enthusiasm and severe reversal during the late 1960s and early 1970s. Some believe that life insurance companies would be well advised to reexamine their basic skills and roles. The development and true real estate equity investment function require strong entrepreneurial skills which are difficult to harness within the framework of a fiduciary organization. Professional managers working within structured organizations will always be subject to some slight disadvantages. Negotiations, political dealings, market feel, and certain patterns of risk taking might not be the proper domain of life insurance company managers.

The key managerial skill which can be developed and maintained is a sense for opportunity. The managers of equity real estate investments should develop a sense for when their organization's resources provide an overwhelming competitive edge. On these occasions, they can seek out highly profitable targets of opportunity. They also have the luxury of being able to retreat from the market when the competition becomes too foolish. This combination of skill and prudence

---

[19] Braun, *Future of Insurance Companies,* p. 13.

[20] Ibid.

[21] Ibid., p. 14.

can make the real estate equity investment an attractive if not grow-ing portion of the investment portfolio.

THE OUTLOOK FOR THE FUTURE

The outlook for real estate equity investment by life insurance companies is uncertain. Both positive and negative aspects are pres-ent. The positive aspects reflect the growing opportunities which seem to be available. The negative factors include the continuing and newly emerging risks.

Positive Aspects

The positive aspects are three-fold. First, there is clearly a demand for new real estate projects. Although there is current overbuilding in many areas, population growth will require at least 15 million new residential housing units over the next decade. With those new units will come the need for the ancillary commercial services. The need for new units is driven by the expected entry of 5.7 million new peo-ple into the work force.[22] Space will have to be provided for their employment. These figures represent only new demand. To this must be added the need to replace the obsolescent stock of residential, commercial, and industrial real estate. Population shifts will further augment demand. All of this activity will require additional equity sources. The demand for the product will be such that many inves-tors will be bound both financially and politically to service this de-mand. In this demand lies opportunity.

The second positive feature is the competition for capital. This development is likely to boost return to all capital sources in most fields. Historically, real estate investment has offered higher than average returns. There is little reason to forecast that this situation will change in the decades to come. Obviously, there have been and will continue to be both good times and bad in this cyclical industry. On balance, however, studies have shown that the returns are better than the alternatives if the investments are adequately managed.

The third positive feature is the result of a perverse forecast. There have been a number of situations such as the Penn Central bank-

---

[22] U.S. Department of Commerce, Bureau of the Census, *Current Population Reports,* "Population Estimates and Projections," Series P–25, No. 476, February 1972, p. 25.

ruptcy, Equity Funding, North American Acceptance, etc., in which the security value of a mortgage or security interest in assets have been challenged and overturned. In other cases, the delay in obtaining control of assets is such that the value of the security is clearly diminished. Unlevered equity positions clearly avoid this risk. Even well-structured joint ventures seem to reduce the problems. The logical consequence is strange. In case of economic difficulties, an equity investor with control of the cash flows may be in a stronger position than a mortgagee.

Negative Aspects

The negative features are reactions to some of the trends identified earlier. There are political risks to equity ownership, and the time horizon is being foreshortened as higher returns are demanded. Projects are requiring more time and management involvement at all stages of their life cycles, and long-duration commitments are difficult to make in times of increasingly rapid change.

Although there has been a clear change from the "buy and hold forever" strategies of the past, real estate is still a long-term investment. This is in clear conflict with the above-mentioned tendency to temporize in the investment posture. High rate of return requirements yield shorter planning horizons.[23]

In order to receive any benefits of hedging against inflation, management attention is required. The benefits of real estate equity ownership are those to be achieved from participating in an operating business. Any less attention will achieve less than totally satisfactory results.

SUMMARY

Successful equity investment in real estate projects offers considerable rewards to a life insurance company investor. A need exists which can be met with adequate compensation for the monetary risks. In the environment of capital scarcity which is predicted for the future, the problem will be to choose among attractive alternatives. Life insurance company management can and should take advantage of these new opportunities.

---

[23] With a 3 percent discount rate, 80 percent of the benefits of an infinite annuity are received within the first 55 years. At a 12 percent rate, 80 percent are received within the first 15 years.

The major factors creating organizational pressure for equity investment have been identified. The response of life insurance companies wishing to take advantage of the opportunities must be coherently thought through. It must include strategic thinking with respect to the following:

Management Strengths and Weaknesses
Diversification Objectives
Economic Risk Analysis of the Properties without Regard to the "Deal"
Time Horizon for Sell-Hold Decision Making, Including Periodic Review
Appropriate Internal Measurement Schemes
Reduced Visibility/Political Liability

These key issues must be resolved in advance. When resolved, they will provide the framework both for enticing a steady flow of possible real estate equity investment opportunities and for selecting those which are most appropriate.

7

Real Estate Investment Trusts and the Life Insurance Industry

*By Peter A. Schulkin**

Real estate investment trusts (REITs) are relatively new financial intermediaries which grew rapidly during the 1969–1973 period. Today, the industry is made up of 213 trusts with total assets in excess of $20 billion. Shares of real estate investment trusts are widely held, and the industry has property and mortgage investments in every state.

Affiliates of life insurance companies are performing management services for 21 trusts, which constitute about 18 percent of the industry's total assets. Life insurance company involvement with trusts has also included the purchase of limited amounts of REIT debt and equity securities for long-term investment.

This chapter is divided into three sections. The first section provides the reader with a brief historical perspective of REIT industry developments. The second section details important characteristics of trusts, while the third section focuses on trust management as a possible life insurance company activity.

HISTORICAL BACKGROUND AND RECENT DEVELOPMENTS

The forerunners of today's REITs were the 19th century Massachusetts real estate trusts with transferable shares, which were pur-

---

* Peter A. Schulkin is vice president of Wells Fargo Realty Advisors.

chased by the general public, often by small investors. When prospective returns from local properties were relatively low, these trusts invested in properties outside of Massachusetts.

After the start of World War II the corporate income tax rate rose significantly, and the small number of existing trusts tried to obtain the same tax benefits that had been afforded mutual funds. Their efforts came to fruition in 1960 when Congress approved the necessary changes in the tax laws.[1]

From 1961, when the new tax law became effective, through 1967 about $300 million of new REIT securities were sold to the public, bringing the total number of REITs to over 50. Most of these early REITs were relatively small in terms of asset size, and they specialized in investment in real property. Only a few specialized in construction and development loans.

During the 1969–1970 tight-money period the traditional real estate lenders (savings and loans, commercial banks, and life insurance companies) were forced to curtail greatly their mortgage lending activities. REIT mortgage lending, on the other hand, grew rapidly during this period as stock market and money market conditions permitted REITs to raise large amounts of funds through the sale of REIT debt and equity securities and through bank borrowings. The formation of new trusts and the growth of existing ones pushed total REIT assets from $1 billion at the start of 1969 to about $5 billion by the end of 1970.

While the monetary situation eased considerably during 1971 and 1972, REIT assets continued to grow, reaching about $14 billion at the end of 1972. When interest rates rose during 1973, REIT assets increased further, reaching about $20 billion by year-end. Most of the asset growth which occurred during this period was concentrated in the construction and development loan area. Among the factors contributing to REIT asset growth of the 1969–1973 period were: (1) a boom in builder construction and development activity and (2) the ability of REITs to obtain funds at low enough cost to make lending profitable.

The coincidence of the oil crisis, record high inflation and interest rates, the most serious post-war recession, and overbuilding in many areas of the country resulted in very difficult times during 1974–1975 for those REITs which were oriented towards construction and development mortgage lending. Much less affected by the adverse eco-

---

[1] Internal Revenue Code Secs. 856–58 deal with REITs.

nomic climate were trusts with portfolios composed largely of long-term mortgage or property ownership investments.

REITs AS FINANCIAL INSTITUTIONS

As financial intermediaries, REITs serve as conduits of funds. They raise capital in the debt and equity markets and channel these funds to the real estate market. REITs are directed by trustees and are usually administered by a separate entity called an *advisor*. They are subject to regulation by both state and Federal authorities.[2]

The Trust Agreement and the Trustees

The legal existence of a trust is established and defined by a document called the *declaration of trust*, which is analogous to the charter of a corporation. The declaration of trust is filed in a specific state under the laws of that state.[3] Among other things, the declaration of trust outlines the investment objectives that are to guide the trustees and may specify certain restrictions on the trust's financial structure or operations.

The trustees of a REIT are elected by, and responsible to, the shareholders. Trustees are generally from the real estate, business, professional, and academic communities. Their function is not unlike that of a board of directors of a corporation. The trustees determine their trust's investment policy within the broad guidelines of the declaration of trust. They also oversee their trust's asset and liability management and approve trust loans and investments. To accomplish some of their tasks, the trustees are often organized into one or more specialized committees such as an investment committee, an audit committee, or an executive committee.

Investment Advisors

The trustees of most REITs contract with an investment advisor, generally on an anuual basis, to run the REIT's day-to-day operations and to present investment opportunities to the trustees for approval or rejection. The trustees are responsible for monitoring the activities

---

[2] For additional background see *REIT Fact Book* (Washington, D.C.: National Association of Real Estate Investment Trusts, annual).

[3] Most REITs have filed their declarations of trust in the Commonwealth of Massachusetts, which historically has been the home of business trusts. Massachusetts recognizes REITs under its common law. Unlike Massachusetts, approximately 15 other states have enacted specific enabling statutes which provide for the creation of REITs.

of the advisor to insure that the advisor is performing its functions competently and within the established policy guidelines.

Many REIT investment advisors are mortgage banking companies or affiliates of financial institutions such as banks and life insurance companies. Other advisors are owned and operated by organizations with real estate backgrounds. In return for its services, the advisor is compensated with an advisory fee which is negotiated between the trustees and the advisor. Most REITs owe their existence to their advisors, for, in most instances, REITs have been organized by the management group that served as the advisor once operations commenced.

In addition to managing the trust's assets and screening investment opportunities, most advisors also are involved in liability management, although in some instances the latter function is handled by personnel of the trust itself. Liability management concerns all aspects of a REIT's capital structure including public offerings or private placements of debt and equity securities and the day-to-day management of commercial paper sales and bank borrowings.

A REIT need not have an advisor—in fact, a number of smaller REITs have not had advisors since their inception. In these cases the advisory functions are performed by employees of the trust when possible. Trust employee activities which are not permitted if the trust is to qualify as a REIT for tax purposes, such as property management, are contracted out to others.

The advisory fees provided in the advisory agreement are negotiated between the trustees and the advisor and are often structured with an incentive feature based on the earnings performance of the trust. The advisory fees are subject to periodic review by the trustees, and on occasion modifications have been made to reflect unforeseen developments. The performance of the advisor is also reviewed. Operating under a contract that can be terminated (with the required advance notice) by either the trustees or the advisor, an advisor which fails to perform satisfactorily can be removed. Advisors may own shares in their own trust subject to restrictions outlined in the REIT sections of the Internal Revenue Code.[4] In practice, most advisors or their principals do not have major share holdings in their REITs.

Operating Capital

Because the Internal Revenue Code requires that a qualified REIT

---

[4] Internal Revenue Code Secs. 856–58.

distribute at least 90 percent of its net income, retained earnings are essentially eliminated as a source of funds. Aside from this significant restriction, REITs may raise funds in any way a corporation might raise funds, including the sale of shares, the sale of debt securities, or bank borrowings.

Most REITs obtain their initial funds through a public offering of securities. Once operational, they have usually obtained additional funds for investment through such means as bank borrowings or placing mortgages on owned properties. When favorable financial market conditions have prevailed, many REITs have financed growth with later public offerings of debt or equity securities.

REIT shares are traded on the major stock exchanges and over-the-counter in the same manner as those of corporations. At the time of writing, 54 REITs representing $13.5 billion in assets, approximately two thirds of the REIT industry total, were listed on the New York Stock Exchange. Thirty-four other REITs were listed on the American Stock Exchange. In all, about 80 percent of the industry's assets were listed on these two exchanges.

REITs have a significantly higher average cost of funds than do the traditional real estate lending institutions such as savings and loan associations and commercial banks. A combination of two factors is largely responsible: (1) much of the "debt" of the traditional lenders consists of relatively low-cost (and usually government insured) deposits not available to REITs as a source of funds; and (2) with debt-to-equity ratios as high as 20 to 1, the traditional real estate lenders are highly leveraged with low-cost debt.

Types of REITs

Within the scope of real estate investments, portfolio objectives may vary widely from one REIT to another. For example, some trusts make investments on a nationwide basis, while others concentrate their investments in one or two regions of the country. Some trusts specialize in one or more types of real estate uses such as shopping centers or apartment buildings; others seek a wider mix of types of structures. Some trusts concentrate their investments in property ownership or certain types of mortgage lending, while others have a broad mix of investments.

Regulation of REITs

REITs are indirectly regulated or monitored by a number of different public and private groups. REIT activities and reporting practices are monitored by the Securities and Exchange Commission (SEC) to insure that REITs are in compliance with Federal securities laws. These are the same laws which apply to corporations whose securities fall under SEC jurisdiction.

If a trust's shares are to be sold publicly, the offering must be approved by the state securities commissioners of those states in which it is to be sold. In contrast to the disclosure requirements of the Federal securities laws, state securities laws give the state commissioners the authority to impose regulatory standards. The state securities commissioners may refuse to allow securities to be sold in their states unless their specified standards are met.[5]

The Midwest Securities Commissioners Association, a group of 24 state securities commissioners, has been particularly active in formulating operating standards, which are applied by its members as guidelines in determining whether or not to permit the sale of a REIT's securities within their states. These policies deal with various aspects of trust operations such as advisory fee charges and investment portfolio composition.

If a trust is listed on a stock exchange, it is subject to the various disclosure requirements of the exchanges in addition to those of the SEC. The exchanges and the SEC require that the trusts notify their shareholders of important developments on a timely basis.

THE LIFE INSURANCE COMPANY AS A REIT ADVISOR

A life insurance company or affiliate may become an advisor to a REIT in one of two basic ways. It may organize a new trust, or it may successfully negotiate to take over the advisory function of an existing REIT. Irrespective of how an insurance company enters this activity, it is similar to other service activities of insurance companies such as mutual fund management, closed-end corporate bond fund management, and commingled investment fund management.

Advantages of Advising a REIT

Aside from whatever net income might be generated from advisory fees, there are a number of other possible incentives for a life insurance company to be an advisor to a REIT. These benefits may be obtained for a minimal investment on the part of the insurance

---

[5] Generally, if a REIT is listed on the New York Stock Exchange, the state standards are waived by the state securities commissioners.

company because the expenses of organizing a REIT are typically charged against the proceeds of the REIT's initial offering.

In addition to advisory fee income, the life insurance company or an affiliate may in some instances earn other types of income as a result of being an advisor to a REIT. For example, mortgage servicing and property management fees are available. The company may also obtain loan placement fees for placing mortgage loans in the trust portfolio. Such fees are normally levied on the borrower by mortgage bankers or mortgage brokers which originate loans.

Being an advisor to a REIT may complement life insurance company activities in ways which do not directly produce income. For instance, the insurance company may, on occasion, find the trust a convenient partner for investments which are larger than the insurance company considers desirable for its own account. In addition, the company may find that serving as a REIT advisor improves the productivity of its real estate department, particularly if the department's expertise is not currently being fully utilized.

Disadvantages of Advising a REIT

The disadvantages of being an advisor to a REIT come under two broad headings—conflicts of interest and the public exposure of the REIT.

Conflicts of Interest. Many of the factors which make an advisor valuable to a trust also give rise to conflicts of interest. For example, if the advisor or an affiliate has real estate-related businesses, there is a potential for conflicts between those businesses and that of the REIT which it advises. On the other hand, an advisor with real estate-related businesses may bring to the trust a wealth of useful experience and through its contacts serve as a source of investment opportunities for the trust.

To eliminate completely such possible conflicts would require that the advisor be connected with the real estate business only in its capacity as advisor to the trust. Since such a restriction may be undesirable, many trusts have taken steps to limit potential conflicts rather than eliminate advisors with real estate-related operations. Such steps usually include a requirement that a majority of the REIT's trustees who are unaffiliated with the advisor or related entities must approve any REIT decisions in which a conflict might be present. Other steps may include a right of first refusal on all investments made by the advisor or affiliates or a requirement that the advisor participate in all investments made by the trust. Life company-sponsored REITs operate with many such provisions in order to insure that conflicts will not be present.

Public Exposure. Publicly held REITs must conform to the various disclosure requirements of publicly held corporations. Obviously, if the portfolio performance of the REIT is poor, extensive publicity will be given to this result. Such publicity may tarnish the life insurance company's reputation. Moreover, the pressure of public exposure may compel the insurance company to aid its REIT if it runs into substantial difficulties. Such aid may create dissatisfaction among the insurance company's shareholders or policyholders.

REITs Affiliated with Life Companies

Tables 7.1 and 7.2, respectively, show the 14 stock and 5 mutual life insurance companies which have been affiliated with the advisor to a REIT. Two of these affiliations were severed in 1975 when the trusts involved became self-administered. Most of the holding companies of the 14 stock life companies have substantial interests in non-insurance businesses. In these instances, the advisory personnel have little or no overlap with the personnel of the life company. In general, the multifaceted holding company trusts are considerably different from those whose advisors are strictly life company related.

In order to focus on those trusts which are closely related to life companies, the five sponsored by mutual life companies were isolated as a group. To supplement financial statement information, officials of these trusts were interviewed. The interviews indicated that these trusts were generally organized to utilize more fully the mortgage departments of the life companies, which had cut back on lending when policy loan demand soared in the late 1960s. Typically, the companies hoped to develop a new, permanent source of funds which could be invested largely in the same type of mortgages made by the parent life company. It was also thought that advising a trust was a logical activity for a life company, similar to other life company activities and consistent with their overall philosophy regarding the appropriate activities for a life company to pursue.

Table 7.3 shows the aggregate balance sheet at the end of the second quarter of 1975 for the five REITs which are affiliated with mutual life companies. For the purpose of making comparisons, the balance sheet of the entire REIT industry is presented in the same table. The table reveals that the life company REITs have made investments largely in the long-term mortgage area. While the total long-term mortgage investments of these REITs, $614 million, are

TABLE 7.1
REITs Sponsored by Stock Life Insurance Companies

Insurance Company	Parent of Insurance Company	Name of REIT	Year of Initial Public Offering	Total Assets of REIT, 12/31/74† (millions)
American Heritage Life Insurance Company	American Heritage Life Investment Corporation	American Century Mortgage Investors	1969	$146.2
Beneficial Standard Life Insurance Company	Beneficial Standard Corporation	Beneficial Standard Mortgage Investors	1970	82.0
Connecticut General Life Insurance Company	Connecticut General Insurance Corporation	Connecticut General Mortgage and Realty Investments	1970	440.9
Continental Assurance Company	CNA Financial Corporation	1. LMI Investors 2. United Realty Trust	1969 1971	148.8 89.6
Diversified Life Insurance Company	First Lincoln Financial Corporation	Lincoln Mortgage Investors	1970	40.5
George Washington Life Insurance Company	George Washington Corporation, of which Peninsular Life Insurance Company is a minority shareholder	Fidelity Mortgage Investors	1969	184.0
Gulf Life Insurance Company	Gulf Life Holding Company	Gulf Mortgage and Realty Investments	1971	144.3

Insurance Company	Advisor	Trust	Year	Assets
Life Investors Insurance Company of America	Life Investors	1. American Equity Investment Trust	1968	90.2
		2. USP Real Estate Investment Trust	1970	17.0
IDS Life Insurance Company	Investors Diversified Services	IDS Realty Trust	1972	356.8
Nationwide Life Insurance Company	Nationwide Corporation*	Nationwide Real Estate Investors	1974	55.9
Northwestern Security Life Insurance Company	Northwestern Financial Corporation	Northwestern Financial Investors	1972	46.8
Occidental Life Insurance Company of California	Transamerica Corporation	Mortgage Trust of America	1969	151.4
Peoples-Home Life Insurance Company of Indiana	City Investing Company	1. C. I. Mortgage Group	1969	329.2
		2. C. I. Realty Investors	1972	181.7
United Investors Life Insurance Company (U.S.) and United Investment Life Assurance Company (Canada)†	Continental Investment Corporation which owns Waddell and Read†	Diversified Mortgage Investors	1969	358.0

* Succeeded Galbreath Mortgage Company as advisor in 1974. The trust was founded in 1969 as Galbreath First Mortgage Investments.

† Relationship with trust discontinued in 1975 when trust became self-administered.

‡ Assets for quarter ending closest to 12/31/74.

TABLE 7.2
REITs Sponsored by Mutual Life Insurance Companies

Insurance Company	Name of REIT	Year of Initial Public Offering	Total Assets of REIT, 12/31/74* (millions)
The Equitable Life Assurance Society of the United States	The Equitable Life Mortgage and Realty Investors	1970	$359.0
Massachusetts Mutual Life Insurance Company	MassMutual Mortgage and Realty Investors	1970	219.7
The Mutual Life Insurance Company of New York	MONY Mortgage Investors	1970	250.4
The Northwestern Mutual Life Insurance Company	Northwestern Mutual Life Mortgage and Realty Investors	1971	265.9
State Mutual Life Assurance Company of America	State Mutual Investors	1971	137.9

* Assets for quarter ending closest to 12/31/74.

TABLE 7.3
Aggregate Balance Sheets of All REITs and Mutual Life Company Sponsored REITs (second quarter, 1975)

	Assets (millions)			Liabilities (millions)	
	Mutual REITs	All REITs		Mutual REITs	All REITs
First mortgages:			Commercial paper	$ 295.3	$ 839.8
Land	$ 23.9	$ 827.9	Bank term loans and		
Development	123.9	2,438.6	revolving credits in use	241.6	8,332.8
Construction	248.5	6,675.0	Bank lines in use	103.3	2,506.0
Completed properties:			Sen. non-convertible debt	12.4	356.0
Short and intermediate-term	58.4	1,634.6	Sub. non-convertible debt	25.0	1,080.7
Long-term	614.2	1,870.7	Convertible debt	98.5	681.7
Junior mortgages:			Mortgages on property		
Land, development and construction	6.8	374.9	owned	28.4	1,827.4
Completed properties	44.0	1,070.4	Other liabilities	15.6	474.8
Loan loss allowance	(28.4)	(1,456.4)		820.1	16,099.2
Land leasebacks	3.9	531.7			
Property owned	107.5	4,996.4			
Cash and other assets	47.1	1,372.0	Shareholders equity	429.7	4,236.6
	$1,249.8	$20,335.8		$1,249.8	$20,335.8

Source: Published balance sheets of the 213 REITs of which the National Association of Real Estate Investment Trusts has any record and the balance sheets of the mutual life insurance company sponsored REITs listed in Table 7.2.

currently equal to only 5 percent of the long-term mortgage holdings of the five parent life companies, the companies generally intended that this figure would grow to be much larger.

The Performance of Life Company-Sponsored REITs

Four of the five mutual-sponsored REITs have performed well in comparison to the average REIT. In late 1975, the non-earning investments of all five totalled about 14 percent of invested assets compared with an industry average of nearly 50 percent. The prices of their shares in late 1975 were among the highest in the industry in relation to initial offering price or current book value per share.

By contrast, the performance of the REITs sponsored by multi-faceted holding companies which include a life company has been poor. As indicated earlier, the advisory companies of these REITs were not staffed by life company personnel. The portfolio objectives of these REITs were, as a rule, less conservative than was the case with those REITs whose advisors were staffed by life company employees.

SUMMARY

REITs are financial intermediaries which obtain funds by offering debt or equity securities in the capital markets. These funds are then invested by the REITs in the real estate market. REITs operate under declarations of trust, which are analogous to corporate charters. They are directed by trustees, but their day-to-day operations are conducted by advisors which receive advisory fees in return for their services. Advisors generally carry out both asset and liability management for their REITs. REITs are regulated by the Securities and Exchange Commission and by state securities commissioners.

Life insurance companies may be attracted to REIT advising by advisory fees and other income opportunities. In addition, life companies may find that REIT operations complement their own mortgage activities and enable them to utilize their real estate personnel more effectively. However, insurance companies engaged in REIT advisory activities may encounter conflicts of interest and adverse public exposure. Nineteen life insurance companies were affiliated with a REIT advisor in early 1975.

If one considers only REITs directly advised by life company personnel, life company REITs are a small factor in the REIT industry in terms of assets. However, during the past two years, they have proven to be among the more profitable REITs due to their conservative underwriting practices and emphasis on long-term mortgage investments. Generally, their life company advisors intended that they would represent a steady source of new funds for their mortgage departments to invest, in part offsetting the diminished inflow of funds caused by increased policy loans and other factors.

8

Separate Accounts

By Meyer Melnikoff*

Until 1962, every U.S. life insurance company had a single portfolio of investments which was used for all the various kinds of business in which it engaged, ranging from individual life insurance
products to group annuity contracts. This primary portfolio, used for
guaranteed fixed-dollar contracts, is now referred to as the *general
account*. During the 1950s, interest began to develop in segregated
portfolios to be available for use under specially designed contracts,
primarily for pension plans and individual annuities. The initial emphasis was on separate portfolios invested primarily in common
stocks, because the insurance law in most states imposed very stringent limits on the proportion of a company's general account which
could be held in that type of investment.

A *separate account* of an insurance company is a separate portfolio
of investments, the results of which are segregated from the results of
all other investments of the company. The term is now in general use,
but similar terms are sometimes used in state statutes, and the term
"segregated asset account" is used in the Internal Revenue Code.[1] A
separate account is defined in the Federal securities laws to mean "an
account . . . under which income, gains and losses, whether or not
realized, from assets allocated to such account, are, in accordance
with the applicable contract, credited to or charged against such ac-

---

* Meyer Melnikoff is senior vice president and actuary of the Prudential Insurance Company of America.

[1] Section 801(g).

count without regard to other income, gains, or losses of the insurance company."[2] The separate account business of a life insurance company involves the performance of all the principal functions normally carried on by the company. Accordingly, this discussion refers to aspects of product design and administration, as well as to investment operations.

HISTORY OF SEPARATE ACCOUNTS

The dawn of separate accounts in the United States may well be set at July 1, 1952, the date on which the College Retirement Equities Fund (CREF) became operational. This is suggested even though, in form, CREF is a completely separate entity—an organization which is separate from, but coordinated with, the Teachers Insurance and Annuity Association (TIAA)—rather than a separate account of a life insurance company. In 1950, William Greenough, now chairman of TIAA-CREF, before seeking the special legislation in New York to provide for the creation of CREF, discussed with the heads of the major life insurance companies the desirability of a basic amendment to the general insurance law to permit all life insurance companies to offer contracts based on separate accounts. He was advised by them to proceed instead with the CREF special legislation, as they considered the subject so controversial that an amendment to the insurance law might take 15 years. This prediction turned out to be precisely correct. Although the New York insurance law was amended to permit the use of separate accounts in 1962, it was not until 1965 that variable annuity benefits, similar to those provided by CREF since 1952, were permitted under the insurance law of the state of New York.[3]

In the earliest days of the separate account field, life insurance companies were faced with the possible applicability of three major

---

[2] Securities Act of 1933, Section 2(14).

[3] Paragraph 1 of Section 227 of the New York insurance law now authorizes the establishment of separate accounts which may provide for variable benefits. Another observation is pertinent at this point. In 1960, when the New York Insurance Department conducted hearings to determine the desirability of permitting life insurance companies to establish separate accounts, Geoffrey Calvert, then a consulting actuary in New York, asked for the opportunity to testify. The gist of his statement was that it would be a disservice to the public if insurance companies were denied the opportunity to develop separate account business, for the investment officers, actuaries, and other specialists in life insurance companies represented a degree of collective competence in these fields which could serve the public well. The great variety of developments in a relatively short time bears witness to his insight.

areas of governmental regulation: (1) state insurance law, (2) Federal tax law, and (3) Federal securities law. Perhaps it is not surprising, therefore, that over the years there were many discouraging times. Efforts to bring about the necessary separate account legislation at the state level began in New Jersey in 1953. In 1959, major developments occurred in all three areas—one favorable and two unfavorable to the use of separate accounts. In that year, several important states, including New Jersey and Connecticut, adopted their first separate account laws. On the other hand, the enactment of the Life Insurance Company Income Tax Act of 1959, which was hailed at the time as a boon for life insurance, was harmful to separate accounts because it included a life insurance company capital gains tax for the first time. Furthermore, the U.S. Supreme Court, by a 5–4 vote, held that variable annuity contracts were subject to regulation as securities.[4]

During the ensuing years, many of these handicaps were gradually overcome. For example, in 1960, a Securities and Exchange Commission (SEC) no-action letter permitted life insurance companies to begin offering certain types of separate account contracts. In 1962, a new tax bill exempted separate account capital gains allocable to qualified retirement plan assets. In the next few years, the variety of separate account contracts permitted by the SEC was broadened; and in 1970, amendments to the securities laws exempted separate accounts used only for qualified retirement plans from the Investment Company Act of 1940 (the 1940 Act). These amendments also exempted separate accounts from substantially all the requirements of the Securities Act of 1933 (the 1933 Act) and the Securities Exchange Act of 1934 (the 1934 Act).

As of the beginning of 1977, significant difficulties with some uses of separate accounts still remain. A very discouraging event took place in 1975 when the SEC withdrew previously proposed rules that would have exempted separate accounts used for variable life insurance from the Investment Company Act of 1940. Nevertheless, a great deal of progress has taken place in a relatively few years.

The first separate accounts were activated in 1962. At the end of that year, the assets held in all separate accounts in the industry were less than $10 million. Only a few states allowed separate account contracts to be issued, in most cases with rather severe limitations

---

[4] *Securities and Exchange Commission* v. *Variable Annuity Life Insurance Company of America,* 359 U.S. 65 (1959). As there was little question about their status as insurance contracts, the Supreme Court decision meant that variable annuities would be subject to dual regulation under both the insurance and the securities laws.

on the contract forms permitted. By the end of 1976, separate account contracts, both group and individual, could be issued in all U.S. jurisdictions. At that time, over 120 companies were issuing such contracts, and total separate account assets were about $16 billion. This was only about 5 percent of total life insurance company assets in the United States, but it is a safe prediction that this sector of the life insurance business has substantial growth ahead.

TYPES OF SEPARATE ACCOUNTS

A separate account of an insurance company is generally established by resolution of the company's board of directors, pursuant to provisions of the insurance law of the state(s) in which it will be marketed. (In many states, it may also be subject to the approval of the commissioner of insurance of the company's state of domicile.) The investments of a separate account are segregated from other assets of the company and are selected in accordance with the investment policy for the separate account. The company's obligations under separate account contracts *generally* vary in value with the investment performance of the accounts, including market value changes as well as investment income, but this is not so in every case.

The most widespread type of account, at the end of 1975, was the commingled, or pooled, common stock account; but several other important forms of separate accounts have been established. Separate accounts can be classified according to whether they are used: (1) for qualified or nonqualified pension plans and (2) for group or individual contracts.

Group Contracts for Qualified Plans

By far the larger portion of separate account assets at this time is held in separate accounts which are used only for group contracts issued for qualified pension and profit sharing plans and which are substantially exempt from SEC regulation. Such accounts are an integral part of the pension business of most large life insurance companies. A typical group pension contract may provide for the use of several separate accounts, as well as the company's general account. Group pension separate accounts may be further divided into: (1) commingled, or pooled accounts, and (2) single-customer accounts. In most companies, the bulk of the group pension separate account assets is held in pooled accounts. These may be classified in accordance with investment policy.

Pooled Common Stock Accounts. At the end of 1976, about $12 billion was held in common stock accounts used under group contracts for qualified plans, with pooled accounts representing the major share. Many companies have several pooled common stock accounts which are used only for group pension purposes. They may be distinguished by: (1) investment objective, such as conservative, aggressive, or special situations; (2) the contract form for which they are used, e.g., variable benefits to individuals as distinguished from equity funding on an unallocated basis for pension trust funds; and (3) SEC requirements, e.g., separate account contracts for HR–10 plans require the use of a prospectus, which is not required for variable annuities under employer pension plans.

Customarily, in pooled common stock accounts participating interests are expressed in terms of units which are valued daily. The change in the value of a unit incorporates both income and changes in the market value of the assets. Accounts used solely for qualified pension plans are free of tax on all investment income and market value gains which are allocated to contractual obligations.

Separate account investment management expense procedures differ considerably among companies. Some companies make a charge at the end of each month on the basis of the current market value of the units held, using a decremental fee schedule. One company levies a charge on a daily basis which may be of the order of ¼ of 1 percent per year. Thus, the changes in unit value over any period of time reflect the effects of investment results, reduced by the investment management fee on a "gross" basis. This company provides an experience rating credit for contracts that have assets exceeding a predetermined amount, such as $20 million. For example, the experience rating credit may reduce the overall investment management fee to the equivalent of an annual rate of ¼ of 1 percent of the first $20 million of assets and ⅛ of 1 percent of the excess.

It is generally not necessary to limit the rate of inflow of funds into a pooled common stock account, but companies often exercise some control over the rate at which funds can be withdrawn from such an account. The purpose of such provisions, of course, is to limit the extent to which the company may be forced to liquidate common stocks in a very short time in order to make funds available for withdrawal. This permits the company to manage the account more effectively. Accordingly, the company may require a minimum advance notice of withdrawal and may retain the right to limit the amount which can be withdrawn in any interval.

When an account is used to provide variable annuities, a lag is generally introduced between the date of valuation of the variable annuity units and the effective date of the payments which are linked to the unit value. Such lags are necessitated by administrative considerations. A lag such as a month and a day is typical; e.g., the unit value determined as of March 31 will establish the annuity payment due May 1.

A single pooled common stock account may be used for many different purposes and may have several sets of unit values. For example, a number of different variable annuity unit values, each applicable to a specified form of annuity, as well as a set of unit values for equity funding purposes may all be linked to the investment results of the same separate account portfolio. Generally, the holder of the group contract, but not the individual participant, is given a choice with respect to the form of annuity payout, thus establishing the series of variable annuity unit values to be used.

Pooled Publicly Traded Bond Accounts. In the last few years, several companies have developed pooled publicly traded bond accounts. These accounts operate in a manner very similar to the pooled common stock accounts but with some differences arising from the nature of the underlying investment asset. For example, there is a relatively small volume of bond trading taking place on the exchanges. Accordingly, for some issues, there may be no current market values available from recent trades. Therefore, another procedure must be used for determining the current market value of some of the assets that enter into the determination of the unit values. One approach is to use market values established by companies which perform such valuations as a regular part of their business, such as Telstat, or Merrill Lynch.

In general, determining market values is more difficult, and more time consuming, for bonds than for common stocks. Accordingly, unit values generally are determined only on a monthly or weekly basis. Daily valuations are seldom encountered. Transactions, representing transfers in or out, may take place only on dates for which unit values are determined. In view of the thinness of the markets for these bonds, even greater controls are desirable over the rate at which funds can be withdrawn from such an account than would be needed for a common stock account. Variable annuity pay-out benefits linked to the investment performance of a bond account would be feasible, but the author is aware of no instance in which this practice has been employed.

Pooled Private Placement Bond Accounts. Several major companies now offer pooled accounts invested in privately placed bonds. Such accounts consist primarily of fixed income securities privately negotiated with the borrowers. The objective of these accounts is to obtain a more favorable overall yield, consistent with safety of principal, than that available on publicly issued debt securities, even when these are actively traded.

For privately placed bonds, of course, no market values are established by public trading. Accordingly, the insurance company itself establishes the current market value of each private placement debt security on the basis of a procedure which calls for: (1) rating the current quality of each issue; (2) establishing a current set of "yield curves" for issues of different quality and duration to maturity; and (3) discounting, at an appropriate interest rate, the interest and principal payments due. Occasionally, these separate accounts acquire privately placed bonds with equity participation features, such as conversion terms or detachable warrants. Accordingly, procedures must be established for placing market values on warrants for the purchase of unregistered shares of common stocks and on other equity interests for which there is no public market. In view of the complexity of the procedure for determining unit values, they may be established at monthly intervals or perhaps even less frequently, such as quarterly.

Privately placed bond transactions frequently involve a long time lag between the date on which the commitment is made to invest in a specific security and the date on which the funds are actually disbursed. Procedures may thus be necessary in the allocation of investments to the separate accounts to recognize the fact that the separate account cash flow may be less predictable than that of the general account. Furthermore, it may be desirable to correlate the inflows of funds into the account, which can take place only on valuation dates, with the timing of investment disbursements. The relatively illiquid nature of privately placed bonds requires that controls be established on the right of contract holders to withdraw funds from such an account. This in turn leads to the need for underwriting rules on the type of pension plans which may be eligible to participate in such an account and on the extent of their participation.

Other Types of Pooled Accounts. At the end of 1976, one major company offered a pooled real estate mortgage account with total assets of about $80 million. The assets of the account consisted primarily of mortgages on apartment houses, office buildings, and commercial and industrial buildings, as well as motels, shopping centers, and land. The market value of the assets in the account was determined on an aggregate basis, recognizing the relationship between the overall yield on the mortgages held and current interest levels considered applicable to the portfolio. The previous comments on controlling the inflow and outflow of funds, the allocation of investments, and the need for limitations on participating plans are applicable to this type of account.

During the last five years, several companies have established pooled accounts invested primarily in equity ownership of income producing property. At the end of 1976, net assets in such accounts exceeded $850 million. The allocation of property investments between a company's general account and a separate account requires careful consideration. Several companies have followed the approach of maintaining complete separation between the investments of the two accounts. At least one company has been sharing property investments between the two accounts.

Perhaps to a greater extent than other types of accounts, the property account requires a procedure for limiting the inflow of funds, as the availability of property for acquisition fluctuates considerably in response to economic considerations and other factors. Accordingly, such accounts usually incorporate provisions for determining the contributions that will be accepted at any time from a pension fund.

The unit values for property accounts are based on appraisal techniques rather than on either published or calculated market values. Some state insurance departments require, as a condition of approval of such an account, that an independent appraiser value each property at least once each year. In view of the complexities of the valuation process, unit values for property accounts are customarily determined less frequently than those for other types of accounts. Quarterly valuation is probably typical. The investment management fee for such accounts is substantially higher than for stock or bond accounts and may be 1 percent or more, per year, of the value of total assets. In view of the relative illiquidity of property investments, restrictions must be placed on the withdrawal of funds from pooled property accounts and, therefore, on the participation of pension plans in such accounts.

At the end of 1976, several companies were offering pooled short-term investment accounts. The purpose of such accounts is to provide a temporary investment outlet for funds that may be destined for common stocks, bonds, or property. Such accounts are invested primarily in certificates of deposit, commercial paper, and Treasury bills. It is customary to determine the account values on a daily basis by accruing the interest on the investments but not to recognize day-to-day changes in the market value of the underlying assets. The temporary investments which form a part of all non-registered separate accounts are frequently invested together as part of an overall short-term pool. A registered separate account, which is an investment company, may not, under the Investment Company Act of 1940, participate in such a pool.

Among the other types of pooled account arrangements are the following:

1. An account which holds both stocks and bonds, with the insurance company given the authority to vary the percentage distribution at its discretion.
2. An account which contains both publicly traded and privately placed bonds.
3. A special situations common stock account, units of which are held as assets by other common stock accounts.
4. An account which holds both mortgages and properties.

Single-Customer Separate Accounts. Single-customer separate accounts are of two basic types. They may exist solely for the purpose of liquidating an existing portfolio; or they may be active, ongoing accounts making new investments and receiving new funds.

A single-customer liquidation account comes into existence when a pension plan which has been using another funding arrangement, such as a trust fund managed by an investment counselor, decides to transfer its funds to an insurance company and to utilize the insurance company's investment facilities, such as pooled separate accounts. In order to obtain the services of the insurance company in the liquidation of the existing assets, the assets are transferred in kind and held in a single-customer separate account. The insurance company is given the authority to liquidate the assets, with all investment income and the proceeds of all sales allocated to other investment accounts of the company either on a predetermined basis or in accordance with the discretion of the insurance company.

Ongoing single-customer separate accounts arise for different reasons and may or may not begin with a transfer of assets from another funding agency. Among the reasons for a single-customer separate account are:

1. Legal restrictions, as in the case of a public employee retirement system which operates under a law which requires it to keep its assets separate from those of any other pension plan.
2. Mobility; e.g., a large pension plan may wish to be in a position to move its assets in kind from an insurance company to another investment manager on short notice.
3. Investment policy; i.e., a plan may wish to have a portfolio with some characteristics that differ from those of accounts used by other clients of the insurance company. As an extreme example,

at least one insurance company has established a separate account invested entirely in the common stock of a single employer, whose thrift plan includes an option to direct contributions into employer stock. In this case, the insurance company is acting essentially as a custodian.

In one company, single-customer separate accounts may be under the investment management of an outside investment counselor. In view of the state laws which normally require all investments of an insurance company to be approved by the board of directors or a committee of the board, such arrangements may require that the outside investment counselor submit a list of all securities he intends to use. In this case, the insurance company retains the ultimate responsibility for the investments that are selected. Thus, in effect, an "approved list" procedure is established, although the insurance company, as a practical matter, may exercise only a veto power. One company has established a common stock account that is used only to provide HR–10 benefits for the members of a large professional association.

Group Contracts for Nonqualified Plans

Several companies have established common stock separate accounts to be used for funding tax-sheltered annuities, satisfying the requirements of Section 403(b) of the Internal Revenue Code,[5] under group annuity contracts. The life insurance company tax law gives such contracts the same exemption from taxes as applies to qualified plans, and there is no essential distinction under state insurance laws. However, the Federal securities laws draw a major distinction between qualified plans and tax-sheltered variable annuities, and the full weight of all major securities laws is placed on the latter type of instrument. Accordingly, a separate account to be used for such purposes must be set up as a registered investment company and must comply with the Investment Company Act of 1940. In addition, it must comply with the Securities Act of 1933, which requires the use of a prospectus; and the sales of such contracts must comply with the Securities Act of 1934, which requires that any sales personnel be registered securities representatives. Many other, fairly onerous requirements flow from these basic facts.

---

[5] Section 403(b) provides for tax deferred pensions for employees of certain nonprofit educational, charitable, and religious organizations. These plans are discussed in Charles C. Hinckley, "Tax Deferred Annuities," in *Life and Health Insurance Handbook*, 3d ed., ed. Davis W. Gregg and Vane B. Lucas (Homewood, Ill.: Richard D. Irwin, 1973), pp. 575–86.

Perhaps the most significant problem has been the need to reconcile two conflicting laws:

1. State insurance law, which, among other things, sets forth procedures for the election of the board of directors of the insurance company and specifies the duties of the board, including the requirement that all investments be made by the board, by a committee of the board, or in accordance with guidelines adopted by the board or a committee of the board.
2. The Investment Company Act of 1940 which, among other things, requires that the individuals who hold the interests in the *investment* company, and only those individuals, have specific rights, including the right to select their own board of directors and their investment manager.

This reconciliation has been accomplished in many cases by amending state insurance laws to authorize the establishment of a separate account as a management type of investment company with its own board of directors.[6] The Investment Company Act of 1940 stipulates that a majority of the separate account board must be individuals who are not otherwise affiliated with the insurance company (if, as in the typical situation, the insurance company is also the principal underwriter of the contracts based on the separate account).[7] Initially, these independent directors may be named by the insurance company.[8] After an initial period of no more than one year, the directors must be elected by the persons participating in the account in the same manner as the election of the board of directors of any other corporation; i.e., the investment company board solicits proxies from the participants through a proxy statement cleared by the SEC, with each participant having the right to vote in proportion to the amount of his or her interest in the account.

This investment company board acts on behalf of the separate account as though it were a separate company (which it is considered to be for purposes of Federal securities law, even though it is a part of the insurance company for state insurance law). It contracts with the insurance company to be the investment manager of the separate account. The contract is subject at any time to termination upon 60 days notice by the investment company board or by vote of the participants. Furthermore, the board, which under the Investment

---

[6] Paragraph 6 of Section 227 of the New York Insurance Law is an example of this type of provision.

[7] Investment Company Act of 1940, Section 10(b)(2).

[8] Investment Company Act of 1940, Rule 16a–1.

Company Act must have ultimate supervision of the investment management of the account, adopts the investment policy of the account. The investment company board also selects the independent public accountant for the account, who certifies the financial statements which are furnished participants and filed with the SEC.

The participants in the account each year have the right to elect the board of directors of the investment company and to approve the selection of the independent public accountant. The participants must also approve any fundamental change in the investment policy of the account.

In most other respects, separate accounts used for such purposes do not differ significantly from the pooled common stock accounts described previously. The insurance company carries out all operations, including sales activities, issuance of contracts and coverage, administration, physical possession of assets, and the disbursement of funds to participants.

Similar accounts have been established by some companies to invest in publicly traded bonds. Generally, participants may freely transfer the cash value of their accumulations between the company's bond and stock accounts without expense or tax charges. Some of the requirements of the Investment Company Act, especially the requirement for payment on withdrawal within seven days of receipt of notice therefor, would probably bar the use of the other investment forms, such as direct placement bonds, mortgages, or real property.

The Investment Company Act imposes a great many other requirements. Most important from a marketing standpoint are the limitations on sales charges. For example, on separate account contracts (which are deemed to be periodic payment contracts), the total sales charges may not exceed 9 percent of total considerations. Other limitations are also present. The issuer may elect one of two alternatives:[9]

1. No more than 50 percent may be deducted for sales expenses in the first year. Under this alternative, the issuer must refund any sales charges in excess of 15 percent of the gross purchase payments if the contract is surrendered within the first 18 months after issuance.
2. The total percentage deductions in the first four years of the contract may not add up to more than 64 percent (i.e., an average of 16 percent a year) with no more than 20 percent deducted in any year.

Both alternatives must include a "free look" provision under which

---

[9] Investment Company Act of 1940, Section 27.

all sales charges are refunded if the contract is surrendered by the policyholder within 45 days after he receives a notice which must be mailed by the company within 60 days of issuance. The application of these rules is quite complex; and, of course, many other restrictions result from the basic requirement to comply with the major Federal securities laws.

Individual Contracts

An insurance company which issues individual contracts for qualified pension and profit sharing plans (but not for HR–10 plans, tax-sheltered annuities, or individual retirement accounts) may utilize any of the separate account arrangements available to qualified group contract plans. However, in most cases individual contracts are used only in fairly small pension plans, which require a high degree of liquidity. This means, in effect, that only common stocks and publicly traded bonds are suitable investment vehicles for individual contract separate account plans.

Most companies interested in offering individual contracts based on separate accounts would not want to limit their markets to qualified plans. However, operating in the nonqualified market is extremely complex. Most of the complications arise not from investment matters but from SEC and tax regulations. The key regulatory considerations are summarized in Table 8.1.

Several alternative approaches are available for dealing with the regulatory structure outlined in the table. If one considers only common stock based contracts, the following options are present:

1. A different separate account with its own portfolio may be established for each set of requirements:
    a. Four separate accounts may be set up with one for each of the four classes described in Table 8.1. This approach is rarely, if ever, used in practice.
    b. Three separate accounts may be set up by combining the first two classes of plans in the table. A prospectus would then be issued for the HR–10 plans which would describe the portfolio used for both the HR–10 and the qualified pension plans but would incur no disadvantage for the qualified plans. Some companies have, in effect, followed this procedure.
    c. Two separate accounts may be set up, with one serving the first three classes above. This would impose the requirements of the Investment Company Act of 1940 on the first two classes, to which it need not apply. This approach has disadvantages, but it has been utilized by some companies.

TABLE 8.1
Federal Regulatory Status of Individual Separate Account Contracts

Type of Plan	Account Interests Exempt from Securities Laws?			Exempt from Tax?
	1933	1934	1940	
Qualified pension plans	Yes	Essentially yes	Yes	Yes
HR-10 plans	No	No	Yes	Yes
Tax-sheltered annuities and individual retirement accounts	No	No	No	Yes
Nonqualified, non-tax-exempt	No	No	No	No

    d. Only one separate account may be established, complying with the Investment Company Act of 1940 and providing for two sets of unit values, applicable to: tax-exempt plans, i.e., the first three classes in Table 8.1; and non-tax exempt plans, i.e., the fourth class. There are some disadvantages to this approach, but some companies have adopted it.

2. The foregoing options may be employed without the use of multiple investment portfolios. Instead, an investment company is established as a separate corporation *outside* the insurance company. The investment company complies with the Investment Company Act of 1940, as an open-end management company (i.e., a mutual fund). This company offers its shares to separate accounts of the insurance company (perhaps exclusively) which operate as unit investment trusts and invest only in shares of the investment company. This approach involves only one common stock portfolio (the mutual fund) which is used for various purposes. Under this arrangement, there may be three separate accounts within the insurance company:

    a. An account for qualified plans—for fund accumulation as well as annuity payout. This account would not have to register as an investment company.

    b. An account for nonqualified plans—fund accumulation only.

    c. An account for nonqualified plans—annuity payout only.

    The fund accumulation account for nonqualified plans (item *b* above) may be established on a basis which provides for the same tax treatment as a conventional mutual fund. Individual participants are able to add to their own tax base any long-term gains which are realized and upon which tax is paid or payable. By contrast, under the "internal mutual fund" options listed under item 1 above, a nonqualified participant may in some cases be unable to recognize in his tax base any taxes paid by the insurance company on realized long-term gains or set aside as a reserve on unrealized long-term gains. About 20 companies have followed the unit trust approach. One of these companies markets shares of the "external" mutual fund directly to the public as well as indirectly through variable contracts based on a separate account.

3. A subsidiary insurance company is established to do separate account business. The subsidiary may then follow any of the approaches described above. A few companies have followed this approach.

4. Separate accounts are established, as deemed desirable, to do the type of business proposed; and all separate account liabilities are reinsured with another life insurance company. The reinsurer provides for the investment management of portfolios, which are used by many different insurance companies, as well as record-keeping and other administrative functions. This approach was developed for use with individual variable life insurance and is not believed to be in effect at this time in the United States (it is in use in Germany).

INVESTMENT LIMITATIONS

In most state separate account legislation, the qualitative limitations applicable to insurance company investments under state insurance law were generally applied unchanged; but most of the quantitative restrictions on particular forms of investment (e.g., the requirement that not more than 10 percent of assets could be invested in common stocks) were removed. Some quantitative limits still apply, however. In New Jersey, for example, no more than 8 percent of the outstanding voting stock of any corporation may be held in all of a company's investment accounts—general and separate combined —with the exception of any shares for which voting rights are passed on to the contract holders.[10] Furthermore, depending on the state law and the form of separate account, there may be a limit on the portion of the market value of any account that may be invested in the securities of one corporation (e.g., not more than 10 percent).

For some accounts, in some states, there may be dividend or earnings tests which must be met by each common stock acquired. Some states provide for "basket" clauses under which a portion of an account may be invested in stocks which otherwise would not be eligible for the account. Some states have imposed qualitative restrictions on certain types of separate accounts which they do not impose

---

[10] New Jersey Insurance Laws, Sections 17B: 20–2 and 17B: 28–9.

on general accounts. For example, stock in such separate accounts may be limited to stock registered on a securities exchange or quoted in the National Association of Securities Dealers (NASD) over-the-counter list.

Other separate accounts, such as single-customer separate accounts, or pooled accounts in which participation is limited to specified types of contracts, may be free of all qualitative and quantitative restrictions, except the limit on overall voting stock for which voting rights are held by the company. When an insurance company uses the unit trust approach, as described earlier, the "external" mutual fund may, in some states, be required to comply with the investment law applicable to separate accounts; and the life insurance company may be required to be the investment adviser at the time the account is established.

RECENT DEVELOPMENTS

An important recent development is the use of separate accounts in the United States for variable life insurance. One major company entered this field in early 1976, using a subsidiary with a separate account which registered as an investment company and which complied with most of the requirements of the Federal securities laws. However, the SEC has granted some exemptions, especially from the limitations on sales charges and voting rights. Major tax questions still remain for both the insurance company and its policyholders.

The investment variety of separate accounts continues to expand. A possibility which exists under the laws of several states, including Massachusetts, New Jersey, and New York, is a separate account to be used for guaranteed, fixed-dollar contracts, as distinguished from variable contracts under which obligations are linked to investment performance. Assets held in such accounts might resemble the assets of general accounts and would be valued on the same basis as general account assets. During 1976, a separate account of this type was established by a major New York company. The objective of this account is to permit the insurance company to offer guaranteed interest return products for pension and profit-sharing plans based on a portfolio of investments which would be managed to meet the special requirements of this type of business. Other than having a separate portfolio of investments, such an account would differ significantly from other separate accounts.

Although the terminology differs in each country, separate account business is now conducted by life insurance companies in Australia, Canada, the United Kingdom, Holland, France, Germany, and

South Africa. In most of these countries, both individual and group contracts are available, as well as many forms of variable life insurance, linked to a wide variety of investment portfolios. Consideration also has been given to such possibilities in Japan, but no separate account business has yet been authorized there.

SUMMARY AND CONCLUSIONS

The origin of separate accounts in the United States can be traced to the College Retirement Equities Fund, which commenced operations on July 1, 1952. However, due to state and Federal regulatory restrictions, the widespread use of separate accounts by commercial life insurance companies did not begin until the early 1960s. Separate accounts have grown considerably since that time and now exist in many different forms for a multiplicity of purposes.

Separate accounts are used as funding vehicles for qualified pension and profit sharing plans, for tax-sheltered (section 403(b)) annuities, for HR-10 plans, and for nonqualified, non-tax-exempt annuities. Those developed for use with qualified plans are the most flexible, and some insurance companies maintain distinct separate accounts to invest in stocks, publicly traded bonds, privately placed bonds, and several other types of assets. Separate accounts are usually pooled; i.e., they include funds from a number of contract holders. However, in some instances separate accounts have been established for the exclusive use of one group contract-holder.

Even though the regulation of separate accounts has been liberalized considerably during the past 15 years, significant regulatory problems remain, particularly with respect to individual contract separate accounts, which are strictly regulated under the Federal securities laws. In order to comply with these laws, insurance companies have developed some extremely complex separate account and subsidiary arrangements. For example, an insurer may maintain distinct separate accounts, each with its own portfolio, for each of two or three classes of individual contract plans. An alternative approach is to establish a mutual fund which maintains a single portfolio and sells shares to each of several separate accounts within the parent insurer.

Separate accounts are exempt from most quantitative investment restrictions imposed by state insurance laws but are still subject to many qualitative requirements. Among the most recent developments is the use of separate accounts for variable life insurance, which may become an important product in the years to come.

9

Measurement of Investment Performance of Life Insurance Company General Accounts and Other Fixed-Dollar Investment Funds

By Irwin T. Vanderhoof*

The subject matter of this chapter can hardly be considered new. After all, it is traditional to examine the relationship between the investment yields of various companies based on the information in exhibits 2 and 3 of the life insurance convention blank. But work on a scientific method of measuring performance on fixed-dollar funds has lagged far behind the work on common stock funds that has culminated in the capital asset pricing model.

Part of the reason for this situation is the great diversity of investment instruments and terms of payment involved in bond and mortgage work. In the last few years, some work has been published which attempts to develop methods for reducing the diversity of factors by setting up adjustments which can bring the different types of investment instruments to a common basis.[1] While these contributions have been valuable, they are not aimed at measuring performance for the particular kinds of funds under discussion here, namely, fixed-dollar pension funds and life insurance company general accounts. The nature of these business organizations is such that per-

---

* Irwin T. Vanderhoof is vice president of the Equitable Life Assurance Society of the United States.

[1] John J. Garand, "Fixed Income Portfolio Performance: A Discussion of the Issues," in *C.F.A. Readings in Financial Analysis*, 3d ed. (Homewood, Ill.: Richard D. Irwin, 1975), pp. 389–417.

formance measures of use to them must take their unique characteristics into consideration.

THE NEED FOR A PERFORMANCE MEASURE

The Bank Administration Institute report on the measurement of
pension and profit sharing fund investment performance emphasizes
the fact that risk and return are inseparable in assessing performance.[2] Although this is not a novel conclusion, the life insurance industry has traditionally measured its return by a single criterion, the
earned interest rate. This measure, which is computed by dividing
earned interest by mean assets, not only ignores risk but is not even
appropriately adjusted for the unevenness in the receipt of funds during the year. In periods when companies were severely restricted in
their choice of investments, this might have been justifiable; but with
the investment freedom and technical expertise available today, it
should not remain an accepted procedure.

There are clear practical reasons for determining risk levels associated with differing portfolio strategies. A Gresham's law exists for
investments as well as for money. The bad will eventually drive out
the good, as long as the distinction between the two is not recognized. Especially in the area of fixed-dollar investments, pressures to
improve performance, in terms of yield, can be met by reductions in
quality. The default rates are inherently very low on this type of investment. Since the accounting methods used recognize default only
when realized, a portfolio can become very risky, compared with the
level of return being realized, for a long period before the losses actually appear. The easy answer to the problem of performance, when
performance is only yield, is to reduce quality covertly.

A better method of assessing performance has been recommended
by the Bank Administration Institute. This method measures the total return over a period of time, namely, interest income plus market
value at the end of a period divided by the market value at the beginning of the period. This approach allows the use of linked indices
(time weighted rates of return) to overcome the problem of investment timing. The measure of risk applied to these returns may be the
standard deviation or, as the Bank Administration Institute recom-
mends, the mean absolute deviation. This method has been given
some impetus by Salomon Brothers and other firms which regularly
publish a total bond return index.

---

[2] Randall S. Robinson, "Measuring the Risk Dimension of Investment Performance," *Journal of Finance*, vol. 25, no. 2 (May 1970), pp. 455–67.

While the Bank Administration Institute approach is sound, it is not well adapted to the investment portfolios of life insurance companies for two major reasons. First, it does not recognize the fund risk which is an important characteristic of life insurance companies and pension plans; and, second, many of the investments of life insurance companies are essentially nonmarketable. Conventional mortgages and private placements can rarely be tested for changes in value against the price on an open market. The need for a performance measure that is specially adapted to this particular type of fund should thus be apparent.

Such a performance measure would be useful to insurance companies and pension funds in several ways. First, it would assist investment managers in evaluating their own performance. In most fixed-dollar funds, each investment department has developed expertise about specific types of investments. However, no generally accepted standard exists against which the investment officer can compare his decisions. For the investment manager, a performance standard is not only the end of the investment process, it is also the beginning. Unless such a standard has been developed, it is difficult for the manager to improve his performance; and once such a standard has been settled upon, it can serve as a set of directions as to what constitutes acceptable performance.

A second use of a performance measure would be to assist the actuary in his work. The assurance funds which are under discussion are the joint creation of the investment operation, handling the assets, and the actuarial operation, handling the liabilities. The actuary for a stock life insurance company must make assumptions as to the level of interest earnings for periods of 20 years or more into the future. Not only are assumptions made with respect to money already in hand, but such assumptions must be made with respect to monies to be received 10 or 20 years from now. Pension fund assumptions are for even longer periods. Since the actuarial assumption is always that the contractual benefits will be paid, the interest rate used may not be one which includes any "risk" premium. The amount of risk premium and risk of loss in the portfolio must be known. An acceptable performance measure should provide this type of information.

Finally, an appropriate performance measure could be used by the trustees (in the case of a pension fund) or by top management (in the life insurance company) in judging the quality of the investment officer. When used properly, it should not be a threat to the manager. Rather, it should constitute a basis for him to report to the higher echelons that, subject to the constraints placed upon him by the nature of the fund, he has performed satisfactorily. If the fund were managed to maximize the performance measure, the operation would be following a scientific investment theory; and the measurement of performance should constitute a vindication of the investment operation.

FUND RISK

The special nature of assurance funds eliminates from consideration some kinds of risks that are normally considered important and creates what Robinson refers to as *fund risk*.[3] Fund risk refers to the probability that the fund will not be able to honor its future commitments. There are two different types of fund risk. The first occurs when the assets of the fund are invested in instruments whose terms are not suitable for the liabilities of the fund. To illustrate, consider a fund which is obligated to make payments only to retirees and has no inflow of funds from other sources. Such a fund will steadily decline in size. If the assets are invested in very long-term bonds (no matter what the quality), then payments from the fund can only be accomplished in later years by the liquidation of some of these assets in the general market. If interest rates have risen during the period, then the market value of the bonds may not be sufficient to support the payments when due. In this case, the quantity and quality of the assets may originally have been sufficient; but the fund was unable to meet its obligations because the maturity structure of the assets was inappropriate for its liabilities.

The reverse situation can also exist. A fund, or insurance company, can accept monies for investment over a long period of years and guarantee a rate of return to be earned on money received over the entire period. If the investments of the fund are very long-term bonds and perhaps some common stocks, the fund may be able to plan on meeting its obligations. If the assets of the fund are Treasury bills, however, then the variations in return over a period of years make the guarantee a highly significant source of risk to the fund.

The fund may experience a second kind of fund risk. This risk is that of apparent insolvency, created by the combination of accounting rules that govern the valuation of assets and the normal fluctuations in market value of assets. Bonds in good standing are carried on an insurance company's books at amortized cost, but equities are carried at market. Insurance companies usually have a surplus of only about 10 percent of assets. Uninsured pension funds, though

---

[3] Ibid., p. 465.

they do not make guarantees and though modifications in the market values of equities are possible for them, may have to call for changes in employer contributions under circumstances that would imply an even smaller margin for error.

Consider an example of this second type of fund risk. Soldofsky and Miller concluded that the mean return (using the total return method) on U.S. government bonds over the period 1950 to 1966 was 1.67 percent per year and that the standard deviation of this return was 5.12 percent.[4] Yet to the extent that the liabilities of the fund matched against the cash flows from government bonds, there was no fund risk. On the other hand, Soldofsky and Miller also concluded that the mean return on common stocks was 16.6 percent per year with a standard deviation of 16.5 percent. This seems to be a better risk-return relationship. However, if the total funds of a life insurance company were so invested, it would have plunged into insolvency during the period. The fund risk is thus created by the high leverage characterizing life insurance companies and by the nature of their liabilities.[5]

This risk is aggravated by insurance company valuation practices for bonds and equities. In the case of the government bonds described above, the market yield rose during the period under study, the market price at the end of each period was lowered, and the total return was thereby reduced. Insurance company valuation procedures ignore this market fluctuation. In the case of common stock, however, market values are used. Since liabilities are calculated using the same low interest rate during the entire period, government bonds are safe and stocks are not.

The accounting treatment described above can be justified. While common stocks can fluctuate in market price for reasons of changes in earnings or even the mood of investors, government bonds change only because of interest rate movements. If the bond interest rate changes and one accepts this change by using market values in the

[4] Robert M. Soldofsky and Roger L. Miller, "Risk Premium Curves for Different Classes of Long-Term Securities, 1950–1966," *Journal of Finance,* vol. 24, no. 3 (June 1969), pp. 429–45.

[5] A more extensive discussion of the elimination of fund risk through the proper selection of asset maturities is presented in Irwin T. Vanderhoof, "The Interest Rate Assumption and the Maturity Structure of the Assets of a Life Insurance Company," *Transactions of the Society of Actuaries,* vol. 24, Meetings Nos. 69A and 69B (May and June 1972); Irwin T. Vanderhoof, "Choice and Justification of an Interest Rate," *Transactions of the Society of Actuaries,* vol. 25, Meeting No. 73 (March 1974); and Irwin T. Vanderhoof, "Inflation, Expenses, Interest Rates, and Benefits," International Congress of Actuaries, Tokyo, Japan, October 25–November 1, 1976.

calculations, then to preserve consistency of treatment in the valuation of the fund surplus the interest rate used to calculate liabilities should also be changed.

But this would create a new problem. A government bond changes about 8 or 10 percent in market price with a 1 percent change in the interest rate. The value of the liabilities of a fund changes at least 15 percent with a 1 percent change in the valuation interest rate.[6] If both assets and liabilities were valued at the market rate of interest and if interest rates fell by as much as 2 percent, the surplus of the fund would probably be wiped out. While no method of accounting produces an ideal solution, the use of amortized cost for fixed-dollar investments and market value for equities at least permits the companies to continue to function.[7]

The fund risk threat has two clear-cut implications with respect to performance measurement. First, the portfolio should have constraints as to possible ranges of maturities and risk levels that will prevent the portfolio manager from exercising complete freedom in his choice of investments. Performance measurements must then be based upon the choices that could actually have been made. If only Aa discount bonds were acceptable, the fact that higher yields on Baa new issues were available would be irrelevant. Secondly, if one accepts the current life insurance accounting system, the use of risk-return measures based on varying market prices for obligations is not possible.

These restrictions suggest the need for a system of performance measurement that is based upon a comparison of actual and potential results, considering all the existing constraints. The system must be based upon prospective measures of risk rather than the determination of risk in retrospect based on market valuations. And, because

---

[6] This factor of 15 percent is significantly larger than the 10 percent implied in the Life Insurance Company Income Tax Act of 1959. The reason for the difference is that the "10 for 1" rule is concerned with statutory life insurance reserves. It is inappropriate for long-term pension funds and also for the valuation of life insurance company asset shares. This is the case because the asset share of a newly issued policy is generally negative. These negative values make asset shares more sensitive to interest rate changes than reserves, as reserves are always positive.

[7] Some pensions use funding techniques like *frozen initial liability*, where investment gains or losses are automatically spread out over future contributions to the fund. This funding technique would seem to allow the use of market values in all cases. However, if the unfunded liability is small, the effect on future contributions could become so large as to be onerous to the organizations making the contributions.

the discussion focuses on fixed-dollar instruments, which have minimal capital gain possibilities in insurance funds, the analysis of risk is limited to potential losses of principal and interest through default.

THE PROPOSED PERFORMANCE MEASURES

The proposed performance measures are developed by analyzing the transactions of each specific sector of the investment portfolio to compare the promised yield on the investments made during the year with an average promised yield on that type of investment available at the approximate time each investment was made. The next step is to identify "best buys" for each such time period by comparing the risk premium offered on each risk of default class with a minimum acceptable risk premium for that category. The classes with the largest such differences constitute the best buys. The comparison of the first two yields measures timing, while the best buy yields measure the selection of risk classes. The final step is to compare the results actually achieved within a sector with those which could have been achieved by a different allocation of funds. This produces a measure of the profits or costs of the particular allocation made during the period. The proposed method may be applied on a monthly basis so that investment results can be evaluated continuously.

The proposed measure focuses upon the performance of securities purchased during a particular period rather than that of the entire portfolio. This is significant because life insurance companies and pension funds generally adopt a buy and hold philosophy so that active trading of existing fixed-dollar investment holdings does not take place.

The buy and hold approach may not be as unsophisticated as it sounds since an assumption of efficiency in the capital market would seem to imply that such a policy should be as good as one of active trading. Even though the evidence for efficiency is not as strong in the debt market as it is in the auction market for stocks, practical problems may prevent active portfolio management. State insurance department examiners have been known to express the feeling that active portfolio management is "speculation with policyholder funds." The threat of having such a statement inserted in an examination report has stopped at least one company from such procedures. Additional comments are made at the end of this chapter concerning the applicability of the proposed method to an actively managed portfolio.

The formulas for the proposed performance measures appear below:

$$\frac{\sum\limits_{i} P_i r_i}{\sum\limits_{i} P_i} = \text{Actual average promised yield} \qquad (9.1)$$

$$\frac{\sum\limits_{i} P_i\, _s r_i}{\sum\limits_{i} P_i} = \text{Possible average yield available} \qquad (9.2)$$

$$\frac{\sum\limits_{i} P_i m_i}{\sum\limits_{i} P_i} = \text{Extra risk premium received} \qquad (9.3)$$

$$\frac{\sum\limits_{i} P_i\, _b m_i}{\sum\limits_{i} P_i} = \text{Extra risk premium available} \qquad (9.4)$$

$$\sum\limits_{i} P_i(\, _s r_i - r_i) = \begin{array}{l}\text{Dollar performance above or}\\ \text{below average available}\\ \text{yield}\end{array} \qquad (9.5)$$

$$\sum\limits_{i} P_i(\, _b m_i - m_i) = \begin{array}{l}\text{Dollar performance above or}\\ \text{below best buy extra risk}\\ \text{yield}\end{array} \qquad (9.6)$$

where

P_i = the actual cost of security i,
r_i = the rate which the security is purchased to yield,
$_s r_i$ = the average performance standard with which the ith security is compared,
m_i = the margin over the minimum risk premium achieved on the ith security, and
$_b m_i$ = the margin over the minimum risk premium on best buys.

The manager could reasonably be expected to perform as well as the average yield actually available on each risk class, but one could only hope that he would maximize the extra risk premiums actually achieved. He could not be expected to allocate funds perfectly among risk classes.

For the average yield performance standard [Equation (9.2)] to be feasible it is only necessary that an adequate variety of standards are available so that the comparison can actually be made. Such a set of standards is available, though they are not perfect in all cases. The available standards are discussed below in connection with the discussion of each investment sector. For the extra risk yield standard [Equation (9.4)] to be meaningful, the capital markets must be reasonably efficient but must depart from perfect efficiency often enough to make the procedure worthwhile.

The Average Yield Performance Criterion

The use of the average yield criterion is possible if techniques are available to predict with reasonable accuracy the probability of default losses and to assess in advance the value of such losses. In other words, the capital market, or at least some segments of it, must be not only efficient but accurate in its assessment of the future. The only really definitive studies of this issue have concentrated on the market for publicly traded bonds, and it is to these studies that one must turn for examples.

One such study, conducted by Hickman, investigated the accuracy of the rating agencies in predicting bond default.[8] The information presented in that study forms the basis for Table 9.1.

TABLE 9.1
The Performance of Agency Bond Ratings from
1900 to 1943

Agency Rating	Default Rate	Promised Yield	Modified Realized Yield
I	5.9%	4.5%	4.3%
II	6.0	4.5	4.3
III	13.4	4.9	4.3
IV	19.1	5.4	4.5

Source: W. Braddock Hickman, *Corporate Bond Quality and Investor Experience* (Princeton: Princeton University Press, 1958) as presented in Harold G. Fraine, *Valuation of Securities of Life Insurance Companies* (Homewood, Ill.: Richard D. Irwin, 1962).

The agency rating grade shown in the table is a combination of the ratings of the four agencies existing during the 1900–1943 period of the study.[9] The modified realized yield figures differ from those originally shown by Hickman in that the capital gains on called bonds

---

[8] W. Braddock Hickman, *Corporate Bond Quality and Investor Experience* (Princeton, N.J.: Princeton University Press, 1958).

[9] The four agencies were Standard Statistics, Poor's, Fitch, and Moody's. Since the period covered by the study, the first two have become Standard & Poor's and Fitch has merged into Moody's.

have been removed. Since these gains were created by the low interest rates during the Depression, the yield after their removal more
properly recognizes the loss factors of concern here.

Although the reputation of the agencies would lead one to expect
them to predict relative default probabilities with reasonable accuracy, the relationship between the actual realized yields on different
classes of securities is rather remarkable; and it is possible that part
of this precision is attributable to historical factors or to chance.
Nonetheless, it does seem evident that over the entire period of the
Hickman Study the rating agencies exhibited an ability to classify
risks of loss such that the risk premium reasonably related to the
probability of loss. When the data are broken down into rails, industrials, and utilities, however, the relationships are far less precise.

A second part of the demonstration of the feasibility of the average yield performance criterion should show that the market in general was able to recognize differences in default probabilities and to
make an additional charge for them that was reasonably related to
the level of risk. Table 9.2 provides evidence on this point.

TABLE 9.2
The Performance of Market Bond Ratings from
1900 to 1943

Market Rating*	Default Rate	Promised Yield	Modified Realized Yield
Under 0.5%	10.5%	3.8%	3.4%
0.5–1.0	13.9	4.5	4.0
1.0–1.5	18.9	5.1	4.6
1.5–2.0	23.8	5.9	4.7
2.0–2.5	27.8	6.6	5.6
2.5 and over	39.1	7.8	6.4

* The market rating is the additional return available on a given security in excess of the return on the lowest yielding security available
at the same time.

Source: W. Braddock Hickman, *Corporate Bond Quality and Investor Experience.*

The data in the table also support the thesis that the market was
reasonably able to predict relative risks of default and charge for
them. It should be mentioned in this connection that there were several real advantages to the market rating approach. This system,
based upon the additional return available on a given security in
excess of that on the lowest yielding security with the same maturity
available at the same time, was better than the agency ratings at

durations long after issue and immediately prior to default. It also worked more consistently among the major groups of industrials, utilities, and rails than the agency ratings. The agencies rated the rails far too highly for the subsequent defaults experienced.

The Extra Risk Yield Criterion

The data seem to support the hypothesis that the level of losses can be predicted in advance. In addition, it is also evident that the investment manager must establish a risk premium level which is sufficient to compensate his fund for the level of risk in the securities purchased. Because the portfolio manager frequently must decide between high- and low-quality bonds, some standard must be available to assist him in setting the minimum risk premium to compensate for the higher probable default levels of lower-quality obligations.

Since the period covered by the Hickman study, there have been almost no defaults of bonds rated as high as Baa. Thus, a lower risk premium than is implied by the Hickman study can probably be justified. A premium of about half of that level might serve as a reasonable rule of thumb. However, this is a matter that must be determined on the basis of the characteristics of the individual fund. For example, a fund with a surplus of 3 percent of assets should require a higher risk premium than one with a surplus of 11 percent of assets. A greater level of return is necessary because the level of risk to the fund and the utilities of additional return are different.

The preceding discussion has shown that prior determination of the risk of loss level is possible and that the establishment of a minimum risk premium for each level is necessary. It must now be shown that opportunities exist to make profits on variations in risk premiums. That yield spreads vary greatly over periods of time can be established by the examination of any such series. The Moody's yields by class are easily obtainable. Using these data on a quarterly basis over the period 1954 to 1969, Jaffee has shown that the yield spread for all corporate bonds was 0.65 percent and the standard deviation of the spread was 0.18 percent.[10] (Unpublished studies by the present author indicate that the variations in new issues are larger.)

Jaffee's study is interesting in several other ways. For example, he establishes that a factor having a great effect on this yield spread is the general attitude of consumers, as measured by the University of

---

[10] Dwight M. Jaffee, "Cyclical Variations in the Risk Structure of Interest Rates," *Journal of Monetary Economics,* vol. 1 (1975), pp. 309–25.

Michigan Survey Research Center. This means that variations in the yield spread from the long-range average can be explained at least in part by the varying emotional climate of the country. While there are some unsatisfactory statistical results in the Jaffee study (most particularly, low Durbin-Watson statistics for many of the regressions), his overall conclusions seem adequately documented. Another of his conclusions which is relevant in the present context is that if the mean of the yield spread were known with certainty, substantial improvement in the overall portfolio yield could be achieved.

Other Considerations

Besides average yields and extra risk premiums, two additional factors should be considered. One is the company's requirement for liquidity and marketability in its portfolio. This is largely determined by the susceptibility of the company to policy loans. As pointed out in Chapter 10 of this volume, policy loan demand is largely determined by the interest rates in the economy. However, all life insurance companies are not affected to the same extent. Each company must carefully estimate the amount of its portfolio that should be held in short-term liquid securities to accommodate this possible demand.

Finally, one must always include the effect of income taxes in the calculations. Pension funds are normally free of any such assessments but insurance companies are not. The life companies' share of interest income is taxed at regular corporate rates. Since high risk securities produce high taxable interest returns and possible capital losses, and since capital gains are typically minimal, tax considerations may become crucial. This is particularly true when determining the risk premium required for the purchase of lower-quality securities. The calculation of the required additional risk premium must recognize the facts that the risk premium is reduced by taxes and that losses must be compensated for by after-tax proceeds.

MEASURING PERFORMANCE OF SPECIFIC CLASSES OF INVESTMENTS

Cash and Bank Deposits

The basic need for cash and bank deposits relates to the operating requirements of risk businesses. A negative yield may actually result from bank charges. As there is no convenient source for "average" bank charges, the average yield criterion is not functional in this case.

The best buy would compare the actual charges with the net return obtainable by lowering cash and bank balances and investing the released funds in commercial paper or Treasury bills.

Short-Term Money Market Instruments

The basic comparison for short-term money market instruments is between the actual instrument chosen and the available yield during the month. The best buys are determined by comparison with other money market instruments. Salomon Brothers reports data on Treasury bills, bankers acceptances, Federal agency securities, finance paper, commercial paper, certificates of deposit, and Eurodollar deposits.[11] The agencies rate many of these obligations, and this is a valuable source of risk assessment data. However, the agencies are not always able to keep their ratings up to date; and one should thus be aware of other methods of predicting bankruptcy as an indication of possible problems in commercial paper.

Altman has used the technique of multiple discriminant analysis to relate probability of bankruptcy to various financial ratios of a firm.[12] While an actual calculation of the additional yield necessary from a given risk class to compensate for the inherent risk has not been conducted, it can be developed utilizing Altman's method and similar information. This procedure should not be considered an attempt to replace the judgment of the investment officer with a mechanical formula. The person purchasing the paper is still assumed to have the ability to make better decisions than could be made by mechanical means. He is expected, however, to be able to demonstrate that he is in fact achieving a superior result.

Bonds

Bonds are the largest investment of most life insurance companies, usually accounting for about 40 percent of assets; but the market for publicly issued bonds is not dominated by insurance companies. Pension funds and, more specifically, municipal pension funds are a major factor in this market. The treasurer of the New York

---

[11] *An Analytical Record of Yields and Yield Spreads* (New York: Salomon Brothers, quarterly).

[12] Edward I. Altman, "Financial Ratios, Discriminant Analysis, and the Prediction of Corporate Bankruptcy," *Journal of Finance*, vol. 23, no. 4 (September 1968), pp. 589–609. See also Craig G. Johnson, "Comment," and E. I. Altman, "Reply," *Journal of Finance*, vol. 25, no. 5 (December 1970).

State pension fund once addressed the New York Society of Security Analysts. One of his complaints was that he had a small staff and that no real analysis of purchases was possible, but he had to buy $1 million of bonds a day. If he missed a day, then he would have to buy $2 million the next day. The fact that the bond market is not perfectly efficient can be partly attributed to this type of situation.

The basic reference for information about standards in the bond market is a publication of Salomon Brothers.[13] It includes data by maturity so that the yield curve can be observed, data by coupon so that the coupon effect (both tax and call) can be valued, and data showing the new yields on various graded industrial and utility securities. Just about every needed standard can be developed from this source. Moody's series of bond yields by rating class also provide a basis for judging risk premium levels.

To determine the relationship between the two series, regressions were run between them on a monthly basis for the period 1971 to 1974 (the Salomon Brothers data do not go back any further). The resulting Durbin-Watson statistics were almost universally unsatisfactory and the coefficients of determination ranged from 1 percent to 89 percent on the yield spreads. The series thus appear to be far from coincident. There are two major reasons to believe that the Salomon Brothers data are to be preferred.

First, these data are based on yield rates in the new issues market, where money is invested in large amounts. The Moody's data are based on the aftermarket. Second, the Salomon Brothers values are adjusted to some extent by the traders on the bond desks, whose grasp of market conditions should enable them to produce better results than those obtained by the simple averaging of numbers. In spite of Moody's efforts to the contrary, their figures may be affected by a few transactions which reflect conditions specific to a particular bond issue. Thus, until better explanations of the poor relationship between the two series have been developed, reliance on the Salomon Brothers data seems wiser.

Yield differentials for private placements must be developed from the data on traded bonds. Data on the public issues can provide a basis for determining the appropriate rates for variations in coupon, callability, and term. The question of the additional premium for nonmarketability and the determination of the risk level are more complex. In recent years, the yield rate premium for private placements has ranged from 0.5 to 1.0 percent. Some data on the levels of

---

[13] *An Analytical Record of Yields and Yield Spreads.*

this spread are available through the American Council of Life Insurance (ACLI).

The question of the determination of risk on private placements remains. Ang and Patel have conducted studies on the relative accuracy of four mechanical methods of developing, from published financial data, the equivalent of agency ratings.[14] The system proposed by Pogue and Soldofsky,[15] was found to be superior to the other three. Ang and Patel also concluded that the Pogue-Soldofsky algorithms, when tested against the Hickman samples, were superior to the agency ratings in predicting default. On the basis of this study, some confidence seems justified in the ability of mathematical formulas to provide the kind of data necessary to classify the risk level of a particular private placement. Altman and Katz have recently devised yet another series of equations that purports to provide the equivalent of agency ratings for electric utilities.[16]

These mechanical methods may do more than merely provide substitutes for ratings. One researcher has concluded that differences between the agency ratings and the results of a mechanical rating method were caused by the agencies' failure to update the rating promptly with the emergence of new data.[17] This finding implies that there are considerable opportunities for profit in more accurately and promptly judging the risk factor in bonds.

Mortgages

Mortgages constitute about one third of the assets of the life insurance industry and may be subdivided into three general categories. The first is government guaranteed home mortgages—FHA and VA. These are essentially riskless investments, and the rates at which they are being placed are published in the Salomon Brothers report.[18] The second broad category is conventional home loans

---

[14] James S. Ang and Koritkuman A. Patel, "Bond Rating Methods: Comparison and Validation," *Journal of Finance,* vol. 30, no. 2 (May 1975), pp. 631–40.

[15] Thomas F. Pogue and Robert M. Soldofsky, "What's in a Bond Rating?" *Journal of Financial and Quantitative Analysis,* vol. 4, no. 2 (June 1969).

[16] Edward I. Altman and Steven Katz, "An Analysis of Bond Ratings in the Electric Public Utility Industry," working paper 74–69(s), Salomon Brothers Center for the Study of Financial Institutions, Graduate School of Business Administration, New York University, n.d.

[17] Hugh W. Long, "An Analysis of the Determinants and Predictability of Agency Ratings of Domestic Utility Bond Quality" (Ph.D. diss., Stanford University, 1973).

[18] *An Analytical Record of Yields and Yield Spreads.*

on which information is usually available from the mortgage bankers association.[19] Data on recent foreclosure experience, from which the current levels of risk can be determined, are available from the ACLI. Basic patterns of default can be developed from the work of von Furstenberg,[20] and Sandor and Sosin have recently published information on the risk premium structure.[21]

The final mortgage category, income property mortgages, accounts for the majority of mortgage funds invested by the life insurance industry. The principal source of data on these mortgages is the ACLI, which compiles information on loan to value ratios, default rates, and other important characteristics. While these data are not as extensive as one might like, they should be sufficient to permit the identification of the market opportunities for income property mortgage loans on different types of real estate.

Identifying the best buys for this class of investment is somewhat more difficult. However, a reasonable approximate solution might be to divide income property mortgages into two major categories—those for which the principal base of security is the borrower and those for which the primary security basis is the quality of the property itself. In the former case, the mortgage could be rated using the method suggested above for corporate bonds. In the latter case, analysis of quality is really the analysis of the equity value of the underlying property. Thus, these mortgages might best be analyzed as equities with a fixed return and a safety margin in the event of default equivalent to the excess of equity in the building over the amount of the mortgage.

The best buy standard for income property mortgages might well be the best buys from the bond analysis above. However, the analysis should consider the fact that many companies maintain their activity in the income property mortgage market even during periods when its relative returns are unattractive. The rationale for this behavior is that it takes a long time for relationships to be developed. A company retiring from the market may have to wait several years to reestablish its position.

---

[19] See also, *Federal Reserve Bulletin,* table entitled "Terms on Conventional First Mortgages."

[20] George M. von Furstenberg, "Default Risk on FHA Insured Home Mortgages as a Function of the Terms of Financing: A Quantitative Analysis," *Journal of Finance,* vol. 24, no. 3 (June 1969), pp. 459–77.

[21] Richard L. Sandor and Howard B. Sosin, "The Determinants of Mortgage Risk Premium: A Case Study of the Portfolio of a Savings and Loan Association," *Journal of Business,* vol. 48, no. 1 (January 1975), pp. 27–38.

COMPARISON OF CLASSES OF INVESTMENTS

The most convenient basis for comparison of alternative investment classes is to compare each of the other types of investment with the opportunities available at the same time in the publicly traded bond market. The most complete information is available in this market, and once the data have been set up there is little problem in running additional presumed purchases through the process. In each case, the computations will reveal the yield that could have been obtained if the amounts of money actually were invested in average investments in the public bond market. In addition, the actual yields and risk premiums achieved may be compared with the best buys available in the public sector.

While these methods should be adequate for the espoused purposes, additional studies can be conducted to improve the results. Practically no defaults have taken place among publicly issued bonds, but many have occurred in the private home mortgage field, and some are apparently developing in the income property mortgage market. Studies of the risk premiums and rates in these investment categories would be useful in developing the needed risk charges.

ANALYSIS OF THE ENTIRE PORTFOLIO

Since life insurance companies and pension funds have traditionally been opposed to active management of their fixed-dollar portfolios, analyses of the portfolio opportunities that were missed during a year are usually rather academic. If a portfolio is being actively managed, the various steps described above can actually be applied in reverse; and the opportunities for profitable switches can be observed. These switches are usually defined in terms of tax advantages, best buys, and best sales resulting from temporary aberrations in the yield spreads.

The procedure can also be applied if an analysis is to be made to determine the opportunity costs of not managing actively. Such an analysis can indicate the relative efficiency of the extensive use of private placements in the portfolio, since they virtually preclude active management.

The final use of a comprehensive analysis of the portfolio, even if activity is not contemplated, is that it would yield estimates of the total risk of loss inherent in the portfolio and of the level of risk premium inherent in the return. This information is necessary in trying to balance toward what has been established as the optimum risk level of the trend. It would also be helpful to the actuary in determining the "risk free" yield on the fund.

CONCLUSION

This discussion has attempted to show that the nature of life insurance companies and pension funds requires performance measuring techniques that are adapted to these institutions. Total return methods do not interface with the fund risk, which is the basic problem in the management of both the assets and liabilities of these funds. The methods described in this chapter are designed to provide information adapted to the nature of these funds that is useful to the investment manager. Application of these techniques should go far toward allowing the investment manager, working with the actuary, to estimate the risk of insolvency of the entire operation. Comparison of this risk level with the tolerable risk level for the particular fund would provide additional information for future management of the fund.

10

Cash Flow and Cash Flow Forecasting in the Life Insurance Industry

By Francis H. Schott*

Cash flow is a term of art in corporate finance. Its most general meaning is "funds that can be ploughed back into the business." The standard definition, for nonfinancial corporations, is "retained earnings plus depreciation allowances."[1]

As is typical, standard manufacturing corporation concepts need considerable redefinition to become applicable to financial or service corporations. In the case at hand, that of life insurance companies, the most significant differences should be mentioned individually since they also explain the importance of investments and investment policy in the life insurance industry.

1. Life insurance companies are not only operating corporations with "sales" (new and renewal premiums) and "costs" (benefits and expenses), they are large pools of capital. Hence, investment income constitutes a significant part of total income (and

---

* Francis H. Schott is vice president and economist of the Equitable Life Assurance Society of the United States.

The author is deeply indebted to William Gobbo, Jr., and Rita Scholze, associate economists, and to Rita Morris, investment statistician, all of the Equitable, for their assistance in the preparation of this paper. All errors are the sole responsibility of the author.

[1] *The McGraw-Hill Dictionary of Modern Economics,* 2d ed. (New York: McGraw Hill, 1973), pp. 85–86. Naturally, there is a valid distinction between *total* earnings and *retained* earnings which will be recognized in several of the tables in this chapter.

hence of the excess of sales over costs). It follows that investment policy plays a much larger role in life insurance than in manufacturing concerns. It is in fact a primary activity inherent in any funded insurance product.

2. For essentially the same reason, in the life insurance case "amortization receipts and other repayments" rather than the provision for replacement of physical assets constitute the bulk of the item called "depreciation" in the manufacturing-concern cash flow statement. Once more, it follows that investment policy assumes special importance in life insurance company cash flow analysis.

3. The existence of a large portfolio implies active management beyond original investment, collection of interest and dividends, and reinvestment. Sales and purchases of securities are undertaken for investment reasons, and sales add to cash flow.

4. Finally, while several of the preceding statements also apply to other nonmanufacturing enterprises, there is one item—policy loans—which is peculiar to life insurance companies and which constitutes a volatile drain on cash flow.

Cash flow is the life blood of a life insurance company's investment activity. Its proper analysis, forecasting, and, above all, its use to produce income are vital supplements to the insurance side of the business.

LIFE INSURANCE CASH FLOW—A REVIEW

Accounting for Cash Flow

The following aggregate summary of life insurance companies' cash flow for the 13 years ending in 1974 (see Table 10.1) is designed to conform conceptually to the general corporate cash flow concept, adjusted for the distinctions drawn in the introductory section.

In Table 10.1, the figures under heading A (lines 1–8) comprise the net results of operations, divided into income and outgo, and add up to the annual increase in admitted assets—a concept roughly comparable to retained earnings.[2] The figures under heading B (lines 9–13) "gross up" this result, after the required adjustment to ledger assets from admitted assets. Thus, additional investable funds become available through repayments of outstanding loans and sales

---

[2] The principal distinction is that a manufacturing corporation typically deducts depreciation allowances before arriving at retained earnings.

from the portfolio (i.e., the crude equivalent of a manufacturing corporation's depreciation allowances). The items listed under heading C (lines 14–16) make the required adjustments for policy loans and for changes in the cash position to obtain the grand total of cash flow (heading D, line 17).

The cash flow statement is specifically designed to be an aid to the investment policy maker and administrator. It provides information on the aggregate amounts that must be put to use. When projected, the cash flow information enables the administrator to plan the allocation of available funds among competitive investment outlets such as bonds, mortgages, and equities.

This is a somewhat parochial view of the matter, however, as in actual fact company-wide policy decisions take precedence over investment decisions. Thus, cash flow may be utilized for investments in subsidiaries and expanded insurance operations as well as purchases of capital market instruments.

Historical Survey

By focusing on row 17 of Table 10.1, it is possible to draw some interesting conclusions about recent cash flow patterns. Total cash flow has gone through three phases during the past 10 to 15 years. The first of these periods, 1962–1965, was one of significant but unspectacular growth at roughly 10 percent per annum. Actually, these years were the tail end of very similar trend growth throughout the earlier post-World War II years. The second period, 1966–1970, was one of irregular fluctuations around the 1966 figure, which was well below that of 1965. Thus, cash flow during these years was severely constricted and totally off-trend. The third period, 1971–1972, was one of spectacular expansion. In 1971 alone, cash flow grew almost enough to return to the pre-1966 trend line, making up for five "lost" years. This expansion continued in 1972. The most recent period covered in the table, 1973–1974, was characterized by renewed volatility similar to that of 1966–1970 but around the higher level established in 1971–1972.[3]

---

[3] A brief examination of the life insurance industry cash flow figures for 1975 and 1976, conducted just before this book went to press, suggests that these were extremely strong years for the cash flow and investments of life insurance companies. This development reflected the increased competitiveness of life companies in the pension area, the fiduciary rules established for pension funds by the Employee Retirement Income Security Act of 1974, and the desire of non-financial corporations to refund on a long-term basis some of their short-term debt.

TABLE 10.1
U.S. Life Insurance Companies Cash Flow by Source

Cash Flow Item	Billions of Dollars												
	1962	1963	1964	1965	1966	1967	1968	1969	1970	1971	1972	1973	1974
A. Operating results													
1. Premium receipts	$19.4	$21.1	$22.7	$24.6	$26.8	$28.7	$31.1	$34.0	$36.8	$40.7	$44.5	$48.7	$52.6
2. Net investment income	5.4	5.8	6.3	6.8	7.4	7.9	8.6	9.4	10.1	11.0	12.1	13.7	15.1
3. Other income*	1.6	1.6	1.7	1.8	2.0	2.1	2.2	2.3	2.1	2.4	2.2	2.4	2.3
4. Total income	26.4	28.5	30.7	33.2	36.1	38.6	41.9	45.6	49.1	54.2	58.8	64.8	70.0
5. Benefit payments	14.5	16.0	17.0	18.2	20.1	21.4	23.2	25.4	27.7	29.5	31.4	34.4	37.1
6. Operating expenses, taxes, and other	4.9	5.3	5.8	6.0	7.0	7.7	8.7	10.0	10.6	11.4	12.1	12.9	15.3
7. Total outgo	19.4	21.3	22.8	24.2	27.2	29.1	32.0	35.4	38.3	41.0	43.5	47.3	52.4
8. Increase in admitted assets† (net of market valuation)	6.9	7.3	7.9	8.9	8.9	9.5	9.9	10.2	10.8	13.3	15.3	17.4	17.6
B. Operating results plus reinvestment													
9. Increase in ledger assets	6.5	6.7	7.1	8.0	7.9	8.3	8.5	7.9	9.2	12.0	13.7	15.0	15.8
10. Amortization receipts‡	4.5	5.1	5.2	5.7	5.5	5.5	5.9	6.3	6.7	7.7	8.1	8.3	8.4
11. Other repayments§	1.9	2.3	2.4	2.5	1.8	1.8	1.7	1.4	1.1	2.3	3.0	2.7	2.0
12. Sales from portfolio	1.1	2.0	2.0	2.5	3.4	2.2	2.3	2.2	2.7	4.5	7.1	7.0	3.8
12a. (Sales of equities)‖									(1.6)	(3.0)	(4.8)	(4.6)	(2.6)
13. Subtotal	14.0	16.1	16.7	18.7	18.6	17.8	18.4	17.8	19.7	26.5	31.9	33.0	30.0

C. Adjustments for policy loans and liquidity

14. Policy loan increases (−)		0.5	0.4	0.5	1.4	0.9	1.2	2.5	2.2	1.0	0.9	2.2	2.7
15. Net increase (−) or decrease (+) in cash position		−0.3	0.0	+0.1	−0.2	−0.1	−0.2	−0.8	−0.9	−0.5	−0.6	−0.1	−1.0
16. Other#		0.2	0.0	0.4	−0.1	0.0	0.3	0.4	0.0	0.3	0.4	0.3	−0.3

D. Grand total

17. Cash flow for market investments	13.4	15.7	16.7	18.2	16.9	16.8	17.3	14.9	16.6	25.3	30.8	31.0	26.0

* Primarily dividends and benefits left on deposit.

† Lines 8 and 9 differ because net premiums uncollected and deferred, plus due and accrued investment income, are included in admitted assets but not in ledger assets. The latter concept corresponds to cash flow availability. For a detailed discussion of the reconciliation, see Joseph C. Noback, *Life Insurance Accounting* (Homewood, Ill.: Richard D. Irwin, 1969), pp. 87–92.

‡ Includes amortization and partial prepayments of mortgages plus maturities and calls of securities.

§ Prepayments in full of mortgages.

‖ Not available prior to 1970.

Primarily includes changes in borrowing (increase = +) and statistical discrepancies.

Sources: Lines (1) through (4): American Council of Life Insurance, *Life Insurance Fact Book* (Washington, D.C., annual).

Lines (5) through (8): derived from data available from the American Council of Life Insurance, Washington, D.C. (table entitled "Flow of Funds through U.S. Life Insurance Companies—Accrual Basis").

Lines (9) through (17): for 1965–1970, George A. Bishop, *The Response of Life Insurance Investments to Changes in Monetary Policy, 1965–1970* (New York: Life Insurance Association of America, 1971). Since 1971, industry totals are estimated by the American Council of Life Insurance (formerly the Life Insurance Association of America) based on quarterly surveys of companies representing approximately 80 percent of total U.S. life insurance company assets.

These periods can be used in a crude first attempt to identify the major factors influencing cash flow. One important observation is that life insurance is ordinarily one of the most steadily growing businesses in the United States. While life insurance has not been impervious to wars, recessions, and economic and regulatory changes, some fundamentals have not changed. These include the persistence of the family as the social unit and the need for family protection against contingencies; the long-term growth in real terms of the U.S. economy, partly expressed in improved benefits such as pensions; and adaptive management in an industry long acquainted with a competitive environment. Thus, at least in the past, a solid growth trend could virtually be taken for granted. This observation is particularly relevant to the period before 1966.

A second generalization is that external circumstances can disrupt the growth trend sharply, at least as regards total cash flow—the "bottom line" for the purposes of this paper. During 1966–1970, the United States experienced two "credit crunches," 1966 and 1969–1970, when "disintermediation" and "borrower problems" became household words. Several investigators have explored the mechanisms through which Federal Reserve monetary restraint is transmitted to life insurance cash flow.[4]

However, even a quick glance at the details of Table 10.1 reveals that the 1966–1970 slowdown can be traced to several interrelated items in the accounting statement. The items which are most sensitive to financial market conditions are policy loans (line 14), unscheduled repayments (line 11 and parts of line 10), receivables as represented by the difference between lines 8 and 9 (admitted versus ledger assets), and the liquidity position (line 15). There is much less variation from the growth trend in the operating results (section A) than in the more strictly financial items (sections B and C).

A third observation relates to the cash flow resurgence of 1971–1972. It is possible to trace this resurgence largely to an improvement in the cash flow items singled out above in explaining the 1966–1970 standstill. Furthermore, the slowdown in cash flow growth in 1973 and 1974 suggests once again the considerable relevance of external economic and financial conditions.

Attention should also be directed to changes in "institutional parameters." The degree of turnover of a portfolio can vary over time with changes in the proportions of various assets in the portfolio and with changes in the maturity and other characteristics of the instru-

---

[4] Several of these studies are discussed below, pp. 232–39.

ments within each asset category. One important change has been the gain in life insurance company equity holdings as a percentage of the portfolio, which can in turn be traced to the gradual liberalization of the relevant regulations applicable to general accounts and the rapid growth of separate accounts.[5] An increased role for equities in the portfolio almost necessarily causes a rise in cash flow since equities are typically managed more actively than bonds and mortgages. As Table 10.1 clearly indicates, the turnover in equities was an important component of cash flow in 1971–1974. Thus, the large "bottom line" increases since 1970 have to be interpreted as reflecting in part institutional change.

Along the same lines, there is an excellent case for conducting an item-by-item check of "structural changes" before stretching for either internal or external explanations of fluctuations in specific cash flow components. Such a systematic examination would be beyond the scope of this chapter, but institutional changes besides the one just mentioned are singled out occasionally. These are sufficient in number and importance to warn against the validity of a strictly statistical analysis, no matter how sophisticated. Here, one further illustration will have to suffice.

The question of portfolio churning is a major obstacle to unambiguous conclusions in the cash flow analysis of any financial institution. Besides being explicitly recognized in sales from the portfolio (lines 12 and 12a) such turnover also has a bearing on changes in the cash position (line 15), although in this case the problem is solved arbitrarily by defining the change as net. The problem with this solution is that the management of the liquidity position may in fact have become a much larger (or smaller) portion of total investment activity, either from one year to the next or in trend-line fashion. Such changes are washed out by the net definition. Although practicality must prevail in data collection and presentation, such issues could conceivably be studied using individual company records.

CASH FLOW ANALYSIS

Background

The last two decades have witnessed rapid development of statistical analysis in economics and finance. The computer has per-

---

[5] The investment regulations applicable to life insurance companies are explained in more detail in Chapter 14.

mitted the storage of vast quantities of data and the testing of associative relationships on a reasonably cost-efficient basis. Very broadly speaking, the decade of the 1950s was devoted to aggregate economic model building on the basis of national income account variables and without close attention to financial variables. This initial direction reflected the emphasis on Keynesian economics in business cycle analysis as fiscal policy and business capital investment were judged the crucial variables determining the course of the economy. Financial factors were believed to be secondary, although interest rates always played some role in Keynesian models.[6]

The attention to financial variables that developed in the early 1960s can be traced directly to the emergence of "monetarism" as a potent force in cyclical analysis. Various monetary aggregates, such as the money supply, were advanced by theorists as the main determinant of the course of the economy.[7]

By the late 1960s, the battle of rival theories had been fought sufficiently to permit attempts at synthesis by the more eclectic of the aspiring model builders. One very practical consideration was that commercial services seeking to satisfy the demands of a variegated clientele simply could not afford a strictly theoretical (or doctrinaire) view of economic relationships. In the course of the developing inflation storm, business in general and financial institutions in particular were becoming more cognizant—if not to say painfully aware —of the interrelationships between real and financial "outside" variables that might affect them.

Throughout the early years of large-scale econometric model building, there has been a nagging question of the proper approach to individual-industry analysis. Almost without exception, the line of investigation has led from the general to the specific. Thus, most industry analyses are the outgrowth of larger-scale models. This in turn means that such analyses have only recently been undertaken with any degree of sophistication. In this context, "sophistication" means that the investigator should be familiar with the institutional peculi-

---

[6] An example of an econometric model built largely along Keynesian lines is the Brookings model. See J. S. Duesenberry et al., eds., The Brookings Quarterly Econometric Model of the United States (Chicago: Rand McNally & Co., 1965).

[7] One leading monetarist model of the U.S. economy is that of the St. Louis Federal Reserve Bank. See L. C. Andersen and J. L. Jordan, "Monetary and Fiscal Actions: A Test of Their Relative Importance in Economic Stabilization," Federal Reserve Bank of St. Louis, Review, vol. 68, no. 11 (November 1968), pp. 11–24; and L. C. Andersen and K. M. Carlson, "A Monetarist Model for Economic Stabilization," Federal Reserve Bank of St. Louis, Review, vol. 52, no. 4 (April 1970), pp. 7–25.

arities of the industry studied to the point where "inside" variables (intra-industry relationships) can be combined with "outside" variables (from the aggregate model). This is a difficult objective to accomplish, especially in a multifaceted industry such as life insurance.

Another step must be taken to make new mathematical techniques fully applicable to a specific problem, i.e., the step from the industry to the company level. It is at this point, of course, that precise inside knowledge becomes truly crucial. It is also at this point, however, that outside model-building expertise can be obtained only through very considerable interaction between inside and outside experts or, alternatively, through a full-scale internal study that takes outside studies into account.

Current Status of Industry Studies

Although statistical work on life insurance cash flow as a whole is just getting underway, much initial progress has been made. As this work has proceeded and some models have gone into the testing stage, however, it has become clear that a rigorous generalized cash flow model of strong past explanatory and future predictive power will prove very difficult to achieve.

Statistical cash flow research must contend with two principal problems. Cash flow is composed of elements subject to both very long-run and very short-run influences. On the long-term side, institutional parameters will change. Thus, premium income over the longer term depends on the perceived need for protection (and its proper form) relative to personal income and on trends in corporate benefit plans. Long-run premium income is also affected by the competition for the consumer's dollar among consumption and savings alternatives. The stability of premium income relative to national income account aggregates may therefore hide institutional changes that are extremely difficult both to envisage and to specify properly for purposes of long-term forecasting. Yet, much planning in life insurance does require a long-time horizon.

A second problem, this one on the short-run side, is that the economic and financial variables that make most of the short-horizon models tick have exhibited a degree of pathological behavior ever since these models were developed, largely because of mounting inflation. Thus, while there has been no dearth of fluctuations in the variables subject to testing, the stability of the functional relationships established is open to doubt. Naturally, the two problems just enumerated merge in a sense—the more the current environment is outside the range of traditional experience, the more likely it is that this environment will also create problems in the cash flow items initially believed to be characterized by stable long-term growth.

Single-Line Financial Models. Considering the impediments to accurate cash flow forecasting, it is not surprising that most investigators have begun with limited objectives. One reasonable proposition is to take a single item in the industry cash flow statement and test it for statistical associations with life insurance or external economic and financial variables. One early example of this type of analysis was conducted by the author of this chapter.[8] Reflecting on the experiences of 1966 and 1969–1970, when it appeared that runups in policy loans were closely correlated in timing with the general "credit crunches" of these periods, the author undertook a systematic examination of the functional relationship between changes in policy loans at 15 large life insurance companies and various outside variables.

The results of this study clearly illustrate the occasional triumphs and frequent frustrations which tend to accompany such exercises. On the positive side, it was possible to establish beyond reasonable doubt the statistical validity of what had by then become obvious— policy loans are the single most important linkage between life insurance cash flow and outside economic variables. Among the hypotheses tested, quite a number performed well. The best multiple regression linked quarterly changes in policy loans (the dependent variable) with an average interest rate (the prime commercial paper rate) and the rate of change in the narrowly defined money supply (demand deposits plus currency in circulation). The findings indicated that policy loans are directly related to interest rate changes and inversely related to fluctuations in the money supply. It was possible to explain more than 96 percent of the variation in past policy loan demand, and the equations passed the standard statistical tests regarding the significance of coefficients (t-ratios) and the absence of serial correlation (Durbin-Watson statistic).

On the other hand, frustrations were also encountered. First and foremost, the power to explain past changes is not equivalent to predictive ability because coincident variations in dependent and independent variables require forecasts of the independent variables. The problem can be alleviated by lagging the independent variables at the

---

8 Francis H. Schott, "Disintermediation through Policy Loans at Life Insurance Companies," *Journal of Finance,* vol. 26, no. 3 (June 1971), pp. 720–29.

deliberate sacrifice of some strength of the correlation, but that deterioration may become severe well within the time frame indispensable for business decisions. The alternative is to involve oneself fully with the aggregate models, so as to obtain statistical or judgmental capability in forecasting the independent variables on a par with the best the experts can offer. But in recent years, forecasting interest rates and money supply changes has not been a happy experience even among presumed experts.

A second problem is the high degree of multicollinearity among most economic time series, which suggests that a variety of explanatory factors is involved in each phenomenon one seeks to elucidate. Also, relatively slight changes in outside parameters can lead to considerable shifts in the relative ranking of statistical explanations. A simple example is the multicollinearity of interest rates, many of which perform almost equally well in explaining policy loans. In this instance, at least, the main underlying hypothesis is the same, regardless of the precise specification of the statistical test.

A more complex problem arises when clearly distinguishable alternative hypotheses perform almost equally well or even take turns at performing better depending on the time period examined. In the initial study of policy loans, lagged consumer price index changes, combined with current money supply changes, had a weaker initial effect on policy loans, but one that lasted longer, than did lagged interest rates. (Changes in the consumer price index were positively related to policy loan demand.) These explanations do not contradict each other; inflation has a more gradual effect on policy loans than do interest rates. However, both the logic and the statistics become increasingly fuzzy as one seeks to replicate real life in multiple correlations.

A third problem is the required reliance upon the stability of functional relationships based on past experience. For statistical reasons, one prefers long time series and many observations. This generates the impression of validity of the eventual "best" explanation for the period as a whole, but each sub-period might have had a much different explanation if examined separately.[9] In the example at hand, this phenomenon has found expression in a marked deterioration of the associative relationship of policy loans with the independent variables found "best" at any one time, despite the capability (and prac-

---

[9] Statistical techniques exist to test for the possibility of significant changes in functional relationships by sub-periods. One such test, the Chow test, is described in J. Johnston, *Econometric Methods*, 2d ed. (New York: McGraw-Hill Book Co.), p. 207.

tice) of permitting coefficients to change as new observations are entered.

A fourth frustration, which follows from the preceding ones, is the need for continued hypothesizing and reexamination. The misfiring of predictions (including those of independent variables), the closeness of the statistical choices, and the nagging question of possible changes in institutional parameters all combine to keep the analyst and the computer busy. This problem in turn raises questions of cost effectiveness throughout the exercise.[10]

Multi-Line Financial Models. Judgmental analysis has had and will continue to have a very significant part in cash flow research and, for that matter, in all aspects of life insurance. The borderline between statistical and qualitative evaluation is actually quite narrow once one steps past the distinction between papers containing formal equations as against those that are largely literary. Analytical insights can be obtained either way.

An excellent judgmental analysis of life insurance cash flows during the period 1965–1970 has been conducted by George Bishop.[11] Stimulated by the events of that period, Bishop systematically studied the cash flow components for their responsiveness to monetary policy. His time frame is, in effect, the monetary policy cycle, which for the period studied meant alternating periods of monetary restraint (1966 and 1969–1970) and monetary ease (1965 and 1967–1968). Bishop thus deals with periods of four to eight quarters each.

While Bishop was primarily interested in the measurable effects of monetary policy changes on the cash flow of life insurance companies, he devoted some attention to the channels of transmission. In a sense, Bishop's major contribution was to bring out into the open the under-

---

[10] An additional problem is that computer programs virtually have to be written so as to obtain the best statistical fit, regardless of whether a reasonable hypothesis can be formulated to conform with the results. Naturally, this problem should be minimized by submitting to tests only those relationships that could be justified logically. The advice is easy to follow on major points but not always on the refinements in which the statistician revels. For example, if a statistical test shows a higher correlation between two variables if one of them is lagged by two quarters rather than one or three, one should then seek a behavioral explanation of the result rather than simply accept it. This is more easily said than done.

[11] George A. Bishop, *The Response of Life Insurance Investments to Changes in Monetary Policy* (New York: Life Insurance Association of America, 1971). The basic cash flow data presented in Bishop are carried forward annually and analyzed in Kenneth M. Wright, *Economic and Investment Report* (Washington, D.C.: American Council of Life Insurance, annual). Bishop's study considerably extends and deepens some closely related observations offered in Francis H. Schott, "Monetary Policy and Life Insurance Companies," Business and Economic Statistics Section, American Statistical Association, *Proceedings* (1970), pp. 335–41.

lying difficulty of defining monetary policy so as to facilitate future quantitative analysis on the basis of that alleged key variable. It is entirely plausible to define changes in monetary policy on the basis of stated changes in the Federal Reserve Open Market Committee's directives, as Bishop did; but changes cannot be quantified in an unequivocal and conclusive fashion.[12]

An attempt at summarizing Bishop's results has been made in Table 10.2.[13] In essence, Bishop classified the cash flow items of Table 10.1—first with respect to the presence or absence of sensitivity to monetary policy and second with respect to the degree and timing of such responsiveness in the relevant cases. Thus, Bishop showed that operating results (section A of Table 10.1) are relatively stable but that monetary policy has an influence that extends beyond policy loans to unscheduled repayments, sales from portfolios, and adjustments in the liquidity position. Bishop also went beyond the bottom line of Table 10.1 to investigate the effect of cash flow variations on new commitment activity. He observed that such activity reflects monetary-policy-induced swings in cash flow in an accentuated manner, with a moderate time lag. This relationship is evidenced by the commitment statistics which comprise the last row of Table 10.2.

Bishop's study did not address the critical problem of quantitative precision and the acid test of predictive power. Nevertheless, his work is the foundation on which an econometrician with limited knowledge of the life insurance industry should build his formulation of testable hypotheses in the financial-cyclical area. The proper measurement of monetary policy, however, remains an obstacle that will require extensive experimentation without any guarantee of success.

Special mention should also be made of J. David Cummins' "allocation of funds" studies.[14] These studies utilize the insurance sector of the Federal Reserve's quarterly flow of funds accounts as a basic framework. The Federal Reserve accounts aim at capturing the net

---

[12] There are two major problems—one of classifying judgments, one of finding the correct measurement. As regards the judgment question, the Federal Reserve moves by degrees of ease and restraint so that some arbitrariness is involved in classifying Federal Reserve policy by intent. As regards the measurement question, there is a long-standing problem of whether the intent and/or the result should be judged by interest rates (such as the Federal funds rate) or by monetary aggregates (such as the narrowly or more broadly defined money supply). The problem exceeds the scope of this chapter.

[13] For the sake of simplicity, annual figures are given although these are not as discriminating as Bishop's quarterly peak-and-trough analysis. Also, the years 1971–1974 have been added.

[14] J. David Cummins, *An Econometric Model of the Life Insurance Sector of the U.S. Economy* (Lexington, Mass.: D. C. Heath, Lexington Books, 1975).

TABLE 10.2
Percentage Changes in Selected Volatile Elements of Life Insurance Cash Flow (annual rates of growth)

Cash Flow Element	1963–1965 Period of Steadily Rising Cash Flow (average annual rate of growth)	Period of Increasing Volatility in Cash Flow					Resurgence in Cash Flow		Renewed Volatility	
		1966	1967	1968	1969	1970	1971	1972	1973	1974
Stable elements										
Increase in ledger assets	7.2%	− 1.8%	5.7%	1.8%	− 6.5%	15.8%	30.6%	14.6%	9.5%	5.4%
Amortization receipts	8.3	− 4.7	0.8	8.2	6.0	6.4	15.1	5.2	2.8	0.2
Monetary policy sensitive elements										
Other repayments	9.9	−27.1	− 1.9	− 3.9	−18.4	−21.9	109.5	30.0	− 8.8	−26.4
Sales from portfolio	35.6	33.5	−36.2	7.7	− 5.4	21.7	69.4	58.0	− 1.5	−45.7
Net increase in policy loans	3.4	167.5	−34.5	32.4	102.0	−11.1	−55.3	− 6.3	134.1	21.3
Total cash flow available for market investments	10.8	− 6.9	− 1.1	3.4	−14.1	11.5	52.4	21.9	0.6	−16.1
Change in total new investment commitments	12.0	−21.0	5.1	− 8.6	−17.3	−24.3	85.1	29.7	3.9	−27.1

Note: Changes in cash position are monetary-policy sensitive but have been omitted since the small dollar amounts involved lead to gyrations in the percentage computations.

Source: Based on industry totals shown in Table 10.1 and sources there cited, plus commitment data available from the American Council of Life Insurance, Washington, D.C.

sources and uses of funds by major categories in an internally consistent matrix for the entire economy. Hence, adjustment of the model to the accounts means as much emphasis on the "output" as on "input" of the life insurance industry. In fact, Cummins' multi-line model has two equations for net inflows (life insurance reserves and pension reserves) and five equations for net outflows (policy loans, corporate bonds, home mortgages, commercial mortgages, and equities). The model can generate simulations of past performance as well as forecasts for as many periods ahead as one is willing to forecast the required independent variables.

One of the great advantages of university-based studies is that the scholars involved are liberal in dispensing information. The published description supplied by Cummins need not be replicated here, but some observations may be in order. First, every one of the explanatory equations obviously reflects reasonable hypotheses, considerable experimentation, and acceptable compromises between stretching for relevant variables and the degree of explanation achieved. The discussion of the hypotheses and the choice among possible independent variables and their exact specification is intriguing and educational. If one compares Bishop's suggestive qualitative insights with the careful quantitative approach of Cummins, the question could well be raised whether Bishop's study could be quantified in a similar manner.

The question also arises in part because the flow-of-funds framework is not easily understood by life insurance executives as directly relevant to their cash flow problems (nor are such problems necessarily Cummins' direct concern). Perhaps the main drawback of the flow-of-funds accounts in a highly practical context is the excessive netting-out of cash flow. Amortization and reinvestment are omitted. But the operator calculating total cash availability, total investment capability, and allocations among competing uses of those funds is interested in gross flows.[15] Thus, the net change in various types of assets upon which Cummins' analysis focuses is by and large a residual, rather than an objective, in actual investment management. Cummins, of course, recognized this drawback and points to other uses of his model. One especially intriguing potential aim might be to examine the changing role of the life insurance industry in various investment markets on the basis of changing relative yield incentives.

---

[15] A model of gross rather than net flows is presented in James E. Pesando, "The Interest Sensitivity of the Flow of Funds through Life Insurance Companies: An Econometric Analysis," *Journal of Finance*, vol. 29, no. 4 (September 1974), pp. 1105–21.

A third and hardly surprising observation is that Cummins' model exposes the user to the statistical frustrations already described in the case of the single-line policy loan model. There is, for example, very little lag in many of his explanatory variables, most of which are exogenous to the industry. This in turn again means that the quality of his forecasts is heavily dependent upon the performance of the aggregate model with which Wharton Econometric Forecasting Associates work; and the coefficients of the equations—if not the equations themselves—would have to be revised regularly if forecasting rather than explanation of the past were to be a major aim.

Finally, Cummins includes quite a few independent variables in his multiple regressions (five in the case of policy loans). Naturally, this may represent real life more adequately than simpler explanations; but in the absence of a tabulation of the partial correlation coefficients it is difficult to tell the relative importance of his variables—helpful information in further experimentation by others.

An Initial Full-Line Study. At the outset of this section, it was noted that the aggregate economic model builders are only now, in the mid-1970s, getting around to detailed studies of the individual industries of their multifaceted clientele. Once engaged in the exercise, the large-scale operator does not hesitate to take a broad swing at all major aggregates of interest to the client—partly because of his experience in dealing with the economy as a whole; partly because of implicit faith in the averaging-out of errors in the subtotals of the aggregates; and party because he is as yet unencumbered with the fine points that may or may not be crucial to the clientele. It is, at any rate, a reasonable approach in acquiring and demonstrating the required specialized competence.

The first such attempt was made by Chase Econometrics.[16] The distinguishing characteristics of the Chase model are: (1) its long-term forecasting orientation—ten years ahead; (2) the inclusion of property-casualty operations, in recognition of the increasing overlap between life and property-casualty insurers; and (3) its concentration on the operating results part of the cash flow statement (section A of Table 10.1). In fact, the expected change in total assets becomes the bottom line of the forecast. However, financial market variables

---

[16] See Chase Manhattan Bank, *The Long-Term Outlook for the Insurance Industry* (New York, 1974) and D. Nemeroff and L. Taub, "An Econometric Appraisal of the Insurance Industry," *Best's Review: Life/Health Insurance Edition,* vol. 74, no. 8 (December 1973), pp. 10, 82–86.

(and not only the net result of insurance operations) enter into the asset forecasts, which also include "distributive shares" by major asset categories.

The specifications of the 20-equation Chase model are proprietary information, but the hints given are sufficient to obtain an impression of the pluses and minuses of the model. Total premium revenue is said to depend on real disposable income and consumer prices, such that premium income rises 0.5 percent for each percentage point rise in real income and an eventual 1 percent for each percentage point rise in consumer prices (after a lag to bring desired or needed protection in line with price rises). In addition, a cyclical variable, the unemployment rate, enters in the total via group premium income.

This national-income-accounts related equation is valuable because it focuses on several of the main linkages between the insurance industry and the economy at large. But if the equation does in fact perform well for the past, it does so by having averaged out differential developments in various types of premium income by line that are crucial in life insurance company management and planning. Hence, the appraisal of the past is subject to the possible charge of oversimplification, and the forecast is too aggregated to be of much immediate help.

As a minor contribution to future development of measurements, Table 10.3 disaggregates the operating results of Table 10.1 to the point of the major components of special interest. (Chase Econometrics has some but not as many details.) It can readily be determined that, among the major components of premium income, the individual life insurance line experienced a downward trend in its contribution to total premium income over the 1962–1974 period, while the other principal lines (especially annuities, including separate accounts) have trended upward. (Examination of new vs. renewal premiums, not shown in Table 10.3, is also important.) A preliminary study of these trends by the Equitable already shows that Chase Econometrics' "most crucial equation" is indeed the composite of widely different component results in the past, inducing doubts about the future aggregate forecast.

Naturally, the groupings themselves will influence, and should in turn be influenced by, the hypotheses to be tested. Thus, the disbursements could well be grouped by type of benefit payment, e.g., death, annuities, etc. One aspect of these choices is whether it is economic or actuarial hypotheses that are to be tested.

TABLE 10.3
Sources of Asset Change at U.S. Life Insurance Companies

| | Billions of Dollars—Accrual Basis | | | | | | | | | | | | |
	1962	1963	1964	1965	1966	1967	1968	1969	1970	1971	1972	1973	1974
Income													
Premium receipts	$19.4	$21.1	$22.7	$24.6	$26.8	$28.7	$31.1	$34.0	$36.8	$40.7	$44.5	$48.7	$52.6
Ordinary life	9.6	10.4	11.1	11.7	12.5	13.2	14.1	14.8	15.7	16.6	17.7	18.8	19.8
Industrial life	1.5	1.4	1.4	1.4	1.4	1.4	1.4	1.4	1.4	1.3	1.3	1.3	1.3
Group life	2.1	2.4	2.6	2.9	3.2	3.5	3.9	4.3	4.7	5.0	5.6	6.3*	6.6
Annuities (Separate accts.)†	1.5	1.7	1.9	2.3	2.4	2.7	3.0	3.8	3.7	4.9	5.5	6.8	7.7
				(0.1)	(0.2)	(0.3)	(0.6)	(1.1)	(1.0)	(1.2)	(1.4)	(1.9)	(1.9)
Health	4.7	5.1	5.6	6.3	7.2	7.9	8.7	9.7	11.4	12.9	14.3	15.5	17.1
Net investment income	5.4	5.8	6.3	6.8	7.4	7.9	8.6	9.4	10.1	11.0	12.1	13.7	15.1
Other income‡	1.6	1.6	1.7	1.8	2.0	2.1	2.2	2.3	2.1	2.4	2.2	2.4	2.3
Total	26.4	28.5	30.7	33.2	36.1	38.6	41.9	45.6	49.1	54.2	58.8	64.8	70.0
Outgo													
Benefit payments	14.5	16.0	17.0	18.2	20.1	21.4	23.2	25.4	27.7	29.5	31.4	34.4	37.1
Ordinary and group life	8.6	9.2	9.8	10.7	11.8	12.6	13.4	15.1	16.7	18.1	19.1	21.0	23.0
Annuities	1.0	1.1	0.9	1.0	1.1	1.2	1.4	1.5	1.7	1.9	2.2	2.6	2.9
Health	3.5	3.9	4.6	4.9	5.4	5.8	6.4	6.8	7.2	7.5	8.1	8.6	8.9
Payments on supplementary contracts	1.0	1.0	1.1	1.1	1.2	1.2	1.3	1.3	1.3	1.2	1.2	1.3	1.3
Disbursement of dividends left on deposit	0.4	0.8	0.6	0.5	0.6	0.6	0.7	0.7	0.8	0.8	0.8	0.9	1.0
Operating expenses, taxes, and other§	4.9	5.3	5.8	6.0	7.0	7.7	8.7	10.0	10.6	11.4	12.1	12.9	15.3
Total	19.4	21.3	22.8	24.2	27.2	29.1	32.0	35.4	38.3	41.0	43.5	47.3	52.4
Increase in admitted assets (net of market valuation)	6.9	7.3	7.9	8.9	8.9	9.5	9.9	10.2	10.8	13.3	15.3	17.4	17.6

Note: Figures may not add to totals due to rounding.

* Includes $1.2 billion of credit life insurance premiums in both 1973 and 1974; such premiums had previously been included in ordinary life and group life.

† Measured by change in reserves.

‡ Includes considerations for supplementary contracts and dividends left on deposit.

§ Includes dividends to stockholders and interest on policy or contract funds and excludes due and unpaid and adjustment items.

Source: For most income items, the *Life Insurance Fact Book* (New York: American Council of Life Insurance, annually); most benefit items, also

THE EQUITABLE CASH FLOW MODEL

Background

The Equitable Life Assurance Society of the United States (ELAS) has developed a simple quarterly internal cash flow model that is used regularly for forecasting cash flow one to nine quarters ahead. As in other cases, the sharp swings in cash flow availability of the post-1965 period were the initial stimulus. Given reasonable success with the policy loan "line" and given the strong likelihood of similar external influences in other lines of the statement, it appeared desirable to experiment with statistical explanations throughout the statement. There was also good reason to apply formal statistical procedures (including seasonal adjustment) to items that might respond to internal variables (e.g., be largely autoregressive). In effect, the formalized cash flow forecast served as the unifying force in substituting for earlier judgmental appraisals that differed in methodology from department to department.

Internal company forecasts are judged strictly by results. One may thus dispense with formal statistical criteria such as the absence of serial correlation. Nor does multicollinearity of the independent variables matter greatly. Low R^2 values can be accepted for what they may be worth. Nevertheless, improvements in the results should be sought, and can often be achieved, by following the established standards for statistical work.

Perhaps the greatest advantage of "inside" work is that data usually can be compiled and arranged in accordance with the hypotheses to be tested. Thus, accounting aggregates that have components likely to be responsive to different explanatory variables should be disaggregated. In fact, this procedure calls for considerable detective work and judgment. Naturally, cost-benefit considerations set limits on this procedure and on the statistical work that follows the data compilation.

One of the major disadvantages of single-company work is that statistical generalizations that may be both reasonable as hypotheses and provable in industry aggregates are not reflected in one company's experience. Two examples are: (1) receipts and disbursements too irregular and too concentrated in relations with a few clients to permit generalizations from past patterns and (2) autonomous administrative or policy changes by the company, which can be disruptive of historical continuity, and, in fact, could at times be designed to be so because they may be intended to improve a company's intra-industry competitive position. Such changes wash out in industry statistics but not in single-company data. The presence of these factors makes it indispensable to have the assistance of the entire company for proper input.

Description of the Model

A summary description of the ELAS cash flow model is presented in Table 10.4. The table will reward some study. It attempts to cover methodology rather completely while protecting internal ELAS figures and proprietary formulas.

Cash flow is disaggregated to 44 lines from the 17 in the basic industry statement of Table 10.1. The relationship between the two cash flow presentations is sketched in the notes to Table 10.4. The disaggregation shows, for example, that individual company records permit a superior categorization of amortization receipts and other repayments (lines 10 and 11 in Table 10.1). The ELAS categorization permits scheduled and unscheduled repayments (lines 29 and 35 of Table 10.4) to be distinguished clearly enough to "read off" *all* contractually mandatory repayments from company records while subjecting *all* unscheduled repayments to economic analysis. In addition, the breakdown by type of loan (corresponding to investment departments) in lines 36–39 permits differential analysis of factors affecting unscheduled prepayments of various types of mortgages and bonds.

Next, attention should be directed to the explanatory equations and their past performance. The table shows exactly which lines of the cash flow statement have been subjected to reasonably successful statistical analysis on the basis of 1965–1974 quarterly data. It also indicates the nature of the independent variables as well as their explanatory power and their "track record." Careful examination of the table reveals that it has been possible to find fairly satisfactory statistical approximations for a variety of cash flow items that had never before been thus examined either at the Equitable or (to the author's knowledge) elsewhere.

The procedure for use of the model is quite simple once the format and data are stored in the computer. Each quarter, new observations are entered as data are received. The coefficients of the independent variables, but not the structure of the equations, are revised on the basis of the new data; and the model is then run for one to nine quarters ahead, utilizing the required forecasts of the independent variables. The output becomes a vital aid in planning the company's commitment posture, both in the aggregate and by investment departments, and its portfolio management, including the liquidity position. The forecasts have generally outperformed the six-months'-ahead cash flow estimates compiled from a large sample of companies by the American Council of Life Insurance.

Problems with the Model

The student of industry cash flow studies would expect a variety of problems in the use of the ELAS cash flow model, and this expectation would not prove to be in error. The single most important problem is unquestionably the dependence of the forecast upon the quality of the forecast of the independent variables. The Equitable is representative of the industry in that certain financial market variables impact with virtually no lag upon a large proportion of its cash flow. In particular, interest rates play a crucial role. A variation of 1 percentage point in the interest rate forecast, if maintained over a year's time, can make a difference of 8 to 10 percent in that year's bottom line forecast (line 44 of Table 10.4). Thus, the most significant potential improvement in the accuracy of the forecast lies, in a sense, outside ELAS and the insurance industry. Top quality economic and financial forecasting is needed.

Second, the areas not yet satisfactorily explained by statistical analysis are disconcertingly large. These include such noteworthy items as separate account inflows and outflows, including transfers between the general account and separate accounts.[17] Separate account operations are heavily subject to current developments in business relations with individual clients. Hence, it is more useful in forecasting to survey the executives in charge of client relations rather than to use any past statistical associations which may exist. For basically the same reason, general account group annuity considerations are also difficult to forecast econometrically. The Equitable has very substantial separate account and general account group annuity operations. The omissions stated thus are major when measured against cash flow. Of course, from a company point of view there is no significance per se to the presence or absence of a series in the statistical model. If the forecasts are satisfactorily close, the method used does not matter. However, group annuity inflows are difficult to predict by any presently known method.

A third problem is the need to reexamine all functional relation-

---

[17] Assets in the Equitable's separate accounts totaled $1.6 billion at the end of 1974, as against general account assets of $16.0 billion.

TABLE 10.4
Summary Description and Results of the Equitable Life Assurance Society General Account Cash Flow Model

Cash Flow Item	Components of Table 1 Line	Independent Variables Used (see Notes)		Statistical Fit of Forecast Equations 1965.1–1974.2			Mean Error of Four Recent 1-Quarter-Ahead Forecasts (percent)	Proportion of Total Gross Cash Flow 1973.3–1974.2 (percent)
		"Internal"	"External"	$\bar{R}^2$	D.W.	Standard Error/Dependent Mean* (percent)		
Insurance income								
1 Insurance income								
2 Group annuity considerations								
3 Less: Cash returns								
4 Separate accounts								
5 General account considerations	1							27.7
6 Individual annuity considerations			1,2	0.785	1.31	10.1	19.8	—
7 Less: Separate accounts							10.5	—
8 General account considerations			1,2	0.233	−0.87	12.7	13.9	4.0
9 Group life premiums	1	1		0.954	1.45	4.1	19.3	32.8
10 Individual life premiums	1	1		0.954	2.53	2.4	4.7	55.7
11 Health insurance premiums	1	1		0.980	1.40	4.0	4.3	53.8
12 Considerations for supplemental contracts	1	2		0.245	1.05	7.9	6.8	4.9
13 Dividend and annuity payment deposits	3	1		0.831	2.19	2.7	7.9	5.9
14 Other income	3						2.3	1.0

#	Item								
15	Total insurance income							4.3	(185.8)
16	*Insurance disbursements*								
17	Surrenders	5	1	0.938	1.05	1	5.3	5.9	−15.1
18	Dividends	5						16.4	−24.9
19	Death and other benefits	5	1	0.984	1.23		2.6	4.1	−118.0
20	Claims on supplemental contracts	5		0.647	1.42	1,2	3.1	6.6	−6.6
21	Dividend and annuity deposits withdrawn	5		0.640	2.35	2	5.3	10.5	−5.4
22	Expenses: Insurance and investment	6		0.963	1.87	1	3.6	4.7	−37.2
23	Other disbursements	6							−2.4
24	Total disbursements							4.2	(−209.6)
25	Insurance income less disbursements								−23.8
26	Investment income: gross	2	3	0.980	2.48	2	2.4	27.4	67.6
27	New money (L. 25 + 26)							3.8	43.8
28	*Investment principal repaid*	9						14.3	
29	Scheduled repayments							2.0	(40.5)
30	Bond investment department	10						4.6	16.8
31	City mortgage department	10	3	0.904	1.73		5.6	5.7	12.8
32	Residential mortgage department	10	3	0.723	0.48	2	3.8	6.8	6.0
33	Farm mortgage department	10	3	0.802	2.19	1,2	6.1	8.1	4.2

TABLE 10.4 (continued)

Cash Flow Item	Components of Table 1 Line	Independent Variables Used (see Notes) "Internal"	Independent Variables Used (see Notes) "External"	Statistical Fit of Forecast Equations 1965.1–1974.2 $\bar{R}^2$	Statistical Fit of Forecast Equations 1965.1–1974.2 D.W.	Statistical Fit of Forecast Equations 1965.1–1974.2 Standard Error/ Dependent Mean* (percent)	Mean Error of Four Recent Consecutive 1-Quarter-Ahead Forecasts (percent)	Proportion of Total Gross Cash Flow 1973.3–1974.2 (percent)
34 Real estate department	10	3		0.920	2.02	9.4	7.8	0.8
35 Unscheduled repayments							24.2	(15.7)
36 Bond investment department	10						35.7	2.3
37 City mortgage department	11		2,2,3	0.439	0.81	34.6	52.0	3.9
38 Residential mortgage department	11		2,3	0.913	1.36	9.1	19.1	7.0
39 Farm mortgage department	11		1,2,3	0.834	1.75	10.4	24.1	2.4
40 Security sales	12							
41 Total investments repaid							7.7	56.2
42 Gross cash flow (L. 27 + 41)							3.8	100.0
43 Net increase in policy loans	14		2,2	0.852	1.00	23.8	24.1	10.8
44 General account net cash flow	17						6.5	89.2

Notes: "Internal" Variables: 1 = Insurance in force, 2 = Premium income, and 3 = Asset holdings. "External" Variables: 1 = Aggregate income, 2 = Financial market, and 3 = Physical production. The key is deliberately vague to protect proprietary information. The precise variables and functional relationships cannot be revealed. Equations given where applicable. Subtotals in parentheses.

* In the deliberate absence of precision in the definition of the independent variables, there is no reason for giving coefficients and t-ratios of the functional relationships. The stated measure (standard error of the forecasting equation as a percentage of the mean dollar amount of the dependent variables) gives a "standardized" indication of the error factors in the various equations and can therefore be compared equation by equation. Very roughly, the higher this percentage, the more difficult it is to make a good forecast.

Source: Equitable Life Assurance Society, internal data.

ships regularly. The policy loan equation, which is discussed above, is a classic example; but once the model is available, similar questions arise with respect to all other lines. Neither such examinations, nor the forecasting of the exogenous variables, nor indeed the computer time to run the model are costless. Executive time is involved in decisions on such matters, as it is in the understanding and proper use of the model.

Mention might also be made of two items that are not considered special problems by ELAS, but which might be important to other researchers. The first of these is the lack of an explicit forecast for security sales. In effect, this item is treated as a residual within the desired liquidity position at the end of each forecasting period. The model output, plus judgments on other above-the-bottom-line items, becomes input to tentative bottom-line results. A second point is that new ELAS investments for general account (in the aggregate and by type) are not forecast explicitly. Tentative decisions on such allocations are made on the basis of input from model results (plus judgment) and the tentative review of the liquidity position on various future dates. An iterative process follows in which prospective general account cash flow and the desired liquidity position (including security sales) are brought into line with prospective investment commitments (including the dating of forward deliveries of funds).

SUMMARY AND CONCLUSIONS

Cash flow analysis and forecasting through structured statistical methods is a new and promising endeavor in life insurance financial analysis. It would have been valuable to the industry and the financial institution analyst under any circumstances, but the unusual gyrations of the economy and of aggregate monetary variables during the past decade have made the analysis timely and indeed virtually indispensable. The interaction of the economy at large with life insurance cash flow is quite direct and virtually immediate.

Future research should include, at the industry level, analytical attempts such as those the Equitable has made for itself. The results are likely to be beneficial in understanding the role of the industry in the U.S. economy. Ideally, one could imagine a model that would truly simulate the interaction between the economy and the industry in such a way that the repercussions of substantial cash flow variations in the life insurance industry induced by economic and financial developments would in turn show up in subsequent economic variations.

Besides the improved understanding which the industry and scholars would thus obtain, public policy implications might also emerge. One such implication, which is already clear from the exercises undertaken so far, is the following. The alternation of monetary policy "crunches" and excessive ease characteristic of the post-1965 period has unhinged the traditional stability of the flows of funds from the life insurance sector into the long-term capital markets. Among all the troubles caused so far by mounting inflation, this one may not strike the "right-now"-oriented Washington policymaker as a major one; but men and women of longer vision will not downplay the problem.

11

Impact of Inflation on the Life Insurance Industry and Its Investment Policies

By J. Robert Ferrari*

It is extremely difficult to isolate the impact of inflation on an industry as complex as life insurance which is influenced by such a wide range of demographic, political, social, technological, and economic factors. The problem is further complicated by our very incomplete understanding of the economic and financial consequences of sustained high rates of inflation because of limited experience with such episodes in the United States. Some experience on life insurance in other countries suggests that inflation has had a negative effect on cash value life insurance but these data are limited.[1]

The question of the effect of inflation on the demand for life insurance in the United States has received relatively little attention in the literature. In the two most serious efforts, Neumann concludes that demand for savings through life insurance in the post-war period

---

* J. Robert Ferrari is vice president and chief economist of the Prudential Insurance Company of America.

[1] Mark R. Green, *Inflation and Life Insurance,* Ben F. Hadley Distinguished Manuscript Series (Columbus, Ohio: Griffith Foundation for Insurance Education, 1974), p. 13. According to accounts in the *Eighth International Congress of Actuaries* (London 1927), the devastating, run-away post-World War I inflation in Germany essentially wiped out life insurance along with all contracts denominated in what became a worthless currency. This, of course, was a case of a virtually incomprehensible inflation many times worse than the double-digit rates that prevailed in 1974–1975. Dr. Hendrik Houthakker of Harvard has conducted a recent study of world inflationary problems which was sponsored by the American Council of Life Insurance, but the results were not published at the time this chapter was prepared.

1946–1964 did not depend on the "expected" price level, while Fortune, studying the period 1967–1971, suggests that expectations regarding the rate of inflation (and not the price level) depress consumer confidence and hence, in his theoretical construct, the demand for life insurance.[2] These represent not so much conflicting conclusions or results from different time periods as significant disagreement between the authors over the appropriate theoretical framework for assessing the effect of inflation on life insurance.

This chapter represents an attempt to draw some meaningful conclusions from the recent performance of life insurance companies in the U.S. economy, where for the last five to ten years inflation and inflation expectations have been increasingly dominant forces. An assessment of how the life insurance industry has performed in and responded to this economic environment is used as the basis for some reasonable judgments as to how such actions and results are related directly or indirectly to inflation. Several other environmental and institutional influences also are recognized. Both the marketing and investment functions are considered because the nature and relative importance of the savings features in the industry's various financial security products have a profound effect on its investment practices and its role as a financial intermediary.

PERFORMANCE IN THE RECENT INFLATIONARY ENVIRONMENT

A recent survey of life insurance industry data points to two general conclusions: (1) The life insurance industry has been maintaining its relative importance in its economic role as an *insuring* institution as indicated by the stability of the share of the public's dollar allocated to providing protection against the financial consequences of death, disability, and superannuation, and (2) the industry has been declining in relative importance in its economic role as a *savings* institution as indicated by its ability to attract only a declining share of the public's saving dollar. The trends that underlie these conclusions were evident several years ago, have been suggested by others,[3] and are reinforced by the more recent evidence.

---

[2] Seev Neumann, "Inflation and Savings through Life Insurance," *Journal of Risk and Insurance,* vol. 36, no. 5 (December 1969), pp. 567–82; Comment on this article by Peter Fortune, *Journal of Risk and Insurance,* vol. 39, no. 2 (June 1972), pp. 317–30; and Peter Fortune, "A Theory of Optimal Life Insurance: Development and Tests," *Journal of Finance* (June 1973), pp. 587–600.

[3] See, for example, Green, *Inflation and Life Insurance;* Francis H. Schott, "Monetary Policy and Life Insurance Companies—Panel on the Impact of Mone-

So far in the 1970s, total life insurance in force in the United States has increased at an 8.9 percent annual rate, reaching more than $2.1 trillion and outpacing the growth in GNP. Life insurance protection per family has remained steady at about two times average family income. Attitude surveys continue to show that life insurance is considered a basic necessity by the vast majority of people. As recently as the fall of 1974, when the consumer confidence indexes were registering all-time lows, the consumers surveyed by the Conference Board in its study of value received from money spent ranked life insurance sixth out of 45 basic products, behind only small appliances, black and white and color television sets, eggs, and poultry.[4] The respectable performance of the industry in recent years is best summed up by noting that total premium and annuity receipts have averaged a relatively stable 5.4 percent of disposable personal income. This represents an improvement from about 5 percent in the early 1960s and provides the basis for the first conclusion.

The second conclusion derives from an analysis of household savings which shows that the share going to life insurance companies has been diminishing. In 1974 and 1975, savings through life insurance companies, as measured by the increase in life insurance and insurance company pension reserves, averaged about 10.4 percent of household savings, as measured by total financial asset acquisitions of households. While this is a significant increase over the prior two years, it remains to be seen whether it represents an end to the fairly steady downward trend from a 14.9 percent share in 1960.

The explanation for these divergent trends in the share of income and the share of savings going to life insurance companies lies in changes in the life insurance company product mix. Table 11.1 shows receipts from the principal product categories and indicates that individual life insurance has not kept pace with the growth in health insurance and group life insurance, while individual and

---

tary Policy on Financial Institutions: Gurley/Shaw Revisited," Business and Economic Statistics Section, American Statistical Association, *Proceedings* (1970), pp. 335–41. Francis H. Schott, "The Life Insurance Role in Consumer Spending and Savings and in the Financial Markets: Another View," *Journal of Risk and Insurance,* vol. 38, no. 3 (September 1971), pp. 463–76; Francis H. Schott, "Continuity and Change at Life Insurance Companies," *Business Economics* (May 1970), pp. 44–47; and Eleanor S. Daniel and Frances N. Jennings, "Consumer Saving through Life Insurance Companies," paper presented to the twelfth annual Forecasting Conference, American Statistical Association, New York Chapter, 1970.

[4] Fabian Linden, "The Consumer's View of Value Received—1974," *The Conference Board Record* (November 1974), pp. 48–53.

group annuity considerations have displayed by far the fastest rate of increase. Table 11.2 relates receipts to disposable personal income.

TABLE 11.1
Life Insurance Company Receipts by Line of Business

	Receipts (millions)			Compound Annual Rates of Growth	
Line of Business	1965	1970	1975	1965–1975	1970–1975
Individual life	$13,155	$17,016	$22,541	5.5%	5.8%
Group life	2,928	4,663	6,795	8.8	7.8
Health insurance	6,261	11,367	19,074	11.8	10.9
Individual annuities	548	960	2,664	17.1	22.6
Group annuities	1,712	2,761	7,501	15.9	22.1
Totals	24,604	36,767	58,575	9.1	9.8

Source: *Life Insurance Fact Book* (New York: American Council of Life Insurance, annually).

TABLE 11.2
Ratio of Premiums and Annuity Considerations to Disposable Personal Income

Year	Individual Life Insurance Premiums	Group Life Insurance Premiums	Health Insurance Premiums	Annuity Consider-ations	Total Premiums and Consid-erations
1960	2.90%	0.53%	1.15%	0.38%	4.96%
1965	2.79	0.62	1.33	0.48	5.21
1970	2.48	0.68	1.66	0.54	5.36
1971	2.41	0.68	1.74	0.66	5.48
1972	2.38	0.70	1.79	0.68	5.55
1973	2.25	0.67	1.72	0.76	5.40
1974	2.17	0.64	1.74	0.79	5.35
1975	2.09	0.63	1.76	0.94	5.42

Source: *Life Insurance Fact Book* (New York: American Council of Life Insurance, annually).

This table reveals that the increasing relative importance of receipts from health insurance and annuities, along with stable group life premiums, has been more than enough to offset the relative decline in individual insurance premiums. These developments account for the relatively stable income share of total receipts in the last five years which was mentioned above.

The picture is somewhat different, however, when considering the effects of product mix on savings flows. Health insurance and group life insurance, which is predominantly term insurance, do not generate any significant amount of reserves; and the premiums for such coverage can generally be viewed as current consumption rather than savings. Furthermore, within the individual insurance product line, cash value life insurance has been growing in absolute terms but declining in importance relative to term insurance. This trend is indicated in Table 11.3 by the upward drift in the term insurance proportion of total life insurance sales.

TABLE 11.3
Distribution of Individual Ordinary Life Insurance Purchases between Permanent and Term Policies

Type of Insurance	Percent of Total Face Amount				
	1955	1959	1964	1969	1975
Permanent (cash value)	66%	60%	60%	57%	55%
Term	34	40	40	43	45

Source: *Life Insurance Fact Book* (New York: American Council of Life Insurance, annually).

The impact of shifts in the individual policy mix on savings flows to life insurance companies is even more pronounced than suggested by these data because since the mid-1950s within the cash value category there has been some shift away from endowment, limited payment, and retirement income policies, which have a relatively heavy

TABLE 11.4
Percent of Household Saving by Financial Asset Type

Year	Life Insurance Reserves	Insurance Co. Pension Reserves	Total Life Company Reserves*	Time and Savings Accounts	Credit Market Instruments
1960	10.7%	4.2%	14.9%	40.1%	22.5%
1965	8.3	3.6	11.8	48.0	8.4
1966	7.9	3.5	11.5	32.3	29.0
1967	7.6	3.0	10.6	53.2	5.1
1968	6.3	4.0	10.4	42.7	16.7
1969	8.4	4.9	13.3	15.4	52.9
1970	6.9	4.3	11.2	57.1	−1.2
1971	6.1	4.4	10.5	66.8	−0.8
1972	5.4	3.5	8.8	58.1	10.0
1973	5.3	4.0	9.4	49.9	23.1
1974	5.2	5.0	10.2	46.7	28.8
1975	4.9	5.6	10.5	54.8	17.6

Note: Share of saving is derived by calculating the net increase in the financial asset type as a percentage of the net acquisitions of financial assets for the household sector.

* These figures are the sum of those in columns (1) and (2) but may not add exactly due to rounding.

Source: Flow of Funds data, available from Flow of Funds section, Board of Governors of the Federal Reserve System.

savings element.[5] The rapid growth of saving through life insurance company pension, retirement, and savings plans has not been enough to offset the slower growth of savings flows to individual life insurance products. As shown in Table 11.4, increases in life company pension reserves show a discernible moderate upward trend and in 1975 for the first time exceeded the share of savings going into life insurance. Increases in life insurance policy reserves averaged about 5 percent of household savings in 1974 and 1975. However, this represents a relatively steady downward trend from 10.7 percent in 1960 and accounts for the secular decline in the industry's share of total savings.

THE SPECIAL PROBLEM OF DISINTERMEDIATION AND POLICY LOANS

During the last decade, the economy has experienced unexpectedly high and volatile rates of inflation and no less than three "credit crunch" periods. Any discussion of life insurance savings flows during this period would be incomplete without mention of disintermediation through policy loans. Disintermediation is a term used most frequently to describe the withdrawal of deposits from thrift institutions for the purpose of investing the funds in open-market instruments offering higher yields. The surge in savings going into credit market instruments in 1966, 1969, 1973, and 1974 provides a clear illustration of the disintermediation phenomenon.

As Table 11.4 indicates, much of this disintermediation occurred at the expense of the share of savings going into time and savings accounts at commercial and savings banks and savings and loan associations. The life insurance company data in Table 11.4 do not show a comparable cyclical response to the wide interest rate swings that plagued the deposit-thrift institutions, and this is partly explained by the contractual nature of these savings. The insurers have been far from immune to financial market strains, however, and have experienced their own special disintermediation problems in the form of policy loans.

The figures on life insurance reserves shown in Table 11.4 are not reduced by increases in policy loans because these loans are treated as increases in liabilities in the household sector of the Federal Reserve Flow of Funds Accounts and because such an adjustment raises

---

[5] This trend may be reversed, at least temporarily, since the Employee Retirement Income Security Act of 1974 (ERISA) has spurred the sale of endowment and retirement income policies for use in tax-sheltered individual retirement accounts along with individual annuities.

a host of sticky technical arguments regarding consistent treatment of other household liabilities such as consumer credit, mortgages, etc. Still, policy loans are a form of disinvestment in the savings element of life insurance. The dimensions of the problem are shown in Table 11.5 by the sharp rise in net increases in policy loans in 1973 and 1974

TABLE 11.5
Life Insurance Reserves and Policy Loans

Year	Net Increases in Life Insurance Reserves (billions)	Net Increases in Policy Loans (billions)	Increase in Loans as Percent of Increase in Reserves
1959	$3.4	$0.4	13%
1965	4.8	0.5	11
1966	4.7	1.4	31
1967	5.1	0.9	19
1968	4.6	1.2	27
1969	5.0	2.5	51
1970	5.2	2.2	43
1971	6.2	1.0	16
1972	6.6	0.9	14
1973	7.3	2.2	30
1974	6.4	2.7	41
1975	7.6	1.6	21

Source: Flow of Funds data, available from Flow of Funds section, Board of Governors of the Federal Reserve System.

and also in two earlier periods, 1966 and 1969–1970. In these years, which were characterized by high rates of inflation and high interest rates, anywhere from 30 to 50 percent of the industry's new investment funds from life insurance reserve growth were absorbed by increases in policy loans and hence were not available for investment in financial market instruments. Therefore, the investable funds of life insurance companies have been reduced both by the secular downward trend in the share of savings going into life insurance and by the diversion to policy loans of cash flow otherwise available for investment.

ISOLATING THE IMPACT OF INFLATION

While it would be extremely difficult to sort out with any precision the effects of inflation from all of the other factors influencing life insurance companies, there are some reasonable propositions that appear to be consistent with the performance data and observed actions of the companies. For example, the relatively constant share of income going to life insurance companies in recent years supports the view that the demand for financial protection is income elastic. As incomes and prices rise, increases in the amounts necessary to provide for survivors, the disabled, and retirees require individuals to adjust by purchasing additional protection. Furthermore, when financial security is being provided through a group arrangement, there is often a direct linkage of insurance coverage and retirement benefits with current wages and salaries. Contracts of this type produce increased benefit amounts and premium income as an almost automatic adjustment to inflation.

Another logical proposition is that, like all forms of fixed-dollar savings, the cash values of life insurance contracts lose purchasing power when prices rise faster than the interest rates credited to such accounts. And, in recent years, market interest rates associated with accelerating rates of inflation have risen much faster than the portfolio yields on the long-term, fixed-debt asset holdings of the life insurance companies. This, of course, has been true for the mortgage-lending thrift institutions as well. Hence, the declining share of individual saving through life insurance can be attributed at least in part to an inability to offer competitive returns as open-market rates have moved to significantly higher levels. These financial conditions have also spawned the creation and/or aggressive promotion of competing institutional savings vehicles. Some of these are discussed in a later section of this chapter.

Statistical analysis of policy loans indicates a high degree of positive correlation with interest rate movements.[6] It is reasonable, therefore, to attribute much of the companies' policy loan problems to the inflation which has pushed nominal interest rates to high levels because of the increased inflation premiums incorporated into rates and/or anti-inflationary monetary policy responses.[7] Prepayments on

---

[6] See Chapter 10, p. 232 in this volume; Francis H. Schott, "Disintermediation through Policy Loans at Life Insurance Companies," *Journal of Finance*, vol. 26, no. 3 (June 1971), pp. 720–29; and J. David Cummins, *An Econometric Model of the Life Insurance Sector of the U.S. Economy* (Lexington, Mass.: D. C. Heath, Lexington Books, 1975), pp. 85–88.

[7] The linkage between inflation rates and interest rates and the notion of an inflation premium in nominal interest rates has been the subject of considerable research. See, for example, Irving Fisher, *The Theory of Interest* (New York: Macmillan, 1930); Martin Feldstein and Otto Eckstein, "The Fundamental Determinants of the Interest Rate," *Review of Economics and Statistics*, vol. 52 (November 1970), pp. 363–76; D. H. Pyle, "Observed Price Expectations and Interest Rates," *Review of Economics and Statistics*, vol. 54 (August 1972), pp. 275–80; and Thomas Sargent, "Interest Rates and Prices in the Long-Run: A Study of the Gibson Paradox," *Journal of Money, Credit and Banking*, vol. 5 (February 1974), pp. 385–447.

existing mortgages also fall off sharply under such conditions, further reducing investable cash flow, especially in companies having relatively large mortgage holdings. At the same time that inflation has contributed to investable funds shortfalls, it has bloated the financial needs of firms dependent on the life insurance companies for financing.

Accelerating rates of inflation and rising interest rates also were primary contributors to the deep stock market decline in 1973–1974. In many companies, unrealized losses in general account common stocks, which are valued at market, completely absorbed the stock component of their valuation reserves and reduced surplus significantly before the market finally bottomed out. The market decline caused values of common stock separate accounts to plunge and, ironically, has had a detrimental effect on the common stock-based products designed by life insurers to provide a hedge against inflation. While the economic values of bonds and mortgages also decline when interest rates rise, these assets are carried on the balance sheet at amortized value and thus do not reflect swings in the market. This practice, of course, is consistent with the surplus limitations imposed by regulation on mutual life insurance companies.

Other factors influencing the market for cash value life insurance include the trends toward more dependence by individuals on social security and private pension plans to provide retirement income and more emphasis on group employee thrift plans. While these basic trends have not necessarily been a function of inflation, the increasing reliance on social security is sure to be accelerated under the current law if inflation rates remain high in the future. This will occur because social security benefits are now adjusted to reflect both increases in the Consumer Price Index and increases in average wages. A group of prominent investigators has charged that these "double indexing" provisions are irrationally designed and make the benefit formulas hypersensitive to changes in the rate of inflation.[8] The impetus for this criticism was the potential effect of double indexing on the financial structure and viability of the social security system. However, indexing also threatens to erode significantly the market for those private life insurance products that provide survivorship and retirement benefits.

Beyond this direct "crowding out" effect related to life insurance

---

[8] *Report of the Panel on Social Security Financing to the Committee on Finance, United States Senate* (Washington, D.C.: U.S. Government Printing Office, 1975).

companies, there is serious concern regarding the impact of social security on private saving in general. Recent studies at Harvard University suggest that social security has reduced total potential private savings in the United States by as much as 40 percent with a consequent impact on the volume of savings available for capital investment.[9] While more research in this area is badly needed, these findings are significant because they contradict both previous empirical evidence that social security and private pension plans have stimulated personal saving[10] and a more recent analysis suggesting that social security has had a neutral effect on saving.[11]

INSURANCE COMPANY RESPONSES TO INFLATION

A number of developments in the recent history of life insurance regarding new products, investment policies, and other operations represent to varying degrees attempts to adapt to inflation and its consequences. The introduction of the major medical policy in the 1950s was a response to mounting medical bills. Group life insurance, while partially a response to pressures by organized labor and to trends in the non-union labor markets, has registered a good deal of success because of its flexibility in adjusting coverage to rising price and income levels.

During the 1950s and 1960s, increasing awareness of the attractive long-term average return on common stocks and acceptance of the notion that common stocks were a hedge against inflation contributed to the steady rise in the proportion of life insurance company assets in common stock. Many companies developed and marketed individual mutual fund, variable annuity, and other equity-based products. More recently some companies have been actively engaged in introducing variable life insurance products in which the investment element will consist of common stocks. During the period from 1966 to

[9] Martin Feldstein, "Social Security, Induced Retirement and Aggregate Capital Accumulation," *Journal of Political Economy* (September–October 1974), 905–26.

[10] Philip Cagan, *The Effect of Pension Plans on Aggregate Saving: Evidence from a Sample Survey*, National Bureau of Economic Research, Occasional Paper No. 95 (New York: Columbia University Press, 1965); and George Katona, *Private Pensions and Individual Saving*, Monograph No. 40 (Ann Arbor: Survey Research Center, Institute for Social Research, University of Michigan, 1965).

[11] Alicia H. Munnell, "The Impact of Social Security on Personal Saving," *New England Economic Review* (January–February 1975), pp. 27–41. This article is based on the author's book of the same title (Cambridge, Mass.: Ballinger Publishing Co., 1974).

1971 (approximately) there was a sharp increase in the use of income and equity participation features, or so-called equity kickers, with life insurance company bond and mortgage investments. The interest in the total return and inflation-hedge aspects of equity investments also was, and to a lesser extent still is, prevalent in the private pension field. This interest has spurred the development by insurance companies of equity-linked group variable annuities and separate accounts for investment in common stocks and, more recently, in real estate.

In the marketing of traditional insurance, increased emphasis has been placed on the virtues of keeping the level of protection in line with changing family needs and income in a period of rapidly rising prices. Some approaches stress a dollar averaging concept of budgeting a fixed percentage of income for life insurance, while others stress using dividend options, riders, and "inflation guard" endorsements to boost coverage in line with inflation.

The present income tax structure for life insurance companies creates an increasing burden as a general rise in interest rates has accompanied inflation. The problem is highly technical, but essentially it arises because the "10-for-1" approximation rule for determining the portion of investment income which can reasonably be considered reserved for policyholders and thereby not included in taxable investment income has become increasingly inaccurate with the widening gap between reserve valuation interest rates and the earned rate on invested assets.[12] As a result, many companies are paying taxes on interest earnings at a relatively higher rate than they did in the past. Thus, there is a greater incentive to consider investments with special tax features or with capital gains potential.

During the last several years, because of the reduced predictability of cash flow and wide swings in interest rates, the companies have become much more cautious about entering into forward investment commitments at rates established at the time of commitment. Some efforts have also been made to reduce loan maturities and increase flexibility in light of the difficulty in forecasting financial market conditions. While these do not yet represent extreme changes, one re-

---

[12] For a discussion of the general features of the Life Insurance Company Tax Act, see Dan M. McGill, *Life Insurance,* rev. ed. (Homewood, Ill.: Richard D. Irwin, 1967), pp. 910–28. The effect of rising interest rates on the "Phase 1" calculation is described in John C. Fraser, "Income Tax and Reserve Valuation," *The Actuary,* Newsletter of the Society of Actuaries; Chicago, Ill. (November 1972) and is also discussed along with other issues in Peter W. Plumley, "Certain Inequities in the Life Insurance Company Income Tax Act of 1959," forthcoming in the *Transactions of the Society of Actuaries.*

spected industry commentator has speculated that if inflation and inflation expectations do not diminish, the transformation in the product mix and consequently the asset-liability structure of life insurers could result in a considerable shift to shorter-term assets or variable-rate, long-term assets whose rates move with the market.[13]

Some companies have attempted to reduce the extent of disintermediation through policy loans by establishing higher contractual policy loan interest rates, typically 8 percent, on newly issued policies in those states that allow such modification. Finally, insurance companies, like most other businesses, must contend with the serious cost problems associated with inflation in all aspects of administration. To deal with these cost problems, the companies have attempted to increase sales productivity, improve budgeting procedures, and mechanize servicing operations.

FINANCIAL ASSETS AND CAPITAL MARKET PARTICIPATION

As noted above, the decline in savings through life insurance and policy loan problems have had a significant effect on the industry's role in the capital markets and its position as an intermediary. Over

TABLE 11.6
Annual Rate of Growth of Financial Assets at Financial Institutions

	Growth Rate		
Institution	1971–75	1966–70	1960–65
Commercial banks	10.80%	7.90%	8.40%
Mutual savings banks	9.00	6.20	7.40
Saving and loan associations	13.90	6.40	12.60
Total: Depository institutions	11.40	7.30	9.20
Life insurance companies	7.10	5.40	5.70
Non-insured pension funds	8.30	9.10	10.00
State and local government retirement funds	12.10	11.80	11.10
Open-end investment companies	−2.80	8.30	7.40
Credit unions	15.50	10.30	12.00
Total: Non-depository institutions	7.90	7.50	7.50
Grand total	10.20	7.40	8.60

Note: Outstanding assets were computed by cumulating flows on a 1959 asset value base to remove the effects of equity value changes on end-of-year outstanding assets.

Source: Flow of Funds data, available from Flow of Funds section, Board of Governors of the Federal Reserve System.

---

[13] Eli Shapiro, "The Future Role of Insurance Company Capital," Paper presented at the Conference Board's Annual Financial Conference, New York, February 1975.

the last 15 years, life insurance companies have consistently experienced a slower rate of financial asset growth than all other major financial intermediaries with the exception of open-end investment companies. This trend is illustrated in Table 11.6.

Although the table reveals that insurance company asset growth accelerated in the 1970s, it did not match that of several other intermediaries, particularly depository institutions. These institutions have bid very aggressively for funds through the issuance of savings certificates. The commercial banks have also borrowed huge sums through certificates of deposit and commercial paper and in Eurodollar markets, while the savings and loan associations have had access to Federal Home Loan Bank advances.

Coinciding with this slower asset growth is a decline in the industry's relative participation in the overall capital market and certain of its sectors, although factors other than availability of investable funds explain some of these shifts. As Table 11.7 indicates, the life

TABLE 11.7
Selected Asset Flows of Life Insurance Companies as a Percentage of Selected Asset Flows of the Aggregate Economy

Period	Total Financial Assets	Corporate Bonds	Corporate Equities	Multifamily, Commercial, and Farm Mortgages	1–4 Family Residential Mortgages
1961–1965	10.7%	41.3%	15.8%	27.7%	6.0%
1966–1970	8.9	17.8	16.1	29.1	−3.1
1971–1975	7.5	29.2	30.7	19.0	−4.8

Note: The figures in the table are five-year annual averages.

Source: Flow of Funds data, available from Flow of Funds section, Board of Governors of the Federal Reserve System.

insurance industry's annual net new investments in the 1970s have averaged about 7.5 percent of total funds raised in financial markets. This represents a downward trend from annual averages of 10.7 percent in 1961–1965 and 8.9 percent in 1966–1970.

Significant changes have also taken place in the industry's participation in its traditional investment outlets.[14] In 1971–1975 life insurance companies' net acquisitions of corporate bonds represented 29 percent of total new corporate bond financing. Thus, the industry

---

[14] An exhaustive treatment is available in George A. Bishop, *Capital Formation through Life Insurance* (Homewood, Ill.: Richard D. Irwin, 1976).

continued to be an important factor in this segment of the capital markets although to a much lesser extent than in the early 1960s. In the last five years, the industry accounted for over 19 percent of net new multifamily residential, commercial, and farm mortgages. This was a substantial participation but was down significantly from the 1960s.

The most dramatic changes have occurred in the home mortgage category (see Table 11.7) where the share of net total financing by life insurers fell from 6.0 percent in the early 1960s to a significant net disinvestment position in the 1970s (i.e., repayments exceeded new investments). This deemphasis of home mortgages resulted from a significant erosion of their yield attractiveness. For example, in the early 1960s home mortgages typically yielded more than 100 basis points (1 percent) more than Baa bonds, but within just a few years this spread was reversed and bonds offered a substantial advantage. This changing market environment was caused by a host of factors including a rapid increase in business demands for funds, statutory limits on insured and conventional mortgage rates, growth of the specialized mortgage-lending thrift institutions, and the increasing role of Federal credit agencies. In essence, the insurers were literally pushed out of the home mortgage market. Their departure, however, did allow them to play a more significant role in the other mortgage and bond sectors than would otherwise have been the case in view of their relatively slow asset growth.

The other significant behavioral change revealed in Table 11.7 is the dramatic rise in the life companies' share of the net total of equity financing. This reflects the sharp increase in common stock holdings, primarily in separate accounts, as well as increased purchases of preferred stock.

INSTITUTIONAL COMPETITION FOR SAVINGS

Since there is a declining share of savings going into life insurance and since this is reflected in the industry's slower asset growth relative to other institutions, it is relevant to consider the past and future role of life insurance companies in the competition with other intermediaries for the public's savings dollar. During the 1960s life insurance companies faced increasing competition from common stock mutual funds. Because of subsequent bear markets, the funds have fallen out of favor; and, while they will probably stage something of a comeback as the stock market recovers, many investors who pursued the slogan "buy term and invest the difference" are sure to remember losing much of the difference.

There are more recent and perhaps more interesting developments in the competitive race among financial institutions for the savings dollar of an increasingly return-conscious saver. In the last several years there has been an intense, widespread, and generally successful promotion of relatively convenient fixed-dollar savings media such as the savings certificates of banks and deposit-thrift institutions, money market mutual funds which invest short-term in U.S. government securities, bank certificates of deposit, high grade commercial paper, and, for a time in the summer of 1974, even small-denomination, floating-rate bank notes.

On the surface, these developments would appear to present serious competition for cash value life insurance. Surely, at least some of the relative decline in the share of individual savings through life insurance must be attributed to the availability of such fixed-dollar investment alternatives. However, to assess properly the implications of this competition for life insurers in general and for cash value insurance in particular, the primary economic and social role of the industry and of this particular product must be clearly understood.

Life insurance companies are in essence marketing organizations offering a wide range of products to fulfill their primary role of providing protection against the financial insecurities associated with death, disability, retirement, and other emergency needs. Certain of these products, such as those providing temporary-term death protection and medical care expense and disability income benefits do not produce any significant annual reserve build-up. Other products, which provide for retirement income needs and permanent life insurance protection, do require and produce a significant year-to-year increase in reserve funds, which can be viewed as a form of contractual savings. This distinction between reserve creating and non-reserve creating financial security products is critical to understanding that the declining relative importance of cash value life insurance is not necessarily occurring because the insurance companies are gradually relinquishing one of their primary functions, namely, providing death protection. Rather, the trends reflect the fact that the companies are providing, and individuals by a revealed preference seem to desire, more and more death protection on a temporary rather than a permanent basis, that is, through individual and group term life insurance that does not require any significant accumulated reserve.

The trends in providing insurance protection are related to interinstitutional competition for savings to the extent that funds that might otherwise have gone into cash value life insurance are lost to the array of fixed-income, market-rate sensitive, alternative savings forms introduced and aggressively promoted by other institutions in recent years. The exact impact of this increased competition for savings cannot be measured but neither can the implications for insurance companies be ignored.

These implications are best understood by first recognizing that the cash value life insurance contract is designed for the basic purpose of providing permanent protection with a level premium even though the mortality risk increases with age. The savings element in life insurance is only incidental to this purpose and is a by-product of the reserves arising out of the level-premium and increasing-risk arrangement. While the design of permanent life insurance is ingenious, the arrangement makes it extremely difficult to separate the cost of protection from the investment portion of the premium dollar for purposes of measuring the rate of return on savings in life insurance.[15] Several published attempts to do so have suggested that the rate of return on straight life insurance policies for selected ages over 20-year policy durations has been the equivalent of 4 to 5 percent.[16] This is a relatively attractive yield since it is essentially an after-tax return because of the favorable personal income tax treatment afforded cash value build-ups.

These same studies, however, show negative or very low returns in the early policy years and, in general, the results for any duration can vary significantly depending on assumptions regarding the dividends on participating policies, the cost of alternative term insurance

---

[15] Indeed, it can be argued persuasively that it is inappropriate even to consider the cash value life insurance policy as two divisible parts, that is, protection and savings elements. For example, see *The Nature of the Whole Life Contract* (New York: Institute of Life Insurance, 1974); and Robert I. Mehr, "The Concept of the Level-Premium Whole Life Insurance Policy—Reexamined," *Journal of Risk and Insurance*, vol. 42, no. 4 (September 1975), pp. 419–31.

[16] For example, see M. Albert Linton, "Life Insurance as an Investment," in *Life and Health Insurance Handbook*, 2d ed., ed. Davis M. Gregg (Homewood, Ill.: Richard D. Irwin, 1964); J. Robert Ferrari, "Investment Life Insurance versus Term Insurance and Separate Investment: A Determination of Expected-Return Equivalents," *Journal of Risk and Insurance*, vol. 35, no. 2 (June 1968), pp. 181–98; Joseph M. Belth, "The Rate of Return on the Savings Element in Cash-Value Life Insurance," *Journal of Risk and Insurance*, vol. 35, no. 4 (December 1968), pp. 569–81; Stuart Schwarzschild, "Rates of Return on the Investment Differentials between Life Insurance Policies," *Journal of Risk and Insurance*, vol. 35, no. 4 (December 1968), pp. 583–95; Robert C. Hutchins and Charles E. Quenneville, "Rate of Return versus Interest-Adjusted Cost," *Journal of Risk and Insurance*, vol. 42, no. 1 (March 1975), pp. 69–79.

protection, and other variables. Moreover, these determinations do not appear to have much practical marketing use since they are the results of highly technical and complex calculations published for the most part by actuaries, economists, and insurance or finance professors in the professional insurance literature and scholarly journals.

Given these features of the cash value life insurance product, it appears reasonable to conclude that it is not designed to compete head on with many institutional savings instruments now available (or for that matter with open-market instruments). The rate of return on the investment element cannot simply be measured and advertised for the purpose of attracting return-sensitive investors who have access to clearer and more explicit rates of return on alternative forms of savings. Saving dollars can appropriately be committed to cash value life insurance but not for the primary purpose of achieving the most attractive, relatively risk-free return in a narrow investment sense. Rather, such dollars are committed to a broader arrangement and secure what may be a lesser return in conjunction with the considerable benefits of permanent death protection and associated surrender, loan, and settlement features.

In taking this view, savings flows into cash values will continue to be determined, as they have in the past, primarily by the perceived financial security needs of individuals and businesses for insurance protection through the structure and flexibility of permanent policies and by the relative success of the industry in selling the need for and advantages of such policies. The other individual savings forms discussed above do not provide a substitute for the unique permanent life insurance product. The investment returns provided by other media do, however, affect the opportunity cost of utilizing savings dollars to secure the benefits of permanent protection; and this cost is a critical determinant of the life insurance purchase decision. In an inflationary environment which is typically accompanied by high market interest rates, this opportunity cost can become a very significant factor.

The product mix of the life insurance industry is, of course, affected by the extent to which the companies satisfy insurance needs with products other than cash value insurance. As noted earlier, the declining relative importance of cash value insurance in individual savings has been very much a function of the changing manner in which basic life insurance is being provided, namely, with greater emphasis on individual and group term insurance. Viewed in this way, life insurance companies are fulfilling their *primary* economic and social function of providing death protection even if it is being done in a manner that is attracting a reduced share of individual savings. This, of course, has significant implications for agency operations. An example of one response is the move by some of the large mutual companies into the property and casualty insurance field. These lines of insurance do not capture any savings dollars, but they do provide opportunities for increased sales of the pure-protection type of insurance.

THE FUTURE OF SAVINGS THROUGH LIFE INSURANCE COMPANIES

While life insurance companies obviously face stiff competition for the saving dollar, there are many reasons to expect them to continue to be important and viable financial intermediaries. The relative decline in cash value insurance is not favorable for the industry, but rising sales figures indicate that a substantial and growing market for this product still exists. Furthermore, sales of high cash value policies and individual annuities are currently receiving a significant boost from the Employee Retirement Income Security Act of 1974 (ERISA), which encourages retirement savings by the self-employed and by individuals not covered by a company pension plan.

The pension sector constitutes a major area for advancement of consumer savings through life insurance companies. As noted earlier, annual increases in insured pension reserves have maintained a steady share of total household savings since 1960. The new pension reform legislation provides a timely opportunity to increase this share of savings. Added support for strong pension growth will come from continuing increases in the labor force and accompanying advances in employment. Group pension innovations such as separate accounts for real estate and private placements have also proved to be attractive to clients desiring more diversification in their pension fund investments.

Equally important, the life insurance companies can compete aggressively for the individual's return-sensitive savings dollar by taking advantage of their investment expertise and experience with group arrangements to participate on an important scale in the trends toward collective personal savings. Such plans can be and are being promoted, marketed, and administered within a framework of explicit and competitive rates of return. Furthermore, the computer technology now exists to provide an employee with an individual savings plan incorporating flexible options for fixed-income investments or equities in addition to the traditional convenience and effi-

ciencies of payroll-related thrift plans. Insurance company administered, collective thrift plans can offer formidable competition for and
provide attractive alternatives to other individual savings outlets.
These arrangements, however, require careful consideration of the
types of investments that will match the nature of these liabilities
and at the same time provide a competitive rate of return.

As for inflation in general, even though the rate of price increases
has moderated to about one half of the double-digit rates experienced
during much of 1974–1975, there remains the grave danger of reac-
celeration, this time starting from an even higher base than before.
The policy mistakes, economic processes, and plain bad luck that
might bring about another inflationary spiral are clearly beyond the
scope of this chapter, as are the numerous arguments against inflation generally. The implications of a reoccurrence of double-digit
inflation, however, are far-reaching for life insurance and deposit-
thrift institutions which hold predominately long-term assets.

The damaging effects of double-digit inflation would again stem
from the related rise of short-term money market yields to levels well
above institutional asset portfolio rates. This occurred in the summer
of 1974 when the Treasury bill rate soared to almost 9.5 percent.
Rapid disintermediation would again result through withdrawals of
savings deposits in banks and savings and loan associations and
through policy loans and surrenders in the insurance industry.

The companies survived the tense situation in 1974, but a continuing danger exists that inflation may pierce some "threshold" rate,
which will drive short-term interest rates to such levels that massive
disintermediation will rupture our huge thrift-institution system. This
would likely be accompanied by plummeting stock prices and a confidence crisis in financial markets that could lead to widespread bankruptcies. It is hoped that the painful lessons of recent years will be
enough to prevent us from ever finding out where this threshold
really is and from experiencing the other serious economic and social
consequences of a renewed inflationary spiral.

12

Investment Problems and Policies of Small and Medium-Size Life Insurance Companies

By Frank A. Cappiello, Jr.*

A common fallacy is to view the investment policies and problems of the smaller life insurance companies merely as scaled-down versions of those of the larger companies. While there are superficial similarities, the differences are significant in a wide range of areas including the competitive investment environment, staffing, and risk-taking. The views expressed in this chapter are based on the author's experience with the investment operations of his own company (Monumental Capital Management) as well as his observation of similar size operations in other life insurance companies.

The investment operation of the author's company is somewhat different in structure but otherwise basically similar to the investment operations of other medium-size companies. Investment activities are conducted within the holding company framework. Monumental Capital Management is an investment management subsidiary of Monumental Corporation and manages the invested assets of its affiliates, Monumental Life and Volunteer State Life. At the end of 1975, these invested assets totaled $666 million, and the company had an investable cash flow of between $55 and $60 million during that year. Thus, according to the criteria set forth below, Monumental can be considered a medium-size company.

---

* Frank A. Cappiello, Jr., is president of Monumental Capital Management, Inc., and financial vice president of Monumental Corporation.

LIFE INSURANCE COMPANY SIZE CATEGORIES

In order to conduct a meaningful discussion of the investment problems and policies of "medium-size" and "small" life insurance companies, objective definitions of these and other relevant size categories are necessary. Because the focus of this analysis is on investments, it seems most appropriate to subdivide the life insurance industry on the basis of total assets. For the purposes of this discussion, the firms in the industry have been categorized into four size groups: super-large, large, medium-size, and small.

The *super-large* group consists of the five largest life insurance companies in the United States—the Prudential with assets of $39 billion, the Metropolitan with $35 billion, the Equitable ($20 billion), New York Life ($14 billion), and John Hancock ($13 billion). These five giants have such enormous assets and investable cash flow that they encounter a unique set of problems and should be considered separately from the remainder of the industry.

Following the super-large companies are those which are characterized here as *large*. The large company category encompasses the 6th through the 40th largest life insurance companies in the United States. The firms in this group range in size from the Aetna Life with $10 billion in assets to Union Central Life of Cincinnati, Ohio, with just over $1 billion.[1]

Medium-size companies are those with assets of less than $1 billion but more than $200 million. The largest company in this group (Minnesota Mutual) has assets of $965 million, while several smaller firms have assets in the neighborhood of $200 million.

Companies with assets of less than $200 million can be classified as *small* companies. These firms utilize one- or two-man investment operations and are characterized by limited risk-taking ability and a high propensity toward market liquidity. This is reflected in the high percentage of publicly issued bonds and secured mortgages in their portfolios and a notable absence of private placements and common stocks.

THE IMPORTANCE OF AVERAGE INVESTMENT SIZE

The implications of size for investable cash flow and the magnitude of individual investments are apparent when one contrasts large and medium-size companies with respect to these parameters. In a

---

[1] "The Fifty Largest Life Insurance Companies Ranked by Assets," *Fortune*, vol. 101, no. 1 (July 1976), pp. 206–7.

hypothetical life insurance company with assets of $5 billion, annual investable cash flow would range from $550 to $600 million and the average individual investment would be anywhere from $4.5 to $6 million. The individual investment size is strongly influenced by staffing considerations since the number of investment deals must be held to manageable proportions. Other factors affecting the size of the average investment are legal limits[2] (in particular, the requirement that individual investments not exceed some percentage of total assets) and investment prudence.

In contrast to the situation in the large company, a typical medium-size life insurance company in the range of, say, $400 to $500 million in assets would have annual investable cash flow of between $40 and $50 million. Typically, this would mean that for the medium-size life company the average single investment would be between $1 and $2 million.

The small and medium-size life insurance companies clearly deal with smaller average investments than their larger counterparts. However, a lower average investment size has different implications depending upon the type of asset which is being considered. This section discusses these implications with respect to privately placed bonds, mortgages, and common stocks.

Privately Placed Bonds

In the private placement field, the size of the single investment is important because it determines whether the firm is a "lead" lender or a follower in bond offerings. The larger the company's average investment, the more likely it is that it will be a "lead" lender with the ability to negotiate the rate, the term, and other important loan provisions. Companies which are "followers" are generally required to accept the format established by the lead or keystone lender.

The medium-size life insurance company usually cannot negotiate terms. Such companies must, of necessity, be tag-ons, following in the wake of the large companies such as Mutual of New York, Connecticut General, and Massachusetts Mutual. The medium-size company must accept what the lead lender does and accept or reject loans within the investment format of the large life insurance companies. There are a number of procedures which medium-size companies can follow in order to offset this limitation and do a good investment job.

---

[2] Investment regulations are discussed in Chapter 14 of this book.

First, it is important for the company to define the loan parameters which it considers acceptable and to have access to a large supply of private placement loans with these parameters. The more loans one sees, the more improved will be the opportunity to select the ones with the highest potential which meet the selection standards. Most private placement loans are brought to the attention of the medium-size insurance company through investment banking firms, and the company's analysts thus must develop and maintain strong contacts with these firms. These contacts should include not only the major Wall Street firms but also the regional firms in major metropolitan areas such as Atlanta, Baltimore, Dallas, and Chicago. These regional firms have the potential for becoming active sources of loans. Finally, there is the direct placement loan, that is, keeping in close contact with previous borrowers in the event that they wish either to enlarge their loan or to develop a new loan.

Identifying sources of investment supply is relatively easy. Developing and maintaining strong contacts is more difficult. It is an unfortunate fact that the medium-size and smaller life companies need the investment bankers more than the bankers need them. Success for a medium-size company in maintaining a constant supply of loan submissions from investment bankers is directly correlated with "quick service," constant communication, and fairness.

A rapid response—"quick service"—is essential; sometimes a fast "no" is far better than a slow "maybe." Most insurance companies find that investment bankers like to operate on this basis. Being quick to say "no" and equally fast to "circle" an investment when it appears to meet quality parameters as well as other aspects of one's current investment policy is the key to seeing a large and better flow of investment options. For example, once an investment is circled by the Monumental, it is 95 percent certain that investment committee approval will be forthcoming.

Constant communication is accomplished primarily by personal visits as frequently as required. More importantly, through frequent telephone conversations, the smaller life company seeks to let its investment banking sources know of any changes in its investment philosophy, e.g., changes related to call protection, payout requirements, or term of the loan. The most important variable, of course, is the target interest rate, and this parameter changes constantly. The smaller company promptly notes any adjustments in its rate expectations. These communications relate to "good service" because they inform the investment supply sources where they should be spending their time. If the insurance company's minimum acceptable rate is 8.5 percent and the investment banker is offering loans yielding 8.25 percent, then the banker should be aware that the company is not interested in this particular issue. The smaller company finds that this kind of communication goes a long way toward maintaining sound relationships.

Finally, fairness in dealings is essential. The smaller companies must try harder; they simply have to be accommodating in their negotiations with investment bankers. This was particularly important during the tight money period of 1970 when many of the larger companies in the life insurance business had the opportunity to become very demanding in stipulating term and rate. During this period many smaller companies kept a longer range perspective and developed a reputation for "reasonableness."

In summary, the private placement market is too important as a source of investments to be ignored by the smaller-size companies. The future growth of private placement financing appears assured since it is attractive to both the lender and the borrower. Privacy in this type of financing is of primary advantage in an era of securities market volatility. A second major advantage to both lender and borrower is the ability to commit on a forward basis, including the "locking in" of a fixed interest rate. For the smaller insurance company, matching takedowns to the borrower's needs and matching commitments to future cash flows is a definite plus. Finally, there is the relative speed and efficiency of private placement deals, with the consequent lessening of market risk and distribution costs. In the energy field alone there seems to be considerable scope for imaginative private placement financing, and this area will continue to supplement the other segments of the private placement market.

Mortgage Loans

In the mortgage market, the medium-size company occupies a different position than it does in the bond market. In the former market, medium-size firms are on a par with larger companies simply because a $1 to $2 million mortgage is sufficient to finance an efficient-size garden apartment, a suburban office building, or a free-standing retail store (such as a K-Mart) in a shopping center. Being able to lend in the $2 to $5 million range does not enhance the bargaining power of the lender or enable it to improve the quality of its mortgage portfolio.

The breakpoint for significantly better terms appears to be above the $5 million level. Few life insurance companies can invest in a project of this size, and here the super-large companies do have the advantage. For example, there are only a handful of life companies who have the cash flow and, more importantly, the expertise to invest in regional shopping centers with enclosed malls. These centers may require anywhere from $15 to $30 million in loanable funds. The very scarceness of this kind of investment ability allows the super-large companies to engage in refined and generally more favorable negotiations with respect to interest rates and terms. Aside from the rarified atmosphere of the super-large loan, however, the mortgage size characteristics of a medium-size life insurer do not differ significantly from those of the larger company.

In mortgages, as in private placements, sources of investment supply are important. Primarily, investment supply means mortgage bankers, and the smaller companies must stress the same quick service and constant communication they give to their brokers. An additional factor to contend with in the mortgages case is the need for geographic diversity. From time to time, overbuilding creates unstable situations in various metropolitan areas. In these areas, vacancy rates are likely to be high and growing. At this point, the investor temporarily suspends mortgage investing in these areas and shifts to other, more productive areas where the commercial market is capable of absorbing the present capacity.

Finally, there may be times when the company believes that interest rates will be moving higher over the near term. In such instances, the investor would prefer to pull out of the mortgage market for a period. Unfortunately, this is extremely difficult to do without impairing mortgage banking relationships. One has to keep a minimum flow of mortgage submissions coming in in order to maintain healthy correspondent relationships. This is less true with private placement brokers.

In summary, the mortgage operations of medium-size companies are relatively similar to those of larger companies. In mortgages, the smaller company can structure the terms and has a type of "origination" capability through its mortgage correspondent network. As a result, smaller companies frequently find themselves acting as lead lenders in this market and are not at a serious competitive disadvantage vis-a-vis the larger companies. However, as discussed below, their reliance on mortgage correspondents may create difficulties in the years to come.

Corporate Equities

With regard to equities, particularly common stocks, investment size is less a function of cash flow than of the target ratio of common stocks to total assets which the company has established. A life insurance company with assets of $1 billion which has targeted 5 percent of those assets to be invested in common stocks would then determine whether the common stock list should consist of 50 names of $1 million each or 25 names of $2 million each. Thus, the company's total assets dictate the overall magnitude of the equity portfolio, but prudence and diversification determine the size of each investment.

INVESTMENT PERSONNEL PROBLEMS IN THE MEDIUM-SIZE LIFE COMPANY

The size effect and its relationship to differences in investing approach and operations between large and smaller-size life companies simply mean that a smaller insurance company has to work harder. In order to do a superior job one needs superior people. In terms of investment personnel in smaller companies, the most serious problem is that such companies cannot afford the specialization, i.e., the comparting of the investment department into various disciplines such as bond, stock, real estate, and mortgage investing, which is common to the large and super-large life insurance companies. A large life insurance company can, by the very nature of its assets, its cash flow, and its activity level, support a larger, more specialized investment staff. The larger company's size allows the investment department to have more titles available with more potential promotion possibilities. Finally, there is a better attitude toward salaries in a larger operation.

A good example of a large life insurance company investment operation is that of the John Hancock.[3] As the fifth largest life insurer in the United States, the Hancock combines size with effectiveness. Investment activities range from monitoring the company's multibillion dollar general account to the management of corporate pension funds, which are partly in the general account and partly in separate accounts. Hancock's investment responsibility and authority begins with its committee of finance. The committee includes outside directors and is headed by the company's chairman of the board. In-

---

[3] Francis E. Wylie, "John Hancock: A Wide-Awake Giant Shows Its Muscle," *Finance* (March 1974), pp. 38–40.

vestment submissions flow from the major departments: bond, common stock, mortgage loan, and agribusiness.

The stock group includes professionals such as security analysts (there are 12 in the analysis department) and portfolio managers as well as supporting staff, including sophisticated computer experts. An investment strategy committee sets the broad policies within which stock investment decisions are made both as to groups, commitment levels, and timing.[4]

In the fixed income area, the bond department's operations cover public bond purchases and the more rewarding private placements. The mortgage department invests in the usual range of commercial real estate such as garden apartments, office buildings, and shopping centers. The scale of lending may range from a $3.5 million shopping center in Birmingham, Alabama, to a loan of nearly $10 million on an office building in Washington, D.C. Further, agricultural-oriented lending (agribusiness) has received increasing emphasis and has encompassed such exotic investments as a joint venture in a California almond grove. Additionally, the Hancock investment complex includes mutual fund appendages among which are a growth fund, an income fund, and a bond fund. Finally, supporting the overall investment operation is the treasury department which conducts economic forecasts that cover the principal elements of the national economy and provides the base for Hancock's overall investment strategy.

This complex and diverse investment operation contrasts markedly with that of a typical smaller company. Here the central problem is the inability to afford investment specialization; and yet, ironically, there is a greater need for high-quality talent and flexibility in the securities analyst and the mortgage analyst. A medium-size or smaller company needs better people simply because these people have to do double duty. The securities analyst, for example, has to be at home both in bonds and equities; but his title and promotion possibilities are limited as compared with those in a larger company. A summary of the functions of a typical security analyst in a medium-size life insurance company should help to illustrate the problem.

The security analyst in this type of operation must not only monitor a certain number of common stocks but must come up with good stock ideas. He is also charged with the duty of working on private placement securities. Both of these basic requirements demand a considerable amount of judgment. Remember too that the security

---

[4] Liz Gallese, "Under the Gun—How Fund Managers at John Hancock Life Seek Safety Gains," *Wall Street Journal* (February 26, 1975), pp. 1 and 18.

analyst is under pressure to evaluate loan submissions as quickly as possible to provide fast service to investment bankers. But coupled with the pressure to complete the job quickly is the need for a thorough analysis. To combine successfully private placement investing and common stock research requires a unique individual—one with imagination, a flair for figures, and the ability to organize his workload.

The medium-size company may have two or three security analysts like the one described—analysts who can exercise good judgment and can work quickly and effectively in private placements, common stocks, and preferred stocks. It also must have mortgage analysts who are thoroughly familiar with the intricacies of commercial leasing, garden apartments, and office buildings, with all of the attendant legal problems.

An analyst of this quality is not only difficult to find but difficult to retain. A recurring problem is hiring a talented analyst, who works for several years, becomes knowledgeable about the company's operations, and then, just at the point when he is becoming effective, leaves to work for someone else. In a typical smaller life insurance company investment operation, the loss of one security analyst might reduce the staff by 20 percent. The loss of a mortgage analyst in Monumental Capital Management would reduce the effective force by one third. To conceptualize the impact of this type of loss, think what it would mean to Connecticut General or John Hancock if it lost 20 percent of its securities staff or one third of its mortgage staff. Yet the effect is the same.

One of the reasons that an analyst might leave a medium-size company is the limited opportunity for promotion, as meaningful titles are scarce. If the company cannot afford the titles and the promotion visibility, the only answer is salary. And salary brings up a host of problems in any life insurance company structure. The life insurance industry is not known for its high salaries. The worst possible situation in a smaller life insurance company is to have the investment department salaries arrayed against those of the underwriting department, the group department, or even the actuarial department. The competition to attract and retain the kind of security analysts the company needs comes not from other insurance companies but from investment bankers and investment advisors, pension funds, mutual funds, and, to a lesser extent, from the larger banks.

In the mortgage area there have historically been two centers of competition for personnel—mortgage correspondent firms and real estate investment trusts. Both of these areas are temporarily depressed. Nevertheless, the good analyst who can make sound judgments on mortgages and on common stocks or private placement bonds is worth considerably more than an individual of equal ability in another department of the company. The "investing industry" is always looking for good people who can exercise the kind of judgment that can make or save money for institutions; and the competition will be increasing from all sources, particularly from pension funds and banks.

Essentially, the salary structure of the investment operation cannot be set within the framework of the other insurance operations. One cannot compare a good security analyst with a top underwriter or actuary. This is true not only for competitive reasons but because of the functions being performed. Good analysts—mortgage or security—can make or save substantial amounts of money for their company. In many instances, their efforts can be evaluated rather quickly in the stock or bond markets. The security or mortgage analyst imposes his judgment on "dynamic dollars." The impact of decision makers in other departments is more difficult to evaluate except on a longer-term basis.

One way to remove the salary structure of the investment operation from typical life insurance company personnel considerations is to place the investment operation in a wholly-owned subsidiary. This has been the trend in recent years for large companies; and the medium-size companies are sure to follow, as the salary problem is even more important for them. An example of this is Capital Holding Corporation, which has centralized its securities operations in the holding company through which it now provides investment counseling services to its life insurance affiliates.

Capital's approach is to coordinate investment operations for its seven principal subsidiaries through a centralized securities investment system at corporate headquarters in Louisville. The first stage of Capital's investment process involves estimating each subsidiary's cash flow for the following year. After analyzing these reports, the corporate staff develops an overall strategy as well as tactics tailored to the needs of each subsidiary (this is necessary owing to differences in state regulation and tax status). The staff determines the amount to be invested in each type of security and in the specific issues. A holding company finance committee screens private placement opportunities and acts as a liaison for the private placement approval committees of the subsidiaries.

In this fashion, the smaller subsidiaries, which previously could invest only in marketable bonds because of size considerations, can

avail themselves of the generally higher yields in the private placement market. Mortgage lending is only partially centralized. While
the overall policy and the general amount of mortgage lending is
determined by the finance committee, selection of individual issues
is left to the mortgage departments of each affiliate. Capital encourages each subsidiary to aid in the development of its region by investing mortgage funds locally whenever possible. Further, allowing
the subsidiaries to direct their mortgage lending on a regional basis
enables them to take advantage of their knowledge of local real estate
and credit conditions.

CORPORATE EQUITY INVESTING

The Rationale for Life Insurance Company Common Stock Ownership

Whether a life insurance company is large or small, a basic function of common stock ownership is to develop capital appreciation
and thereby to increase assets and to add to surplus in order to support expansion of the underwriting portfolio. More importantly, common stock profits allow the life company to offset bond losses. This is
a simple but commonly misunderstood function. Life insurance companies have heavy concentrations of assets in fixed income securities.
Typically the life insurance company's asset distribution will be 30
to 40 percent mortgages and 30 to 40 percent bonds with the balance
in stocks and other investments.

This reliance on fixed income securities can be justified economically by relating the company's liabilities to its investing process.
Nearly all life insurance policies are agreements to pay a stipulated
amount of money at a contingent future date. As a consequence, inflation is not a serious problem as it relates to meeting contractual
obligations. Inflation does have an impact on the bond portfolio in the
sense that increases in the rate of inflation result in a gradual upward
trend in interest rates. This has a negative effect on the market value
of the bond portfolio.

Even though life insurers carry bonds on their balance sheets at
amortized value, the theoretical market losses reflect a real loss of
potential earning power. Because the company is always trying to
improve its yield, the technique is to sell bonds, take the loss, offset
the loss with stock profits, and reinvest the proceeds in bonds (or in
some other fixed income security) at higher rates.

Typically, life insurance companies have a percentage concentration of 2 to 10 percent of their assets in common stocks. For the medium-size company, the objective is to work every common stock dollar as hard as possible. This requires a talented staff, a dedication to excellence, and a definitive objective. The objective is as important as the overall strategy employed to meet the objective.

When considering possible objectives for the common stock portfolios of medium-size life insurance companies, it is important to recall that such portfolios generally range in size from $10 to $50 million. This is not a large amount, and its impact on the company's financial performance depends on the skill with which it is used. In the author's view, the proper goal is total return, i.e., a combination of dividend yield and capital appreciation (the latter measured over a reasonable period of time). The base comparison point for measuring total return should be Moody's AA industrial bond interest rate. This can be considered the "riskless" rate and is the minimum acceptable return for the stock portfolio. One must do considerably better than this to justify the risk of stock investing.

Other possible standards of measurement are the market indices, such as the Dow Jones Industrial Average (DJIA) or the Standard & Poor's 500 stock index (S&P 500). Not too long ago, the objective of any equity money manager was to do 25 percent better than the S&P 500. At present, this may be too ambitious a standard except perhaps over a long period of time. Certainly, one should be measured against the standard indices, but the common stock portfolio should also stand up against alternate methods of investing. Portfolio appreciation of 5 percent in a year in which the DJIA and S&P averages were down 10 percent cannot be considered satisfactory if the company could have gained 10 percent at virtually no risk by placing the money in bonds.

A thorough study of the results of common stock investing is the so-called Fisher-Lorie Study conducted at the University of Chicago.[5] This study measured rates of return on investments in common stocks over a series of time periods from 1926 to 1965. One of these periods ranged from January 1926 through December 1960. The average rate of return compounded annually (assuming tax exemption and reinvestment) during this period was about 9 percent. The study was based on hypothetical equal initial investments in common stocks listed on the New York Stock Exchange during this period. On the

[5] L. Fisher and J. H. Lorie, "Rates of Return on Investments in Common Stock, the Year by Year Record, 1926–65," *Journal of Business*, vol. 40, no. 3 (July 1968), pp. 1–26.

basis of this result and subsequent studies, 9 percent is often cited as the typically expected experience over a long period of time under the assumption that past conditions prevail.[6] This assumption is critical, as future conditions will probably not duplicate the bull market of the late 1920s, the bear market and the depression of the 1930s, and so on. Nevertheless, realistic expectations as to investment in the stock market are an important facet of any equity investment program.

The history of the stock market does not warrant an expectation of a rate of return higher than 9 percent for most investors. There have been scattered instances of inspired portfolio managers who have done extremely well. For example, during the period extending from 1956 through 1969, Warren Buffett compounded a substantial amount of money on an annualized basis of 31 percent a year. A $10,000 investment in his partnership in 1956 would have appreciated to $260,000 by 1969. His record and those of a few others demonstrate that superior money management is possible, but it is rare and not available to the average company.

Support for this thesis is provided by the fact that over an 11-year period ending on December 31, 1972, only nine management groups have done better than 9 percent on a compounded annualized basis. Among these nine were David Babson, T. Rowe Price, General American Investors, and the Chemical Fund. But, 9 percent is not bad when one considers the time period from 1961 through 1972 or the longer time period from 1926 through 1960, both of which encompassed several bear markets. The compounded 9 percent annualized rate of return looks attractive when compared to the compounded annualized interest rates available during these years. Against all of this, and considering the present level of stock prices and the probable scenarios of economic activity over the next three to five years, it is the author's view that a common stock investing program can achieve a total return rate between 10 and 12 percent.

Implementing the Investment Strategy

In developing an investment strategy to achieve the established objective, one must assess the talent—i.e., the human resources—that is available to achieve this objective. Since the medium-size life insurance company has a small staff, it is important to realize what this staff can do, and even more importantly, what it cannot do. In general,

---

[6] Later, Fisher and Lorie examined common stock returns for the period 1926–1965, obtaining an average return of 9.3 percent.

the staff will not be able to predict short-term or long-term stock market fluctuations, the timing or the duration of business cycles (even the economists have not been able to do this), the course of international development, or political events, especially on the national scene.

The amount of effort expended on trying to predict the unpredictable is totally unproductive when compared with the investment results. Even if the analyst were able to predict short-term developments successfully, he probably could not gauge the impact of the predicted events on the securities market. While political and economic forecasting thus appears to be futile, a competent securities staff should be able to follow individual stocks on a detailed basis and to develop original ideas on stock investing. The investment department of a medium-size life company thus should eschew forecasting in favor of securities analysis.

The investment staff of the medium-size life insurer should search for stocks which have good prospects for increasing earnings and dividends over a period of years. In many cases, however, such stocks are already recognized and have been bid up to premiums over normal values. Consequently, the staff must work diligently to select stocks that have not been institutionally accepted, i.e., valid growth stocks that are up for election by the institutions but have not yet been purchased in a major way. The same benefit can be realized by buying institutionally accepted growth stocks during a major shake-out when they dip down to a reasonable valuation. Given the volatility of the securities markets and the number of experts in the field, any other strategy requires far more expertise and staff than the medium-size company can afford.

Structuring the Common Stock Portfolio

Successful equity investing really involves being invested in the right stocks at the right time. The central point is portfolio exposure, i.e., emphasis, diversification, and so on. Thus, the portfolio must be properly structured in order to achieve the investment objectives. Selecting the right stocks is perhaps less important than investing in the proper group. In this regard, the portfolio exposure must be known, not in terms of banks, savings and loan companies, etc., but in terms of, say, interest sensitive stocks.[7]

---

[7] Claude N. Rosenberg, Jr., "Portfolio Structure: The Way You Look at What You Have Can Make a Difference," *Institutional Investor* (November 1972). The article espouses a somewhat different approach to portfolio structuring, but it is equally valid and provocative.

Traditionally, portfolio managers have categorized their portfolio positions by industry group to indicate both concentration and diversification. Convenient percentages are derived based on each group's relationship to the total investment position. A typical stock portfolio classified on this basis is presented in Table 12.1.

TABLE 12.1
A Hypothetical Stock Portfolio Categorized by Industry Group

Industry Group	Stocks Held	Industry Group	Stocks Held
Autos	Ford General Motors	Hotels	Marriott
Banks	Citicorp Philadelphia National	Oil	Exxon Atlantic Richfield
Chemicals	DuPont Hercules	Photography	Eastman Kodak Polaroid
Drugs	A. H. Robins Merck Syntex	Retailing	May Department Stores S. S. Kresge
Electronics	Hewlett-Packard Fairchild Camera	Utilities	Baltimore Gas and Electric
Food	Pillsbury Standard Brands		Kansas City Power and Light

The list presented in Table 12.1 looks reasonable in terms of market exposure and diversification, and one can quickly make a risk assessment relative to market exposure. However, a better and more effective way of looking at the portfolio might be to categorize stocks not by stratified industry group, but by broader economic and market segments such as various types of growth stocks, interest sensitive stocks, energy stocks, etc. On this basis the portfolio would take on a strikingly different orientation, as shown in Table 12.2.

The portfolio structuring portrayed in Table 12.2 allows the manager to assess his common stock exposure in relationship to expectations with regard to the national economy and stock market psychology. To illustrate, a fully invested portfolio has been developed based on the market levels of late 1974 and on the assumption that a growing recession in 1975 would bottom-out in the third quarter, accompanied by falling short-term rates and a gradual unwinding of inflation. This portfolio is presented in Table 12.3.

TABLE 12.2
A Hypothetical Stock Portfolio Categorized by Economic and Market Characteristics

Classification	Stocks Held	Classification	Stocks Held
Quality growth stocks	Merck Hewlett-Packard	Interest sensitive stocks	Baltimore Gas and Electric Citicorp
Medium quality growth stocks	S. S. Kresge Syntex		Kansas City Gas and Electric Philadelphia National Bank
Cyclical growth stocks	Eastman Kodak DuPont Fairchild Camera	Energy stocks	Atlantic Richfield Exxon
Depressed growth stocks	Polaroid Marriott A. H. Robins	Consumer non-durables and services	Pillsbury Standard Brands
Raw materials and intermediate goods stocks	Hercules	Consumer durables	Ford General Motors

TABLE 12.3
Distribution of Assets among Stock Categories
in a Hypothetical Portfolio

Stock Grouping	Percent of Total Portfolio
Quality growth	10%
Medium growth	10
Depressed growth	15
Interest sensitive (banks, savings and loans, utilities)	15
Energy (coal, domestic oils)	15
Consumer non-durables and services (insurance, food, retailing, tobacco)	15
Construction (cement, housing, etc.)	12
Raw materials and intermediate goods (fertilizers, chemicals, metals)	8
Total	100

One may quarrel about the possible redundancy in Kresge (as a growth and retail stock) and challenge the emphasis on interest sensitive stocks and the absence of consumer durable stocks. This is precisely the advantage of the portfolio grouping; i.e., it forces the staff to justify its proposals in the context of the overall portfolio mix. This approach seems to be valuable in staff meetings in defining problems in the portfolio and in assisting with the development of satisfactory solutions.[8]

Convertibles

The volatile securities markets of the 1970–1976 period have resulted in an increasing focus on risk management rather than rate of return management. On this basis, convertible securities may be an appropriate outlet for a portion of the medium-size insurance company's funds. They could well provide a major alternative to a part of the common stock segment of the portfolio because convertibles

---

[8] An excellent approach to the cultivation of idea-generating and problem-solving abilities that can be useful for the investment analyst can be found in James L. Adams, *Conceptual Blockbusting* (Stanford, Calif.: The Portable Stanford, The Stanford Alumni Association, 1974).

are supposed to involve less risk than the underlying common stock.

The problem is that the relative safety depends on the price of the convertible securities—the higher the price, the more they tend to act as equity instead of debt instruments. Further, many convertible issues are not sufficiently large for substantial purchases—say, 500 to 800 bonds. Not only is the "size" of the market a problem, but a wide spread sometimes exists between the bid-and-asked quotations. Additionally, evaluating a convertible is usually much more difficult than evaluating a straight bond or stock. The analyst must evaluate the fundamentals underlying the stock and then he must evaluate the relationship of the convertible's price to its value purely as a fixed income security.

Equity-Oriented Private Placements

Around 1968, a number of life insurance companies began to stress equity-oriented private placements. This focus on privately placed securities with equity features seemed to be a spectacular way to gain capital appreciation. The companies were influenced by well-documented records of convertibles or bonds with warrants (either public or private) that did extremely well. Some investment officers were pushed into these programs by top management, who came back from industry meetings with fantastic stories of the returns to be derived from this type of investment. The most successful companies in this field appeared to be Massachusetts Mutual, Northwest National, and State Mutual. State Mutual gained acclaim by investing in the late 1950s in equity-oriented private placements issued by Russell Stover and McDonald's.

Companies which followed the trend toward equity-oriented private placements after about 1968 soon found their successes offset by significant losses on issues by firms such as Visual Electronics, Black Watch Farms, and Four Seasons Nursing Homes. As a result, this kind of investing suddenly went out of fashion and a pall was cast over the entire concept. The state of the securities markets in the past several years and the negative attitude of investors toward the bonds and stocks of smaller companies have reinforced this retrenchment with respect to equity-oriented private placements. Further, the high interest rates available on straight bonds have made it difficult to justify diverting funds to this area. Accordingly, given the limitations of human and financial resources of the smaller life companies, this does not appear to be a productive investment sector.

PROBLEMS IN MORTGAGE LENDING

The single characteristic that distinguishes large and medium-size insurance companies in developing mortgage loan sources is the scope and intensity of their effort. Highly intense mortgage loan generation is epitomized by Prudential, Equitable, and Jefferson Standard Life. These companies lend direct; that is, they find, screen, analyze, and close the loans and then service them (collecting the interest and principal directly). The alternative is a mortgage correspondent network, i.e., intermediaries that develop loans geographically for a fee and feed these loans to the central or regional office of the life insurance company.

The principal advantage of direct lending is its efficiency in terms of loan generation. More importantly, it eliminates the mortgage correspondent's loan development and servicing fee, which could equate to one point on the loan amount and ⅛ of 1 percent on the interest rate. Presumably, this total savings of ¼ of 1 percent (one point being equivalent to ⅛ of 1 percent) is shared by both the borrower and the lender. Accordingly, the direct lenders receive a higher return than they would if mortgage correspondents were used.

The Prudential's system of direct loan generation is in many ways the most structured. Both the home office and a number of regional offices service loans. The regional offices also oversee a number of field offices, which are really production offices staffed by from two to five mortgage men who spend the majority of their time developing mortgage loan sources.

Metropolitan Life and Aetna Life have adopted a combination approach. These companies have mortgage correspondents but also do a fair amount of direct lending. On complex real estate deals, these companies may utilize their mortgage correspondents' advice and/or underwriting ability. Usually correspondents are relied on when evaluating special-use properties which call for a quality of entrepreneurial judgment lacking in the insurance company but available in the mortgage correspondent staff. The third and final category of large lenders are those that do not (as a matter of policy) make direct loans—the borrower must utilize their correspondents under all circumstances.

Whichever approach is selected, the larger companies are potentially able to generate all or a substantial portion of their mortgage loan requirements internally without reliance on mortgage correspondents. Further, large companies which utilize correspondents are increasingly likely to supplement their efforts with direct lending in key metropolitan areas.

In contrast, the medium-size insurance company's mortgage origination options are rather limited. Typically, most of its mortgage loans have flowed through a mortgage correspondent network. This network has been developed geographically at no small cost in time and effort. Monumental Capital Management does business with 29 mortgage correspondents of which perhaps a dozen are very active. Its network ranges throughout most of the United States. Over the past four or five years, many of these mortgage correspondents have been acquired by major bank holding companies.

This may pose a problem in the future. At some point, the supply of good commercial mortgages may diminish; and at that point the bank, through its mortgage correspondents, may have a tendency to retain the better mortgages and divert the increasingly marginal mortgages to the life insurance companies. In any event, more and more mortgage correspondents are leaving the independent ranks as their management grows older and as the competition increases. These developments could well have a significant influence on the future investment strategy of the medium-size life insurance company.

BOND MANAGEMENT

During the past several years, institutional investors have become increasingly involved in the bond market. Traditionally, this was a market dominated by banks and insurance companies. The new entrants are pension funds, endowment funds, and the larger mutual funds. A number of reasons for this trend exist, but primarily it is based on two factors: (1) Investors perceive less risk in the bond market relative to the stock market, particularly after the horrendous experience of 1973–1974. (2) At the interest levels prevailing in recent years, bonds offer returns comparable to those available in stocks on a total return basis.

Significantly, most of the attention has centered on the public bond market at the expense of the private placement market. This has been based on a desire for both liquidity and flexibility. Flexibility is the chief motivation. There has been and will continue to be pressure on those who manage money to improve investment performance. Most stock programs experienced poor results on the average, and managers have responded by thinking more creatively about flexible strategies for investing assets and a broader mix in their investment portfolios.

From the standpoint of the life insurance industry, two significant trends have been developing: a growing resistance to lower quality bond offerings and a greater attraction to medium-term securities with maturities ranging from five to ten years. While life companies are willing to buy issues with high coupon rates to offset the impact of future inflation, they are anxious to avoid significant credit risks. Growing fears of corporate bankruptcies, illustrated by the difficulties of real estate investment trusts and highlighted by the collapse of the Franklin National Bank, have led to an increased aversion to lesser quality securities.

Fear of future inflation and the risk of being "locked in" to fixed bond rates, which depreciate in real value over the years, have impelled many investors to favor shorter maturities in their bond purchases during recent quarters. Medium-term offerings, with maturities of 5 to 10 years rather than the usual 25 or 30 years, accounted for close to 40 percent of all public bond issues in 1975, compared with 30 percent in 1974, less than 8 percent in 1973, and about 20 percent in 1972.[9]

Arrayed against this backdrop of a more popular bond market, a drive toward liquidity, and an aversion to significant credit risks, the medium-size life insurance company must decide whether to emphasize research or trading when attempting to optimize its bond operation. In the opinion of the author, the emphasis should be on research rather than bond trading. There are three types of research which could be stressed—interest rate research, market research, and research on credits. Of the three types, research concerning interest rates or the ability to predict rates is the most profitable. However, it is also the most difficult type of research; and, on balance, market research and research on credits tend to yield the more certain and attainable improvements in the portfolio.

Careful attention to credit and market research may enable the company to take advantage of yield disparities or of temporary under- or over-valuations of particular credits. In addition, such research may facilitate trading to take advantage of special situations and may alert the company to the need to improve call protection.

Yield disparities may exist within the same rating class or may involve a general upgrading or downgrading. Among the factors which must be assessed and weighted are: (1) how close or how distant one

---

[9] Kenneth M. Wright, *1975 Economic & Investment Report* (Washington, D.C.: American Council of Life Insurance, 1975), p. 3.

feels the spreads are between bond ratings, (2) the characteristics of the new issue calendar, (3) the immediate outlook for interest rates, and (4) the amount of money destined for the long-term public bond market.

In order to take advantage of temporary under- or over-valuation of a credit, the company must stay one step ahead of the rating services. This, of course, is based on the premise that the market has not already discounted the change.

Trading to take advantage of special situations covers that area in the market where gaps in the selling structure exist. Bids can be substantially different from dealer to dealer, particularly where small pieces (several hundred bonds) are involved. Splits or anomalies of this nature may involve as much as three points. Since these spreads exist only for brief periods, close attention and prompt action are required. Over a period of time these small increments can add up to a considerable improvement in overall yield.

Improving call protection is the least immediate and most controversial tactic in bond trading. Its advantage obviously depends on the correctness of interest rate judgments many years out. The prudent portfolio manager simply must hedge his position in this area.

CONCLUSION

All institutional investors will have to possess flexibility to operate in the securities markets of the future. This will be particularly true of the smaller life insurance companies. Improving yield on invested assets has been and will continue to be an important offset to the constantly rising costs of selling and administration. In order to continue to enhance yield, investment operations must be successful within the difficult environment of the market place. The market place of the future will be characterized by a gradual decline in market liquidity as fewer and fewer firms will be able or willing to make markets. Further, increasingly volatile price movements will occur as investors will continue to be much more sensitive to short-term developments and to react much more quickly. Finally, widening price differentials can be expected in terms of quality and maturity, particularly in the bond market.

Under these conditions, widespread uncertainty could result in the near avoidance of all but the top quality issues; and the prices of medium-grade issues could well be attractive. Historically, such situations have created opportunities for the flexible and aggressive investor. By displaying these two qualities the smaller life insurance company can maximize its probability of investment success.

13

The Social Responsibilities of Life Insurance Companies as Investors

By Robert H. Mundheim*

In recent years, the concept of corporate social responsibility has become more important to business enterprises of all types. The life insurance industry has not been immune to this development and in some respects has been in the forefront of defining and participating in socially responsible investment activities. This chapter examines several aspects of the social responsibilities of life insurance companies as investors. In the first section, the industry view of its responsibilities is discussed. The second section outlines the legal precedents for socially responsible actions and discusses the limitations placed on such activities by law. In the third section, a new approach to life insurance company social responsibility investing is proposed, which may enable the companies to improve their effectiveness in this area. Finally, the issue of the social obligations stemming from the ownership of common stock is analyzed.

THE INSURANCE INDUSTRY VIEWPOINT

In order to discuss the social responsibilities of life insurance companies as investors, it seems reasonable to begin by examining how insurance companies themselves are defining their social responsi-

---

* Robert H. Mundheim is Fred Carr Professor of Law and Financial Institutions at the University of Pennsylvania and director of the University of Pennsylvania Law School Center for Study of Financial Institutions.

bilities. An excellent example of the company viewpoint is provided by the keynote address at the 1971 Life Insurance Conference on Corporate Social Responsibility given by Donald S. MacNaughton, chairman and chief executive officer of the Prudential Insurance Company of America.[1] MacNaughton served as a member of the steering committee for the conference. Moreover, Prudential was a leader in putting together the original life insurance industry commitment of $1 billion toward the Urban Investment Program.[2] In addition, *Response,* the magazine published by the life insurance industry's Clearinghouse on Corporate Social Responsibility, often lists Prudential projects in its periodic reports of new social responsibility investments.

MacNaughton began his speech by contrasting the smaller, entrepreneur-owned businesses of "the early days" with the modern business corporation. He characterized the latter as a "private enterprise institution" (as opposed to a "private property institution"). The private enterprise institution is "a business organization whose managers act as trustees for *all* who have an interest in the enterprise— the stockholders, employees, suppliers, consumers and the public."[3] (Emphasis in original.) Under this definition, the private enterprise institution is seen as a social force with all the duties and responsibilities of a social organization.

MacNaughton also commented on the change in public demands on the modern business corporation. Originally, the demand was primarily economic in nature. But, he observed:

> The time has come . . . for us to recognize that the future role of business must be social as well as economic. We can't ignore, nor can we reject, this public demand. Instead, we must adapt our corporations to their new role, and we must develop a whole new set of performance measures for determining company viability and vitality.[4]

---

[1] Donald S. MacNaughton, "A Responsible Business," Keynote address presented at the Life Insurance Conference on Corporate Social Responsibility, October 10–11, 1971 (New York: Institute of Life Insurance).

[2] This program is discussed in Karen Orren, *Corporate Power and Social Change: The Politics of the Life Insurance Industry* (Baltimore: Johns Hopkins University Press, 1974), chap. 6. See also, Clearinghouse on Corporate Social Responsibility, *A Report on the $2 Billion Urban Investment Program of the Life Insurance Business: 1967–1972* (New York: Institute of Life Insurance, 1973).

[3] MacNaughton, "A Responsible Business," p. 3.

[4] Ibid., p. 9.

Although MacNaughton recognized the absence of mechanisms for conducting audits to measure the success of business enterprises in meeting social demands which are not reflected in the willingness of society to pay higher prices, he urged insurance companies to:

> . . . get on with the work. If each of us will pursue the social problems in his own way, with the customary vigor and enthusiasm of businessmen, the job will somehow get done, and society will be adequately served. This assumes that the philosophy of Adam Smith is applicable to social development, as well as economic development.[5]

Finally, MacNaughton addressed himself specifically to the investment activities of insurance companies.

> We must be particularly sensitive to the social effects of our investment activities. Our traditional investment policy has been to maximize investment return. If a literal translation of the policy encourages investment in antisocial activities, or activities which return only a short-term benefit, it doesn't make sense and is wrong. But I'm sure that's not a proper translation. Surely we know that we can't operate effectively in a society which is not functioning well. We have a responsibility to place our investment funds (and they are considerable) where they will inure to society's benefit. This is not inconsistent with maximum yield because in determining yield, we must take into consideration the effect of our investments on society as a whole, and over the long, not the short, haul.
>
> We must also determine our responsibilities with respect to the power which flows to us as institutional investors. As we increase our equity holdings, this becomes even more significant.[6]

MacNaughton creates an expansive mood for the definition of an insurance company's social responsibilities; but his specific discussion of investment activities focuses on maximization of investment return (presumably, relative to risk). He points out that maximization neither requires nor results from a preoccupation with short-term benefits. The shareholders of a stock life insurance company expect it to be in business for a long period of time. The policyholders of a mutual life insurance company expect to pay their premiums and receive benefits over long periods of time.

To the extent that MacNaughton looks at social responsibility as an aspect of profit maximization, he does not introduce any significant conceptual change in evaluating the way in which life insurance companies go about their business. He realistically stresses the rapid

---

[5] Ibid., p. 11.
[6] Ibid., pp. 14–15.

changes in society's values and desires which a long-term enterprise must take into account in formulating its business strategy. The congruence between doing well and doing good is not a new insight.

For example, life insurance companies invest in pollution control bonds without sacrificing yield or safety. One life insurance company made substantial commitments to the financing of one of the "new town" developments. The company analyzed the project as an existing venture which pioneered an important concept in structuring communities of the future. It also saw substantial, favorable investment opportunities if the project proved successful. Although the project was not commercially successful, it was undertaken in a spirit totally compatible with profit maximizing principles.

This aspect of socially responsible action urges the investment officials of a life insurance company to be open-minded in evaluating projects which are not the traditional investment media of the company. If society generally will pay for those things it wants, an ability to predict the direction of society's demands should enhance portfolio profitability. The compilation of "investments for socially desirable purposes," produced by the Clearinghouse on Corporate Social Responsibility includes those investments which would not normally be made under the customary company practices.[7] The Clearinghouse designates certain types of investments (e.g., housing for low and moderate income families, health and social service facilities in inner city and rural areas, and funds to finance anti-pollution facilities) as having a "prima facie socially desirable purpose."[8] However, inclusion in the Clearinghouse's category of investments for socially desirable purposes does not require that there be any financial sacrifice.

Long-term profit considerations also mandate recognition of existing and emerging social demands in order to minimize costs which may be imposed on the company. The public has come to demand socially responsive action from corporations and may punish those enterprises which do not behave responsibly. For example, it may make good business sense for an insurance company not to finance or otherwise be connected with a project undertaken by a developer who is not adhering to existing or projected anti-pollution requirements.

The Massachusetts Mutual Life Insurance Company has adopted

---

[7] Clearinghouse on Corporate Social Responsibility, "1974 Reporting Program of Life and Health Insurance Companies on Corporate Social Responsibility Activities" (New York: Institute of Life Insurance, September 1974), p. 47.

[8] Ibid.

certain requirements with respect to its real estate investment operations which are designed to keep it from being involved with potentially troublesome situations. Applicants for loans are required to certify that they are not in violation of any Federal, state, or local environmental, fair employment, or occupational safety and health statutes and that the investment property now and as proposed conforms to the requirements of such statutes. In addition, applicants are asked to indicate whether the investment project:

1. is opposed by individuals, groups, or governmental bodies;
2. involves individuals or organizations that have a controversial product or otherwise engage in operating practices considered to be discriminatory or controversial;
3. is liable to destroy or damage historic places or installations or affect historically or architecturally significant buildings;
4. will cause water, air, noise, nuclear, or scenic pollution; reduce or destroy existing wetlands or create wetlands or impoundment areas where none is desired; or destroy or have any detrimental effect on present or desirable wildlife or plant life;
5. is liable to affect the supply and disposition of water and sewage, streams or rivers, natural surface drainage and underground water supply, traffic flow or congestion and resultant air pollution; or
6. is subject to Federal or environmental controls.[9]

In some cases, maintenance of good will may require an insurance company to act affirmatively, e.g., by joining in the financing of an economically non-qualifying project which community leaders have persuaded other local insurance companies to sponsor. At times, insurance companies have been willing to make investments which yield less than other available opportunities to forestall threatened governmental action which might have much greater potential impact on the company's long-run profitability. Thus, life insurance companies made residential loans under the Voluntary Home Mortgage Credit Program in rural and remote areas to head off a threatened program of direct governmental loans even though the greater difficulty of field appraisals, credit checks, and loan servicing made these loans less profitable than other types of loans.[10] Similar motiva-

---

[9] See *Response* (January 1975), p. 13. The report in *Response* indicates that no loan applications had been rejected for failure to meet the standards implied by the questions.

[10] Kenneth M. Wright, "Social Concerns, Public Policy and Life Insurance Investments," *C.L.U. Journal* (January 1972).

tion may help to explain the major financial sacrifices incurred by some insurance companies through investments in projects designed to rebuild the decaying cities in which they are headquartered. The costs have been justified, in substantial part, as a less expensive alternative to relocating the headquarters.

LEGAL IMPLICATIONS OF SOCIAL RESPONSIBILITY INVESTMENTS

Since all of the activities described above are premised on the basis that they contribute to long-term profit maximization of the life insurance company, they probably cannot be successfully challenged as legally improper. The common law has traditionally recognized that corporations may expend money for public purposes if the expenditure can reasonably be expected to benefit the corporation. The benefit need not be immediate; also it need not be direct.[11] The courts have not had to define how long-term or how indirect the benefits may be. The imprecision in court guidance on these important questions arises from the judiciary's unwillingness to second-guess management's judgment that specific, socially responsible activities tend to further the corporation's purposes.

In the latter half of the 1960s, a shareholder of the corporation owning the Chicago Cubs baseball team sued management for failure to install lights in Wrigley Field so that night baseball could be played there. The shareholder alleged that night baseball would increase attendance at Chicago Cub games and thus enhance the profits of the corporation. He asserted that failure to install lights derived from the dominating shareholder's personal judgment that baseball is a daytime game and that the installation of lights and night baseball games would have a deteriorating impact on the neighborhood surrounding the ball park. In affirming dismissal of the complaint, the Illinois Appellate Court refused to look behind management's judgment not to install lights in Wrigley Field because the complaint did not alleged fraud, illegality, or conflict of interest in the decision-making process.[12] The court said that management concerns properly embraced the possible deterioration of the neighborhood and its potential impact on the patrons of Chicago Cub

---

[11] E.g., A. P. Smith Mfg. Co. v. Barlow, 13 N.J. 145, 98 A. 2d 581 (1953). See also Ruder, "Public Obligations of Private Corporations," *University of Pennsylvania Law Review*, vol. 114 (1965), p. 209.

[12] *Shlensky* v. *Wrigley*, 95 Ill. App. 2d 173, 237 N.E. 2d 776 (1968).

baseball games and on the value of Wrigley Field to the corporation. The court concluded:

> By these thoughts we do not mean to say that we have decided that the decision of the directors was a correct one. That is beyond our jurisdiction and ability. We are merely saying that the decision is one properly before directors. . . .[13]

Court attitudes thus give management great leeway, within the profit maximizing framework, to respond to social demands. Perhaps the only clear cases for questioning a particular management action occur when the corporation is going out of business or, as explained below, when management fails to link the action to a business purpose. Nevertheless, an honest application of the profit maximization rationale should make management feel subject to the discipline of asking in a cold-blooded way whether a particular, socially responsible course of action will maximize economic returns in the foreseeable future. It does not permit management merely to ask, as suggested by some portions of MacNaughton's address, whether a particular course of action is the right thing to do.

MacNaughton's reference to managers acting as trustees for all (including the public) who have an interest in the enterprise suggests that management has the right (even the duty) to disregard long-term profit maximization. However, management's deliberate sacrifice of shareholder (or in mutual life insurance companies, policyholder) economic interests so that the company can take action management thinks is "right" raises troubling issues of law and policy.

The propriety of such action was squarely raised in *Dodge* v. *Ford Motor Company*.[14] In that case the Dodge brothers sought to compel the directors of Ford to declare a dividend. The corporation could well afford to do so. It had a $112 million surplus, roughly half of it in cash and marketable securities. Projected expansion plans called for expenditures of only $20 million. Henry Ford wanted the company to share its profits with the public by making substantial reductions in the price of the cars sold. Market conditions did not appear to require any reduction. The court found that "certain sentiments, philanthropic and altruistic, creditable to Mr. Ford, had a large influence in determining the policy to be pursued by the Ford Motor Company. . . ."[15] In its affirmance of the lower court decision to com-

---

[13] *Id.*, at 181, 237 N.E. 2d, at 780.
[14] 204 Mich. 459, 170 N.W. 668 (1919).
[15] *Id.*, at 505–506, 170 N.W., at 684.

pel declaration of $19 million in dividends, the Supreme Court of
Michigan ringingly asserted:

> A business corporation is organized and carried on primarily for the
> profit of the stockholders. The powers of the directors are to be em-
> ployed for that end. The discretion of directors is to be exercised in
> the choice of means to attain that end and does not extend to change
> in the end itself, to the reduction of profits or to the non-distribution
> of profits among stockholders in order to devote them to other
> purposes.[16]

The adverse judgment in the *Ford Motor Company* case probably
could have been avoided if Henry Ford had linked the proposed reduction in car prices to a desire to broaden the market for future production. In that event the court probably would not have tested this
exercise of director discretion to determine whether such a reduction
would in fact result in ultimately greater profitability for the stockholders.

Substantial inroads into the significance of the holding of *Ford
Motor Company* for business corporations have been made by the
proliferation of provisions in state corporation statutes giving corporations the power to make donations for the public welfare or for
charitable, scientific, or educational purposes.[17] In some states these
provisions apply to life insurance companies,[18] while in others, the
insurance law specifically provides comparable power.[19] Typically,
these statutory provisions impose no explicit limitation on the power
of the corporation to give away corporate assets. However, counsel
usually tend to imply into the statutory grant of power a limit of reasonable contributions. One commonly accepted test of reasonableness
is the 5 percent of net income which the Internal Revenue Code permits as an income tax deduction for corporations.[20] In fact, average
corporate donations have tended to amount to 1 percent or less of net
corporate income.[21]

Corporate power to make donations has also been upheld in sweep-
ing language under the common law. The New Jersey Supreme Court
was asked to examine the propriety of a $1,500 contribution by the

---

[16] *Id.*, at 507, 170 N.W., at 684.

[17] See Model Bus. Corp. Act Ann. 2d (1973 Supp.) §4(m), §6. As of January
1, 1973, all jurisdictions except Arizona and Idaho had statutes on the subject of
donations.

[18] E.g., Delaware Ins. Code, 4903.

[19] E.g., Illinois Ins. Code, 1053(d).

[20] Int. Rev. Code of 1954, 170(b)(2), 26 U.S.C. 170(b)(2). *Theodora Holding Corp. v. Henderson*, 257 A. 2d 398 (Del. ch. 1969).

[21] American Association of Fund-Raising Counsel, *Giving USA* 17 (1975).

A. P. Smith Company to Princeton University's annual giving campaign.[22] The court found the gift to be for at least the indirect benefit of the corporation. It viewed free, nongovernmental educational institutions as essential to the economic and social environment for private business enterprise. This broad articulation of the benefit standard invites inclusion of almost any welfare contribution as an appropriate object of corporate concern.

The court went on to find an even broader basis for sustaining the gift, noting that "modern conditions require that corporations acknowledge and discharge social as well as private responsibilities as members of the community in which they operate."[23] That language was not necessary to sustain the modest gift made. It is also not clear that this broad justification was meant to go beyond providing a rationale for traditional corporate charitable giving, an activity which had acquired statutory sanction in New Jersey, the state where A. P. Smith was domiciled and the university was located.

Even if a life insurance company is permitted to donate a portion of its assets for the public welfare, should it be barred from making investments (at below market yields or at above normal risks) in activities it believes serve the public welfare? Can the financial sacrifice involved in such investments be viewed as a contribution to the public welfare? The major practical difference between such public welfare investments and charitable contributions is the potentially open-ended nature of the former. Not only is it difficult to evaluate how much of the investment may be lost, but pressure may arise to invest additional funds to save the enterprise or project. Moreover, these investments often cost investment officials substantial, but hard to identify, amounts of time and energy. The author has heard a number of life insurance company officials complain about the extra time and frustrations encountered in doing business with many of the projects (particularly minority businesses) funded in the course of the industry's $2 billion Urban Investment Program. Finally, corporate charitable giving tends to be limited to organizations qualifying as exempt organizations under Section 501(c) of the Internal Revenue Code. Section 501(c) contains a category of organizations which society through the political process has designated as serving the public welfare.

These distinctions do not destroy the charitable contribution precedent as a conceptual justification for non-profit-maximizing corpo-

---

[22] *A. P. Smith Mfg. Co.* v. *Barlow*, 13 N.J. 145, 98 A. 2d 581 (1953).
[23] *Id.*, at 154, 98 A. 2d, at 586.

rate investments in projects contributing to the public welfare. However, they point out practical problems which should be considered in framing a program for making socially responsible investments. For example, insurance companies participating in the Urban Investment Program fulfilled a substantial portion of their commitment by investing in Federally insured or guaranteed housing, because the government guarantee effectively limited the risk of loss from these investments to loss of a few months' interest, potential opportunity costs, and greater administrative expenses.[24]

A PROPOSAL FOR IMPROVING INSURANCE COMPANY EFFORTS

Avoidance of the open-ended cost of a social responsibility investment program seems to argue for life insurance company adoption of techniques for separating out their non-profit-maximizing investments into a separate portfolio. Segregation of such a portfolio (which could be managed within the company or in a separate pool in which several companies could invest) has a number of potential advantages. It encourages the thinking through of the investment effort so that the insurance company's expertise and funds can be deployed in a way that will create the most significant social impact. Much of today's social responsibility investment undoubtedly represents ad hoc reactions to specific pressures. By developing investment officials who will have a continuing need to be concerned about investments in minority enterprises and projects, segregation may also stimulate the exploration of techniques for overcoming some of the management obstacles and frustrations heretofore encountered. Even though the investments will not be made on profit maximizing principles, there is no reason for the program not to be operated on a businesslike basis.

Life insurance companies seem to reject the concept of an industry-wide investment fund for projects which do not meet profit maximizing principles. The Urban Investment Program was an industry-wide commitment to help solve problems which had become painfully acute in the late 1960s. The Program was announced in 1967, the summer of which had seen the riots in Newark (home of the Prudential), Detroit, and other cities. Although the commitment was industry-wide, fulfillment of the pledge was the responsibilty of individual

---

[24] Clearinghouse on Corporate Responsibility, *A Report on the $2 Billion Urban Investment Program of the Life Insurance Business, 1967–1972.*

companies making separate investments.[25] Industry initiatives were undertaken to work out appropriate governmental cooperation for some of the proposed investment projects.[26]

The industry's Committee on Corporate Social Responsibility has sought to initiate other industry-wide investment efforts. However, the only program on which progress has been made is a project to help finance a primary care group medical program. Under this program, the Robert Wood Johnson Foundation will screen and fund certain hospital-related ambulatory care centers. Individual insurance companies will provide mortgage loans for about 30 of the centers selected and funded by the foundation.[27]

Life insurance companies also generally have not moved in the direction of specifically earmarking a certain portion of their portfolios for non-profit-maximizing investments. One reason for not doing so may be a general uneasiness about the propriety of such activity. It is more comfortable and, as the *Ford Motor Company* case illustrates, perhaps legally safer to characterize, to the extent possible, socially responsible action as an aspect of fulfilling the long-run profit making expectations of the owners of the business. Under this view, it may be sensible to commingle all investments on the theory that together they serve to further the objectives of the company. Moreover, such a policy does not expose to shareholder, policyholder, or public view and evaluation the precise nature or amount of the company's investments for primarily social responsibility purposes.

The cry for corporations, including life insurance companies, not to conduct their affairs on bases wholly dictated by profit maximizing considerations but to be socially responsive citizens is appealing and, as indicated above, commands significant support. However, the reaction may be quite different if one puts forth the bald proposition that corporation management has the right to determine priorities among social objectives and to spend other people's money (the shareholders' or policyholders') to underwrite their choices. On this fundamental policy question, many people would prefer that, except for de minimus matters such as relatively modest charitable contributions, management of business enterprises should limit itself to business judgments, and the political process should make social judgments. The argument is that this clear allocation of responsibility

---

[25] Ibid., p. 25.

[26] Ibid., pp. 31–35.

[27] See *Response* (January 1975), p. 3.

may make it easier to hold people accountable for failure to meet objectives.

The most compelling reason to reject this approach is the rigidity inherent in leaving questions of defining priorities solely to government regulation. Society's problems are too numerous and diverse for government regulation to deal with them all. Moreover, government regulation frequently appears not to work well in assessing society's will and often is limited in the imagination with which it can respond to problems. In addition, government may be subject to disproportionate pressures from special interests on particular issues. Corporate responsibility notions encourage a diversity of approach to solving society's problems and promote a desirable dispersion of power. In the event that a particular problem looms large enough, the political process can take the ultimate judgment away from the corporation and return it to society as a whole.

Indeed, in this country society does not forbid private aggregations of wealth from affecting priorities among social objectives. On the contrary, U.S. tax laws encourage the creation of foundations whose financial resources have allowed them to support those efforts to improve society which they consider worthwhile. However, foundations generally seem better structured than business corporations to engage in non-profit-maximizing activities. The management of the large, ongoing foundations tend to be chosen because of their familiarity with the social problems to which the foundation addresses itself. In contrast, corporate management is chosen for its business expertise. Moreover, foundations normally are staffed by persons with professional qualifications for carrying out the primary purposes of the foundations. Most business corporations, including insurance companies, assign their normal business staff to take on the social responsibility projects in which the company may become interested. Further, the work of the foundation is subject to public scrutiny and discipline because information about its aims and its activities are publicly available.[28] Business corporations tend to be judged by their

---

[28] Private foundations having at least $5,000 of assets at any time during a taxable year must file an annual report containing among other items of information:

> an itemized list of all grants and contributions made or approved for future payment during the year, showing the amount of each such grant or contribution, the name and address of the recipient, any relationship between any individual recipient and the foundation's managers or substantial contributors, and a concise statement of the purpose of each such grant or contribution.

Int. Rev. Code of 1954, §6056(b)(7).
These annual reports are made available for public inspection. *Id.* §6104(b).

financial results. The cost of the corporation's social responsibility activities will not normally be a material item and will, therefore, be buried in its profit and loss statement. Moreover, the corporation is not obligated to make any specific disclosure about its non-profit-maximizing activities.

In addition to the lack of public disclosure, management and the board of directors are not forced to face squarely the question of whether they should depart from profit maximizing standards in evaluating specific investments as long as courts will not question the expenditure of funds for purposes which produce an arguably long-term indirect benefit to the corporation. As a practical matter, management is under no greater restraint than it would be under an explicit recognition that corporate assets can be given away to a reasonable extent. Unfortunately, the prevailing indirect standard frustrates the development of mechanisms for imposing some discipline and review on management's exercise of discretion.

Legal developments in this area should emphasize two distinct points. First, profit maximizing activity should be defined in terms of relatively direct benefits to the corporation in the foreseeable future. That is the standard which management ought to apply in judging whether a particular project enhances the business of the enterprise. Second, in the absence of shareholder (policyholder) instructions to the contrary, management should be recognized as having the right to make reasonable expenditures on activities which do not necessarily advance the business of the enterprise. It should be appropriate and, for the reasons suggested previously, sound for life insurance companies to create foundation-like organizations to make non-profit-maximizing, public welfare investments. However, an important corollary of that management right should be the obligation to tell the shareholders, clearly and in as much detail as possible, what it is doing.

An explicit disclosure practice would force management to think through the wisdom of its policy decisions. Does the company really intend to take on activities which, in the foreseeable future, will have a net negative impact on the shareholders? How should such action be justified to the shareholders? Identification and justification should also make management more conscious of the need to develop a well-conceived program for expending corporate assets. Shareholders may expect that corporate generosity should reflect more than the sympathetic reaction of the chief executive to a particular proposal.

Public disclosure not only forces management to think through the difficult problems posed by the call for socially responsible action, but it also serves as the only practical way for management to be held accountable for the response which the corporation ultimately makes. Finally, fairness to the shareholder whose money is being used for non-business purposes suggests that he be told that some of his money is being given away. It is surprising that corporations are not required to describe to shareholders their policy on corporate charitable contributions and to disclose (at least) the aggregate amount donated.

Admittedly, the adoption of this proposal would create the danger that management will cut back (or abandon) support for activities which are not expected to produce relatively direct benefits to the corporation in the foreseeable future. Management may fear that once it is known that the company will support some non-profit-maximizing activities, pressures will build up for it to support other (probably not less worthwhile) activities. Failure to respond to these pressures may create undesirable consequences for the company. Moreover, in some cases management may worry that its willingness to respond to a social need will not be shared by at least some shareholders and will thus create shareholder dissatisfaction.

The disclosure aspects of the views on corporate social responsibility expressed in this chapter could be implemented by the Securities and Exchange Commission (SEC)—at least with respect to those companies whose securities are registered under Section 12 of the Securities Exchange Act. As an initial step, the SEC could require companies to disclose the identity of, and amounts expended or invested in, activities or projects which would not have been undertaken under the narrow profit maximization standard. Although such disclosures might not be material for evaluating the worth of the corporation's securities, this information seems germane to the broader interest of the shareholder in judging the stewardship of management. State insurance commissioners would be able to formulate comparable disclosure requirements for insurance companies whose proxy solicitations they regulate.[29]

THE RESPONSIBILITY OF EQUITY OWNERSHIP

Another important issue in the social responsibility realm is the role of life insurance companies as holders of common stock. At the

---

[29] Although insurance companies are generally exempted from the SEC's proxy rules under §12(g)(2)(G) of the Securities Exchange Act of 1934, similar proxy provisions are applicable to insurance companies under state law. If the SEC adopted the suggested approach in its proxy regulation, it is likely that state practice would follow the SEC lead.

end of 1975, life insurance companies held roughly $20 billion in common stocks.[30] MacNaughton's speech urged companies to take seriously their responsibility to vote such stock.[31] He predicted that the traditional Wall Street rule, vote with management or sell the stock, would be displaced by alternative procedures.

Initial dissatisfaction with the Wall Street rule stemmed from the fear that the large positions in particular stocks accumulated by institutional investors could not be sold without incurring enormous liquidity discounts. Institutions would thus become locked into certain investments and be forced to take a critical interest in management activities and in any proposals presented for shareholder vote. The development of market mechanisms to handle large blocks of stock may make this basis for abandoning the Wall Street rule less applicable for most of the stocks held by life insurance companies. Nevertheless, sale of portfolio stock and purchase of new stock involve transaction costs. Thus, institutions should exercise their shareholder rights thoughtfully in cases where intervention may help make the stock more valuable or prevent a decline in value. For example, institutional investors, including life insurance companies, have voted against or taken less formal action to oppose overly generous management compensation proposals and corporate combinations. Similarly, if abandonment of a portfolio company's activities in South Africa or Namibia is seen as preventing a potentially unfavorable public reaction to the company, shareholder action to bring about such abandonment would be consistent with profit maximizing principles and may be less expensive than following the Wall Street rule.

However, life insurance companies appear to have voted for shareholder proposals even though they contemplated action which, at least in the narrow sense suggested in this chapter, probably would not maximize the profits of the portfolio company. How are such actions justified? The Trustees of the University of Pennsylvania have articulated a justification which may be useful for life insurance companies to consider.[32]

The Trustees accept the premise that all corporations have a duty not to earn their profits at the cost of creating social injury. They think that a shareholder may not sit silently by while the corporation

---

[30] *Life Insurance Fact Book—1976* (New York: American Council of Life Insurance, 1976), p. 75.

[31] MacNaughton, "A Responsible Business," p. 15.

[32] University of Pennsylvania News Bureau, "University of Pennsylvania Guidelines for Investment in Publicly Held Companies," approved by the Trustees October 13, 1972.

of which it is an owner inflicts social injury. (Indeed, it has been argued elsewhere that each shareholder has "the moral minimum responsibility" to take such action as he can to prevent or correct corporate social injury.)[33] The key point in this formulation relates to the definition of social injury. The Trustees have defined it as "any corporate activity which violates the law of the applicable jurisdiction, frustrates its enforcement or implementation, or, in the judgment of the Trustees' Committee on Corporate Responsibility, is unconscionable."[34]

To the extent that the definition proscribes unlawful activities, it reflects judgments formally made by the political process. Inclusion of activities which frustrate the enforcement or implementation of the law continues to tie the concept of social injury closely to formal societal judgments. Further extension of the concept of social injury (which involves independent moral judgments) is limited by the term unconscionable. Use of the unconscionable standard results in proscriptions of only those activities which strike a sufficiently sensitive nerve so that a future formal societal judgment condemning the activity may reasonably be expected.

A wider concept of social injury has been developed by others. For example, Simon, Powers, and Gunnemann define social injury as:

> the injurious impact which the activities of a company are found to have on consumers, employees, or other persons, particularly including activities which violate, or frustrate the enforcement of rules of domestic or international law intended to protect individuals against deprivations of health, safety, or basic freedoms; however, social injury does not result from activities limited to doing business with other companies engaged in socially injurious activities.[35]

The social injury concept, as used by Simon, Powers, and Gunnemann or by the University of Pennsylvania Trustees, draws a sharp distinction between shareholder concern for the harm caused by a corporation's activities and the duty or right of a shareholder to use his ownership position to have the corporation promote specific social goals. For example, the concept would sanction voting for a shareholder proposal that a company discontinue certain strip min-

---

[33] John G. Simon, Charles W. Powers, and Jon P. Gunnemann, *The Ethical Investor: Universities and Corporate Responsibility* (New Haven: Yale University Press, 1972), p. 65.

[34] University of Pennsylvania News Bureau, p. 9.

[35] Simon, Powers, and Gunnemann, *The Ethical Investor*, pp. 171–72.

ing activity; but it would not sanction voting for a proposal that a life insurance company invest a specified percentage of its assets in low-income housing. On the other hand, the concept does not limit the investor to reacting to proposals that are presented for shareholder vote. Indeed, Simon, Powers, and Gunnemann assume that the shareholder may initiate action to correct social injury.[36] Also, the shareholder can effect corrective action through a wide variety of techniques: voting on shareholder proposals, informally communicating with management, initiating a shareholder proposal, or commencing litigation.

Before determining whether a life insurance company should accept even this limited responsibility in its stock ownership capacity, the company should assess the costs of doing so. The most obvious cost relates to securing information. Many of the social responsibility issues raised with corporations are complex, and a shareholder must educate itself sufficiently to vote intelligently. A number of organizations have sprung up to produce relevant information. For example, the Investor Responsibility Research Center puts together a review of the arguments for and against each of the major shareholder proposals on social responsibility issues. It also conducts in-depth studies of specific problems. Its most recent study relates to nuclear generating plants. The center also publishes *News for Investors,* a monthly report for investors and others "that make and affect decisions on private sector responsibility." The fees charged for these and similar services are modest. To some extent the information provided would be helpful even for an investor whose sole concern is profit maximization.

An additional cost is the manpower expended in considering the vote on these difficult issues. Obviously, affirmative action beyond voting on shareholder proposals would require even greater expenditures of time and effort. The University of Pennsylvania has a special Trustees' Committee on Corporate Responsibility which is separate from the Investment Committee. Similarly, many institutional investors, including some life insurance companies, have created special groups to deal with social responsibility questions. The creation of a special group (on which a member of the investment committee often sits) underscores the need to consider these questions on a basis other than traditional investment criteria. Such a group may also serve as a way of focusing other social responsibility concerns of the com-

---

[36] Ibid., p. 173.

pany. Another cost of opposing corporate management on social responsibility questions is possible retaliation; e.g., the life insurance company's investment analyst may be denied access to management. Although such actions are possible, the author is aware of only one instance in which it has occurred.

A final cost consideration is the potential loss in value of the portfolio stock if its management follows the socially responsible course of action. In many cases any loss in value will be negligible. However, in some cases voluntary internalization of costs which would otherwise have to be borne by society as a whole will have a material impact on the value of the stock. It may be urged that if the correction of social injury severely impairs the return on the stock, the life insurance company may sell it. However, when management indicates its willingness to correct the social injury, the market will probably reflect that change in information about the corporation. Further, it seems inappropriate (and in certain cases it may violate insider trading prohibitions) for a life insurance company to urge correction of a social injury and then sell the stock because of the potential costs shortly before management signals to the public its willingness to make the corrections.

Thoughtful exercise of a life insurance company's ownership power in accordance with a social injury standard not only imposes costs; it may also provide benefits. For example, the life insurance company's votes and other actions may make portfolio companies more sensitive to widely shared social concerns. Such heightened awareness may discourage the portfolio company from committing funds to activities which social pressure will ultimately restrict, forbid, or place at a relative disadvantage. Further, the process of reviewing the activities of other corporations may have important feedback consequences for the insurance company as an operating business organization. The company may obtain early warning signals about activities it should reconsider under normal profit maximizing principles.

Special attention has been devoted to the exercise of ownership responsibility because it seems a relatively modest commitment to socially responsible action, which may involve a departure from profit maximizing principles. A method for defining the company's commitment has been effectively pioneered by universities which have published guidelines for governing their action. It is hoped that the directors of more life insurance companies will respond to Mr. MacNaughton's call to be responsible in the exercise of their ownership powers.

SUMMARY AND CONCLUSIONS

The prevailing view in the insurance industry seems to be that socially responsible investments should be confined to those projects which are consistent with the goal of long-term profit maximization. In this context, profit maximization is interpreted rather broadly and encompasses such activities as renovation of central city areas surrounding a company's home office to avoid the necessity to relocate. However, this interpretation is not broad enough to include activities which further the public good to the expected net long-term detriment of the company.

The companies' present position is well-supported by legal precedent. In a number of cases, the courts have held that corporations do have the authority to conduct activities which, in the view of their boards of directors, further the companies' long-range interests. Such activities can be undertaken even if the long-term benefits are intangible.

The insurance companies could enhance the effectiveness of their current social responsibility programs by segregating such activities from their other investment operations. This procedure would help to encourage a consistent and well-planned social responsibility investment program. It would be useful to require companies to disclose fully the social responsibility investments made and the results of the program. A more modest expansion of the companies' activities in the social responsibility field could take the form of more vigorous and consistent efforts to enforce social responsibility through the exercise of common stock voting rights. A model for this approach is provided by universities which have adopted guidelines for employing voting rights with regard to social responsibility issues.

14

The Impact of Life Insurance Company Investment Regulation

By Mendes Hershman*

The life insurance company lawyer is often called upon for opinions regarding the compliance of a particular proposed investment with the investment code of the company's home state. He may also be asked to judge its conformity with the laws of other states in which the company does business if, as in New York, substantial compliance with the investment laws of such states is required. He documents the investment decision in notes and loan agreements, trust agreements, bonds, mortgages, and such other instruments and provisions as may be necessary or desirable. Then, in the event of default, he has the task of enforcement through bail-outs, foreclosures, bankruptcies, and other default procedures. He thus obtains a fairly jaundiced view of the investment process. Even when the proposed investment is being made and appears attractive to the investment officer, the lawyer must consider the eventuality of default. This concern is generally expressed in negative covenants designed to mini-

---

* Mendes Hershman is senior vice president and general counsel of the New York Life Insurance Company. He is a member of the Advisory Panel to the New York State Law Revision Commission for Recodification of the New York Insurance Law. The views expressed are personal to the author and do not necessarily represent the views of the company.

This chapter reflects legal developments as of April 1976. At that time, the New York State Law Revision Commission, at the request of the New York legislature, was engaged in a recodification and revision of the insurance laws of the state of New York. The recodification had not progressed sufficiently to be dealt with in this chapter.

mize default probabilities and in the remedies for default for which provision must be made at the outset of the investment.

The lawyer learns economics the hard way, e.g., by witnessing the disappearance of the equity cushions behind loans in periods of deflation and depression and also, as experience has shown, in periods of inflation and recession. He gains a considerable respect for the objectives of regulation as well as considerable impatience with the anachronisms in regulation that outlive the needs and events which evoked them. Justice Holmes put the issue trenchantly when he wrote: "It is revolting to have no better reason for a rule of law than that so it was laid down in the time of Henry IV. It is still more revolting if the grounds upon which it was laid down have vanished long since, and the rule simply persists from blind imitation of the past."[1] He also observed in another connection that "historic continuity with the past is not a duty, it is only a necessity."[2]

The goal of this chapter is to analyze life insurance company investment regulation and to attempt to discern its impact on life company investment policy. Because the investment laws are so deeply rooted in the past, it seems appropriate to begin the analysis by tracing the history of life insurance investment regulation from its beginnings early in the 20th century. To attempt to recount that history in all the states or even those in which the important life companies are domiciled would unduly and unnecessarily lengthen this discussion. The history in New York will suffice. New York is the home state of several of the major life companies and by its substantial compliance rule[3] has had a significant effect on the investments of the foreign companies doing business in New York. New York's investment regulation thus has had a more prominent and pervasive influence on American life insurance companies' investment portfolios than that of any other state.

A SUMMARY HISTORY OF INVESTMENT REGULATION IN NEW YORK

The Armstrong Investigation and Early Investment Rules

Early in the century, "high, wide, and handsome" spending by James Hazen Hyde, first vice president of the Equitable and owner

---

[1] Oliver Wendell Holmes, "Path of the Law," *Harvard Law Review*, vol. 10 (1897), p. 459.

[2] Oliver Wendell Holmes, "Learning and Science," *Speeches*, p. 68 (1913).

[3] N.Y. Insurance Law §42(5) (McKinney 1966) (hereafter cited as Ins. L. §-).

by inheritance of a majority of its stock, touched off a struggle for power in that company and a major scandal that enveloped the industry. Sensational stories in the press followed, replete with charges of self-dealing, secret political contributions, personal loans to officers and directors, and other abuses. Policyholders became apprehensive; and an aroused New York legislature established the famous Armstrong Committee, which retained Charles Evans Hughes as counsel.[4]

The stringent laws enacted in 1906 as a result of the Armstrong investigation limited life companies' investments to government obligations, corporate bonds secured by adequate collateral, and mortgages on unencumbered real estate appraised at 50 percent more than the amount loaned.[5] In the more than 70 years that have followed, the field of eligible investments has been broadened considerably.

Changes in the Law before 1950

The chronology of change in the law mirrors the nation's economic history. Thus, the expansive economy of the 1920s led to the first major change when, in 1928, *unsecured* corporate obligations and preferred or guaranteed stock qualifying under prescribed earnings tests were made eligible.[6] In the 1930s, government intervention to revive a moribund mortgage market and an otherwise depressed economy led to amendments permitting purchases of mortgages insured by the Federal Housing Administration (FHA) despite their high loan-to-value ratios. The 1930s also witnessed the liberalization of earnings tests for investment in unsecured corporate obligations and in preferred and guaranteed stock as well as the authorization of investments in transportation equipment and in housing projects.[7]

The year 1939 was one of general revision of the New York Insurance Law.[8] The basic change was in the statutory approach. Eligible investments were specified rather than those that were ineligible. In 1939, too, express reference was made for the first time to investments in municipal bonds of the special revenue type, a boon to local gov-

---

[4] New York, Senate and Assembly, Concurrent Resolution adopted July 20, 1905. The committee findings are reported in New York, Senate and Assembly, Joint Committee to Investigate the Affairs of Life Insurance Companies, *Testimony, Exhibits, and Report*, 10 vols. (Albany, N.Y.: Brandow Printing Co., 1905–1906).

[5] N.Y. Laws of 1906, ch. 326 (hereafter cited as Laws of —).

[6] Laws of 1928, ch. 539.

[7] *See*, e.g., Laws of 1933, ch. 791; Laws of 1935, chaps. 409 and 413.

[8] Laws of 1939, ch. 882; Ins.L. §81.

ernments laboring under debt ceilings.[9] In 1946, because of declining interest rates and some difficulty in finding eligible investments, the law was amended to permit life companies to invest up to 3 percent of admitted assets in real estate for the production of income.[10]

Changes during the 1950s

By 1951, the cyclical swings in the national economy had apparently become more moderate, large corporations were placing increased emphasis on retained earnings as a source of funds, and other types of investing institutions were beginning to compete more vigorously with life insurers in the corporate bond market. These factors, plus the favorable common stock returns realized by life companies of other states, persuaded the New York legislature to permit investment in common stock. Such investments were initially limited to the lesser of 3 percent of admitted assets or ⅓ of surplus;[11] and strict qualitative standards were imposed; i.e., stocks were required to have ten-year cash dividend histories and to satisfy an earnings test.[12] Another significant change in 1951 was the authorization of mortgages on leaseholds of 21 years or more, amortized within the lesser of 35 years or ⅘ of the unexpired term of the lease.[13]

In 1954, permission was given to receive, in connection with an otherwise eligible investment, "stock warrants, whether detachable or non-detachable, stock options, stock, property interests or other assets of any kind" to be carried on the books at no value.[14] Express recognition was also given to the practice of investing in convertible securities. Such instruments present significant problems for the legal draftsman, such as questions of eventual registration with the Securities and Exchange Commission and how to prevent dilution without impairing the debtor's flexibility for financing future expansion. Another difficulty was the prevention of forced conversion, an exercise that requires the working out of compromises in algebraic prose.

Authorization was granted in 1956 to invest 1 percent of assets in

[9] Laws of 1939, ch. 882; Ins.L. §81(1).

[10] Laws of 1946, ch. 509; Ins.L. §81(7)(h).

[11] Laws of 1951, ch. 400; Ins.L. §81(13).

[12] In 1951, when New York life companies were first permitted to invest in common stocks, the yield on corporate bonds was between 2.75 and 3 percent, while the yield on common stocks which met the qualitative standards varied from 5 to 6 percent.

[13] Laws of 1951, ch. 400; Ins.L. §81(6)(a).

[14] Laws of 1954, ch. 491; Ins.L. §81(14).

any foreign country (Canadian investments up to 10 percent), generally in instruments of the same kind and grade as permitted in the United States.[15] In 1957, the first step was taken to permit leeway investments of no more than 2 percent of admitted assets. *Leeway* investments are those not eligible under any of the existing permitted categories.[16]

In creating the leeway provision, the legislature recognized the potential problem stemming from the combination of a rapidly changing capital market and an investment code which is specific as to the type of investments that can be made. Thus, sound investments may exist which provide an excellent rate of return but for technical reasons may not be made. For example, the acquisition of an oil production payment or the virtually riskless obligation of a highly responsible religious order, which would have no earnings record, would have been barred by the code in the absence of the leeway provision.

While leeway permits investment in categories not otherwise eligible, the quantitative limitations, viz., amounts which may be invested in any one issuer or in any one class, still apply. Of course, the theory of these latter limitations is not the assurance of solidity but the prevention of control.

In 1957, the law was also amended to raise to 5 percent of admitted assets the limitation on investments in real estate held for the production of income.[17] Finally, in that year, the authorized investment in common stock was increased to the lesser of 5 percent of admitted assets or 50 percent of surplus.[18]

In 1959, the then general requirement that mortgage loans may not exceed 66⅔ percent of the appraised value of the mortgaged real property or leasehold was changed by raising the percentage to 75 percent for loans of not more than $30,000, amortized over 30 years or less, on single-family residences.[19] Among the economic developments which led to these changes in the mortgage requirements were the tremendous demand for residential mortgage money and the pronounced tendency for the average home mortgage amount to increase. Other factors included the self-liquidating character of the mortgage, which eroded away the notion that a mortgage was not a liquid investment, and the increased competition for home mortgages

---

[15] Laws of 1956, ch. 530 and ch. 387; Ins.L. §81(8)(a) and (c), respectively.

[16] Laws of 1958, ch. 491; Ins.L. §81(17).

[17] Laws of 1957, ch. 646; Ins.L. §81(7)(h).

[18] Laws of 1957, ch. 646; Ins.L. §81(13).

[19] Laws of 1959, ch. 273; Ins.L. §81(6)(a).

from banks and other savings institutions which did have the ability to lend on a 75 percent or higher loan-to-value basis.

Changes during the 1960s

In 1961, the superintendent of insurance placed limitations on the broad authorization for insurers to invest in corporate obligations which "are adequately secured and have investment qualities and characteristics wherein the speculative elements are not predominate (sic)."[20] In a "Circular Letter" to all insurers authorized to do business in the state of New York, the superintendent focused on so-called "corporate real estate obligations." This term referred to bonds, notes, and other obligations of corporations engaged primarily in the business of owning or holding and leasing real property or formed for the purpose of engaging in such real estate activities.[21] The superintendent stipulated that such investments must satisfy the requirements for real estate loans unless certain conditions were met.

According to the Circular Letter, corporate obligations secured by one or more leases, whether or not additionally secured by one or more mortgages, could qualify if they met the following conditions:

1. the lessees under such leases, or the guarantors, must be those whose obligations would be eligible for direct investment;
2. the leases, not in excess of six, must be assigned as security directly to the insurer and must be non-cancellable; and
3. the aggregate rentals must be sufficient to provide for all operational expenses and for 100 percent of the amortization of the investment.

As a result of the celebrated Connecticut General decision,[22] in 1962 the New York legislature authorized New York life insurance companies to invest in or acquire subsidiaries doing an insurance business and to engage in the business of insurance in a foreign country through a foreign subsidiary. This type of investment was substantially limited to $20 million.[23]

Also in 1962, New York life companies were permitted to estab-

---

[20] Ins.L. §81(2)(a).

[21] N.Y. Superintendent of Insurance, Circular Letter addressed to all insurers authorized to do business in New York, November 27, 1961.

[22] Conn. Gen. Life Ins. Co. v. Sup't of Ins. of N.Y., 10 N.Y.2d 42, 176 N.E.2d 63, 217 S.2d 39 (1961).

[23] Laws of 1962, ch. 627; Ins.L. §46-a.

lish separate accounts pursuant to group contracts under "qualified pension, profit-sharing or annuity plans."[24] Except for the leeway increase to 10 percent for the separate account assets, *qualitative* restrictions on eligibility of investments remained the same as for other investments of the company; but the *quantitative* limitations were changed.[25] Thus, all of the investments allocated to the separate account may consist of common stock; but the common stock must qualify as for the regular portfolio.[26]

Three principal changes in 1964 provided additional latitude for reserve investments:

1. The maximum amount which could be loaned upon *any* conventional mortgage on real estate was increased from 66⅔ percent to 75 percent of the value of the real estate, but minimum principal paydowns were required to be made for loans in excess of 66⅔ percent of value.[27]
2. The percentage of total admitted assets which could be invested in real estate mortgage loans (exclusive of FHA loans and the guaranteed portions of Veterans Administration loans) was increased from 40 to 50 percent.[28]
3. The percentage of total admitted assets which could be invested in leeway was increased from 2 to 3.5 percent.[29]

In 1965, two principal amendments of the insurance law were enacted. First, a further category of corporate unsecured obligations was added whereby a lower average coverage of "net earnings available for its fixed charges" of 1¼ (rather than 1½) times was permitted. This coverage ratio had to be met in four out of the past five and in seven out of the last ten years. The test also requires that the liquid assets of the corporation not be less than 105 percent of liabilities (other than capital stock and surplus).[30]

The law had finally caught up to the business fact that finance companies have higher debt-to-equity ratios than industrial companies and that with the narrowing of the margin of the return on

---

[24] Laws of 1962, ch. 680; Ins.L. §227.

[25] Ins.L. §227(1)(b).

[26] Ibid. The companies were still required to comply with the then existing stricture against holding more than 2 percent of the common stock of any one institution.

[27] Laws of 1964, ch. 799; Ins.L. §81(6)(a).

[28] Ibid.

[29] Laws of 1964, ch. 799; Ins.L. §81(17).

[30] Laws of 1965, ch. 615; Ins.L. §81(2)(d).

money advanced by the finance companies over the cost of money to them, the "1½ times" earnings test was outmoded. The liquidity test would at the same time limit such investments to companies with the kind of assets that permit operation with a high ratio of debt to capital.

Secondly, the 1965 legislature made eligible certain production payments, or interests therein evidenced by trust certificates or other instruments, from oil, gas, or other hydrocarbons. Such investments were permitted if an obligation secured thereby and payable from the production payment or interest therein would qualify as an obligation adequately secured and having investment qualities in which the speculative elements were not predominant.[31]

This was legal recognition of the evolutionary process which had converted oil in the ground from a hazardous and highly speculative risk into a stabilized, bankable commodity. This development in turn was due to advances in engineering knowledge which permitted accurate determination of producible reserves and to the successful administration of regulated production which led to the realization of income in predictable amounts over an extended period.

In 1966, the legislature amended the investment code to clarify the circumstances under which the earnings of a subsidiary could be added to the earnings of the parent corporation to qualify the bonds of the latter as legal investments.[32] Another amendment in that year permitted life companies to invest in the stock and obligations of mortgage loan correspondents under certain conditions.[33] In 1967, additional latitude for investment in common stock was provided by deletion of the requirement that the institution whose shares are being purchased must have paid a cash dividend on such shares for the last ten years.[34] This change indicated recognition of the fact that whether or not a company pays cash dividends does not necessarily determine whether its common stock is a good investment. The modification was also designed to permit investment in relatively recently organized enterprises.

---

[31] Laws of 1965, ch. 850; Ins.L. §81(15).

[32] Laws of 1966, ch. 329; Ins.L. §81(2).

[33] Laws of 1966, ch. 537; Ins.L. §81(16). The obligations are permissible if the correspondent is primarily engaged in making or servicing mortgage loans and is acting as such for the life company making the investment, subject, however, to the approval of the superintendent of insurance. The total of such investments may not exceed ½ of 1 percent of admitted assets and not more than ¹⁄₁₀ of 1 percent of assets may be invested in any one correspondent.

[34] Laws of 1967, ch. 803; Ins.L. §81(13)(a).

The three changes made in 1968 were aimed at enhancing the capability of insurance companies to finance socially desirable projects. They recognized the obligation of large investors to be "good citizens," provided that the resulting investments do not have an important effect on financial solidity. The three changes are as follows:

1. Investment in real property constituting a project of the New York State Urban Development Corporation, or a subsidiary thereof, was authorized. The total cost of such investment may not exceed 5 percent of admitted assets and not more than ½ of 1 percent for one parcel of real property.[35]
2. Investment in stocks and evidences of indebtedness of any subsidiary of the New York State Urban Development Corporation was authorized. These investments are authorized to the extent and upon such conditions as the superintendent of insurance determines.[36]
3. Investment in obligations issued or guaranteed by the Asian Development Bank was authorized. The total of such investments may not exceed 5 percent of admitted assets.[37]

In 1969, four notable changes were made in the law:

1. The authorized common stock investment in any one corporation was increased from 2 to 5 percent of the corporation's outstanding shares. At the same time, the law was liberalized to allow an insurer to have ½ of 1 percent of its admitted assets invested in the common stock of one corporation (increased from ⅕ of 1 percent).[38]
2. Authorization was given for investment in tangible personal property under certain conditions.[39] The total of such investments could not exceed 1 percent of admitted assets, and the total guaranteed or payable by any one governmental unit or institution may not exceed ½ of 1 percent of admitted assets.
3. Investment in adequately secured noncorporate obligations was

[35] Laws of 1968, ch. 174; Ins.L. §81(7)(k).

[36] Laws of 1968, ch. 174; Ins.L. §81(9)(b).

[37] Laws of 1968, ch. 113; Ins.L. §81(11–b).

[38] Laws of 1969, ch. 190; Ins.L. §81(13)(b).

[39] Laws of 1969, ch. 836; Ins.L. §81(18). Such investments are permissible where there is a right to receive rental, purchase, or other payment for the use or purchase of such property adequate to return the investment and where such payments are payable or guaranteed by one or more governmental units or institutions whose obligations would qualify for investment under the insurance law.

authorized.[40] The total of such investments may not exceed 1 percent of admitted assets, and the total guaranteed or payable by any one governmental unit or institution may not exceed ½ of 1 percent of admitted assets.

4. The maximum limit on investment in common stocks was raised to the lesser of 100 percent of surplus or 10 percent of the insurer's admitted assets.[41] This change established a more realistic limit in the euphoric atmosphere of a constantly rising stock market.

Changes during the Early 1970s

The 1970 legislature increased the limit on the amount of real property an insurer can purchase as an investment for production of income from 5 to 10 percent of admitted assets.[42] At the same time, the maximum permitted investment in any one parcel was increased to 1 percent of admitted assets. In 1971, the legislature again focused on socially desirable investments and authorized insurers to invest in obligations guaranteed by the Community Facilities Project Guarantee Fund and participations therein.[43]

The law was amended in 1972 to permit investment in the common stock of companies which are not listed on national exchanges.[44] This amendment indicated recognition of the fact that, by virtue of the 1964 amendment to the Securities Exchange Act of 1934, current financial information, comparable to that available for companies whose stocks are registered on exchanges, has become available on firms which are not so listed. This authorization is subject to the proviso that insurers be limited to those common stocks which are traded actively enough over-the-counter so that prices are quoted regularly.

In 1973, five amendments to the insurance law were enacted:

1. Investments in second mortgages were authorized. Prior to 1973, such investments were qualified only under the leeway provision. To be eligible, however, both the first and the second mort-

---

[40] Laws of 1969, ch. 836; Ins. L. §81(19). Adequate security is provided by (a) an assignment of the right to receive rentals or other payments which are payable or guaranteed by a governmental unit or institution whose obligations would qualify for investment under the insurance law and (b) a mortgage or security interest in the property.

[41] Laws of 1969, ch. 190; Ins.L. §81(13)(c).

[42] Laws of 1970, ch. 945; Ins.L. §81(7)(h).

[43] Laws of 1971, ch. 1030; Ins.L. §81(11–c).

[44] Laws of 1972, ch. 743; Ins.L. §81(13)(a)(iii).

gage combined may not exceed 75 percent of the appraised value of the mortgaged property.[45]

2. The aggregate amount an insurer is permitted to invest in mortgage participation loans was increased from 10 to 15 percent of admitted assets.[46]

3. Investments in notes secured by a mortgage upon real property which is insured by the New York City Rehabilitation Mortgage Insurance Corporation were authorized. There is a maximum on these loans of 95 percent of the value of the real property or leasehold securing the same.[47]

4. The percentage of total admitted assets which may be invested in leeway was increased from 3.5 to 4 percent.[48]

5. Interest paid on deposits by banks and trust companies was expressly excluded from the definition of "fixed charges" as defined in the insurance law to determine the eligibility for investment of the securities of such institutions.[49] Prior to this amendment, many sound and profitable banks and trust companies were unable to satisfy the investment code requirement regarding the ratio of net earnings to fixed charges.

In the 1974 legislative year, the legislature enacted three further amendments to the insurance code. First, the law was amended so as to eliminate the insurance department's requirement that, where the total amount of mortgage loans which are secured by the same property exceeds 75 percent of the appraised value of such property, the aggregate loan amount must be carried as a leeway investment. By virtue of this amendment, only the loan amount in excess of 75 percent of appraised value need be carried as leeway, provided there are separate bonds, notes, or other evidences of indebtedness which are separately transferable.[50]

Second, the law was amended to enable insurers to make first mortgage loans in amounts up to 90 percent of value upon real property improved by a one-to-four family dwelling, including a residential condominium.[51] And, third, the law was amended regarding the corporate obligations of finance companies. In the past, finance com-

---

[45] Laws of 1973, ch. 1020; Ins.L. §81(6)(a).

[46] Laws of 1973, ch. 774; Ins.L. §81(6)(a).

[47] Laws of 1973, ch. 924–5; Ins.L. §81(6)(g).

[48] Laws of 1973, ch. 1020, Ins.L. §81(17).

[49] Laws of 1973, ch. 1020; Ins.L. §81(2).

[50] Laws of 1974, ch. 822; Ins.L. §81(6)(a).

[51] Laws of 1974, ch. 853; Ins.L. §81(6)(a).

panies had to meet an earnings test of 1.25 times fixed charges and a liquid asset test stipulating that such assets could not be less than 105 percent of the company's liabilities. The new legislation, recognizing the specific interests and problems of finance companies as borrowers, eased these tests by requiring either (1) that fixed charges be covered by earnings 1.15 times and liquid assets be 105 percent of liabilities or (2) that fixed charges be covered by earnings 1.25 times and liquid assets be 95 percent of liabilities.[52]

Finally, in 1975, the legislature made two significant changes to the New York Insurance Law. First, the limitation of investments in tangible personal property of 1 percent of admitted assets was raised to 2 percent,[53] as was a similar limitation covering adequately secured noncorporate obligations.[54] The existing limitation of ½ of 1 percent of admitted assets applicable to any single investment of either category remained unchanged. Second, the provisions relating to subsidiaries were revised to equalize the investment limitations applicable to downstream holding company subsidiaries and their affiliates.[55]

SOME LESSONS FROM HISTORY

A number of conclusions can be drawn from this historical perspective. The post-Armstrong years have witnessed a progressive liberalization of the statutory restrictions on management's authority to invest. These changes represent an almost complete swing of the pendulum from the punitive consequences of the Armstrong investigation to an era of sturdy public confidence in life insurance company management. This confidence was earned through the dark days of the Great Depression when the major life companies, almost alone among the financial and industrial corporations of the country, met their obligations with meticulous care.

Whether this history also indicates that the statutory restrictions had a substantial impact on investment decision making is a more difficult issue to resolve. Changes in statutory restrictions were certainly a consequence of active, persistent efforts on the part of the industry to effectuate the changes. Would these strong urgent efforts have been exercised if the companies did not believe that they needed

---

[52] Laws of 1974, ch. 447; Ins.L. §81(2)(e).

[53] Laws of 1975, ch. 562; Ins.L. §81(18).

[54] Laws of 1975, ch. 562; Ins.L. §81(19).

[55] Laws of 1975, ch. 562; Ins.L. §46–a.

the liberalization of the restrictions, i.e., that decision making was being hampered and confined? The subsequent discussion attempts to find a tentative answer to this question.

An Illustration of an Industry Effort to Effect Change

In 1967, 15 years after the original authorization to invest in common stock, the industry caused the introduction of proposed legislation to liberalize its authority to engage in this type of investment.[56] Five changes were requested:

1. The authorization to invest 5 percent of admitted assets in common stock would be made fully operative by deleting the further limitation that such investments may not exceed 50 percent of surplus to policyholders.
2. The permitted investment in common stock of any one corporation would be increased from 2 to 5 percent of its outstanding shares and, aside from separate accounts, from $\frac{1}{5}$ of 1 percent to $\frac{1}{2}$ of 1 percent of the insurer's admitted assets.
3. The requirement that a common stock must have paid at least a nominal cash dividend in each of the last ten years would be deleted.
4. The 4 percent earnings test period of ten years for common stock would be changed to a five-year period.
5. Investment in common stock of substantial companies registered under the Securities Exchange Act of 1934 and traded over-the-counter would be authorized.

The brief[57] submitted by the industry with respect to the proposed changes serves to illustrate in bold relief how a number of companies chafed under the statutory restriction on equity investment. Two portions of the brief are reproduced in the Appendix to this chapter to demonstrate the thorough and excellent quality of this document and the effort put into the proposed changes by the industry. The arguments advanced included reference to the length of time the proposed changes had been urged, the competition of out-of-state companies with more liberal restrictions, and the great success of

---

[56] Assembly Bill 4311 (Print 4465), February 7, 1967 (Mr. Altman).

[57] Memorandum in Support [of Assembly Bill 4311], Proposed Amendments to Ins. L. §§81(13), 46–a(6) and 227(1)(b), submitted by Life Insurance Association of America (Drafting Committee on New York Investment Legislation), February 1967.

this type of investment for those companies which had taken advantage of the current authorization to invest in common stock. In addition, the industry pointed out that adequate safeguards were provided by other statutory requirements, such as the valuation procedures and the mandatory securities valuation reserve.

The companies also argued that the change in the proportion of one issuer's stock which could be held by a life insurance company would benefit the economy by permitting life insurers to invest in the stock of medium-size firms on a cost-effective basis. Despite the strength of the industry brief, several years elapsed before the authorization to invest in common stock was broadened to the extent requested by the 1967 proposal.

The fact that the arguments were advanced at all, as well as the effort which went into their formulation, reflected a fairly broad consensus in the late 1960s that statutory restrictions were then or soon would be hampering management investment decision making. Whether the restrictions actually had such an effect is not, however, completely clear.

Investment Restrictions and the Purpose of Regulation

In 1967, a distinguished Special Committee was appointed by the superintendent of insurance of the state of New York to look into all aspects of holding companies in the insurance field, particularly "the substantive concerns underlying the holding company phenomenon."[58] The committee's report, published in 1968,[59] was premised "on the assumption, accepted as an axiom among insurance people, that insurance is affected with the public interest and that protection for the policyholder is a paramount public concern."[60] No responsible authority either in industry or in government has expressed disagreement with the axiom.

The two major influences on life insurance company regulation were the Armstrong investigation, which followed a major scandal in the industry, and the 1939 revision of the insurance laws of New York, which followed the most cataclysmic and prolonged period of

---

[58] The committee, appointed on April 28, 1967, consisted of Oscar M. Ruebhausen (chairman), Newell G. Alford, Jr., Samuel C. Cantor, Spencer L. Kimball, Stacy May, and Oren Root.

[59] New York, Insurance Department, *Report of the Special Committee on Insurance Holding Companies* (New York, 1968) (hereafter cited as *Holding Company Report*).

[60] Ibid., p. 7.

economic distress in American history. Neither a scandal nor a depression is likely to produce any appetite for risk-taking by the managers of the industry or its public regulators; and this, of course, is reflected in the statutory scheme of investment regulation in New York.

In the late 1960s, when the Special Committee was making its investigations, it found considerable dissatisfaction, not with the objective of regulation—to assure policyholders virtually riskless protection against insurable risks on fair terms—but with a result blamed to some extent on overly restrictive regulation, i.e., that life insurance companies were losing ground relatively in the American economy. Unquestionably, the life companies were growing, measured both by value of assets and by amounts of premium income. On the other hand, their prominence in mobilizing savings and investing in long-term securities was obviously diminishing. As explained elsewhere in this book, life companies were losing ground to such institutions as banks, savings and loan associations, non-insured pension funds, state and local retirement funds, and investment companies.

In a persistently inflationary economy, there was fear on the part of both the life insurance industry and regulatory representatives that a product which consisted of a promise to pay a fixed amount at an indeterminate date, likely to be far in the future, was losing much of its attractiveness by comparison with other savings media. This gave rise to the interest in the late 1960s in freeing management of statutory stringency with respect to both equity investments and variable payouts. At the time, the lesson of the early 1970s—that equities do not necessarily respond affirmatively to inflationary forces—had not yet been learned.

Several conclusions with respect to investment by life insurance companies and its regulation emerge from the Special Committee's report. Among its other conclusions, the committee reported that:

> A revised approach to insurance investment principles, and particularly to those applicable to investment in common stocks, is another indicated response to the economic realities facing the insurance industry. . . .
>
> While the major obstacle to a new investment approach probably lies in existing legal restrictions, the traditions of the insurance business, at least for life insurance, have not been unimportant. It is a fact that many companies have not taken full advantage of the flexibility that the law already allows. Both the law and these traditional attitudes merit re-thinking.[61]

---

[61] Ibid., p. 21.

In support of this need for re-thinking, both of the law governing investments and of life company investment management, the committee cited "the speeding up of natural tendencies toward inflation and the continuing decline in the real value of money."[62] The committee also noted that basic structural changes in the economy had greatly reduced the likelihood of a 1930s-type depression. Another consideration was the competitive disadvantage of New York domiciled companies because of the greater freedom accorded companies domiciled in other states to invest in common stocks. Finally, the committee noted that "over the long pull, common stocks, on the average, do considerably better than fixed income investments."[63]

In justification of the latter conclusion, which seemed to go quite far based on limited research, the report hedged by noting that common stock may not do as well as fixed income investments for limited periods, "but life insurers, by their institutional nature, are able to ride out short recessions, since life insurer investment programs are of long duration and life insurers may engage in continuous long-range dollar cost averaging. Moreover, the cash flow and the cash requirements of life insurers are such that they seldom are required to liquidate investments in a bad market to provide cash for their insurance operations."[64]

The committee then faced the crucial question of how much liberalization is advisable in the light of the paramount objective of regulation which is that the promises of life insurers, essentially expressed in fixed-dollar terms, be kept. Comparison was made with bank trust departments, which maintain at least ⅓ of their assets in equities, and with state retirement systems and certain private retirement systems subject to the New York Insurance Law, which can invest up to 20 percent of their assets in common stock.

The committee concluded from these comparisons and other research that a doubling of the then current limits of investment in common stock would be safe enough, i.e., up to the lesser of 10 percent of admitted assets or 100 percent of surplus. However, these changes were to be subject to a restriction on timing, i.e., "that the pace by which any company may progress in any one year to the new limits be fixed at no more than 2 percent of its admitted assets" or such slower pace as the superintendent may direct.[65]

---

62 Ibid.
63 Ibid., p. 22.
64 Ibid.
65 Ibid., p. 23.

The committee also recommended continuing review by the insurance department of the uses of the increased investment freedom and expressed concern "that investment valuations not distort or frustrate the purpose of the liberalizations we recommend."[66] The committee suggested that "studies of valuations both for the application of investment limits and to ascertain the financial condition of the insurers should precede further loosening of investment restraints."[67] The committee's recommendation regarding the common stock limitations was adopted a year later.[68]

It is a curious commentary on investment regulation that the qualitative and quantitative limitations on investment decisions loom so large in the literature of both industry and legislative commentators, but the impact of the valuation process which is at least as significant has had so low a profile. Perhaps this is because the valuation process is so little understood, even by investment officers, and because its permutations are so tenuously related to reality.[69] All the committee could come up with after its investigations was a precatory injunction to the regulators to make studies of the valuation process before they permitted *further* liberalization of the investment restrictions.

Finally, the committee concluded that the objective of investment regulation, to provide relatively riskless security for the life company's promise to perform, would not be impaired by liberalizing the compulsion to diversify contained in the legal limit on the amount that a life insurer may invest in the stock of any one company. It recommended increasing this limit to 1 percent of admitted assets and also increasing the companion limitation on the maximum permissible percentage of outstanding shares of stock of the company in which the investment is made from 2 to 5 percent.[70]

While industry representatives have from time to time urged various liberalizations in the quantitative and qualitative restriction on long-term debt investments, the committee found only the restrictions on common stock investment as handicapping life insurance companies in serving their policyholders. The committee implicitly assumed that insurance companies should be able to earn an "appropriate" level of return on their policyholders' invested funds. This was a view of the late 1960s, an assertion that the regulators must be

---

66 Ibid., p. 24.
67 Ibid.
68 *Supra*, p. 318.
69 *Supra*, p. 318.
70 *Holding Company Report*, pp. 24–25.

concerned not only with safety of principal but perhaps equally with the level of return on investments.

THE IMPACT OF STATE REGULATION ON INVESTMENT POLICY

Changes in the investment laws generally have been prompted either by industry pressure or by profound changes in the national economy. Thus, the history of changes set forth above would seem to provide some evidence that, at least for certain companies, the changes were needed in order to remove binding constraints on investment management. Other evidence, perhaps of a more subjective nature, would be the record of industry testimony at public hearings or in response to questionnaires. Finally, inferences may be drawn from a comparison of life company portfolio proportions with quantitative legal maximums. This section employs these evidentiary forms in an attempt to gauge the impact of regulation on company investment policies.

Impact on Major Types of Investments

Corporate Debt. Long-term, privately placed highly rated (Baa or better) corporate debt and first lien real estate mortgage loans with an equity "cushion" represent the preponderant bulk of life company assets. No evidence seems to exist either in industry urgings of statutory changes, the testimony of management officials, or responses to questionnaires that the statutory quantitative limitations on the amount which may be invested in the debt obligations of a single corporation (10 percent of the total admitted assets of the insurance company) has had any effect on investment decision making.

Some evidence exists that qualitative limitations have had at least a minimal restraining effect. For example, the fact that the industry successfully sought to have the earnings requirement liberalized by permitting "tacking" of predecessor earnings and by providing the alternative of bonds "adequately secured" with "investment qualities" indicates that at least some influential companies found earnings requirements too restrictive. Actually, the "adequately secured" provision was used largely to permit 90 and sometimes 100 percent of appraised value financing of real estate secured by high-credit net leases. This type of financing is limited to corporations whose obligations would qualify as life company investments.

Undoubtedly, too, the pressure for a leeway provision and subsequently for increasing the leeway percentage was motivated at least in part by a desire to facilitate loans to companies or partnerships which, because of their youth, were badly in need of financing but did not have the earnings history to qualify. Because of their need for funds, such firms often were willing to offer equity participations which were quite attractive to enterprising life insurance companies.

In a survey conducted in 1963, James J. O'Leary found that four amendments of the insurance law were regarded as most urgent by the responding life companies. One of these was "an increase from 2 percent to 5 percent of admitted assets in the amount which may be invested under the 'leeway' provision of the law"[71]—a percentage not yet reached ten years later. In support of this proposed amendment, O'Leary stated:

> Also, the well-established corporation is more likely to rely more heavily on internal funds than the newer, less well-established firms which are in a strong growth period. Such corporations are more likely to rely more heavily on external financing. This is an important reason for some liberalization of the "leeway provision" of the New York law because some of these highly promising, but less well-established firms seeking financing may not be able to meet the strict requirements in the law for eligibility of their bonds.[72]

Most life companies did not take significant advantage of the leeway provision to invest in securities which did not meet earnings requirements. Hence, while the earnings requirements had some restrictive effect on loans to new "growth" companies, it seems clear that the effect was a modest one and that the leeway provision was adequate to meet any excessively restrictive qualitative requirement on corporate bonds.

Mortgage Loans and Real Estate. The two major statutory restrictions on mortgage lending are the maximum loan-to-value ratio (presently 75 percent except for one-to-four family home loans) and the percentage of admitted assets which may be invested in mortgage loans (presently 50 percent).

In his 1964 report, O'Leary studied the sources and uses of loanable funds in the post-World War II period. Based on this analysis, he identified two major implications for life insurance investment regulation. First,

---

[71] James J. O'Leary, "Review of the New York Law Governing Life Insurance," Report to the superintendent of insurance of the State of New York, New York, February 13, 1964, p. 2.

[72] Ibid., p. 17.

the new supply of mortgages of all types has grown very markedly whereas the new supply of corporate bonds has shown little tendency to grow. If life insurance companies are to satisfy their investment requirements in the coming years, they will need to place a greater proportion of their funds in mortgages. The most promising part of the mortgage market for life companies is conventional mortgages on homes and income-producing properties. For these reasons, therefore, the New York law should be amended to permit a higher percentage of assets in conventional mortgages.[73]

The second implication stemmed from the fact that New York law imposed a 66⅔ percent loan-to-value ceiling on most mortgage loans of life insurance companies, while their competitors in the mortgage market were able to make loans on a 75 percent basis. He thus concluded that "there are strong grounds for liberalizing the loan-to-value limit on conventional mortgages . . . as the industry representatives recommend."[74] As indicated above, the industry urging was heeded. The percentage of assets which could be invested was raised to 50 percent and the loan-to-value ratio to 75 percent.[75]

To this day only about 31 percent of aggregate industry assets are invested in mortgages,[76] an amount which is substantially less than the permitted maximum. However, almost as soon as the loan-to-value ratio was raised, it became not only a ceiling but a floor.

Statutory restrictions on mortgage lending have been met in the past by tailoring financing arrangements to comply with statutory requirements. For example, the purchase and leaseback of the fee simple estate, placing a mortgage on the leasehold, is a fairly common financing device. This has the effect of increasing the financing by 25 percent of the property value. If this is insufficient financing, a second mortgage to be placed in the leeway portfolio is available. Some companies also use the installment sale contract device to permit financing beyond the statutory limit. In recent years, the joint venture has become a popular means of financing the real estate developer; and this, of course, means that substantially all of the hard cash comes from the insurance company.

As a rule of thumb, mortgage loan officers generally consider 85 percent of an accurate appraisal to be a reasonable index of the up-

---

[73] Ibid., p. 23.

[74] Ibid., p. 24.

[75] Supra, p. 315.

[76] Life Insurance Fact Book—1976 (New York: American Council of Life Insurance, 1976), p. 64.

per limit of total lending. Exceptions to this rule are often made when, in addition to prime real estate, the security includes a triple-A credit on long-term net lease. In such cases, the financing could go to 100 percent of the cost of land and improvements. Considering all of the evidence on the financing of real estate, it seems reasonable to conclude that the statutory regulation of mortgage lending has had no substantial restrictive impact.

Since 1946, when the New York law first permitted life insurers to purchase commercial and industrial properties as investments, the companies have never reached allowable limits. In housing, their equity holdings have been even further from statutory ceilings. Consequently, it could hardly be said that the regulation of real estate ownership has had a significant restrictive impact. The reason is that the companies have been very reluctant to assume managerial duties and, particularly in housing, found the landlord-tenant relationship not only uncomfortable but much too demanding in terms of executive time and energy.

Preferred and Common Stock. Life companies generally have not been restricted in the amount which they can invest in preferred stock. Limits exist on the amount of a single issuer's preferred stock which a life insurance company can hold. (The limit is currently 20 percent of the total issued and outstanding stock of any one corporation, not to exceed 2 percent of the admitted assets of the insurance company.) The earnings and dividend requirements are similar to the corporate bond restrictions and have met the same arguments for liberalization, resulting in some amelioration over the years.

As noted above, life insurance companies were not permitted to invest in common stock until 1951. Several amendments over the years brought the quantitative limit to the current 10 percent of admitted assets or 100 percent of surplus with limitations on amounts which may be acquired during any calendar year. Stringent earnings requirements and limitations on amounts which may be invested in any one issuer are also present. The history of amendments of the common stock limitations provides some indication that these limits have had an impact on investment policy. Broadly speaking, however, considerable doubt exists that the statutory restrictions made much difference for most companies.

As Orson Hart, chief economist for the New York Life Insurance Company, has pointed out:

> . . . since the time of the Armstrong Investigation in 1905, and actually for pretty much the history of the life insurance business in

this country, American life insurance companies have been predominantly fixed income investors, seeking certainty in investment return and safety of principal over potential appreciation through stock market profits. It is a partly mutual and partly stock business in which the big New York mutuals in effect are required by law to pass along 90 percent or more of their earnings every year to their policyholders, thus exerting an enormous competitive pressure not only on the stock companies but on each other. . . .

This, it seems to me, establishes the investment philosophy of the business, quite apart from the limitations imposed by the insurance laws of New York and other major insurance states. A life insurance company must credit interest to its policyholders' reserves at the rate of 2½ to 3 percent per year. With reserves ranging from 80 to 85 percent of assets and surplus 10 percent or less, it is obvious that continuity of income has to be an essential aspect of the financing planning of all companies. Larger surpluses relative to reserves must be built to accommodate larger equity programs, and in view of the competition that exists in the business today it is obvious that unless the Commissioners ordered a limitation on dividends—a far cry from established life insurance philosophy—most companies would find this a long and difficult job.

The fact is there is little demand from our policyholders, other than employers setting up retirement systems, to invest their reserves in common stocks. Our policyholders may seek appreciation with their own funds by investing them in common stocks. They may even neglect their real insurance needs to provide funds for common stock investment in periods when common stock prices are rising. But when it comes to their life insurance they want what they have to be safe beyond question. Safety is the paramount consideration. Policyholders do not regard their insurance as a vehicle of possible profit through fortunate equity investment. Even in periods when the price level seems to be indicating a sustained rise they do not ask us to move into common stocks, but rather that we oppose easy money, government spending or other developments they believe are responsible for the inflation.[77]

Generally, life companies approve of limits on common stock investment and few, if any, have ever expressed interest in a limitation exceeding 10 percent of admitted assets or 100 percent of surplus. In addition to the ingrained investment philosophy referred to by Hart, there is fear among many that too much management discretion in

[77] Dr. Orson H. Hart, "Life Insurance Companies and the Equity Capital Markets," address delivered before the American Finance Association in Chicago, December 30, 1964. Although this address was delivered more than ten years ago, it is hardly dated in its applicability.

this area would lead to speculation by some small companies, resulting in losses to policyholders which might have to be made good by the industry. Such developments could damage the industry's reputation for financial solidity. Certainly, the recent behavior of the stock market has justified many of the fears of common stock investment and supports the philosophy to which Hart referred more than a decade ago.

Impact of Securities Valuation Rules

According to New York Insurance Law, the superintendent of insurance is authorized to determine the method of establishing values for investments which are eligible for amortization.[78] All others are required to be valued in the discretion of the superintendent at either market or appraised value. Common stocks must be valued at market value when available and, if not, at a value determined by the superintendent. Notwithstanding any of these rules, the superintendent may require valuation to comply with the requirements approved by the National Association of Insurance Commissioners (NAIC).[79]

Under the requirements of the NAIC, bonds and preferred stock (not in default) are valued at amortized cost; but a reserve, the Mandatory Securities Valuation Reserve (MSVR), is required, which calls for an annual contribution from surplus.[80] The amount of this contribution is determined by the annual valuation and classification of bonds and preferred stock made by the Securities Valuation Office of the NAIC based primarily on various financial ratios. In addition to the required contribution, net realized and unrealized capital gains are credited to the reserve so long as the reserve is below its maximum. Net realized and unrealized losses are charged to the reserve until it is reduced to zero and thereafter are charged to surplus. Since bonds not in default are typically carried at amortized cost, unrealized gains and losses result primarily from the revaluation of defaulted securities. The maximum reserve is 20 times the annual contribution.

The common stock component of the MSVR requires an annual contribution from surplus equivalent to 1 percent of the market value of the common stock portfolio on each December 31. In addition, net

---

[78] Ins. L. §91(1).

[79] Ins. L. §91(7).

[80] National Association of Insurance Commissioners, *Valuation of Securities* (1976).

realized and unrealized gains are credited to the reserve so long as it is below the prescribed maximum of 33⅓ percent of the market value of the common stock portfolio. That portion of capital gains which would cause the reserve to exceed its maximum is normally transferred to surplus. Realized and unrealized losses are charged to the reserve until it reaches zero and are thereafter charged to surplus. Inasmuch as common stock is valued at market, unrealized gains and losses have a much greater effect on the mandatory reserve than does the annual contribution.

In short, investment in the typical high-grade, long-term bonds requires minimal contributions to the MSVR and is not likely to exert any strain on surplus except for an occasional catastrophe, such as the collapse of Penn Central. On the other hand, investments in common stock, which are valued at market as of one day in the year, can exert an immediate impact by wiping out the common stock reserve component and drawing on surplus. The valuation system thus enforces the ingrained philosophy of life company management by discouraging investment in lower-quality debt issues and common stock.

THE NEW WISCONSIN APPROACH TO INVESTMENT REGULATION

The 1972 Wisconsin statute[81] liberalizes the limits and conditions upon which insurers can invest in the asset categories specifically enumerated in the statute[82] and adopts a philosophy of investment regulation basically different from the New York type of legislation. The specific limitations of this statute are not aimed at regulating the investment of all assets. Beyond investment of an amount of assets equal to liabilities plus security surplus, the statute provides for virtually complete investment freedom.

Security surplus, as used in the statute, refers to an amount of surplus which an insurer should have in order not to be considered financially hazardous, i.e., an amount which will provide the insurer with a margin of safety in meeting its financial needs.[83] Security surplus represents a variable or flexible requirement to be determined separately for each insurer. Broad discretion regarding this determination has been given to the commissioner of insurance. The only

---

[81] 40E Wisc. Stat. Ann. §§620.01–620.32, §623.11, and §623.12 (West Supp. 1975) (hereafter cited as W.S.A. §–).

[82] The categories are similar to those enumerated in the New York statute.

[83] W.S.A. §623.12.

direction given by the statute is with regard to the general areas which the commissioner must consider.

The comments of the legislative committee which drafted the statute suggest that the following factors should be considered by the commissioner in setting security surplus:

a. The size of the insurer as measured by its assets, capital and surplus, reserves, premium writings, insurance in force and other appropriate criteria.

b. The extent to which the insurer's business is diversified among the several lines of insurance.

c. The number and size of risks insured in each line of business.

d. The extent of the geographical dispersion of the insurer's insured risks.

e. The nature and extent of the insurer's reinsurance program.

f. The quality, diversification, and liquidity of the insurer's investment portfolio.

g. The recent past and projected future trend in the size of the insurer's surplus in relation to policy obligations.

h. The surplus in relation to policy obligations maintained by other comparable insurers.

i. The adequacy of the insurer's reserves.

j. The possibility that surplus may be freely withdrawn by policyholders or subscribers and the probability that they will do so.[84]

Each insurer is required to maintain a level of assets equal to its liabilities plus its security surplus as determined by the commissioner. Assets are counted toward satisfaction of this requirement, however, only insofar as they are invested in accordance with the statute, i.e., in one of the enumerated categories and to the extent permitted. Once this requirement has been met, the specifically enumerated limitations of the statute are no longer applicable. For example, even though the statute limits common stock investment to 20 percent of assets, an insurer which has met the security surplus requirement can have investments in common stock beyond the 20 percent limitation.

A surprising paucity of detail exists in those sections of the statute which set out permitted categories of investments.[85] Among the few percentage limitations are those on common stock investment (20 percent of assets for life insurers, 10 percent for nonlife insurers) and on investment in real property purchased for the purpose of earning income (20 percent of assets for life insurers, 10 percent of assets

---

[84] The comments follow W.S.A. §623.11.

[85] W.S.A. §620.22 and 620.23.

for nonlife insurers). In addition, for life insurers total investment in common stocks and income producing real property should not exceed 30 percent of assets.

Other restrictions are placed on leeway investment (5 percent of assets) and on investments in property needed for the transaction of the insurer's business (20 percent of assets in the case of nonassessable insurers). Also of note is the fact that no limitations or directions are present which deal with the quality of the investments (e.g., earnings tests such as those used in the New York statute). Finally, in addition to the specifically enumerated categories of investment, an authorization is granted for "such other investments as the commissioner authorizes by rule."

Another key aspect of the Wisconsin scheme is that detailed rules and regulations, similar to those which were in effect under the old Wisconsin statute and are now being used under traditional state statutes, are in effect for "new, small, or marginal insurers."[86] Within a broad framework provided by the statute, the responsibility for the establishment and implementation of these regulations has been delegated to the commissioner. This reflects a recognition of the fact that all insurers are not the same and, therefore, that the same amount of regulation will not be appropriate for all insurers.

In addition to these technical differences between the New York and the Wisconsin codes, there are basic differences in philosophy which are highlighted in the Wisconsin code. The introduction to the code states that

> the purpose of this chapter is to protect and to further the interests of insureds, creditors and the public, by providing, with minimum interference with management initiative and judgment, standards for the development and administration of programs for the investment of the assets of insurers. . . .[87]

The Wisconsin statute thus attempts to provide a framework for the development of sound investment programs. The New York statute provides the detailed outline of an investment program and relies minimally on the willingness and ability of the insurer's investment officers to make investment decisions which will provide the highest yield and the most security for insureds. The new Wisconsin statute assumes that the investment managers of strong insurers are for the most part experienced and skilled and in a better position than the

[86] W.S.A. §620.03 and 620.04.
[87] W.S.A. §620.01.

legislature to devise an appropriate investment program for their companies.

Under the Wisconsin statute, new investment vehicles reflecting the changing needs of the economy and society in general can be made permissible in an easy and timely fashion by commissioner rule. This results from the extreme generality of the statute and the increased rule-making power of the commissioner. If a new form of investment would not be permitted under the liberal language of this statute, which seems unlikely, an insurer would not be precluded from participation if (1) its security surplus requirement had already been met, (2) it had not exhausted its leeway amount, or (3) the commissioner authorized the particular investment. In contrast, under the detailed regulation of the New York statute, change can only be reflected through leeway investments and statutory amendments.

The Wisconsin statute may represent the wave of the future; but those accustomed to the more stringent New York type of statute argue that the extremely broad discretion delegated to the commissioner presents considerable and unwarranted risk, not justified by any compelling need. So long as the commissioner is an able and experienced official of complete integrity, the system will, of course, work well and perhaps better than the more rigid New York type of investment code. The latter, however, minimizes the risk of administrative incompetence or worse.

CONCLUSION

The hard facts are scant from which any positive assertions can be made as to the impact of statutory regulation on investment decisions of life company investment managers. The history of pressures for liberalizing amendments is evidence that at least some companies would have experimented earlier with lower-quality securities to achieve higher yields. They would have entered more boldly and much earlier into equities and would have deviated to a greater extent from the portfolio composition of the industry as a whole. This is particularly true of common stock investment during the steady rise of the market in the post-World War II years. For the most part, the pressures produced the desired statutory liberalizations; but the delays affected the timing (and to that extent the consequences, for good or ill) of the investment process.

Without larger surpluses or more stabilized valuations, or both, life companies could not do much more general account investing in common stocks than they are now doing without raising their standards on fixed-interest debt investing. By and large, the inherent conservatism of life company managements would in any event have limited the range and variety of life company investments to the high quality bonds and the real estate mortgages in which the bulk of life company funds has been invested.

Of course, a process of interaction occurs between the subjective attitudes of the investment managers and the statutory framework in which those attitudes are formed. Given a more liberal statutory environment, the investment managers may have had a somewhat different attitude as to the appropriate range of investment outlets. The growth of pension plans with their separate accounts and the advent of variable life insurance, should it come to pass, may work a profound change in investment attitudes and exert greater pressure for a Wisconsin type of legal framework. The author's feeling in the matter is reflected in a wise remark by Mr. Justice Holmes:

> It cannot be helped, it is as it should be, that the law is behind the times.[88]

---

[88] Oliver Wendell Holmes, "Law and the Court," *Speeches*, p. 101 (1913); *Coll. Leg. Pap.* 294.

APPENDIX

Excerpts from the 1967 Life Insurance Industry Brief in Support of Proposed Changes in the Common Stock Sections of the New York Insurance Code*

At the time the brief was filed (February 1967), New York law stipulated that life insurance companies could invest in common stocks to the extent of the lesser of 5 percent of admitted assets or 50 percent of surplus. One of the proposed changes was that the 5 percent of assets provision be made fully operative by repealing the 50 percent of surplus portion of the limitation. The industry brief on this point was as follows:

The 5 percent of admitted assets authorized cannot be exercised by a domestic mutual life insurance company so long as the "½ of surplus" limitation is retained. Its surplus could never be as much as 10 percent of its admitted assets (except in the case of a small company) since §207(1) of the New York Insurance Law limits the surplus of a domestic mutual life insurance company to 10 percent of its policy reserves and policy liabilities or, if greater, $850,000.

It is understandable that the initial authorization in 1951 to invest in common stock tied the aggregate permitted investment to a percentage of surplus as a conservative first step in permitting life insurance companies to enter that investment area. It is also understandable, considering the gradual exercise of the new authorization, that this limitation has not been an obstacle to date. But some life insurance companies which have been carrying on a common stock investment program for several years will soon—within two or three years for one major company—find that their new investments in common stock will be restricted by the "½ of surplus" ceiling to ½ of the annual increase in surplus unless they immediately curtail their present programs. This change was first urged by the industry in 1956 but at that time, with only one New York company having as much as 2 percent of its admitted assets invested in common stocks, then Superintendent of Insurance Holz concluded there was not a "crying need at the moment."[1] The time has come to appraise the need and de-

---

* Memorandum in Support (of Assembly Bill 4311), Proposed Amendments to Ins. L. §§81(13), 46–a(6) and 227(1)(b), submitted by Life Insurance Association of America (Drafting Committee on New York Investment Legislation), February 1967.

[1] Joint Legislative Committee on Insurance Rates and Regulation, Minutes of the Proceedings of a Public Hearing held on September 27 and 28, 1956, p. 175.

sirability of the limitation based on the amount of surplus. An exhibit is attached to the industry brief which sets forth a schedule of the common stock investments (at cost and at market) of the 15 largest life insurance companies in the United States (including four New York companies) as related to their admitted assets and their surplus as at December 31, 1965. Three of the out-of-state companies had common stock investments aggregating (at cost) more than ½ of their surplus (the percentages ranging from 53.4, 57.3, and 66 percent, respectively). For three of the New York companies, the percentages were 38.7, 36.5, and 28.5 percent, respectively. All of the 15 companies had substantial unrealized capital gains—the market values of the portfolios ranging from 123 percent to 318 percent of cost.

A well-diversified portfolio of quality common stocks is a proper part of the long-term investment program of a life insurance company. It follows that determination of the portion of an insurer's assets which should be invested in its common stock portfolio is a matter of bringing about a prudent diversification of all investments rather than a question of the amount of surplus. This is particularly so when an adequate reserve must be established to meet realized and unrealized losses as is provided for in the valuation procedures approved by the National Association of Insurance Commissioners (NAIC).

NAIC procedures currently provide for a mandatory securities valuation reserve with a separate common stock reserve component. Each year there must be credited to that common stock reserve component an amount equal to 1 percent of the statement (market) value of the common stock portfolio; and, also, there must be credited thereto any realized and unrealized capital gains. In addition, an insurer may make additional annual voluntary contributions of up to 2 percent of statement (market) value. The maximum reserve may not, however, exceed 33⅓ percent of the statement (market) value of common stocks (20 percent, however, of common stock of controlled or affiliated companies at book value).

For any type of investment other than common stock, statutory requirements for diversification (as distinguished from percentage requirements to preclude control) have been limited solely to a percentage of admitted assets. This seems proper for common stock too, since surplus is merely the excess of all admitted assets over all liabilities and reserves and does not represent any particuar investment or class of investments. To the extent any special reserve is required for fluctuations in the value of investments or for losses, it can best be met—as it already is met for all securities, including common stock—by the procedure under §91 of the New York Insurance Law for a special reserve of the character prescribed by NAIC valuation procedures. Any provision limiting the amount which may be invested in a particular type of investment to a percentage of surplus ignores §91 and NAIC procedures.

A flat "5 percent of admitted assets" limitation, which would be applicable after the elimination of the "½ of surplus" restriction, will bring New York more in line with other states where major life insurance companies are domiciled.

Another change proposed in 1967 was that the authorized investment in the common stock of any one corporation be increased from 2 to 5 percent of the corporation's total outstanding shares and from ⅕ of 1 percent to ½ of 1 percent of the insurance company's admitted assets. With regard to this proposal, the brief advanced the following argument:

The purpose of placing a limit upon the percentage of common stock of any one corporation which may be acquired is twofold: *first,* to prohibit an insurer from doing, directly through subsidiaries or affiliates, business which cannot be done directly under its charter and the Insurance Law and, *second,* to preclude the control of other business enterprises which might result from owning a substantial stock interest, in fact to avoid any semblance of control that could lead to allegations of imagined abuses. It is not a question of limiting the portion of the insurer's assets at risk in any one enterprise, as that is met by the provision limiting the percentage of admitted assets (which would be increased from ⅕ of 1 percent to ½ of 1 percent) permitted to be invested in the common stock of any one corporation. The increase of that percentage limitation from ⅕ of 1 percent to ½ of 1 percent will be somewhat more realistic, particularly considering that the common stocks of some of the major industrial and utility companies may be expected to constitute substantial percentages of the common stock portfolios of life insurance companies.

In the industry's 1951 proposal for an authorization to invest in common stock, a percentage as low as 2 percent of the common stock of any one corporation was apparently suggested by the life insurance industry to avoid any conceivable possibility of a question. At that time, none of the 34 jurisdictions then permitting investments in common stock set a percentage limit of less than 5 percent and only 4 of those jurisdictions (Connecticut, Delaware, Nebraska, and New Hampshire) had a limit of less than 10 percent. Correspondingly, in 1951 the percentage of admitted assets permitted to be invested in the common stock of any one company was set at $\frac{1}{10}$ of 1 percent (increased in 1957 to the present $\frac{1}{5}$ of 1 percent) when none of those 34 jurisdictions set a limit of less than 2 percent, except that the District of Columbia and Maine had a limit of 1 percent and Delaware, Massachusetts, and Texas had a limit of 10 percent of surplus. Four states had a limit of 2 percent—Illinois, Indiana, New Jersey, and Pennsylvania—and two states had a limit of 5 percent—Maryland and Ohio.[2]

The proposed changes will still leave New York very much on the conservative side as compared to most other major life insurance states.

It will benefit the economy of the nation, as well as result in desirable investments for the life insurance companies, if they were to expand their common stock portfolios to include some stocks of medium-sized companies. To make that a real possibility, it is almost essential to use a percentage limit which would permit an investment of $500,000 to $1 million. It is not feasible for a life insurance company to invest in the common stock of a company unless the investment is or will become sufficiently large to justify the expense of continuous study of the company's current and potential financial position.

In the coming few years, a greater need for this higher percentage limitation may be expected to result from increased investments in common stocks both in the regular portfolios and particularly in separate accounts, which are also counted in applying the percentage limitation. A higher limit will be less likely to block a life insurance company from acquiring a desirable common stock for its regular portfolio simply because the percentage limit has already been exhausted by acquisitions for separate accounts, and vice versa.

---

[2] See Report, dated January 30, 1951, of Life Insurance Association of America and American Life Convention in Support of Proposed Amendments to Article 5, Section 81, of the New York Insurance Law Submitted to the Joint Legislative Committee on Insurance Regulation and Rates of the State of New York, p. 67.

About the Contributors

WILLIAM E. AVERA is assistant professor of finance at the University of Texas at Austin. He holds a B.A. degree from Emory University and a Ph.D. from the University of North Carolina. His previous publications include the coauthored monograph *Investment Companies: Analysis of Current Operations and Future Prospects*, as well as numerous articles in scholarly journals.

FRANK A. CAPPIELLO, JR., is president of Monumental Capital Management, Inc., financial vice president of Monumental Corporation, and chairman of the Investment Committee and director of Fiduciary Counsel, Inc. He holds a B.A. degree from the University of Notre Dame and an M.B.A. degree from Harvard University. Mr. Cappiello has lectured extensively on economic problems and investments at New York University, Southern Methodist University, and the University of Chicago, as well as the Wharton School. He is a faculty member and lecturer at the Johns Hopkins University. He is a director of Equitable Bancorporation, a member of the Advisory Investment Committee for the State of Maryland and the City of Baltimore Retirement Funds. Since 1970, he has been a continuing panel member on the Public Broadcasting System's television series, "Wall Street Week." Mr. Cappiello is an occasional columnist for the *Chicago Tribune*.

J. DAVID CUMMINS is assistant professor of insurance at the Wharton School, University of Pennsylvania, and research director of the S. S. Huebner Foundation for Insurance Education. His academic credentials include a B.A. degree from the University of Nebraska and M.A. and Ph.D.

341

degrees from the University of Pennsylvania. Among his prior publications are *An Econometric Model of the Life Insurance Sector of the U.S. Economy* and *Development of Life Insurance Surrender Values in the United States.* He is a member of the editorial board of the *Journal of Risk and Insurance.*

JAMES L. FARRELL, JR., is an investment officer at the College Retirement Equities Fund. He previously served as a securities analyst at CNA Financial Services Corporation. He holds a B.S. degree from the University of Notre Dame, an M.B.A. from the Wharton School, University of Pennsylvania, and a Ph.D. in economics and finance from New York University where he now serves as adjunct assistant professor of finance. He has written extensively on the subject of modern portfolio theory and its application to investment practice and has published a monograph entitled *The Multi-Index Model and Practical Portfolio Analysis.* He is chairman of Columbia University's Institute for Quantitative Research in Finance.

J. ROBERT FERRARI is vice president and chief economist of the Prudential Life Insurance Company of America. He heads the company's economic and investment research department and is a member of Prudential's investment committees. Formerly an associate professor at the Wharton School, University of Pennsylvania, Dr. Ferrari earned M.B.A. and Ph.D. degrees at the University of Pennsylvania and a B.S. degree in engineering at Penn State University. Among his publications are *The Private Insurance of Home Mortgages* and several articles in academic and professional journals including the *Journal of Risk and Insurance.*

MENDES HERSHMAN is senior vice president and general counsel of New York Life Insurance Company. He holds an A.B. degree from New York University and an LL.B. degree from Harvard Law School. He is a former chairman of the section of corporation, banking, and business law of the American Bar Association and a member of the American Law Institute advisory committee for the real property restatement and land use model code. Among his directorships and trusteeships are those for the New York Bank for Savings and for New York University.

LAWRENCE D. JONES is associate professor of urban land economics in the Faculty of Commerce, University of British Columbia. He holds a Ph.D. in economics from Harvard University. He has previously taught economics and finance at Harvard University, Indiana University, and the University of Pennsylvania, and served as associate director of the Securities and Exchange Commission's *Institutional Investor Study.* Among his other publications are *Investment Policies of Life Insurance Companies* and *Investment Policies and Practices of Public Employee Retirement Systems* (forthcoming).

HENRY A. LATANÉ is Willis Professor of Investment Banking at the University of North Carolina, Chapel Hill. He holds a B.A. degree from the University of Richmond, an M.B.A. from Harvard University, and a Ph.D. from the University of North Carolina. Before entering the academic community, Dr. Latané served as security analyst for the Banker's Trust Company in New York and investment counselor for the Lionel D. Edie Company. He has published many articles in academic and professional journals and is coauthor of *Security Analysis and Portfolio Management*.

MEYER MELNIKOFF is senior vice president and actuary of the Prudential Insurance Company of America. He holds both B.A. and M.A. degrees from Montclair State College and is a Fellow of the Society of Actuaries. Mr. Melnikoff has participated in pension seminars sponsored by New York University, Oklahoma University, Purdue University, and Rutgers University, and is a member of the Wharton School's Pension Research Council. At the Prudential, he has participated in the development of numerous new pension funding concepts including various types of separate accounts and the investment year method of crediting interest earnings to pension funds.

ROBERT H. MUNDHEIM is the Fred Carr Professor of Law and Financial Institutions at the University of Pennsylvania Law School and director of its Center for the Study of Financial Institutions. Mr. Mundheim holds a B.A. degree from Harvard University and an LL.B. degree from Harvard Law School. Prior to joining the University of Pennsylvania faculty, he was associated with Shearman and Sterling in New York, served as special counsel for the Securities and Exchange Commission, and taught at the Duke University Law School. He is a member of the American Bar Association's committee on federal securities regulation and chairman of its subcommittee on securities markets and market structure and also a consultant to the American Law Institute's Federal Securities Code Project.

ROBERT A. RENNIE is senior vice president—investments for the Nationwide Life Insurance Company. Among his academic credentials are an A.B. degree from Wesleyan University and M.A. and Ph.D. degrees from Harvard University. Prior to joining Nationwide in 1951, Dr. Rennie taught economics at the Johns Hopkins University. As a result of his planning, in 1951 Nationwide became the first major insurance company to sell both mutual funds and life insurance through its agency force. Dr. Rennie has published articles in academic and professional journals and has contributed to a previous Huebner Foundation lecture series publication, *All Lines Insurance*.

FRANCIS H. SCHOTT is vice president and economist of the Equitable Life Assurance Society of the United States. Dr. Schott joined the Equitable after a 15-year affiliation with the Federal Reserve Bank of New York where he was research and foreign department officer. He holds a B.A. degree from Oberlin College and a Ph.D. from Princeton University. He has published numerous articles in professional and scholarly journals including the *Journal of Finance* and *Business Economics.*

PETER A. SCHULKIN is vice president of Wells Fargo Realty Advisors. He holds a B.A. Degree from the University of Maryland and a Ph.D. degree from Harvard University. He previously served as economist for the National Association of Real Estate Investment Trusts and taught finance at the George Washington University. Among his publications are *Commercial Bank Construction Lending* and several articles in business and financial publications.

ELI SHAPIRO is vice chairman of The Travelers Corporation, a director, and chairman of the finance committee. In addition, he is Alfred P. Sloan Professor of Management at the Massachusetts Institute of Technology. Prior to joining the Travelers and MIT, Dr. Shapiro served as professor of finance at the Graduate School of Business Administration, Harvard University. He is a director of a number of institutions including the Federal Home Loan Bank of Boston and the National Bureau of Economic Research. Among his previous publications are the coauthored books *Money and Banking* and *The Role of Private Placements in Corporate Finance.*

HOWARD H. STEVENSON is associate professor of business administration at the Graduate School of Business Administration, Harvard University. Prior to joining the Harvard faculty, he was vice president of Simmons Associates, an investment banking firm. He holds a B.S. degree from Stanford University and M.B.A. and D.B.A. degrees from Harvard. Among his directorships and trusteeships are those at Realty Income Trust and Wolfe Industries, Inc. Dr. Stevenson has consulted and written extensively in the fields of business strategy, feasibility analysis, and location problems for real estate ventures including publications in *Sloan Management Review, Real Estate Review,* and *Urban Land.*

IRWIN T. VANDERHOOF is vice president, equi-pension department of the Equitable Life Assurance Society of the United States. He previously served as executive vice president and treasurer of the Standard Security Life Insurance Company. He is a Chartered Financial Analyst and a Fellow of the Society of Actuaries. Among his previous publications are several articles in the *Transactions of the Society of Actuaries.*

Index

347

Corporate bonds—*Cont.*
shares of, in total funds raised in capital markets, 65
yields on, relative to
home mortgages, 42, 45
income property mortgages, 76
Corporate equities; *see* Common stock;
Corporate stock; *and* Preferred
stocks
Corporate stock; *see also* Common
stock *and* Preferred stock
health insurers, as investors in, 23
life insurer acquisitions of, 6, 262
life insurer holdings of, 5, 10–11
life insurers emphasizing pension
plans, as investors in, 23
small and medium size life insurers,
as investors in, 274, 279, 280–
84
yield rates on, 114–15, 209, 279–80,
287
Correspondents; *see* Originators
Credit cruches, 24–25, 228, 232, 254
Credit unions, growth of, 8
Cummins, J. David, 235, 237, 238

D

David, Phillip, 157
Declaration of trust, 176
Default
impact of, on loan terms for income
property mortgages, 81, 86
rates of
on home mortgages, 220–21
on publicly issued bonds, 213–15,
221
risk of, related to participation features, 78
Delinquency rates, on income property
mortgages, 91–92, 95, 102
Demand for life insurance; *see* Life insurance
Deposit administration contracts, 28
Direct placements; *see* Private placements
Disintermediation, 25, 228, 254–55,
260, 267
Diversification
impact of managerial attitudes toward, on life insurer investment
strategy, 30
in the stock portfolio, 105, 118, 144
Dividends, to policyholders, 25, 28,
128

Dodge v. *Ford Motor Company,* 296–
97, 300
Dow Jones Industrial Average, 116,
279

E

Earned interest rate as measure of life
insurer investment performance,
206; *see also* Performance measurement
Earnings test, regulatory
on bonds, 311, 315, 320, 326
on common stock, 312, 321, 329
on preferred stock, 311, 319, 329
Economic indicators, use of, to evaluate stock market, 112
Efficient capital markets, 30, 119, 211,
213
Employee Retirement Income Security
Act of 1974 (ERISA), 225n, 266
Endowment insurance, relative importance of 20, 253
Equitable Life Assurance Society of
the United States (ELAS), 241,
243, 247, 286, 310
"Equity kickers"; *see* Incentive features *and* Participation provisions
Escalator clauses in long-term leases,
87

F

Farm mortgages, life insurer holdings
of, 5; *see also* Income property
mortgages *and* Mortgages
Federal National Mortgage Association, 166
Federally sponsored credit agencies,
71, 166, 262
Finance committee, 109; *see also* Investment committee
Financial intermediaries
competition among
for consumer savings, 8–10, 262–
66
in the investment markets, 10–14,
262
life insurers as, 1, 2–3
Forecasting
of cash flow, 31, 52, 231–47
of interest rates, 32
of separate account flows, 242
of the stock market, 111, 115–17,
281
Foreclosures
impact of, on real estate equity investing, 168

This book has been set in 10 and 9 point Caledonia, leaded 2 points. Chapter numbers are in 42 point Helvetica Regular and chapter titles are in 16 point Helvetica. The size of the type page is 25 by 43½ picas.